INTERGOVERNMENTAL RELATIONS
AND PUBLIC POLICY

INTERGOVERNMENTAL RELATIONS
AND PUBLIC POLICY

Brian Galligan

Owen Hughes

Cliff Walsh

Editors

Allen & Unwin

First published in 1991
Allen & Unwin Pty Ltd
8 Napier Street, North Sydney NSW 2059 Australia

National Library of Australia
Cataloguing-in-Publication entry:

Intergovernmental relations and public policy.
   Includes index.
   ISBN 0 04 442257 1.
   1. Federal government—Australia. 2. Interstate relations—Australia.
   3. Intergovernmental fiscal relations—Australia. I. Galligan, Brian,
   1945– . II. Hughes, Owen E. III. Walsh, Cliff, 1946– .

Printed in Singapore by Chong Moh Offset Printing.

Contents

List of Tables

List of Figures

Contributors

Jim Butler is a Senior Research Fellow in the National Centre for Epidemiology and Population Health, and a Departmental Visitor in the Division of Economics and Politics in the Research School of Social Sciences, Australian National University. He is a co-author of *The Economics of Natural Disaster Relief in Australia* (1979) and is interested in welfare economics, public finance and health economics with particular reference to federalism.

Bruce Davis is Deputy Director of the Institute of Antarctic and Southern Ocean Studies in the University of Tasmania. His research interests are policy studies and environmental management. He acts in an advisory and consulting role to state and commonwealth governments on natural resource issues and was awarded AM (Member of the Order of Australia) in January 1990 for services to conservation of the environment.

Brian Galligan is Deputy Director of the Centre for Research on Federal Financial Relations at The Australian National University and Senior Research Fellow in the Department of Political Science. He is the author of *Politics of the High Court* (1987) and *Utah and Queensland Coal* (1989), and editor of *Comparative State Policies* (1988) and *Australian Federalism* (1989).

Rolf Gerritsen is Senior Lecturer, Graduate Program in Public Policy, The Australian National University and Program Director, Graduate Program in Development Administration, ANU.

Marcus Haward is a Tutor in Political Science, University of Tasmania. He has interests in intergovernmental relations and resource management and has written articles on offshore resources policy and environmental politics.

Judith Healy is a Senior Lecturer in Social Administration, School of Social Sciences, The Flinders University of South Australia. She has been a member of various intergovernmental committees for community services programs in South Australia.

Owen Hughes is Assistant Director at the Public Sector Management Institute at Monash University and Lecturer in Public Administration. His areas of specialisation include public sector reforms, intergovernmental relations and budgeting. Recent publications include *Australian Politics: Realities and Conflicts* (1988), co-authored with H.V. Emy.

Aynsley Kellow is Senior Lecturer in Policy Studies, School of Social Sciences, Deakin University. He has a particular interest in environment and resources policy and in theoretical perspectives on the policy process. He is co-editor of the *Deakin Monograph Series in Public Policy and Administration*.

Neil Marshall is Lecturer in the Department of Administrative, Higher and Adult Education Studies, University of New England. He has published a number of articles in the areas of higher education and public policy.

Ciaran O'Faircheallaigh is a Senior Lecturer in Public Policy in the Division of Commerce and Administration, Griffith University. He is author of *Mining and Development* (1984) and *Mine Infrastructure and Economic Development in North Australia* (1987), co-author of *Uranium in Australia: An Annotated Bibliography 1970—1987* (1989), and author of articles on mineral economics, mineral policy and policy evaluation.

Martin Painter is Senior Lecturer, Department of Government and Public Administration, University of Sydney. He is co-author of *Politics Between Departments* (1979), author of *Steering the Modern State* (1987) and of numerous articles and chapters on the relationships between governmental structures and public policy making in national and sub-national governments.

Andrew Parkin is Senior Lecturer in Politics, and Chair of the Graduate Program in Policy and Administration, at the Flinders University of South Australia. He has written and edited several books on Australian politics, and has contributed many articles on aspects of public policy. He chaired the South Australian Housing Advisory Council from 1985 until 1989.

Will Sanders is a National Research Fellow in the Urban Research Program, Division of Politics and Economics, Research School of Social Sciences, Australian National University. He has published numerous articles on Aboriginal Policy, particularly on the inclusion of Aborigines in the Australian social security system.

Campbell Sharman is a Senior Lecturer in the Department of Politics at the University of Western Australia. He has a long standing research interest in Australian and comparative federalism and has recently published articles on state politics, constitutional design, and the federal process in Australia.

Cheryl Saunders is Professor of Law at the University of Melbourne Faculty of Law and Director of the Centre for Comparative Constitutional Studies. She has a specialist interest in intergovernmental relations. She has been President of the Administrative Review Council since 1987 and is the editor of *Intergovernmental News* and the *Journal of Public Law*.

since 1987 and is the editor of *Intergovernmental News* and the *Journal of Public Law*.

Cliff Walsh is a Professor in the Institute of Advanced Studies and Director of the Centre for Research on Federal Financial Relations, Research School of Social Sciences, Australian National University. He has had extensive experience as an advisor to governments and has been co-author and editor of numerous books on public sector reform, including *Spending and Taxing: Australian Reform Options* (1987) and *Budgetary Stress: The South Australian Experience* (1989).

John Wanna is Senior Lecturer Public Policy, Division of Commerce and Administration, Griffith University, Brisbane. He co-authored *Public Policy in Australia* (1988) and has recently contributed to and co-edited *Budgeting Management and Control* (1990). He has a teaching and research interest in government—business relations in Australia.

Roger Wettenhall is Professor of Administrative Studies at the University of Canberra, and joint editor of *Australian Journal of Public Administration*. His principal work in the field of disaster studies is *Bushfire Disaster: An Australian Community in Crisis* (1975), and he is a member-at-large of the Research Committee on Disasters of the International Sociological Association. He has also written on machinery of government, administrative reform and administrative history issues.

Deil S. Wright is Alumni Distinguished Professor of Political Science and Public Administration at the University of North Carolina at Chapel Hill. He has published books and articles in the fields of federalism, finance, intergovernmental relations, and administrative behaviour including *Understanding Intergovernmental Relations* (3rd ed., 1988).

Preface

Intergovernmental relations have been relatively neglected in the study of Australian federalism and public policy. That is surprising because intergovernmental processes and relations between state and commonwealth governments are essential ingredients in Australian federal politics and public policy. The purpose of this book is to demonstrate this. We have not attempted to give a definitive account of Australian intergovernmental relations or to cover the whole policy field. Rather our purpose has been to open up the area. The Centre for Research on Federal Financial Relations (CRFFR) has an ongoing brief, pursuant to our enhanced funding for the next three years, to promote and develop the study of Australian intergovernmental relations. Accordingly, a series of research seminars and monographs on key policy areas has been planned for 1990, and will take further the study that has been begun here.

The project was jointly sponsored by CRFFR (in the Research School of Social Sciences at the Australian National University [ANU]) and the Public Sector Management Institute of Monash University (PSMI). The scope and diversity of the work was possible because contributors were drawn from fourteen universities throughout Australia. A preliminary workshop for participants was held in Canberra in November 1988 and a conference for presentation of draft papers in April 1989. We were fortunate in being able to attract leading American authority Deil Wright to provide the American perspective on intergovernmental relations for our project, and to take advantage of Martin Painter's sabbatical period in Canada for an up-to-date review of Canadian developments. We should like to put on record our appreciation to all colleagues for their enthusiasm and hard work in carrying through the project.

The three editors have jointly planned the project, collaborated on the framework paper, which focused earlier discussion and in revised form has become chapter 1 of the book, and shared editorial duties. Brian Galligan was responsible for overall co-ordination. The exercise has been enjoyable and, we trust, fruitful.

This is the first of three joint CRFFR/PSMI projects involving the editors: the second, on 'Micro Economic Reform' is to be co-ordinated by Owen Hughes, and the third, on 'Federalism and the Hawke Government', is to be co-ordinated by Cliff Walsh.

As usual, in the organising of workshops and conferences, co-ordinating the research and writing of a large number of participants, Linda Gosnell and Stephanie Hancock have played an indispensable role with the usual cheerful professionalism that we and our team of colleagues have come to admire. As well, we should like to acknowledge the contribution of Gillian O'Loghlin and Sue Dee for editorial assistance, Catherine Baker from Allen & Unwin for copy-editing the final manuscript, and Suzanne Ridley for preparing the index.

Brian Galligan
Owen Hughes
Cliff Walsh
Canberra and Melbourne, February 1990

Acronyms

AAC	Australian Agricultural Council
ACIR	Advisory Council for Inter-government Relations
ACIR-US	Advisory Commission on Intergovernmental Relations
AFZ	Australian (Extended) Fishing Zone
AHMAC	Australian Health Ministers' Advisory Council
AHMC	Australian Health Ministers' Conference
AHSC	Australian Health Services Council
AITC	Australian Industry and Technology Council
ALP	Australian Labor Party
ANU	Australian National University
AUC	Australian University Commission
BCA	Business Council of Australia
BIE	Bureau of Industry Economics
BTEC	The Brucellosis and Tuberculosis Eradication Campaign
CACAE	Commonwealth Advisory Commission on Advanced Education
CAE	College of Advanced Education
CAI	Confederation of Australian Industry
CER	Closer Economic Relations
CONCOM	Council of Nature Conservation Ministers
CRFFR	Centre for Research on Federal Financial Relations
CSHA	Commonwealth—State Housing Agreement
CSO	Community Service Obligation
CTEC	Commonwealth Tertiary Education Commission
DAA	Department of Aboriginal Affairs
DAIA	Department of Aboriginal and Islander Affairs
DCS&H	Department of Community Services and Health
DCW	Department of Community Welfare
DEET	Department of Employment, Education and Training
DOLGAS	Department of Local Government and Administrative Services
DPIE	Department of Primary Industry and Energy

DRE	Department of Resources and Energy
EIS	Environmental Impact Statement
EPF	Established Program Funding
FED	Federalism
GBRMPA	Great Barrier Reef Marine Park Authority
HACC	Home And Community Care
IAC	Industries Assistance Commission
IGM	Intergovernmental management
IGR	Intergovernmental relations
JOG	Joint Officers Group
MTIA	Metal Trades Industry Association
NACAIDS	National Advisory Committee on AIDS
NBEET	National Board of Employment, Education and Training
NCADA	National Campaign Against Drug Abuse
NCSC	National Companies and Securities Commission
NDO	Natural Disasters Organisation
NEP	New Energy Policy
NH&MRC	National Health and Medical Research Council
OCS	Offshore Constitutional Settlement
PCN	Private Communication Network
PSMI	Public Sector Management Institute (Monash University)
RAS	Rural Adjustment Scheme
RRR	Resource Rent Royalty
RRT	Resource Rent Tax
SAAP	Supported Accommodation Assistance Program
SAAP	Supported Accommodation Assistance Program
SCA	Standing Committee on Agriculture
SCOHM	Standing Committee of the Health Ministers' Conference
SES	State Emergency Service
SIA	Social Impact Assessment
SPIREC	State Preference and Industry Restructuring Advisory Committee
SSCCLA	Senate Standing Committee on Constitutional and Legal Affairs
TAFE	College of Technical and Further Education
TEC	Tertiary Education Commission

Part 1: Intergovernmental relations in Australia

1   Perspectives and issues

Brian Galligan, Owen Hughes & Cliff Walsh

The study of federalism in Australia has concentrated on fiscal and constitutional issues, and, to a lesser extent, political issues. The perspective has tended to be essentially federal, focussing on the divisions of powers and responsibilities, and the conflicts to which they give rise. By contrast, the vast network of intergovernmental relations—administrative as well as political, fiscal and legal, and informal as well as formal—that underpin the day-to-day working of the federal system have received relatively little recognition.

Intergovernmental relations in Australia involve a wide range of institutions, processes and interactions, ranging from high profile meetings of peak organisations like the Premiers' Conference and Loan Council to informal contacts between commonwealth and state officials. Others have catalogued the variety and extent of intergovernmental organisations and emphasised their increasing importance in modern federal government (ACIR, 1986; Sharman, 1988). Sharman has attributed 'the luxuriant flowering of intergovernmental relations' in recent times to increased government involvement in economic and social life, and, in particular, the commonwealth's continuing postwar drive to become involved in a range of policy areas outside its formal constitutional jurisdiction (Sharman, 1988:108). While critical of such commonwealth intrusion, Sharman nevertheless welcomes the flowering of intergovernmental relations as evidence of the continuing vitality of the Australian federal system. Others have been more critical of the complexity that the increasing interdependency of governments entails (Wiltshire, 1986).

Although there has not been a systematic study of intergovernmental relations in Australia, several authors have drawn attention to aspects of the subject and analysed select institutions from an intergovernmental perspective. According to Chapman (1988), intergovernmental organisations constitute a 'fourth branch' of government and operate as 'moderating institutions' in the federal policy process. Wettenhall (1985) characterises the National Crime Authority, along with other intergovernmental agencies like the Joint Coal Board, Snowy Mountains Commission and the River Murray Commission, as 'lubricating' the federal system. Such agencies respect the federal character of the system while enabling issues that spill over the boundaries of government jurisdictions to be dealt with adequately.

Despite an extensive literature on Australian federalism and a current mushrooming in policy studies, there is still a lack of information about how intergovernmental relations impinge on particular public areas. Much has been written on the formal division of powers in the federal system by constitutional lawyers, on fiscal federalism by Russell Mathews and others associated with CRFFR, and on the interaction between political leaders at the level of prime minister and premier by political scientists. Less well known are the policy and administrative processes of intergovernmental relations at the bureaucratic level, the interactions involved in decision making in particular programs and policy areas, and how these affect the actual delivery of services.

Besides mapping the institutions and processes of intergovernmental relations, it is also necessary to evaluate how well they are working. Is there overlap and duplication between levels of government? And if so, is this a bad thing? How does one assess effectiveness and efficiency in intergovernmental matters? Are there policy areas in which the current division of responsibility between governments leads to inefficiency? Is a greater degree of centralisation or decentralisation necessary? Or is each policy area sufficiently distinct that it has to be considered separately?

The debate about Australian federalism has been carried on typically in ideologically-charged language and from set-piece positions of being for or against federalism. But rather than there being a general case for or against federalism, there may well be differing answers for different policies or types of policies, or for particular aspects of policies such as planning, management, finance and delivery. In this book an extensive range of policy areas are examined in detail, the focus being on their specific *intergovernmental* aspects. This chapter explores the broader context of intergovernmental relations within the study of Australian federalism.

Some comparisons with other countries

Australia's relative neglect of intergovernmental relations is in sharp contrast to the literature on federalism in both Canada and the United

States. In order to tap the more extensive literature of those two countries and provide a comparative perspective for the study of Australia, we commissioned papers from Deil Wright and Martin Painter on the current state of American and Canadian intergovernmental relations. As well, Campbell Sharman has contributed an overview of Australian approaches to federalism and intergovernmental relations. The different emphases in the literature from the three countries suggest different characteristics in the three federations. The broad categories of Table 1.1 sum up the three in very simple terms.

Table 1.1: Federal characteristics in three countries

	Leading Characteristic	Primary Locus of Power	Focus of Literature
Australia	Fiscal	National government	Fiscal relations with a centralist focus
Canada	Executive	National Provincial balance	Executive intergovernmental relations
United States	Programmatic	Diffuse	Intergovernmental relations of federal grants. Implementation analysis/management

The leading characteristic of Australian federalism in the postwar decades has been fiscal; for Canadian federalism it has been executive; whereas for American federalism it has had to do with the intergovernmental aspects of massive federal aid programs. These various attributes are directly related to the relative strengths or balance of power between national and state or provincial governments in the federations. In Australia, the orthodox view is that the commonwealth has been the leading federal player because of its fiscal dominance; in Canada, the provinces are relatively stronger and more independent so that intergovernmental relations has been more a tussle between equals; and in the United States, the central government is as dominant as in Australia but power is more fragmented so that large federal programs have tended to take on a life of their own. Not surprisingly the federal literature in the three countries has gone where the action is, concentrating on what is central to the functioning of federalism in each country. While much more detail is provided in the chapters by Sharman, Wright and Painter, some broad observations can be made in order to put Australia in perspective.

As is well known, Australia has the most acute vertical fiscal imbalance of any federation because of the commonwealth's monopoly over income tax and preclusion of the states from levying sales taxes on goods. This makes the commonwealth fiscally dominant and more or less ensures that fiscal issues take first place on the intergovernmental agenda

(Grewal, 1989). As well, Australia is the most fiscally equalised of all federations (Mathews, 1986), so the equalisation process and the Commonwealth Grants Commission are important parts of Australian federalism.

All of this has been reflected and, to an extent, exaggerated in the Australian literature on federalism, much of which has come from CRFFR at the Australian National University. This centre was known appropriately as the 'Russell Mathews' Centre, since he was not only its sole professional staff member during most of the time he was Director but also its founding influence. The original proposal was for a centre of intergovernmental relations modelled on the American Advisory Commission on Intergovernmental Relations, but because of public concern with issues of fiscal federalism at the time—the states, and in particular Victoria, were pushing for a growth tax—and Mathews' influence, the proposed centre quickly became one for research on federal financial relations (Mathews, 1974:2). Since Mathews was pre-eminent in the field and also was a member of the Grants Commission, the Centre prospered and its publications and orientation tended to dominate the literature of Australian federalism. Its influence has been in marked contrast to the ill-fated Advisory Council for Inter-government Relations, which emerged from the Fraser Government's half-hearted 'New Federalism' and was unceremoniously abolished by the Hawke Government.

As one might expect in a nation that is forged by political will from diverse regions and across founding peoples with different language and culture, federalism in Canada is centred around political relations. Since the 'key engine of the state' or 'collective central energizing' force in modern Canadian politics, as elsewhere, is the executive, Canadian federalism is, par excellence, 'executive federalism' (Hockin, 1976:7). Executive federalism, according to its authoritative Canadian interpreter, Don Smiley, is 'defined as the relations between elected and appointed officials of the two orders of government in federal–provincial interactions' (1980:91). Where the orders of government are more equal in power and where one represents Canada's second founding people, those relations typically are depicted in the language of diplomacy, the conceptual framework that Simeon (1972) popularised in his classic study of federal policy making in Canada.

Appropriately the Canadians use the term 'intergovernmental relations' more than Australians, and they use it in the literal sense of relations between governments. As we shall see directly, this is quite different from the American use of 'intergovernmental relations' (IGR) to refer to the interrelationships between and within the three levels of government—national, state and local—in administering programs that are broadly planned and financed by national government. The distinctive character of Canadian intergovernmental relations is evident in the

MacDonald Commission's volume of that title in which the contributions from political scientists concentrate on executive dealings between governments and use concepts like summitry, unilateralism, bilateralism and multilateralism (Dupré, 1985; McRoberts, 1985). Underlying Canadian intergovernmental relations and its federal literature is a more evenly balanced federal system with relatively strong provinces. Compared with Australia and the United States, Roger Gibbins reminds us in a recent comparative essay, modern forces of social change have been 'accompanied by growth in the power and stature of provincial governments, by enhanced regional conflict, and, in some respects, by decentralization of the Canadian federal system' (1987:21).

According to some critics the Canadian process of decentralisation and intergovernmental summitry has gone too far. Dupré claims that in recent years the interaction among federal and provincial first ministers has 'fallen into a state of disarray' while federal–provincial relations at the level of ministers and officials 'have become so varied and complex that they defy generalization' (1985:1,15). Such intergovernmental relations have become exercises in showy summitry which are not conducive to addressing Canada's needs for sound fiscal and economic management. Dupré recalls with nostalgia an earlier period of greater co-ordination and workability of federal–provincial relations and calls, not for its reinstatement (which is probably not feasible), but for more 'routinized summitry'. Others, like Albert Breton (1985), however, champion 'competitive federalism' on public choice grounds and are suspicious of co-operative dealings between governments.

The heart of American federalism in the postwar decades, and particularly during the years of the 1960s and 1970s, has been national assistance to states and localities through grant-in-aid programs. The national government assumed more and more responsibility for dealing with domestic issues that had previously been the preserve of state governments and local authorities. Numerous federal aid programs were mounted in areas of health, education and social welfare as well as more specialised programs in a range of particular areas like rural fire protection, meals-on-wheels and urban renewal in 'model city' programs (Stenberg, 1981). Beginning with the Great Society initiatives of the 1960s, federal grants-in-aid quadrupled in real terms between 1960 and 1980, growing at two and one-half times the rate of the US economy. During the 1980s, however, due to fiscal stringency and Reagan's 'New Federalism', such grants have been wound back quite substantially (Petersen et al., 1986:1–2).

The study of American federalism by social scientists from the 1960s on was as intergovernmental relations, or IGR (Elazar, 1962; Grodzins, 1966). Deil Wright, a leading proponent of this new sub-discipline, argued that IGR was 'an alternative way of referring to the multiple, complex, and interdependent interjurisdictional relationships found in the

United States', and had replaced the concept of federalism which was considered too 'value-related' and debased by loose political discourse (1983:418). Moreover, Wright made no bones about claiming that 'Intergovernmental relations is a concept indigenous to the United States' (1975:426), a claim that could only be true if we restrict its meaning to the peculiarly American version that studies federal grant-in-aid programs. Another major strand of the American federal literature in recent decades has focused on implementation. The field is a vast one that includes development of tools for analysing implementation to tracking implementation across governmental organisations and comparing different policy areas and environments (O'Toole, 1986). If IGR is essentially plotting the organisational and policy processes of federal aid programs, implementation analysis is the attempt to critically evaluate their effectiveness (Pressman & Wildavsky, 1984).

As one might have expected in view of their extensive study of the processes of intergovernmental relations and the critical thrust of much of the implementation literature, Americans have led the way in developing the notion of intergovernmental management (Agranoff & Lindsay, 1983). It springs from a period of widespread disillusionment with the effectiveness of many federal programs and was largely an attempt to solve problems in administering and co-ordinating federal grants-in-aid that had come under fire for being both lavish and inefficient.

Federalist critics have always been suspicious of the whole notion of intergovernmental management and its compatibility with federalism (Schechter, 1981). A more radical approach adopted by the Reagan Administration was to cut back federal grant programs quite ruthlessly in the name of fiscal restraint and respect for local autonomy. It seems that such harsh federal measures have given something of a boost to the states in that interest groups are now more inclined to look to the states for action and redress (Nathan & Doolittle, 1987). According to some critics, however, the indiscriminate cutbacks are an inappropriate response since the effectiveness of federal programs depends on the type of program and administration, as will be discussed below. Chapter 4 in this volume gives both an up-to-date account of American intergovernmental relations during the current period of fiscal restraint and a critical analysis of the emergence of intergovernmental management.

Shifting the Australian focus

Although the federal system in Australia has been a perennial source of debate and discussion, little attention has been paid to the way in which the division of responsibility affects either the formulation of public policy or the delivery of particular kinds of government-provided goods and services. The Australian argument about federalism has usually been overlaid with strong ideological and partisan differences (Brugger &

Jaensch, 1985). The Labor party has traditionally favoured a more centralised state, while the non-Labor parties have generally defended federalism. In the past the argument was very much whether we should have a federal system or not, even though abolition was never a realistic option once the federal system had been put in place. Nevertheless, until the 1970s, the Labor party was formally pledged to an abolition plank, and Bob Hawke, before becoming prime minister, preached the demise of federalism in his 1979 Boyer Lectures (1979).

The new focus on policy studies that began in Australia in the 1970s, and has increased greatly in the 1980s, did not lead to the same emphasis on intergovernmental relations as had been the case in the United States. There IGR flourished as an alternative to federalism and preferable to it because it was more amenable to policy studies. Policy studies in Australia, with the exception of the few authors noted earlier, either ignored federalism or assumed the older prejudice that federalism was irrational and inefficient.

A couple of notable examples can serve to illustrate the anti-federal bias that has coloured much of the Australian discussion of federalism and its effect on public policy. Former Prime Minister Whitlam argued: 'It is possible to advance historical or geographical reasons for having a federal system in Australia; but it is impossible to deny that Australians pay for it dearly in delays and duplication' (1983:28). If Whitlam finally brought the federal Labor party to a formal reconciliation with the Australian federal system, he nevertheless sought, while in office, to assert greater central dominance over the states. A recent book by a leading group of Australian policy analysts echoes the Whitlam view that the federal system is incoherent and wasteful:

> The complex division of powers ordained by federalism makes it diffi-
> cult for any administration to implement coherent policy. Essential
> functions may be controlled by another level of government dominated
> by a rival party. How can a federal government formulate plausible
> macroeconomic policy, for example, when the constitution has been
> interpreted to deny Canberra power to set prices and wages, or the right
> to nationalise industries? Similarly, how can Australians expect
> cogent fiscal measures when the power to levy some taxes, such as
> personal income tax, rests with the federal government, but important
> state and payroll taxes belong to seven different states. When a
> government's power is fragmented then so, in consequence, will be its
> policies. (Davis et al., 1988:48)

The overall argument about the costs or benefits of the federal system will no doubt continue, even though there does seem to be a maturing realisation that, for better or worse, the federal system is here to stay. If the states seemed to be administrative backwaters during the 1950s and 1960s, they were provoked to reassert their place within Australian federalism by the Whitlam Government in the 1970s. Extensive mineral resource development in Queensland and Western Australia helped ensure that those two states adopted a more assertive place within the federal system. During the 1980s and often under Labor governments, the states have demonstrated that reform is not necessarily a commonwealth prerogative. Labor premiers, like John Cain of Victoria, have championed a renaissance of federalism and an enhanced role for the states (Birrell, 1987). At the commonwealth end, fiscal restraint, coupled with a new ethos of managerialism and smaller government, has stemmed the postwar expansion of central government programs. As well, the pragmatic Hawke Government, more than any other federal Labor government in Australian history, has been prepared to work within the federal system.

The political resurgence of federalism in Australia coincides with a reorientation in thinking about big government and public administration. At the practical level, attitudes have changed—genuinely federal answers rather than centralist direction or commonwealth takeover are now more likely to be required. At the theoretical level, many are no longer satisfied with the 'Great Society' solutions for complex economic and societal problems.

Consequently, there is also more attention being given to devising better ways of working within, rather than debunking, federal arrangements. Recently, the trend has been towards either the devolution of policy-making powers, or at least devolution of their implementation. In addition, there are arguments made that federalism is not necessarily inefficient, that decentralising public policy may be more efficient, even in narrow terms, than centralisation. Or, there may be some policies better suited to central organisation and others to local organisation. It is more helpful to specify what these might be and to allow that different degrees of centralisation and decentralisation may suit the same policy area at different times.

Allocating functions

Federalism is a complex system of government which allows a variety of centralised and decentralised policy arrangements, but provides no precise criteria for sorting out which arrangements best suit which policy areas. After surveying the literature, the Constitutional Commission's Advisory Committee on the Distribution of Powers argued that 'there are no *a priori* grounds for treating powers as inherently national or as regional in character except in such areas of so called minimum federal competence as defence, foreign affairs, overseas trade and some areas of taxation' (1987:2). However, it did provide a list of factors to be considered in deciding the federal distribution of powers (Appendix F). Wiltshire, who also specifies the appropriate level for a range of functions, concludes that 'virtually all the current political science and public administration literature in Australia, Canada and the United States declares it to be a futile exercise to attempt to identify rigid criteria by which allocations of complete functions of government can be permanently assigned to a particular level of government' (1981:65).

Nevertheless, there have been useful suggestions for sorting out broad types of policy that are more appropriately handled by national or subnational governments. If government economic functions are classified into allocation, stabilisation and redistribution, there is a fairly general view that stabilisation and redistribution are more appropriately handled by the national government while allocation can be shared. For example, Grewal argues:

> The principal responsibility for stabilisation and redistribution should rest with the national government, whereas that for the allocation of resources should be shared among all levels of government. The major criteria which should determine the role of each level of government in the allocation of resources include the range within which the benefits of public goods are enjoyed, i.e. the 'benefit jurisdiction' of public goods, economies of scale, financial autonomy, administrative costs and interjurisdictional spillovers. (1981:36)

One advantage of centralised arrangements that is commonly cited has to do with minimising the externalities or flow-on of benefits beyond the boundaries of lower-level jurisdictions. As well, centralisation may permit economies of scale to be realised in the provision of public goods. For example, each colony before federation maintained its own defence forces, whereas an Australian army and navy are obviously best organised on a national basis. Centralisation also may better save the wishes of the majority of a country's citizens. This is the Laski or Dicey argument, repeated in Australia by notable public figures and commentators like Whitlam and Wilenski, that only a strong national government can implement a reform program for the benefit of the entire nation. The central government is presumed to act as an instrument of the people or a benevolent despot, furthering the national interest and implementing coherent national policy.

Such advantages of centralisation are more often claimed in principle than demonstrated to apply in practical politics and policy making. Belanger points out:

> The conventional approach emphasises the waste and inefficiencies resulting from the spillover effects of decentralised decisions but does not address the other side—the inefficiencies resulting from centralised decisions: the exporting of a very large part of the cost of regional services, standardisation of services, increasing cartelisation of government and a lack of experimentation and flexibility, to mention only a few. (1985:13–14)

Certainly there are some advantages to centralisation but these are in particular kinds or aspects of public policy rather than in all. Moreover, there is no possibility of the Australian federal system being designed anew as a single government, even if general central efficiencies could be shown. But, in any case, the advantages of centralisation need to be weighed against the advantages of decentralisation.

An advantage of decentralisation is that it allows a citizen to cast different votes on different components of public policy. Moreover, by creating a diversity of jurisdictions, it allows a better matching of preferences and policies with political and policy communities. For a sophisticated and regionally diverse nation, the standardisation of many public policies may be neither desirable nor efficient. Benefit jurisdictions may be local or regional, or alternatively spillovers can be provided for through co-operative or centralised arrangements. Nor is it likely that economies of scale for the provision of public goods always favour the national level of government. As Hanf points out, we have become

more aware of the problematic nature of central control. Often such attempts lack political feasibility, considering the political power of decentral units to resist effectively any move to reform or abolish them. At the same time, under conditions of western democracies, effective centralization can be resisted on the grounds that it is normatively undesirable, and, in light of the various 'costs of centralization', that it may be functionally ineffective as well. (1978:2–3)

In putting forward economic principles for determining the division of responsibilities cited above, Grewal also acknowledges that theoretical discussion 'cannot provide definite answers in the absence of detailed information about the variables involved' and that 'empirical investigations are required' (1981:36). And, as we have seen, there are arguments favouring decentralisation as well as centralisation and no certainty as to which is necessarily better. Moreover, it is unlikely that a general case can be made in favour of either. It is more likely that between the various levels of government there are a host of policies and arrangements with varying degrees of centralisation and decentralisation. These need to be understood. It may well be that the optimum solution is for a mix of both centralisation and decentralisation features. In any case, that is the likely result for a functioning federal system with extensive and complex public policies.

Redistributive and developmental policies

A more practical way of sorting out federal policies is in terms of their basic type. By the same token, perhaps a better way of allocating functions between levels of govrnment is on the basis of political and administrative propensities and capabilities. This is essentially the approach taken in a recent innovative study of federalism and public policy by Peterson, Rabe and Wong that focuses on the workings and effectiveness of American federal programs. These authors take issue with the negative implementation literature and report much more positively on the mutually accommodating intergovernmental relationships that operate in many federal programs. Petersen et al. propose a typology for sorting out the likely effectiveness of federal programs based on two distinctions: the extent to which a particular federal policy is redistributive as opposed to developmental, and the extent to which administering agencies are exempt from local political pressures and are staffed by professionals who identify with policy goals. The various combinations of effectiveness and type of program are summarised in Table 1.2.

Table 1.2: The effectiveness of federal programs by type of program and administration

Administration	Developmental programs	Redistributive programs
Professional	Moderately effective	Increasingly effective
Politicised	Effective	Ineffective

Source: Peterson, Rabe & Wong, 1986:7.

From this table it can be seen that developmental programs can be administered in a politicised way but that redistributive programs administered that way will be ineffective. For example, state activity in attracting business could involve cutting corners and being entrepreneurial, whereas this form of administration in a redistributive program would probably fail. The well-known study by Pressman and Wildavsky (1984) of the implementation of a federal program in Oakland was of this kind. It involved relying on local political figures for implementation of a vague, redistributive federal program, one that was seen to fail. On the other hand, professional administration of developmental projects is likely to be less effective than political administration. Developmental policies work well with local political input because local politicians have a special interest in the success of programs that are aimed at improving the economic position of their community in competition with other areas. Peterson et al. found that developmental programs worked well with local input and co-ordination.

Redistributive policies, on the other hand, are those that benefit low-income or otherwise disadvantaged groups. As argued by Grewal, these policies should mainly involve the central government. Problems might emerge when one community provides services to a specific group, such as the elderly, and the next does not. The result would be inequity, and perhaps migration of the needy. The central government can overcome this by providing to all in a professionally administered program. But this does not necessarily mean that the local level is not to be involved in administration. Here there are differences between types of program. Programs involving cash benefits such as social security or medicare payments to doctors may be centrally funded and administered. These programs have very small administrative costs, essentially transferring funds from one section of the community to another. There may be some local problems in that the level of social security payments is likely to be unvarying while economic conditions may vary widely, but transaction costs and the difficulty of setting equitable levels means that this problem is normally ignored.

When redistributive policies involve the supply of goods or services, such as housing, education, medical care, food, legal assistance or social services and the like, there is a case for involving decentralised governments. This may be by way of participation and co-operation in national programs or through joint or shared responsibilities. Tensions can emerge between the levels of administration arising from resource constraints, the autonomy of administrative officials and problems of implementation when redistributive programs become politically visible. Such conflict will probably lead to a new intergovernmental phase in the evolution of program administration as federal bureaucrats modify program guidelines and expectations. If there is tolerance for local interests and adjustment to local pressures, the implementation of such federal programs will be adopted. In that process of adjustment, professional interests and aspirations that are shared by administrators at federal, state and local levels will be important (Peterson et al., 1986:20).

This is very much what has happened in Australia in the administration of health policy by the hospital system and state health departments. This is a form of redistributive policy, as the majority of services are available regardless of means. Strict, rigid implementation of commonwealth health policy has given way to less formal arrangements under the medicare agreements where detailed administration is left to state and hospital administrators with close bureaucratic links with their federal counterparts. There is the further complication that certain key policy areas, housing for example, are both developmental and redistributive. Housing merits particular attention in the study of intergovernmental relations both for that reason and also because it is apparently one of the most harmonious policy areas.

Dynamics

Just as intergovernmental arrangements and processes vary among policy areas, so they can also vary across time in any particular area. There may be more or less involvement by ministers, depending on the political salience at any time, and, as well, different mixes of political and administrative participation. Some policy areas in whole or in part may become routinised while others are more volatile and variable. In Figure 1.1 we suggest a simple framework for analysing intergovernmental relations in Australia. We assume that for each level of government there is a spectrum of policy issues ranging from 'high' to 'low', and that the 'high' will be dealt with at the most senior political level while the 'low' can be routinised in administrative structures and processes.

Figure 1.1

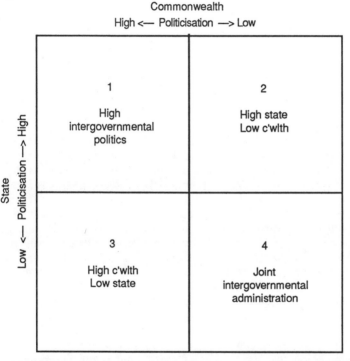

Prime examples of type 1 'high intergovernmental politics' are the Premiers' Conference and Loan Council meetings that are attended by first ministers and treasurers. These meetings have all the characteristics of 'high politics' for both sides. Being predominantly concerned with the big fiscal issues, the commonwealth quite unashamedly asserts its fiscal muscle to enforce decisions regarding the overall level of state reimbursements, public expenditure and borrowing on the states. For their part, the state political leaders use the occasion for political posturing on a grand scale. Those who are more administratively minded downplay the significance of the latter and brand such meetings as a waste of time, but the continued staging of such meetings suggests their political significance.

Examples of type 1 issues have been at various times uranium mining, foreign ownership in mineral resource development, jurisdiction over the offshore, aboriginal land rights and more recently the protection of world heritage environmental areas. When they are highly contentious and political flashpoints, policy areas and issues move into type 1, but once they have been resolved through accommodation or compromise and routinised in intergovernmental procedures, they tend to move to other categories. This will depend on which level of government has the major political role in the policy area. For example, matters of foreign investment in developmental projects will tend to become type 2 and be dealt with by state politics once the commonwealth's foreign investment guidelines have been set at levels that are acceptable to the states. Alternatively, if the two levels of government work out a shared arrangement that deals with ongoing business in a routinised way, such as for the offshore, the policy area becomes type 4.

This is not to suggest that there is a standard cycle from type 1 high politicisation to less politicised categories. Most intergovernmental issues probably never become type 1, or, alternatively, certain aspects may while others continue to be handled by routine intergovernmental administration. For instance, it was not uncommon for strong-man state premiers to indulge in Canberra bashing or agitation on particular issues while their administrative officials continued with cordial and constructive dealings. In fact, it might be preferable to construct a three-dimensional framework that included a second separate tier of administrative management that did not correspond exactly with the commonwealth–state politicisation represented here. However, to introduce the dynamic quality into our broad analysis, it is simpler to use a two-dimensional typology that combines political and administrative in three of the four categories. The particular dynamics of individual policy areas are explained in the following chapters.

Certain high-level political issues of Australian federalism are resolved, not by means of power assertion, bargaining and accommodation that are typical of the normal political process of relations between governments, but by independent bodies. Jurisdictional disputes concerning the respective powers of each level of government are decided by the High Court, and the relative shares of commonwealth grants to the states by the Commonwealth Grants Commission. Neither process, however, is entirely separate from politics. Regardless of how judges decide hard constitutional cases, the decisions still have to feed back into the political system where their impact may be adjusted by political negotiation. The *Offshore* decision is a classic example of an instance in which the Court's decision, in this instance to award offshore jurisdiction entirely to the commonwealth, was modified by insistent state politicians and the accommodating Fraser Government. Through intergovernmental agreement that was enacted in mirror legislation, the states retained a share in the administration of part of the offshore.

The Commonwealth Grants Commission is an independent body, albeit one appointed by the commonwealth, that now decides the states' relative shares of total commonwealth grant funds. The commonwealth retains control of the Grants Commission's terms of reference, as well as key aspects of its procedures such as the inclusion of most specific purpose or section 96 grants in its calculations and, most important of all, whether to implement its final recommendations. Over the last decade the Grants Commission has been given an increasingly significant role in determining relativities for grant allocation. The effect is to partly depoliticise aspects of fiscal decision making, although the Grants Commission's procedures have become more controversial as its role has become more politically significant (Walsh, 1989).

Arguably, the Grants Commission plays an important role in keeping the states onside in their tolerance of special-purpose grants, where the commonwealth is busily engaged in policy areas that would otherwise be the preserve of the states. Through including such payments in the equalisation calculation, the Grants Commission in effect cancels out much of the intrusiveness and political discretion of the commonwealth since a state that misses out on specific-purpose grants gets the equivalent in general grants after some time lag. In other words, the level of specific-purpose payments are not necessarily *prima facie* proof of coercive federalism. Hospital grants have become an exception, however, and have been explicitly excluded from equalisation calculations in the latest review.

Efficiency and effectiveness

Unless objectives neatly coincide between levels of government, against whose policy objectives or what combination of joint objectives are we to assess the successfulness of policy implementation? The question, of course, is simplistic. Once we accept the federal structure as a fact of life, then an important part of the focus must shift from assessing outcomes relative to the priorities of one or other level of government towards assessing the success of intergovernmental arrangements as processes for recognising, accommodating and reconciling differences in policy priorities. This is not to deny that outcomes are an important issue, but rather to indicate that the effectiveness of intergovernmental arrangements as devices for policy formulation are equally important.

The available literature offers little concrete guidance on how such assessments might be made. There is, of course, a huge literature, predominantly of United States origins, on so-called implementation research (O'Toole, 1986; Sabatier, 1986). However, its dominant focus is on 'top-down analysis' of multi-agency (and largely administrative) implementation. Nonetheless, even that literature contains some important lessons that need to be borne clearly in mind—many of them obvious once stated, but often overlooked particularly in more popular discussions. For example, even accepting a top-down perspective, increasing the number of administrative units involved in implementing policies (and hence the extent of 'redundancy' or 'overlap and duplication') may actually increase the reliability of decision-making processes (O'Toole, 1989). What is not clear, however, is how robust this sort of conclusion is either to adoption of a less top-down approach or, more importantly, to the recognition of multi-level political (as opposed to administrative) decision making in the implementation process. Perhaps the point is simply that the language commonly used for intergovernmental relations is usually value-laden—complexity, co-ordination costs, duplication, overlap, redundancy, monitoring costs, etc. In turn this could reflect the misplaced application of concepts relevant to simpler, less politically charged contexts.

At the risk of gross oversimplification, we can identify two polar opposite views prevalent in discussion of intergovernmental relations. Associated with a centralist (or top-down) position is the view that complex multi-layered decision making creates costs arising from the destruction of smooth integrated decision-making processes—costs associated with delays, with conflict, with co-ordination efforts, with additional complexity in monitoring and so on. From a more decentralist (or bottom-up) perspective on the other hand, the costs of intergovernmental arrangements arise from the imposition of 'outside' preferences, and from overlap and duplication in administration, monitoring and approvals systems. In a sense, both perspectives draw on similar models of administrative processes that emphasise the benefits of smooth, integrated and non-duplicative organisational structures. The top-down view dreams of removing lower levels of decision making to make the world fit the model, while the bottom-up view dreams of a neat delineation and separation of functions and responsibilities for similar reasons. And, of course, both presume that in their respective ideal worlds, administrative rationality and political rationality dictate similar arrangements.

It is not only administrative models of federal arrangements that have tended to emphasise the virtues of simplicity. Based on models which concentrate attention on efficiency and co-ordination, economists too have tended to describe federal arrangements which involve a neat division of powers, blurred 'only' by a complementary system of intergovernmental grants to achieve vertical and horizontal balance, and to correct for some of the inevitable spillovers. The implicit models of the political and administrative arrangements that lie behind this vision of the 'federal' system are, at best, obscure. Quite how 'neatness', 'efficiency' and 'co-ordination' are secured and sustained given the complexities introduced by the systems of grants is unclear. Particularly strange, in light of the virtue attached to competition in other contexts by economists, is the fact that overlap and duplication in federal arrangements seems to be automatically dubbed as wasteful, rather than as something to be investigated as a potential source of creative competition, or a necessary part of co-ordination.

On the other hand, there also are those—predominantly political scientists and/or economists with a more public-choice orientation—who see greater value in the growth of complex, unorthodox and overlapping arrangements. Although untidy, such arrangements might be more appropriate mechanisms for accommodating multiple values, encouraging bargaining, facilitating participation and adaptability, and imposing constraints on the exercise of power. At the extreme is an almost axiomatic view that increased complexity in inter-relationships is evidence of increased health in federalism arrangements.

None of these positions can be attributed strictly to any particular writer. Nor can any of them be taken as providing a clear model for use in the evaluation of intergovernmental arrangements. Any evaluative framework would have to draw from the various different perspectives. What does seem clear is that evaluation of intergovernmental arrangements should attempt to incorporate elements of at least three inter-related perspectives:

1 how the arrangements affect the efficiency and effectiveness of policy outcomes (i.e., an output-oriented perspective, which will need to be sensitive both to the differing objectives of different governmental units, and to the implications of more process-oriented perspectives);

2 how the arrangements affect the reliability of policy making and implementation process (i.e., a sort of half-way house between output and process oriented perspectives that seeks to establish whether—viewed top-down or bottom-up—the arrangements might increase confidence that consistency and coherence in outcomes is secured, despite the ostensible costs of overlapping, complex decision making);

3 how the arrangements affect the entire decision-making process (i.e., a perspective on the broader objectives of processes themselves, including the extent to which they accommodate differences in values, by facilitating participation, bargaining and adaptability, and by constraining the exercise of coercive power).

For all of these levels of evaluation, there is the further important question as to how robust are the conclusions (and hence the virtues of the particular intergovernmental arrangements) to changes in the external environment?

Of particular importance in this regard is the question of 'resource availability'. The implementation research literature emphasises the importance of the extent to which resources are made available to encourage policy implementation. This perspective is mirrored in the Australian literature in the view that the states acquiesced in the growth of commonwealth financial dominance because they were richly bribed to do so, rather than strictly coerced. At least since the end of the Whitlam era, there has been a general winding-back in the generosity of commonwealth transfers to the states, with particular acceleration in recent years.

Bibliography

ACIR, 1981. Advisory Council for Inter-government Relations, Information Paper No. 9, *Towards Adaptive Federalism: A Search for Criteria for Responsibility Sharing in a Federal System*, AGPS, Canberra.

—— 1986. *Compendium of Intergovernmental Agreements*, Tasmanian Government Printer, Hobart.

Agranoff, R. & Lindsay, V.A., 1983. 'Intergovernmental Management: Perspectives from Human Services, Problem Solving at the Local Level', *Public Administration Review*, 43(3), 227–37.

Belanger, G., 1985. 'The Division of Powers in a Federal System: A Review of the Economic Literature, with Applications to Canada', in *Division of Powers and Public Policy*, ed. R. Simeon.

Birrell, M. ed., 1987. *The Australian States: Towards a Renaissance*, Longman Cheshire, Melbourne.

Breton, A., 1985. 'Minority Report', in *Report of the Royal Commission on the Economic Union and Development Prospects for Canada*, Canadian Government Printers, Ottawa (reprinted as 'Towards a Theory of Competitive Federalism', in *European Journal of Political Economy*, Special Issue, 3 (Nos 1 & 2) 1987).

Brugger, B. & Jaensch, D., 1985. *Australian Politics: Theory and Practice*, Allen & Unwin, Sydney.

Chapman, R., 1988. 'Inter-governmental Forums and the Policy Process', in *Comparative State Policies*, ed. B. Galligan, 99–121.

Constitutional Commission, 1987. *Report of the Advisory Committee on the Distribution of Powers*, AGPS, Canberra.

Davis, G., Wanna, J., Warhurst, J. & Weller, P., 1988. *Public Policy in Australia*, Sydney, Allen & Unwin, Sydney.

Dupré, J.S., 1985. 'Reflections on the Workability of Executive Federalism', in *Intergovernmental Relations*, MacDonald Commission, 1–32.

Elazar, D.J., 1962. *The American Partnership: Intergovernmental Cooperation in the Nineteenth Century United States*, University of Chicago Press, Chicago.

Galligan B. ed., 1988. *Comparative State Policies*, Longman Cheshire, Melbourne.

—— ed., 1989. *Australian Federalism*, Longman Cheshire, Melbourne.

Gibbins, R., 1987. 'Federal Societies, Institutions, and Politics', in *Federalism and the Role of the State*, eds H. Bakvis & W.M. Chandler, University of Toronto Press, Toronto, 15–31.

Grewal, B.S., 1981. 'Economic Criteria for the Assignment of Functions in a Federal System', in *Towards Adaptive Federalism: A Search for Criteria for Responsibility Sharing in a Federal System*, ACIR, 36.

—— 1989. 'Federal Institutions and Processes: An Economic Perspective', in *Australian Federalism*, ed. B. Galligan, 118–41.

Grodzins, M., 1966. *The American System: A New View of Government in the United States*, ed. D.J. Elazar, Rand McNally, Chicago.

Hanf, K., 1978. 'Introduction', in *Interorganizational Policy Making*, eds K. Hanf & F.W. Scharpf.

Hanf, K., & Scharpf, F.W., eds, 1978. *Interorganizational Policy Making*, Sage Publications, London.

Hawke, R.J.L., 1979. *The Resolution of Conflict*, 1979 Boyer Lectures, Australian Broadcasting Commission.

Hockin, T.A., 1976. *Government in Canada*, McGraw-Hill Rogerson, Toronto.

MacDonald Commission, 1985. *Intergovernmental Relations*, University of Toronto Press, Toronto. (This is Vol. 63 in the series of studies in the research program commissioned by the Royal Commission on the Economic Union and Development Prospects for Canada. Research Coordinator: Richard Simeon.)

McRoberts, K., 1985. 'Unilateralism, Bilateralism and Multilateralism: Approaches to Canadian Federalism', in *Intergovernmental Relations*, MacDonald Commission, 71–129.

Mathews, R., 1986. *Fiscal Federalism in Australia: Past and Future Tense*, Reprint Series No. 74, Centre for Research on Federal Financial Relations, The Australian National University, Canberra.

—— ed., 1974. *Intergovernmental Relations in Australia*, Angus & Robertson, Sydney.

Nathan, R.P., Doolittle, F.C. & Associates 1987. *Reagan and the States*, Princeton University Pess, Princeton, NJ.

O'Toole, L.J., Jr, 1986. 'Policy Recommendations for Multi-Actor Implementation: An Assessment of the Field', *Journal of Public Policy*, 6(2), 181–210.

—— 1989. 'Goal Multiplicity in the Implementation Setting: Some Impact and the Case of Wastewater Treatment Privatisation', Paper presented at American Political Science Association Annual Meeting, Atlanta.

Peterson, P., Rabe, B.G. & Wong, K.K., 1986. *When Federalism Works*, The Brookings Institution, Washington, DC.

Pressman, J. & Wildavsky, A., 1984. *Implementation*, 3rd edn, University of California Press, Berkeley (first edn, 1973).

Sabatier, P.A., 1986. 'Top-Down and Bottom-Up Approaches to Implementation Research: A Critical Analysis and Suggested Synthesis', *Journal of Public Policy* 6(1), 21–48.

Schechter, S.L., 1981. 'On the Compatibility of Federalism and Intergovernmental Management', *Publius*, 11(4), 127–41.

Sharman, C., 1988. 'The Study of the States', in *Comparative State Policies*, ed. B. Galligan, 1–17.

Simeon, R., 1972, *Federal–Provincial Diplomacy*, University of Toronto Press, Toronto.

—— ed., 1985. *Division of Powers and Public Policy*, University of Toronto Press, Toronto.

Smiley, D.V., 1980. *Canada in Question: Federalism in the Eighties*, 3rd edn, McGraw-Hill Rogerson, Toronto.

Stenberg, C., 1981. 'Beyond the Days of Wines and Roses: Intergovernmental Management in a Cutback Environment', *Public Administration Review*, 41(1), 10–20.

Walsh, C. ed., 1989. *Fiscal Equalisation, Allocative Efficiency & State Business Undertakings: The Commonwealth Grants Commission 1988 Report on Relativities*, Centre for Research on Federal Financial Relations, ANU, Canberra.

Wettenhall, R., 1985. 'Intergovernmental Agencies: Lubricating a Federal System', *Current Affairs Bulletin*, April, 28–35.

Whitlam, E.G., 1983. 'The Cost of Federalism', in *Australian Federalism; Future Tense*, eds Allan Patience & Jeffrey Scott, Oxford University Press, Melbourne.

Wiltshire, K., 1981. 'Administrative Criteria for the Allocation of Functions Between Levels of Government in a Federation', in *Towards Adaptive Federalism: A Search for Criteria for Responsibility Sharing in a Federal System*, ACIR.

—— 1986. *Planning and Federalism*, University of Queensland Press, St Lucia, Qld.

Wright, D.S., 1975. 'Intergovernmental Relations and Policy Choice', *Publius*, 5(4), 1–24.

—— 1983. 'Managing the Intergovernmental Scene: The Changing Dramas of Federalism, Intergovernmental Relations, and Intergovernmental Management', in *The Handbook of Organization Management*, ed. W.B. Eddy, Marcel Dekker, New York: 417–54.

2 Executive federalism

Campbell Sharman

The growth of intergovernmental relations—as the interaction between the component governments of a federation are now frequently called—is commonly observed to be one of the most significant changes to have affected federal government since the war. There is similar widespread agreement that this growth has occurred because of the expansion of government involvement with the social and economic life of citizens. The number of agencies designed to exchange information and establish channels of communication between the state and national spheres of government has consequently grown. In addition, the process of increasing government regulation in federations has meant greater jurisdictional overlap. This in turn requires bodies to provide a framework for consultation and the harmonisation of policies. Further, and especially in the Australian case, growing central government involvement in financing state programs has implied a corresponding growth in administrative machinery for consultation in those policy areas.

On closer examination, however, the growth in intergovernmental relations is a more complex phenomenon than might be suggested by the rather bland summary given above. To begin with, the defining characteristics of intergovernmental relations are far from clear. The operation of state and national governments involves such a degree of interpenetration that it is hard to find either an area of commonwealth activity that does not impinge on state policies, or state administration that does not entail some commonwealth involvement. In other words, Australia is a federation with a single citizenry subject to the actions of two spheres of government. It is hard to distinguish the growth of intergovernmental relations from the growth of government in general.

To restrict intergovernmental relations to explicit transactions between governments limits the field a little—to what chapter 4 in this book calls intergovernmental management—but this would still encompass everything from formal agreements between heads of government to casual phone calls between officials. Yet to limit intergovernmental relations to only those transactions between agencies specifically charged with dealing with other spheres of government is clearly too restrictive since it excludes a great deal of the day-to-day consultations shaping policy at all levels of government. As a result, one of the problems of analysing intergovernmental relations is the difficulty of distinguishing them from intragovernment transactions (see Dupre, 1987), and the sporadic contact that all government agencies have with other spheres of government from time to time. A related difficulty is that the single term 'intergovernmental relations' is no more than shorthand for a cluster of highly diverse transactions.

But some of the most contentious aspects of intergovernmental relations, however defined, can be found in attempts to explain and assess the nature and consequences of its growth, its impact on federalism, and its effect on the governmental system in general.

This chapter reviews these issues, following three particular themes. The first examines the extent to which the growth of intergovernmental relations can be seen as a continuation of long-standing characteristics of the Australian version of executive federalism. The second investigates the range of activities covered by the term 'intergovernmental relations' and the variety of explanations for its growth. The final theme concerns attitudes to the impact of intergovernmental relations on federalism and whether its growth should be regarded as a sign of the success or of the failure of the federal system as a whole.

Executive federalism in Australian

Australia is a parliamentary federation—its main characteristics being a combination of a federal division of powers and a parliamentary mode of operation of executive authority.

Yet there is a tension between these characteristics in the sense that each rests on assumptions about the nature of government that are at odds. Federalism implies the dispersal of power between a number of autonomous governmental authorities and a mode of decision making characterised by negotiation and compromise. Contemporary parliamentary government, however, presumes the concentration of power in the executive branch. The executive dominates the parliamentary process through the medium of party discipline and no constraints on policy making arise from the need to accommodate the competing views of others with equal claim to constitutional legitimacy. This conflict is a manifestation of the broader tension between what Lijphart (1984; 1989) has called consensus and majoritarian forms of democratic government.

The implications of this are that while federalism reflects the existence of multiple and autonomous agencies of government, parliamentary government integrates all the agencies of each government into a single hierarchy with the executive at its apex. Consequently, the relations between the component governments in the federation become the realm of executive action alone, and of the chief executive officer, premier or prime minister in particular. This is what Smiley (1987) has described as executive federalism and it is characterised by the channelling of intergovernmental relations into transactions controlled by elected and appointed officials of the executive branch. This contrasts with the much more open and diffuse pattern of intergovernmental relations to be found in the United States (Grodzins, 1966; Wright, 1988), where the separation of powers of a presidential system creates opportunities for a great diversity of intergovernmental relations and includes the legislature as a major independent actor (note Gibbins, 1982).

It could be argued that this picture of executive federalism in Australia is overdrawn to the extent that it ignores a number of factors which work to reduce the effectiveness of the executive monopoly of intergovernmental relations. One is the role of the High Court as a forum for resolving intergovernmental disputes, another is the tradition of strong bicameralism in a majority of Australia's parliaments, and a third is the great diversity of the executive branch itself.

The High Court clearly plays a critical role in setting the framework for government interaction through the Court's interpretations of the commonwealth constitution (Galligan, 1987; Lindell, 1989; Zines, 1989). But it is not itself a major actor in the process of intergovernmental relations. Few intergovernmental transactions involve the courts, partly because most dealings between governments do not involve disputes over jurisdiction, and partly because governments do not wish to invoke the complex, time consuming, and unpredictable procedures of the legal process. Nor do the rules governing legal standing permit easy access to the courts by groups wishing to challenge particular intergovernmental agreements. Recourse to the judicial process is a strategy of last resort and signals the partial or complete breakdown of the usual pattern of intergovernmental relations (see generally Galligan, 1987).

The Australian experience of powerful upper houses does represent a major limitation on the British parliamentary tradition of executive dominance of the legislative process (Sharman, 1987). But strong bicameralism cannot remove the advantages given to the executive by law and custom in the control of parliamentary procedure. The most an upper house can do against the wishes of its executive-dominated lower house is to veto the legislation required to implement executive-negotiated intergovernmental agreements, or to use the power of parliamentary scrutiny to inquire into aspects of intergovernmental relations. The potential for even this indirect involvement of upper houses in intergovernmental relations has been exploited only infrequently (note Sharman, 1982). The reason seems to derive from a belief by members of parliament themselves that intergovernmental relations is primarily a matter for the executive. Only when there is public outcry or strong partisan hostility to a particular measure involving an agreement between governments should recourse to the legislature be considered. It is possible that the Senate and some of the legislative councils in the states may initiate procedures for routine scrutiny of intergovernmental relations, but there are few signs of any real challenge from this direction.

The mixed nature of the executive itself is a further consideration. While one view of the executive is of an orderly hierarchy of executive agencies subject to the direction of the cabinet as a central co-ordinating body, it can also be seen as a very large aggregate of disparate bureaux, each with its own goals, strategies and sets of priorities. Some of these goals will correspond with the interests of the co-ordinating agency but others will conflict. The clash of interests may spill over into relations with other spheres of government, and, in addition, some government agencies may develop closer relations with similar agencies in other governments than with different agencies in their own (note Holmes & Sharman, 1977:117–34).

The fact of intra-executive rivalry is, however, less a criticism of the notion of executive federalism than a caution on the acceptance of a picture of each government in the federation as a hard-edged monolith in its dealings with other governments. A better analogy would be to describe governments, both state and commonwealth, as teams of more or less unruly players (see Sharman, 1977).

The utility of the notion of executive federalism is that it describes the basic logic of intergovernmental relations in parliamentary federations— that the executive branch designs the organisational context of intergovernmental relations and is the dominant actor. In addition, it helps to explain why intergovernmental relations is of special importance to the heads of government, premiers and prime ministers, since it both reflects and reinforces their key positions in the political and administrative process (note Sharman & Stuart, 1982). Nothing shows this more clearly than the most visible mechanism of intergovernmental relations, the Premiers' Conference.

The Premiers' Conferences, ministerial councils
and the Grants Commission

Meetings of heads of government in Australia predate federation and illustrate both the bureaucratic and political functions of intergovernmental relations. Contemporary Premiers' Conferences are held in Canberra at least once a year with one usually held around June before the final deliberations on the commonwealth budget. Formal public presentations by the prime minister and the premiers are followed by one or two days of largely private and informal discussions. The dominant issue at the conference is always the matter of commonwealth–state financial relations, punctuated by news conferences in which participants offer rival views of the proceedings. The Premiers' Conference often concludes with a final statement and a flurry of press releases expressing a range of assessments of the success of the conference.

The major function of the Premiers' Conference might appear to be making decisions about financial transfers from the commonwealth to the states. Decisions are also made on a range of other issues affecting relations between governments that have not been resolved at lower levels. As such, the Premiers' Conference can be seen as the apex of a hierarchy of intergovernmental structures designed to cope with relations between the two spheres of government. But, while there are elements of this, the major function of the Premiers' Conference is political and symbolic rather than administrative.

Some of the reasons for this can be found in the limited room for manoeuvre on key issues. This is especially the case on financial transfers where the outline of the commonwealth budgetary strategy has been set by the cabinet before the Premiers' Conference, and prior consultation between state and commonwealth treasuries has given the states a clear picture of the likely outcome of the conference. Moreover, the commonwealth has usually gone out of its way to deny that the conferences are forums for making negotiated decisions on finance, simply because it is the commonwealth that has assumed the responsibility of raising the funds to be distributed. While the states dispute this view of the Premiers' Conferences, their only remedy is to stress the political consequences of commonwealth actions.

This is similar to non-financial issues. While the room for manoeuvre and bargaining is larger, the Premiers' Conference is primarily a forum for making statements of principle to be referred to committees for further study, or the ratification of agreements already negotiated. It is for this reason that the diplomatic analogy has been so popular in describing Premiers' Conferences, since it stresses that the conferences involve formal transactions between heads of government within an established framework permitting limited bargaining and the deployment of a range of bureaucratic and political resources (Simeon, 1972; and note Sharman, 1977).

The major role of the Premiers' Conference is a political one in that it permits the seven most influential executive officers in Australia to speak to a variety of audiences. The widest audience is the public at large—the Premiers' Conference provides a national forum for each premier to give his or her own view of policies affecting the national interest. This enables a premier to be both a commentator on national affairs and a defender of his or her state's interests. Although the commonwealth government may resent its temporary loss of monopoly access to Canberra's media during Premiers' Conferences, its use of these conferences indicates its awareness that they can be used to publicise and dramatise government concern, as has been the case with such issues as gun control, drugs and housing.

Apart from the general public, there are other audiences for whom Premiers' Conferences are important events. One of these is the conference participants themselves. The conferences provide the opportunity for assessing the personality and political skills of rival players in the national arena. In a similar way, the quality of bureaucratic advice available to the premiers and the prime minister is on display. These elements combine to provide all participating governments with a range of views and information not available to a single government. This is particularly important for prime ministers and premiers who are not accustomed to cope with the face-to-face expression of rival views by politicians of equal status.

The variety of functions performed by Premiers' Conferences goes much of the way to explain the ambivalent attitudes of the press to these meetings. On the one hand they are often described as ritual gatherings with no policy significance, yet the coverage given them indicates their high political salience. The Premiers' Conference is an artefact of a parliamentary federation in that the parliamentary process produces seven heads of government, each playing a key role in their governmental systems, and federation needs a forum for their formal interaction. Hence the fact of their meeting is more important than the substance of their discussions. Nor has this situation changed over the life of the federation. While the procedures of Premiers' Conferences have been modified over the years, and ease of transport has had an effect on the style and frequency of meetings, the dynamics of their operation has remained substantially unaltered.

This description of Premiers' Conferences also applies to ministerial councils. They represent, in the microcosm of a particular policy area, a similar mix of administrative procedures and political considerations, the meetings having a variety of public, bureaucratic and participant audiences. The key players are ministers whose political dominance in certain areas is subject only to the direction of the premier or prime minister, and cabinet. The councils are also underpinned by committees of officials, and their deliberations are also coloured by differing policy, regional and partisan considerations. The numbers of these councils has grown rapidly over the last twenty years to more than 40 (ACIR, 1986a), but their design reflects the basic logic of a parliamentary federation: that such policy forums are an exclusive concern of the executive branch and that the representatives of the political executive—ministers—should have pride of place.

Before leaving the topic of ministerial councils, two institutions need special mention both because of their anomalous position in the federal structure and because each, in its own way, reflects the executive dominance of the federal process. The first of these is the Loan Council whose formal establishment in 1927 was designed to alleviate the problems of raising funds on overseas markets by setting up joint rather than competitive procedures for loan raising and debt servicing. The operation and evolution of the Loan Council are well analysed elsewhere (note Gilbert, 1973; Mathews, 1985:58–60; Mathews & Jay, 1972; Saunders, 1985, 1990; Walsh, 1989:231–34), but its importance in the present context is its congruence with other aspects of intergovernmental relations in Australia. While it is the only intergovernmental body to have constitutional underpinning (section 105A), and its procedures are governed by formal rules in a way which is not characteristic of other ministerial councils, the meeting of state and commonwealth treasurers has many of the features of such bodies. Its meetings are held in camera, its key participants are ministers backed by bureaucratic expertise, and its decisions are not reviewed by the legislatures of either sphere of government, even though Loan Council decisions have had important consequences for public expenditure and the pattern of state capital works (but note Saunders, 1990).

The second institution is the Commonwealth Grants Commission, which is included even though it is not a ministerial council at all but a body established by the commonwealth to advise it on the allocation of commonwealth funds between the states. Its creation in 1933 was a response to a vigorous campaign by the least populous states for compensation for their special financial disabilities (May, 1971; Reid, 1979). Today its role has become that of producing formulas to reflect some notion of regional equity in the allocation of commonwealth funds to the states (CGC, 1983, and Reports; note also Grewal, 1989).

As such, the Commonwealth Grants Commission plays a paradoxical role. It attempts to reduce questions of financial need to objective accounting measures as though basic issues of government expenditure were matters of economic expertise divorced from politics. Yet the Commission has, in fact, played a highly political role in masking the consequences of the central government's pre-eminence in the raising of revenue since the 1940s. In this respect, both the Loan Council and the Commonwealth Grants Commission are agencies which reflect the continued unwillingness of the states to challenge the financial dominance of the commonwealth. The comfortable pattern of intergovernmental transfers are the substitute for direct state responsibility for their own revenue raising.

To the extent that these agencies are key components of the negotiating process for the allocation of commonwealth funds to the states, they are closely tied to the deliberations of the Premiers'

Conference and survive only as long as their role can be harmonised with the political goals of a majority of conference participants. This was also true of the Advisory Council for Inter-government Relations (ACIR) as a body that generated authoritative information. The fact that the ACIR became identified with views on local government that clashed with those of members of the Premiers' Conference does much to explain why the ACIR was wound up (see Chapman, 1988a).

The growth of commonwealth-state consultative machinery

The search for reasons why ministerial councils and such like have proliferated over the last twenty years brings us to why intergovernmental relations in general have grown. Three sets of explanations can be offered.

The first, already discussed, is that the expansion of intergovernmental relations is simply part of the growth of government in general. This explanation fails to deal with the fact that intergovernmental relations appears to have continued on a rising theme since the mid 1960s while the size of government has not. While Emy and Hughes (1989:145–81), for example, demonstrate that the growth of government is a more complex issue than is often assumed, such broad budgetary indicators as public sector outlays as a percentage of gross domestic product show an increase of 10 per cent over the period from 1966 to 1986 (Budget Paper No. 4 1987–88:14). Over the same period, however, data from the ACIR show that the number of ministerial councils has more than doubled (ACIR, 1986a), a pattern reinforced by details of other intergovernmental transactions published by the ACIR (1985, 1986b).

A modification of the growth-of-government argument might be that a critical point was reached in the 1970s where the increase in the volume of intergovernmental transactions led to a qualitative change in intergovernmental relations and a pattern of growth that is now independent of the growth of government in general. There is some plausibility in this since, by almost any measure, there was a rapid growth in the size of government in the years of the Whitlam Government from 1972 to 1975 and a similar increase in intergovernmental relations. While the extent of government expenditure, for example, has grown only slowly since the mid-1970s, the ACIR indicators of intergovernmental activity have continued to rise at a rapid rate (ACIR, 1986a:20).

Unfortunately for this argument, one of the most obvious measures of intergovernmental activity does not follow the trend of the ACIR indicators. Since specific-purpose payments to the states are one of the main ways the commonwealth has become involved in policy making in the states, it might be assumed that an increase in intergovernmental transactions would be mirrored in an increase in specific-purpose payments to the states. This has not occurred: specific-purpose payments, while they grew rapidly under Whitlam, have declined since the mid-1970s, measured either as a proportion of gross domestic product or as a proportion of total commonwealth transfers to the states (Budget Paper No. 4, 1987–88:10).

Clearly, examining the relationship between intergovernmental relations and the size of government raises both conceptual and analytical difficulties as well as questions about the causal links between the two phenomena. However these questions are answered, the point is that attempts to link intergovernmental relations directly to the level of government activity in general ignores the distinctive political goals that are a major component of transactions between governments.

This leads to the second set of explanations, which focus on explicitly political events. There are two strands to this argument, one stressing the partisan goals of national governments, the other the inherently expansionist ambitions of the commonwealth. The first strand points to the great surge in the scale of intergovernmental transactions flowing from the Whitlam Government's new federalism initiatives. The continued growth of intergovernmental relations under the Fraser Governments from 1975 to 1983 stemmed, paradoxically, from a political commitment to reduce commonwealth involvement with state responsibilities (Sharman, 1980). This attempt to extract the national government from open-ended financial commitments to shared-cost programs led to an increase in the extent of commonwealth involvement in intergovernmental relations and an increase, rather than a decrease, in consultative machinery. Similarly, new consultative bodies established by the Hawke Governments since 1983, and the extension of intergovernmental transactions in the areas of the environment, education and drugs, for example, can all be traced to specific political events or the partisan goals of the government or particular ministers.

The second strand points to the pressures for the commonwealth to participate in activities outside its narrow jurisdictional responsibilities, partly because of pressure from interest groups who have not been successful at state level, partly because the states themselves have invited commonwealth participation, and partly because of the wish by all commonwealth politicians to be seen to be involved in any area of high political salience. This explanation sees the growth in intergovernmental relations as a memorial to the inherent expansionism of all commonwealth regimes.

The final set of explanations of the recent growth of intergovernmental relations stresses that the years since the 1970s have seen a change in administrative culture that has led to increasing pressure for greater interaction between state and national governments, and is quite independent of the particular policy goals or scale of expenditure of governments.

This change might be called a shift towards managerialism. Although this term is an imprecise one, in this context it is used to refer to three characteristic concepts of contemporary executive government: first, a concern with using resources to achieve goals at the least economic cost; secondly, a concern with the co-ordination of government activities so that they are consistent with the overall direction of government policy; and thirdly, a concern with the design of the organisation of government itself.

These concerns have been strongly influenced by the decline in the belief of the virtues of big government and the eclipse of both socialism as a political ideology and Keynesian economics as the basis for government regulation of the economy. In Australia this corresponded roughly with the defeat of the Whitlam Government and the rise of a conservative, market-oriented view of the role of government, which has captured the leadership of both the Labor and Liberal parties. These developments have had major implications for the conduct of intergovernmental relations because of the change in both the nature of governmental concerns and the style of coping with them.

It had been realised during the term of the Whitlam Government that the massive increase in intergovernmental transactions prompted by Whitlam's new federalism had created major problems of administrative overload. The range of commonwealth initiatives in health, education, and urban development, for example, even when welcomed by state governments, caught them unprepared for the flood of funds and the multiplicity of demands for a corresponding flow of information. The lack of established procedures and trained personnel, the extent and variety of the new programs, the political demands for rapid implementation and the fact that most of the biggest programs were in areas that had been outside the previous ambit of intergovernmental relations, all contributed to a sense of pressure and confusion that was exacerbated by the growing political tension between the states and the national government (note Sharman, 1984). By the close of the Whitlam period in 1975, two responses to this situation could be seen. The first was the establishment of new routines and standard operating procedures in areas that had previously been outside the scope of intergovernmental relations, and the creation of groups of officials at both levels of government with specific responsibilities for the conduct of intergovernmental relations (Warhurst, 1987).

The second was a concern with monitoring intergovernmental relations and co-ordinating government responses across programs. The principal motivation for this was a need to supervise and co-ordinate the activities of one's own government. This not only restored some order to the conduct of intergovernmental transactions, but enabled the premiers and prime minister to maintain their administrative dominance in a forum of major importance to them. The detail required to monitor the inter-governmental aspects of a department's activities both enabled a premier or prime minister to harmonise one department's intergovernmental relations programs with the general goals of the government as a whole, and gave the premiers' and prime minister's departments a useful insight into the running of all departments in the ministry.

These trends were reinforced by the Fraser Government when budgetary pressures on the commonwealth forced a major reassessment of commonwealth financial transfers to the states. This meant the end of an era of new big spending intergovernmental programs and radical initiatives, and the beginning of the politics of low expectations and incremental change. Initially, the attempt by the commonwealth under Fraser to reduce its commitment to many existing programs was seen by the states as a major attack on the rules of intergovernmental relations, but, by the accession of the Hawke Government in 1983, the states had accepted that financial stringency was here to stay.

The new concern with parsimony further accentuated the need for effective control of administration. The public goal of heads of government was to be good managers of existing programs rather than bold innovators. Indeed, the thrust of the managerial explanation of recent changes is that there has been a shift in the nature of intergovernmental relations because it is being driven by administrative concerns rather than partisan politics. If this is true, it raises the question of whether this marks a change in substance or style.

In broad terms, the dynamics of intergovernmental relations have not changed in that the principal participants have not altered nor have the basic characteristics of executive federalism been changed. What has altered has been the removal of intergovernmental relations from the central position it occupied in the 1970s as a result of an overall decline in partisan tension (note Sharman, 1989). This has been accompanied by a much more modest view of the role and extent of commonwealth-sponsored initiatives, and the establishment of procedures to cope with intergovernmental relations at all levels of government. In sum, in dealings between spheres of government it can be argued that there has been a clear shift from a partisan to a bureaucratic mode of interaction and an increasing stress on administrative rather than financial and partisan resources (note Wright, 1988:99–112).

All three of these explanations for the growth of intergovernmental relations—the expansion of government activities, the political agenda of successive governments, and the shift in stress from partisan to bureaucratic politics—are, of course, closely related to the attitudes of the commentators.

Attitudes to intergovernmental relations

The notion of managerialism raises an issue that is critical to attitudes regarding intergovernmental relations. It is also relevant to discussions of the existing pattern of transactions between the two spheres of government and whether the administrative structures of intergovernmental relations should be regarded as beneficial or dysfunctional aspects of federalism.

Those who take a beneficial view stress that federalism, by creating a variety of jurisdictions, fosters the growth of multi-agency government. The interaction between a variety of government agencies and the quasi-market context provided by competition for support produces a highly responsive governmental structure, both in terms of the allocation of resources and in reflecting the political preferences of citizens. This view represents an important element in commentary on the federal system of the United States (for example, Elazar, 1987; Grodzins, 1966; Ostrom, 1973) but it has been almost entirely absent from analyses of the Australian system until very recently (see Galligan, 1989b, and note chapter 1 in this volume).

In Australia, together with Canada, the growth of intergovernmental relations has been seen at best as a way of overcoming problems in the allocation of jurisdiction between governments and at worst as a symptom of the failure of the federal system as a whole. Part of this has stemmed from views of federalism that have been strongly influenced by Wheare (1946). In defining the federal principle in terms of the independence of the two spheres of government, Wheare suggested any degree of interdependence is a breach of federalism. Given the postwar influence of Wheare in parliamentary federations, this immediately cast intergovernmental relations as an illegitimate and almost furtive component of the federal system and, for some, a symptom of the intrinsic unsuitability of federalism to cope with the problems of modern government.

This was modified by Birch (1957, 1966), for example, who argued that Wheare's definition of federalism was much too restrictive. What was important was the interdependence of the two spheres of government, not their independence. Even this approach, however, implied that a process of intergovernmental accommodation was a second-best solution forced on a federation by the growth of government intervention in the social and economic life of the public. Intergovernmental relations was the remedy for a federal division of jurisdictions in a collectivist age.

This theme was reinforced by those who distrusted the inherent untidiness of federalism. From the perspective of public finance, for example, the open disagreements and piecemeal competition for political support that characterise the public face of intergovernmental relations was seen as inconsistent with an orderly process of fitting tax revenue to public needs. The notion of co-operative federalism became popular precisely because it implied the subordination of the unruly political aspects of federalism to the reasoned processes of administrative accommodation. As a consequence, intergovernmental relations would become an administrative forum where conflict between spheres of government could be resolved before it led to open political dispute. Such a view saw intergovernmental relations as a poultice for the political wounds created by federalism.

This attitude towards intergovernmental relations is widespread among those who participate in transactions between governments and many of those who comment on them. They see the role of intergovernmental relations as the management and resolution of potential conflict, and as harmonising the policies of state and commonwealth governments (for example, Chapman, 1988b; Wettenhall, 1985; Wiltshire, 1986; and note Mathews, 1974). Yet the benefits claimed by some for this process of managed accommodation are seen by others to be a major drawback of the present pattern of intergovernmental relations.

From very different standpoints, Smiley (1987) and Breton (1985) have argued that this stress on intergovernmental relations as a process of bureaucratic management in Canada signals a failure in the operation of other aspects of the federal system. Smiley points to the importance of executive federalism and intergovernmental relations as a response to the eclipse of Canadian parties as forums for the resolution of critical questions in the political life of Canada, while Breton sees the growth of the administrative management of intergovernmental relations as an attempt to establish oligopolistic control of the essentially competitive nature of the federal process. Both authors see the managerialist nature of intergovernmental relations as a threat to the efficiency of government and to the processes of representative democracy.

These themes have been muted in Australia (but note Saunders, 1987) and where they have surfaced in the past they have done so in the form of a concern with the relationship between intergovernmental relations and British-style responsible parliamentary government (for example Reid, 1974; Spann, 1972). Such discussions, however, often became lost in the labyrinth of debates over the nature of responsible government.

The fact that these concerns have received little attention in Australia does not reduce their importance. If nothing else, they point to a double ambiguity in the nature of intergovernmental relations. On one hand intergovernmental relations is a manifestation of the open and competitive interaction of governments in a federation, and on the other it can be seen as a way of suppressing such open competition. Similarly, intergovernmental relations is viewed both as an intrinsic part of federalism and the liberal democratic values on which it is based, and as a substantial modification of federalism and a threat to such values. Perhaps these conceptual differences are yet another version of the debate over the merits of federalism itself, discussion of the nature of intergovernmental relations becoming a proxy for the analysis of the normative bases of the federal system.

The critical element may be found in the nature of executive federalism itself. Ambiguities in attitudes to intergovernmental relations in Australia simply mirror the fact that, in a parliamentary federation with a small number of states, it is possible to form a cartel of executive governments to manage transactions between them. By greatly constricting the avenues for interaction between governments, executive federalism exacerbates political tensions (note Riker & Schapps, 1957) even though it provides the opportunity for their partial resolution. Accordingly, it can be argued that the diversity of the federal system of the United States makes intergovernmental relations in that country inherently open, political and competitive, while executive federalism in Australia makes intergovernmental relations inherently closed, bureaucratic and collusive. If this is so, intergovernmental relations in Australia is yet another example of the incomplete accommodation between the rival constitutional traditions of federalism and parliamentary government. It also follows that intergovernmental relations is neither a recent nor a peripheral phenomenon in the operation of Australian federalism, but has been an inherent part of the governmental process in Australia since 1901.

Bibliography

ACIR (Advisory Council for Inter-government Relations), 1985. *Register of Commonwealth–State Co-operative Arrangements*, 3rd edn, Information Paper No. 10, Government Printer, Hobart.

—— 1986a. *Operating Procedures of Inter-Jurisdictional Ministerial Councils 1986*, Information Paper No. 13, Government Printer, Hobart.

—— 1986b. *Compendium of Intergovernmental Agreements*, Information Paper No. 12, Government Printer, Hobart.

Bakvis, H. & Chandler, W.M., eds, 1987. *Federalism and the Role of the State*, University of Toronto Press, Toronto.

Birch, A.H., 1957. *Federalism, Finance and Social Legislation in Canada, Australia and the United States*, Oxford University Press, London.

—— 1966. 'Approaches to the Study of Federalism', *Political Studies* 14(1), 15–33.

Breton, A., 1985. 'Supplementary Statement', Royal Commission on the Economic Union and Development Prospects for Canada, *Report*, Volume 3, 486–526, CGPS, Ottawa.

Budget Paper No. 4 1987–88 (Commonwealth of Australia, Budget Paper No. 4) *Commonwealth Financial Relations with Other Levels of Government*, AGPS, Canberra.

CGC (Commonwealth Grants Commission), 1983. *Equality in Diversity: Fifty Years of the Commonwealth Grants Commission*, AGPS, Canberra.

Chapman, R.J.K., 1988a. 'The Australian Advisory Council for Inter-Government Relations as a Moderating Institution', *Australian Journal of Public Administration* 47(2), 130–6.

—— 1988b. 'Inter-government Forums and the Policy Process', in *Comparative State Policies*, ed. Brian Galligan, Longman Cheshire, Melbourne.

Dupre, J.S., 1987. 'The Workability of Executive Federalism in Canada', in Bakvis & Chandler.

Elazar, D.J., 1987. *Exploring Federalism*, University of Alabama Press, Tuscaloosa.

Emy, H.V. & Hughes, O.E., 1989. *Australian Politics: Realities in Conflict*, Macmillan, Melbourne.

Galligan, B., 1987. *Politics of the High Court: A Study of the Judicial Branch of Government in Australia*, University of Queensland Press, Brisbane.

—— ed., 1989a. *Australian Federalism*, Longman Cheshire, Melbourne

—— 1989b. 'Federal Theory and Australian Federalism—A Political Science Perspective', in Galligan, 1989a.

Gibbins, R., 1982. *Regionalism: Territorial Politics in Canada and the United States*, Butterworths, Toronto.

Gilbert, R.S., 1973. *The Australian Loan Council in Federal Fiscal Adjustments 1890–1965*, Australian National University Press, Canberra.

Grewal, B., 1989. 'Federal Institutions and Process—An Economic Perspective', in Galligan, 1989a.

Grodzins, M., 1966. *The American System: A New View of Government in the United States*, ed. D.J. Elazar, Rand McNally, Chicago.

Holmes, J.& Sharman, C., 1977. *The Australian Federal System*, Allen & Unwin, Sydney.

Lijphart, A., 1984. *Democracies: Patterns of Majoritarian and Consensus Government in Twenty-One Countries*, Yale University Press, New Haven.

—— 1989. 'Democratic Political Systems: Types, Cases, Causes and Consequences', *Journal of Theoretical Politics*, 1(1), 33–48.

Lindell, G., 1989. 'Federal Institutions and Processes—A Legal Perspective', in Galligan, 1989a.

Mathews, R.L. ed., 1974. *Intergovernmental Relations in Australia*, Angus & Robertson, Sydney.

—— 1985. 'Federal State Fiscal Arrangements in Australia', in *Federalism and Resource Development: the Australian Case*, eds P. Drysdale & H. Shibata, Allen & Unwin, Sydney.

Mathews, R.L. & Jay, W.R.C., 1972. *Federal Finance: Intergovernmental Financial Relations in Australia Since Federation*, Nelson, Melbourne.

May, R.J., 1971. *Financing the Small States in Australian Federalism*, Oxford University Press, Melbourne.

Ostrom, V., 1973. 'Can Federalism Make a Difference?' *Publius*, 3(2), 179–238.

Reid, G.S., 1974. 'Political Decentralization, Co-operative Federalism and Responsible Government', in Mathews, 1974.

—— 1979. 'Western Australia and the Federation', in *Essays on Western Australian Politics*, eds R. Pervan & C. Sharman, University of Western Australia Press, Perth.

Riker, W.H, & Schapps, R., 1957. 'Disharmony in Federal Governments', *Behavioral Science* 2(4), 276–90.

Saunders, C., 1985. 'The Expiry of the Financial Agreement', Reprint Series No. 64, Centre for Research on Federal Financial Relations, Australian National University, Canberra.

—— 1987. 'The Federal System', in *Australian State Politics*, ed. Brian Galligan, Longman Cheshire, Melbourne.

—— 1990. 'Government Borrowing in Australia', *Publius*, forthcoming.

Sharman, C., 1977. *The Premiers' Conference: An Essay in Federal State Interaction*, Occasional Paper No. 13, Department of Political Science, Research School of Social Sciences, Australian National University, Canberra.

—— 1980. 'Fraser, the States and Federalism', *Australian Quarterly*, 52(2), 9–19.

—— 1982. 'Parliaments and Commonwealth–State Relations', in *Parliament and Bureaucracy*, ed. J.R. Nethercote, Hale & Iremonger, Sydney.

—— 1984. 'Grappling with Proteus: A Survey of Intergovernmental Relations', *Australian Journal of Public Administration* 43, 287–96.

—— 1987. 'Second Chambers', in Bakvis & Chandler, 1987.

—— 1989. 'Federal Institutions and Processes—A Political Science Perspective', in Galligan, 1989a.

Sharman, C. & Stuart, J., 1982, 'Premiers' Departments: Patterns of Growth and Change', *Politics* 17, 46–58.

Simeon, R., 1972. *Federal Provincial Diplomacy: The Making of Recent Policy in Canada,* University of Toronto, Toronto.

Smiley, D.V., 1987. *The Federal Condition in Canada*, McGraw-Hill Ryerson, Toronto.

Spann, R.N., 1972. 'Responsibility in Federal Systems', in Mathews, 1974.

Walsh, C., 1989. 'Federalism, The States and Economic Policy—An Economic Perspective', in Galligan, 1989a.

Warhurst, J., 1987. 'Managing Intergovernmental Relations', in Bakvis & Chandler, 1987.

Wettenhall, R., 1985. 'Intergovernmental Agencies Lubricating a Federal System', *Current Affairs Bulletin* 61(11), 28–35.

Wheare, R.C., 1946. *Federal Government*, Oxford University Press, London.

Wiltshire, K.W., 1986. *Planning and Federalism: Australian and Canadian Experience,* University of Queensland Press, Brisbane.

Wright, D.S., 1988. *Understanding Intergovernmental Relations* 3rd edn, Brooks Cole, Pacific Grove, California.

Zines, L., 1989. 'Federal Theory and Australian Federalism—A Legal Perspective', in Galligan, 1989.

3 Constitutional and legal aspects

Cheryl Saunders

The constitutional structure is an essential starting point for consideration of the legal aspects of intergovernmental relations. It also has a major influence on the extent of intergovernmental relations and the form which such arrangements take. This chapter does not attempt to deal comprehensively with the constitutional structure, but focuses instead on those aspects of it which have particular relevance to intergovernmental relations.

Division of legislative powers

The commonwealth constitution follows the United States model in allocating specific legislative powers to the commonwealth and leaving the undefined residue to the states. Most commonwealth powers are concurrent and thus exercisable by either the commonwealth or the states. Under section 109 of the constitution, in the event of inconsistency a commonwealth Act will prevail. The High Court has held that inconsistency is created not only when there is direct conflict between commonwealth and state legislation, but also when a commonwealth Act is construed by the court as intending to cover an entire legislative field, into which a state Act intrudes (*Viskauskas'* case, 1983).

Some uncertainty and disruption may be expected whenever the commonwealth moves into a legislative field hitherto occupied only by the states. This suggests the need for consultation and, if possible, co-operation between the levels of government on such occasions, although tactical considerations may dictate otherwise. An example of the confusion that may ensue when such considerations prevail was provided recently by the saga of the unilateral commonwealth companies and securities industry legislation.

Since federation, companies and the securities industry have been subject primarily to state legislation, despite the commonwealth power in section 51(ii) of the constitution to legislate for 'Foreign corporations, and trading or financial corporations formed within the limits of the Commonwealth'. In the face of mounting pressure for uniformity, the state legislation has been channelled, for the past 30 years, through increasingly complex intergovernmental schemes. In 1987 the commonwealth Attorney-General announced his intention to promote commonwealth legislation which would cover as comprehensively as possible the companies and securities industry fields. The proposal was opposed by the states. Protracted negotiations took place in the Ministerial Council for Companies and Securities, in which various modifications to the commonwealth proposals were suggested. No agreement was reached before the Corporations and Australian Securities Commission Bills were passed by the parliament in May 1989.

The validity of the legislation subsequently was challenged by three states. By agreement, the subject matter of the challenge was limited to those parts of the legislation which required trading and financial corporations to incorporate under the Commonwealth Act and forbad them from incorporating under state legislation. The challenge was successful (*New South Wales* v. *Commonwealth* (1990) 64 ALJR 157) and state co-operation became more essential than ever. At the time of writing, negotiations over a more centralised version of the previous co-operative scheme are still proceeding, with the allocation of company fees a major outstanding item, although final agreement is expected shortly. By the time it is reached, Australian company law will have been through a period of largely unnecessary turmoil for more than two years.

Problems of a lesser order arise whenever the commonwealth legislates in an area with potential for conflict with state legislation. They are likely to be exacerbated where the commonwealth legislation can be construed to cover the field. Where the potential for conflict is recognised the commonwealth Act will often expressly exclude, or expressly save, state law. Where conflict is not foreseen, however, the consequences for state law which follow may be undesired, as well as unintended. This was most clearly demonstrated by the extraordinary saga of the *Viskauskas* and *Metwally* cases. In the former, the High Court held that the Racial Discrimination 1975 (Cth) covered the relevant field, rendering inoperative the sections of the Racial Discrimination Act 1977 (NSW) on which the applicant relied. In the latter, the High Court held that the new section 6A speedily inserted in the commonwealth Act to save state laws following the *Viskauskas* decision could not have a retrospective operation. The result was that Mr Metwally's action failed as well.

In 1984 the Fiscal Powers Sub-Committee of the Australian Constitutional Convention sought to discover the steps that are taken by the commonwealth to anticipate these difficulties in drafting new laws. It was told that:

> Regrettably the pressures of the Government's legislative timetable rarely allow the officer drafting a Commonwealth Bill the luxury of considering in detail its possible effect on State law. Reliance has to be placed on the instructing officers to ensure that there will be no untoward effects. In many cases, of course, Bills are publicly circulated before being introduced, or are introduced and allowed to lie for a particular period, to permit public scrutiny, including scrutiny by State officers. (Fiscal Powers, 1984:67)

The sub-committee ultimately recommended legislation to provide that a commonwealth Act should not be construed to cover the field 'unless such an intention appears by express statement in the commonwealth law or its existence is logically necessary' (Fiscal Powers, 1984:73).

The operation of the federal distribution of legislative power is complicated further where there are gaps in the subject matter of the powers allocated to the commonwealth or where the meaning or scope of a power is unclear. One example of a gap was the failure of the powers over marriage and matrimonial causes in section 51(xxi) and (xxii) of the constitution to cover custody of ex-nuptial children (*Russell* v. *Russell*, 1976). Its consequences were manifested from time to time in the Family Court of Australia, when the court found itself unable to deal with all the custody issues arising from the marriage breakdown that was before it (*Re F.*, 1986). This particular problem has recently been largely overcome by a reference of power to the commonwealth by four states over a range of family law matters, including the custody of children.[1] A fifth state, Western Australia, had avoided many of the practical problems of divided power in family law matters by using the facility available under section 41 of the Family Law Act 1975 (Cth) to create a state Family Court. The Family Court of Western Australia exercises both federal and state jurisdiction in family law matters.

There is no shortage of examples of uncertainty in meaning or scope of commonwealth legislative powers. Two, which are both topical and important, are the taxation and corporations powers. In the case of taxation the critical question is whether the power in section 51(ii) of the constitution to legislate with respect to 'taxation...' refers only to commonwealth taxation, or whether it applies to taxation generally, empowering the commonwealth to override state taxation laws. Although there are some suggestions to the contrary (*Hematite* case, 1983:617, 631, 639, 661), so far the case law supports the more limited interpretation of the power (Fiscal Powers, 1984:35–36). The broader interpretation would force a great deal more interaction between governments in taxation than exists at present. Nevertheless, the experience of revenue redistribution in Australia suggests that it would not be a healthy result for the responsibility of government at both levels unless more genuinely co-operative arrangements and attitudes were put in place. At least three key aspects of the corporations power are affected by uncertainty. The most fundamental of all is the continuing problem of when an Act which mentions corporations can properly be characterised as 'with respect to' corporations and thus within the scope of the power, and when the connection between the law and the power is too remote. Two other more limited issues, from which the states derived much of their bargaining power in negotiations over the national companies legislation, are the definition of 'trading or financial' corporations and the question whether the power extends to the incorporation of companies. The latter eventually will be resolved by judicial decision, one way or the other. The definition of trading or financial corporations is likely always to remain uncertain in relation to particular companies, however, suggesting again the need for co-operation or co-ordination between the levels of government.

Even where the scope of commonwealth power is relatively clear, there may be interaction with state power which makes some form of intergovernmental arrangement desirable or necessary. A topical example is immigration, which has the potential to impinge on a range of state powers in areas such as housing, education and health. The conference of Ministers for Immigration and Ethnic Affairs reached tentative agreement at its meeting in April 1989 on closer co-operation in migration policy for this reason (*Intergovernmental News*, April 1989:14). These developments had some parallel in the Meech Lake Constitutional Accord reached between the Canadian and provincial governments in 1987, which in the event was not ratified. Clauses 95A and 95B of the draft constitutional amendments would have provided a framework for agreement between governments on migration matters which would have had the force of law, subject to any Canadian Act setting national standards and objectives and to the Canadian Charter of Rights and Freedoms (Meech Lake, 1987).

Another striking example, of a somewhat different kind, is the provision of legal aid. Joint commonwealth–state funding arrangements implemented under the commonwealth Legal Aid Commission Act 1977 recognised the responsibility of the commonwealth to provide legal aid for persons in the 'Federal area' including 'members or discharged members of the Defence Force or their dependants, migrants, persons in receipt of benefits under the Social Services legislation of the Commonwealth, Aboriginals or students' (Legal Aid Agreement, 1979:cl.4.4). In practice, it proved impossible to quarantine these categories of people from the rest of the community using legal services, with the result, in the commonwealth's view, that the states' contribution towards legal aid funding was disproportionately small (Discussion Papers on Legal Aid, 1989:39–40). New arrangements negotiated with the states from 1987, in conjunction with the commonwealth Legal Aid Amendment Act 1988, are designed to specify the proportion of operating costs which each government will provide towards legal aid services in that state (CPD (S), 3 November 1987:1598).

Constitutional recognition of intergovernmental relations

The commonwealth constitution is somewhat unusual amongst older-style federal constitutions in explicitly recognising certain forms of intergovernmental relations. The structure of the Australian judicature provides one major, important example. Unlike the Supreme Court of the United States, the High Court is the final court of appeal from all Australian courts in matters of both commonwealth and state law. This feature of the Australian structure has had a significant unifying effect on Australian law. Integration of the judicial branch is further reinforced by section 77(3) of the constitution, which explicitly authorises state courts to be vested with federal jurisdiction, a facility which has been used extensively since federation. Cross-vesting legislation enacted by the commonwealth and all states in 1987 is designed to build upon this mechanism by enabling any court, whether federal or state, to deal with the whole of a matter properly before it which raises issues in both commonwealth and state law.[2] The scheme came into effect on 1 July 1988. It assumes, without encouragement from the text of the constitution itself, that the states can constitutionally vest federal courts with state jurisdiction.

A further example of constitutional recognition of intergovernmental cooperation is section 51(xxxvii) of the constitution, which expressly contemplates that the states may refer legislative powers to the commonwealth. The power has not been used often, partly, but not solely, because of legal uncertainties about its operation (Saunders, 1978a). In fact it seems likely that the legal uncertainties could be largely overcome by a more sophisticated approach to drafting both the reference and any agreement made pursuant to it than has generally been taken in the past. Despite real or imagined defects, the reference power remains a potentially useful mechanism for intergovernmental co-operation. It was the vehicle through which the adjustments of family law powers were made in 1986–87. It has been one of the options canvassed in the debate over the national companies legislation, and may still provide the means whereby a comprehensive regulatory structure is created.

A third provision, section 105A, was inserted in the constitution at a later stage in 1928. Section 105A authorises the commonwealth to make agreements with the states with respect to the public debts of the states. Such an agreement will override anything in commonwealth or state constitutions or laws. The section provides the constitutional foundation for the Financial Agreement of 1927, which establishes the Loan Council and ostensibly regulates government borrowing in Australia.

Finally, many of the fiscal provisions of the constitution assume continuing interaction between governments in fiscal matters. Thus section 87 required the commonwealth to distribute three-quarters of the customs and excise revenue to the states for at least the first ten years after federation; section 94 provides for the commonwealth to distribute its surplus revenue to the states; section 105 authorises it to take over state debts; and section 96 empowers the commonwealth parliament to grant financial assistance to the states 'on such terms and conditions as the Parliament thinks fit'. With hindsight, these provisions made inevitable the fiscal emphasis in intergovernmental relations in Australia to which Galligan, Hughes and Walsh refer in chapter 1. Ironically, the presence in the constitution of such a clear and apparently unrestricted provision to make conditional grants to the states may have inhibited the development of the commonwealth power to make grants directly to other recipients for purposes otherwise outside commonwealth power. One result is the sometimes purely formal involvement of the states in commonwealth spending programs. The best, but by no means the only example, is university funding, currently authorised by the Higher Education Funding Act 1988 (Cth).

Somewhat unexpectedly, the High Court has developed a greater tolerance to the constitutional validity of schemes with an intergovernmental flavour. A clear expression of this attitude emerged in *Re Duncan: ex parte Australian Iron and Steel*, in which the court upheld the validity of the Coal Industry Tribunal under the joint coal industry arrangements between the commonwealth and New South Wales. The Court confirmed that the executive power is likely to be interpreted flexibly under co-operative arrangements and in particular that it could be employed in the operation of a scheme of the type in question under which both the commonwealth and the state vest power in the same authority. It was also made clear that the court would be unlikely to interpret a commonwealth Act constituting part of such a scheme as intending to 'cover the field', thereby possibly invalidating a complementary state Act, in any event where the commonwealth Act specifically authorised the investiture of the joint authority with state power.

Scope of intergovernmental relations in Australia

Much of Australian intergovernmental relations continues to have a fiscal character. Its complexity from an intergovernmental point of view is greater where the commonwealth role extends to specifying the purposes for which moneys can be spent and other related matters. The emphasis on general as opposed to specific-purpose transfers has see-sawed throughout Australian federal history: there appears to be a pronounced tilt towards the specific-purpose end at present, although it has not been sufficient to cause major comment.

It is possible to detect developments in the methodology of specific-purpose grant arrangements which are interesting and have the potential to make intergovernmental arrangements in Australia more sophisticated than has been the case in the past. The attention paid to the appropriate roles of the commonwealth, state and local governments in the Supported Accommodation Assistance Program (SAAP) is one example. The approach recently taken in the States and Northern Territory Grants (Rural Adjustment) Act 1988 is another.

In the latter case, the recitals to the Agreement, scheduled to the Act, refer to the need to redirect the scheme 'towards enabling rural industries to better contribute to the national economy through increased efficiency and consequent international competitiveness and to this end to enhance the role and thereby the responsibility of the States and the Northern Territory in relation to the scheme.' The agreement accordingly identifies quite precisely the objectives of the scheme, the strategies to be adopted to meet them and the roles to be performed by the commonwealth and the states respectively. The commonwealth is confined to 'setting broad policy guidelines' leaving 'total managerial and financial responsibility' to the states, subject to general accountability mechanisms. In his second reading speech, Minister Kerin claimed the Bill as 'a landmark piece of legislation in terms of being the first attempt at applying, in the context of cooperative Commonwealth–State relations, the principles of devolution of financial management encapsulated in concepts such as program budgeting and the financial management improvement program' (CPD (H), 12 October 1988:1463). He explained the particular allocation of responsibilities on the basis that 'it has been demonstrated, by the experience of the last three years, that it is impractical for the Commonwealth to control the detailed financial and managerial operations of the State adjustment authorities.'

Nevertheless, it would be a mistake to assume that all intergovernmental arrangements in Australia are primarily fiscal in character. A large and significant group is designed primarily for the sharing or rationalising of the use of legislative power and/or administrative action. Examples exist in companies legislation, the offshore areas, industrial relations, and drug regulation. Mechanisms used for intergovernmental relations in this area include the following:

1 Co-operation in legislation, ranging from simple agreement to try to keep the relevant legislation of the participating jurisdictions as uniform as possible, to the device presently used in the co-operative companies scheme under which the commonwealth enacts comprehensive legislation for the Australian Capital Territory on the basis of the territories' power in section 122 and each of the states

enacts legislation to adopt by reference the commonwealth law, as varied from time to time. The Australian Capital Territory (Self-Government) Act 1988 specifically excludes companies and securities law from the powers conferred upon the new Legislative Assembly, presumably to protect the integrity of this device.

2 Intergovernmental agreements with varying degrees of formality, which may or may not be ratified by legislation, scheduled to legislation, authorised by legislation, or tabled in the respective parliaments.

3 Joint administrative bodies, established by one government (typically, the commonwealth) and invested with power by the others. The National Companies and Securities Commission is an example. The offshore arrangements offer a variation, whereby the Petroleum (Submerged Lands) Act 1967 (Cth) provides for the appointment of a 'designated authority' who may in fact be the minister of the relevant participating state. Under the same legislation, the commonwealth and state ministers combine to constitute a 'joint authority' for particular administrative purposes (Crommelin, 1987:15).

4 Meetings of the relevant ministers from each jurisdiction, called ministerial councils or conferences, run across all these arrangements, providing a forum in which intergovernmental relations may be negotiated and settled.

Some legal issues

Section 96 grants

In the latest edition of his book *Understanding Intergovernmental Relations* Deil Wright describes the emergence of juridical federalism in the United States (Wright, 1988). The first example given is the development of a recognised area of law known as federal grant law. A comparable body of law has not yet emerged in Australia, much less under that name, although it may be on the way. Some questions related to the development of Australian federal grant law are discussed below, in the context of administrative review.

There is a discrete question about the enforceability of section 96 arrangements, however, which should logically be considered first. The problems raised may be distinctively Australian because of the peculiarities of section 96 itself. On the one hand section 96 confers power on the parliament, and therefore presumably is legislative in character. On the other hand, the nature of the arrangement which it contemplates has obvious contractual overtones. In this regard it is necessary to remember that the High Court has insisted that a grant arrangement under section 96 is voluntary (*Second Uniform Tax* case,

1957:605). Whatever else that means, it implies at least that a state may, theoretically, decide whether to accept a grant or not.

The problem of the enforceability of grants arrangements potentially arises either way: in relation to a state seeking to enforce payment of a grant by the commonwealth, or in relation to the commonwealth seeking to enforce compliance by a state with conditions attached to a grant, or, at least, repayment of the grant. One of the reasons why the uncertainty about these questions has not yet presented major practical problems is that the commonwealth can threaten to withhold future grants from a recalcitrant state. This may not be as universally effective a solution as is generally assumed, however, and in any event, the legal question is an interesting one. It is possible to present only a bare outline of the arguments here. They have been examined more fully elsewhere (Saunders, 1987; Saunders, 1988).

In brief, the hybrid nature of section 96 suggests two possible models, neither of which alone is entirely satisfactory. The first draws its inspiration from the principles and remedies of public law. This model treats a section 96 grants Act as far as possible as an ordinary Act of the parliament. The approach is complicated a little by the superficial similarity between a grants Act and an appropriation Act. Courts have traditionally been unwilling to recognise rights based solely on the latter type of legislation (*AAP* case, 1975). There is a question whether this attitude is correct (Saunders, 1978b), but in any event it can readily be argued that the constitutional power for the parliament to attach conditions to a grant distinguishes grants from appropriation legislation.

The public law model has some application to enforcement of grants legislation by a state against the commonwealth, although even for this purpose its application is limited. If a grants Act clearly creates an entitlement to a grant, which is not paid, principles of public law suggest that the state concerned would be able to enforce the grant. Legislation of this kind is relatively rare, however, although by no means unknown: the former revenue redistribution arrangements under the States Grants (General Revenue) Act 1985 created an entitlement of this kind.

Enforceability of a condition by the commonwealth against the state is complicated by the voluntary character of an exercise of section 96. In the face of that doctrine it is difficult, if not impossible, to argue that section 109 applies to a condition in a grants Act to override inconsistent state legislation. Even if section 109 were to apply, however, it would not resolve all problems of non-compliance by a state, many of which are more likely to involve default in executive, rather than legislative action.

It is possible, however, that ancillary provisions in grants legislation, and in particular provisions requiring repayment of a grant if the conditions are not met, represent an exercise of the incidental power in section 51(xxxix), rather than of section 96 itself. In this case the analysis might be different, enabling the commonwealth to enforce repayment of a grant in appropriate cases.

The second model relies on private-law concepts and draws the obvious analogy with contract. Its principal difficulty is the reluctance of the courts in the past to enforce intergovernmental agreements, on the grounds that they are not justiciable (*Railway Standardisation*, 1962). The courts have never issued a blanket denial of the enforceability of such agreements, however. It is both possible and appropriate to argue that where the terms of an agreement are sufficiently certain and the circumstances otherwise enable a court to conclude that the parties intended to enter into legal relations, an agreement is enforceable. Again, this model would not provide a basis for enforcement of all section 96 grants arrangements, but it could be pressed into use for some. An interesting by-product would force greater attention to be paid to the point at which and the conditions on which states accept grants, which would be no bad thing.

Parliamentary government and accountability

Intergovernmental relations raise a range of issues for accountability generally and for the system of parliamentary government in particular.

The first is the chronic absence of information about all aspects of intergovernmental relations: the existence and operations of ministerial councils, the conditions of grants legislation, the substance of intergovernmental agreements. To a large degree this appears to be an oversight on the part of the institutions involved: a convenient oversight, no doubt, from the standpoint of executive government, but one which is at least partly attributable to the fact that intergovernmental arrangements do not fit the usual framework of governmental activity. This is becoming an increasingly less convincing explanation, however, as intergovernmental activity grows in size and significance. And the strange myopia of the commonwealth parliament in relation to the conditions of grants has always been difficult to explain when the responsibility of the parliament is apparent on the face of the constitution.

In this connection, the debate that took place in Queensland in 1989 about misallocation of moneys for drought assistance should be noted. The problem was attributed by one witness before the state Public Accounts Committee to the fact that 'There was no Act of Parliament they were working to, no written objectives or guidelines' (*Courier Mail* 13 July 1989:1). It is possible, however, that the problem originated at a much earlier stage, in the original grant of financial assistance from the commonwealth, which also had no legislative basis other than a one-line appropriation in Appropriation Bill No. 2 and a power for the Minister for Finance to attach terms and conditions to the grants.

Whatever the explanation, it remains difficult and labour intensive to collect systematic and reliable information about intergovernmental arrangements. The quarterly *Intergovernmental News* now provides a regular source of information about grants, councils and agreements, compiled with some difficulty from the public record and a network of contacts. The Senate Standing Committee on Finance and Public Administration recently asked again that a list of all commonwealth–state consultative bodies be included in a current central register of non-statutory bodies, at least until a separate register of commonwealth–state bodies 'of the type published in a number of federations is developed' (SSCFPA, 1988:23). It did not accept the government's proposed exclusion from the register of 'commonwealth–state consultative bodies with high level *ex officio* membership only'. It may be presumed to have rejected the government's explanation that the exclusion was 'intended not to qualify the government's commitment to public sector accountability but to provide for cases where other forms of reporting are more appropriate' in the absence of any such mechanisms (SSCFPA, 1988:7).

The paucity of information about intergovernmental relations in Australia also has a more formal and deliberate basis which is less readily overcome. There is a widespread view, which deserves re-evaluation, that intergovernmental arrangements require some special protection from the public gaze. Thus in *Sankey* v. *Whitlam* (1978) the only documents on which, in the end, the High Court was prepared to confer any special protection were the Loan Council minutes. Freedom of Information legislation also typically includes a special public interest exemption for intergovernmental arrangements.[3]

Secondly, intergovernmental arrangements notoriously impede the ability of the parliaments to perform any sort of scrutiny or review function, although the parliaments themselves seem to recognise this only in relation to legislative, rather than fiscal arrangements. In this sense, intergovernmental relations in Australia are as executive in character as they are in Canada, although in Australia the executive of one level of government, the commonwealth, occupies a more dominant position. Typically, the concern is that where governments have agreed that legislation will be enacted in a particular form, the parliaments have no opportunity to make alterations to it. The objection rings somewhat hollow in the face of the customary *modus operandi* of parliaments, but can be accepted to have some force in principle, at least. A similar objection may be directed to regulations which form part of an intergovernmental scheme where scrutiny by the subordinate legislation committee or its equivalent may be purely formal (Craven, 1989).

A recent example of objection to an intergovernmental scheme on these grounds is once again provided by the versatile area of companies and securities industry regulation. The criticism of the co-operative scheme by the Senate Committee was a powerful impetus for the move to unilateral commonwealth legislation (SSCLCA, 1987). More recently, on considering a Bill introduced into the parliament under the co-operative scheme, the Scrutiny of Bills committee commented that:

> the whole of the Bill can be seen as an inappropriate delegation of legislative power, since...the Bill has been approved by the Ministerial Council. Parliament now has the option of approving the Bill as it stands or, if any changes are proposed, delaying passage of the Bill until the Ministerial Council also approves the changes. (SSCSB, D4/1989:16)

Intergovernmental mechanisms tend to create problems for the state parliaments to an even greater degree, particularly where such mechanisms take the relatively sophisticated form used for the purposes of the companies scheme of an option of legislation by reference. The commonwealth parliament at least plays a role in the passage of amending legislation: state parliaments may never be exposed to the legislation again, once the adopting Act is passed, although theirs is the authority on which the regime rests. State parliaments also are less likely than their commonwealth counterpart to have systematic access to intergovernmental agreements or to the proceedings of ministerial council meetings.

Cabinet government also is affected, particularly at the state level, by intergovernmental arrangements. It appears now to be regular practice for commonwealth ministers to obtain cabinet endorsement, if that would otherwise be necessary for their negotiating position in a ministerial council. The instances in which this occurs at the state level are still relatively rare. In the case of at least some councils this is because the states are not made aware of the issues to be raised in time to obtain cabinet endorsement. In other cases, perhaps, it may not occur to them to do so. There are some signs of change: the 1988–89 Victorian Budget Papers report a formal procedure for the acceptance or renewal of specific purpose payments, which requires consultation with the premier and treasurer and, in appropriate circumstances, cabinet or a cabinet committee (Victoria, 1988:39). If these procedures are to be followed, some modification of ministerial council practices would be inevitable.

Once again, the Premiers' Conference provides an extreme example of the problem. The commonwealth position at the Premiers' Conference certainly is subject to the commonwealth cabinet process: the need for cabinet endorsement, indeed, is sometimes given as a reason for not firming the commonwealth position in time for prior circulation of papers. But the very failure to circulate papers prior to the conference, resulting in the notorious 'package under the door' before breakfast, deprives the states of the opportunity for state cabinet deliberation or for any prior analysis of the issues at all. The recent debacle over the emergency relief program, devolved by the commonwealth to the states with no prior consultation in 1988 (*Intergovernmental News*, April

1989:11), and taken back in 1989 following protests not only from state ministers and departments but also client groups, was a not particularly surprising product of this process.

Administrative review

Review of government decisions by the courts gives effect to the fundamental principle that governments are subject to law. In recent decades additional mechanisms have been introduced for external review of government decisions in recognition of the relative difficulty of using the traditional processes of judicial review and of the importance of government decisions to individuals affected by them. Thus the commonwealth and all Australian states have created the position of ombudsman to deal with complaints of maladministration. Some jurisdictions have introduced other reforms as well. At the commonwealth level these have taken the form of an integrated package of measures which have modernised and rationalised the law and procedures for review of administrative action. In addition to the ombudsman, the commonwealth system comprises codification of the principles and remedies of judicial review, including a right to reasons, in the Administrative Decisions (Judicial Review) Act 1977; and an Administrative Appeals Tribunal hearing appeals on the merits from primary decision makers. It has become accepted that there is a *prima facie* case for tribunal jurisdiction where the interests of a person are affected by a decision (ARC, 1986–87:51)

The operation of systems for administrative review are complicated where decisions are made in the course of intergovernmental schemes. Sometimes the intergovernmental character of the primary decision making process itself creates a legal impediment to review. At the commonwealth level, for example, both the federal court exercising jurisdiction under the AD (JR) Act and the Administrative Appeals Tribunal require a decision to be taken under a commonwealth enactment before they can exercise their functions. If, on analysis, a decision turns out to have been made in fact under a state enactment, these mechanisms do not apply. Similarly the other source of authority for federal judicial review, section 75(v) of the constitution, which gives the High Court jurisdiction over decisions made by an 'officer of the commonwealth', cannot apply where the decision maker is an officer of a state, even when acting under commonwealth law. Under the Ombudsman Act 1976 the commonwealth ombudsman has jurisdiction over commonwealth departments or prescribed authorities. The definition of prescribed authority is broad, but nevertheless requires a commonwealth enactment, appointment by the governor-general or a commonwealth minister, or incorporation by the commonwealth government (section 3).

These factors do not necessarily make review of decisions under intergovernmental schemes impossible, but they complicate the choice of both the law and the forum for review. In partial response to these problems, some co-operation between commonwealth and state ombudsmen now takes place, following an agreement reached between the prime minister and state premiers in the late 1970s (*Commonwealth Ombudsman*, 1980:79). Section 8A of the Ombudsman Act 1976 (Cth) provides formal legislative authority for the commonwealth ombudsman to enter into arrangements with the ombudsman of a state for the purpose of an investigation.

In many cases impediments to external review of decisions made in the course of intergovernmental arrangements are the result of deliberate exclusion of the decisions from review, rather than difficult or insurmountable problems of jurisdiction. Thus decisions of the National Companies and Securities Commission in the exercise of power under state law, and all decisions of the Ministerial Council for Companies and Securities, are excluded from the AD (JR) Act[4] in accordance with an Administrative Remedies Agreement entered into by the participants in the co-operative companies scheme in 1982 (Saunders, 1982:28-39). Similarly, decisions of the Joint Authorities under the petroleum mining[5] and fisheries schemes[6] are not subjected to AAT review, even where the nature of the decision would normally be considered appropriate for review on the merits; a matter on which the Senate committee has commented unfavourably from time to time (SSCSB, D12184:38; D3:85, 13). The reason which most commonly underlies exclusions of this kind seems to be some sort of intergovernmental protocol which has never been clearly articulated for its validity to be assessed. While it may be accepted that review of decisions of one level of government by agencies of another should be avoided in the interests of comity, it would be desirable in such cases to ensure that review was provided in some other acceptable form, in the interests of individuals affected by such decisions.

Particular issues are raised in relation to review of decisions made in the context of specific-purpose grants. They may exist at either the commonwealth or the state level, or both. While a decision about the conditions which should be attached to a grant appear to be legislative in character (Saunders, 1987:11), there are some programs under which the commonwealth minister is authorised to make administrative decisions within the scope of broad conditions. An example was the power under the States Grants (Schools Assistance) Act 1983 to approve individual building projects by non-government schools for the purpose of the schools grants program.

On the assumption that such a power is administrative in character, there is a question whether its exercise is subject to judicial review. In theory, there is a problem: the power of the commonwealth is limited to attaching conditions to grants which states are not bound to accept (*Second Uniform Tax* case, 1957). It might be argued, therefore, that the commonwealth action has no substantive effect to attract judicial review. The reality is of course very different. An exercise of power by the commonwealth under state grant programs may have a very significant practical effect on individuals. In the case of the schools grants, a school could not receive a grant without commonwealth ministerial approval and once approval had been given a recipient state was bound, 'without undue delay', to pass the moneys on (section 21). The theoretical prerogative of a state to refuse a grant is rarely, if ever, exercised.

These questions have not yet been resolved. They have been raised in one or two cases but the fundamental problems suggested by the character of grants legislation so far have been avoided. Most interesting was the *Peninsula Boys School* case (1985) in which the Federal Court held that an exercise of power to approve projects under the States Grants (Schools Assistance) Act attracted the obligation to accord natural justice in view of the 'legitimate expection' of applicants. The force of that conclusion has since been strengthened considerably by the decision of the High Court in *Kioa* (1985). The issues were not canvassed comprehensively in *Peninsula Boys*, however, possibly because the court held that an adequate standard of natural justice had been met. The increasing number of grant programs which confer power on commonwealth ministers with significant practical implications for individuals makes it inevitable that these issues will be raised again.

Questions of review under grant programs also arise at the state level, at the point at which a service is provided under the program to the end user. In some cases the state itself will provide the service. In others the service will be provided by yet another party: typically, a local government body or a private-sector organisation. Several issues arise. If the service is provided by a state, should decisions taken by administrators in the course of doing so be subject to review and, if so, in what form? If the service provider is a party other than the state, what kind of review arrangements are appropriate and practicable? Should the commonwealth make provision for review a condition of its grants to the states? And what sanctions can or should be applied for breach of such conditions: or, indeed, of any others?

These issues have, as yet, barely been addressed, although the debate has started. The new agreement for the Supported Accommodation Assistance Program requires the commonwealth and the states to agree within two years on 'mechanisms for resolving breaches of individual rights', including 'principles and strategies for the protection of users' rights' (CPD (H), 4 May 1989:2009). The Administrative Review Council is currently conducting a major project on review of decisions in the Community Services and Health portfolio, many of which involve commonwealth–state programs (*Admin Review*, 1989:41). The United States experience with juridical federalism will be a useful guide, if not a model, in establishing satisfactory systems.

Conclusion

From a constitutional and legal standpoint, intergovernmental relations is a major and intricate area of governmental activity. It affects almost all operations of government. It uses a wide and expanding variety of mechanisms. It is in a constant state of flux, in the face of changing attitudes and practices of governments. It owes at least some of its form and substance to the terms of the constitution itself and, more recently, to judicial decision.

In these circumstances it is remarkable that relatively little attention has so far been paid to legal aspects of intergovernmental relations and their constitutional significance. One consequence has been the absence of both impetus and opportunity for the development of broad underlying principles about the structure and purpose of intergovernmental arrangements. In their absence, most decisions on such issues are *ad hoc*. This in turn has had some cost for the accountability and efficiency of Australian government.

These attitudes may be changing. Signs of greater interest in underlying principle are manifested by developments in relation to administrative review of intergovernmental arrangements, reflecting the greater importance now attached to open government and the rights of individuals *vis-à-vis* government and the bureaucracy. The structure of some new grant programs suggests a concern to identify the proper role of all participants in the interests of both efficiency and accountability. The stand of the Senate on the co-operative companies scheme may indicate more thoughtful consideration of the implications of intergovernmental arrangements for parliament: generalisation from a single instance may be unwise, but the recent establishment of the Australian Council of Public Accounts Committees, which will provide a vehicle for more effective parliamentary involvement in grants issues (*Intergovernmental News*, June 1989:10), is also relevant in this regard. And the debate which has taken place over the respective merits of constitutional change and intergovernmental co-operation in respect of the environment may be another sign of the times.[7] Co-operation is unlikely to yield satisfactory results on difficult and sensitive issues of this kind unless mechanisms with a fair degree of sophistication are put in place. Even that long-term denizen of the too-hard basket, the federal financial arrangements, may eventually yield to critical analysis and substantial change in recognition of its significance in constitutional as well as economic terms.

Endnotes

1 Commonwealth Powers (Family Law—Children) Act 1986 (NSW); Commonwealth Powers (Family Law—Children) Act 1986 (Vic.); Commonwealth Powers (Family Law) Act 1986 (SA); Commonwealth Powers (Family Law) Act 1987 (Tas.).

2 Jurisdiction of Courts (Cross-vesting) 1987 (Cth, all states and the Northern Territory).

3 Freedom of Information Act 1982 (Cth), section 33A; Freedom of Information Act 1982 (Vic.) section 29; Freedom of Information Act 1989 (NSW), schedule 1, clause 5.

4 By schedule 1, paras (m), (n).

5 For example, Petroleum (Submerged Lands) Amendment Act 1984, section 140C; Petroleum (Submerged Lands) (Cash Bidding) Amendment Act 1985, section 22B. Decisions of the Designated Authority, who in fact is a state minister, similarly are not made subject to AAT review.

6 For example, Fishing Legislation Amendment Act 1984 (Cth). Decisions of state officers acting as delegates of the commonwealth minister under the legislation are not directly subject to AAT review; an appeal lies to the commonwealth minister, however, and thence to the AAT.

7 A decision whether to support a referendum to amend the constitution to confer specific power over the environment was reported to have been 'put on hold' by the federal cabinet on 13 July (*Courier Mail*, 14 July 1989). The newly appointed ambassador for the environment, Sir Ninian Stephen, suggested subsequently in an interview that the eventual decision on the referendum would depend on the effectiveness of the co-operation between the commonwealth and the states over the next two years on environmental matters (*The Age*, 24 July 1989).

Case references

AAP case: *Victoria* v. *Commonwealth & Hayden* (1975) 134 CLR 338.

Re Duncan; ex parte Australian Iron and Steel Pty Ltd (1983) 158 CLR 153.

Re F; ex parte F (1986) 161 CLR 376.

Hematite Petroleum Pty Ltd v. *Victoria* (1983) 151 CLR 599.

Kioa v. *West* (1985) 159 CLR 264.

Metwally: University of Wollongong v. *Metwally* (1984) 158 CLR 447.

Peninsula Anglican Boys' School v. *Ryan* (1985) 69 ALR 555.

Railway Standardisation case: *South Australia* v. *Commonwealth* (1962) 108 CLR 130.

Russell v. *Russell, Farrell* v. *Farrell* (1976) 134 CLR 495.

Sankey v.*Whitlam* (1978) 142 CLR 1.

Second Uniform Tax case: *Victoria* v. *Commonwealth* (1957) 99 CLR 575.

Viskauskas v. *Niland* (1983) 153 CLR 280.

Bibliography

Admin Review, Administrative Review Council, AGPS.

ARC: Adminitrative Review Council, *Eleventh Annual Report. 1986–87*, AGPS.

Commonwealth Ombudsman, 1980. *Fourth Annual Report*, AGPS.

CPD (H): Commonwealth Parliamentary Debates (House of Representatives).

CPD (S): Commonwealth Parliamentary Debates (Senate).

Craven, G., 1989. *Consultation and the Making of Subordinate Legislation— A Victorian Initiative*, Monash University Law Review (forthcoming).

Crommelin, M., 1987. *Commonwealth Involvement in Environment Policy: Past, Present and Future*, Papers on Federalism 10, Intergovernmental Relations in Victoria Program, Law School, University of Melbourne.

Fiscal Powers Sub-Committee of the Australian Constitutional Convention, *Report to the Standing Committee, 1984*, Government Printer, Brisbane.

Intergovernmental News, Vol. 1—Intergovernmental Relations in Victoria Program, Law School, University of Melbourne. ISSN 1032–441.

Legal Aid Agreement: Agreement Between the Commonwealth of Australia and the State of Victoria in Relation to the Provision of Legal Aid, 1979.

Meech Lake: Government of Canada, 1987. *A Guide to the Meech Lake Constitutional Accord*, August.

National Legal Aid Advisory Committee, 1989. *Funding, Providing and Supplying Legal Aid Services*, Discussion Paper on Legal Aid: AGPS, Canberra.

Saunders, C., 1978a. 'The Interchange of Powers Proposal' (Part 1) 52 *Australian Law Journal* 187–97; (Part 2) 52 *Australian Law Journal*, 254–63.

—— 1978b. 'The Development of the Commonwealth Spending Power, 11 *Melbourne University Law Review*, 369.

—— 1982. *The Co-operative Companies and Securities Scheme*, Information Paper 4, Intergovernmental Relations in Victoria Program, Law School, University of Melbourne.

—— 1987. 'Towards a Theory for Section 96: Part 1', 16 *Melbourne University Law Review*, 1.

—— 1988. 'Towards a Theory for Section 96: Part 2', 16 *Melbourne University Law Review*, 699.

SSCFPA: Senate Standing Committee on Finance and Public Administration, 1988. *Further Report on Non-Statutory Bodies*, AGPS.

SSCLCA: Senate Standing Committee on Legal and Constitutional Affairs, 1987. *The Role of Parliament in Relation to the National Companies Scheme*, AGPS.

SSCSB, Senate Standing Committee for the Scrutiny of Bills, *Alert Digest*.

Victoria, 1988: Budget Information Paper No. 2, *Commonwealth Payments to or for Victoria 1988–89*, Government Printer.

Wright, D.S., 1988. *Understanding Intergovernmental Relations*, University of North Carolina, Chapel Hill.

Part 2: Comparative overviews

4 The United States

Deil S. Wright

This chapter serves two purposes. First, it describes contemporary patterns of intergovernmental relations (IGR) in the USA and, second, it explores features of a relatively new term that has emerged in America— intergovernmental management (IGM). Both IGM and IGR are grounded in analytic and applied efforts to deal with significant shifts in interjurisdictional relationships in the United States federal system. Whether this new term, IGM, has relevance for boundary-spanning relationships in Australia is a topic still to be explored.

Contemporary IGR

It has been a common if not a conventional practice to review historical developments in federalism and IGR in the United States in terms of phases or patterns (Elazar, 1965; Wright, 1974). It is not necessary here to evaluate this approach in order to understand the current dynamics of the American political system. Rather, it is sufficient to note that the 1980s have been widely regarded as marking a significant shift in the character and content of IGR (Nathan, 1982, 1986; Nathan & Doolittle, 1983, 1987). That shift forms the departure point for the 'contractive' phase of IGR—starting in the 1980s but clearly extending into the 1990s.

In the third edition of *American Federalism: The View from the States* (1984:252), Daniel Elazar says 'the American federal system may be passing into a new phase', and that in this new phase federal grants 'no longer set the tone in intergovernmental relations'. In place of fiscal issues, Elazar (1984:252) observes that 'now the move seems to be in the direction of new relationships in the field of government regulation'. His view is an appropriate starting point for a discussion of the contractive features of contemporary IGR.

The word *contractive* is defined by Webster's *New Universal Dictionary* (unabridged, 1976) as 'producing or tending to produce contraction'. There are four ways in which contraction applies to IGR in the 1980s:

1 Federal aid is shrinking. In fiscal 1982 federal aid to state and local governments declined to $88 billion from $95 billion in the year before. Furthermore, federal aid is dropping quite regularly when measured in constant dollars, as a percentage of GNP, or as a percentage of state and local revenues (ACIR-US, 1989). The demise of General Revenue Sharing in 1986 should be mentioned specifically. There are the added consequences of the 1986 changes in the United States Internal Revenue Code (known as 'tax reform') that have altered the so-called tax expenditure advantages enjoyed by state and local governments (Wright, 1988:142–8).

2 State–local relations is a second area where contraction has occurred. One researcher uses the term 'the erosion of local autonomy' (Stephens, 1974). Using a variety of financial, employment and service measures for each of the 50 states, one analysis found a long-term trend toward the greater concentration of resources, services and personnel at the *state* rather than the local level. These multiple measures were used to form a composite index of state centralisation, for which the results are shown in Table 4.1.

Table 4.1: State centralisation in the USA

	Aggregate centralisation index (%)	Number of states in centralised category (above 60%)
1957	47	4
1969	52	6
1972	53	8
1977	54	9
1982	57	16

Source: Stephens (1985)

In short, there has been a tightening or contraction of the connections between state governments and their respective local jurisdictions.

3 Court decisions and congressional statutes have also contributed to a contracted intergovernmental system. Expert legal advice is among the most valued information resources needed by public administrators, elected officials, and governing bodies and boards at the state–local levels. Several United States Supreme Court decisions plus numerous problems precipitated by other litigation have constricted the range of action by state and local governments.

Federal courts have intervened to review and limit state–local actions in ways that seem to have few precedents. One author has labelled this new phenomenon 'juridical federalism' (Carroll, 1982). Another way to describe these changes metaphorically is to suggest that the intergovernmental system has been legally telescoped to an unprecedented degree. Federal courts are looking through telescopes that focus on detailed, specific, judgmental and policy actions by state and local officials. Examples abound, especially involving schools (under desegregation orders), prisons and mental health facilities.

4 A fourth meaning of the word *contractive* is not associated with shrinking or restrictions. Instead, it refers to the increasing tendency of governmental agencies at all levels to enter into contracts for the purchase and delivery of services. The contracts may be for the provision of 'hardware' services such as sanitation, refuse collection or transportation. Increasingly, however, contracting-out patterns have developed in human services and social program areas that are extensively intergovernmental in character, for example, employment training and social services. One observer termed this trend 'the fourth face of federalism' (Kettl, 1981). His broad observations were drawn from a detailed and thoughtful analysis of patterns and practices in local government where a city manager acknowledged that 'the more you get involved and try to play the federal game, the more you have to go outside (of city agencies)' (Kettl, 1981:367).

The manager's comment about 'outside' links raises an important aspect associated with this fourth meaning of *contractive*. It refers to the active involvement of *private* entities, both non-profit and for-profit, in IGR decisions, actions and impacts. This is part of a larger movement or policy theme in the 1980s called *privatisation* (Savas, 1982, 1987).

Another facet of this fourth meaning of *contractive* focuses on the management of the contracting process. The term *intergovernmental management* (IGM) has been used with increasing frequency to describe the problem-solving efforts of people involved in implementation activities. We only mention the term here; its features and significance are discussed later. This meaning of contractive was well stated by a researcher (Kettl, 1981:371) who noted that grant programs have shifted local governments (and officials) from the 'direct provision of services to the management of contracted services. This not only means a change in some of what local governments do but also a shift in who does it. Accountants, contract specialists, environmental engineers, and equal opportunity experts have moved into a key role in helping to govern urban America.' Privatisation and management (of interjurisdictional disputes and of contracts) have assumed increasing importance during the current contractive phase of IGR.

Main problems

What are the main IGR problems confronting United States public officials in the contractive phase of IGR? Each researcher and participant could construct a list that might be different from the four discussed below. They may serve as a provisional list for discussion, however.

Borrowing and budget balancing. The size and persistence of the national government's deficit is a problem that exerts an omnipresent influence on IGR. Huge and continuing deficits cast a dark shadow over the current and long-term IGR fiscal scene. At the national level Congress has confronted the politically uncomfortable circumstance of where, how and when to reduce overall outlays. This created an atmosphere of forced trade-offs: a zero-sum situation in which any new initiative had to be carved out of existing resources and programs. Congress laboured hard in 1985 to pass a law, Gramm-Rudman-Hollings, that would move toward a balanced budget over a five-year period. The law was described by one of its sponsors, Rudman, as 'a bad idea whose time had come'. The results achieved by the legislation have fallen far short of expectations.

The impact of national austerity measures has been immense. The actual dollar consequences have been noteworthy, but of greater significance is the resulting shift in attitudes. On domestic and intergovernmental programs the agenda of choices for Congress and agency administrators involves efforts to balance equity and neutrality in program contractions. Ideas for new or expanded programs or for innovative intergovernmental strategies fail to gain much attention or high priority for legislative or executive action. One observer, writing about prospects for state and local governments during the new George Bush Administration, noted that 'the only certainty is that federal money will be in short supply' (Shribman, 1989).

Fiscal constraints, borrowing and budget balancing problems have not been confined to the national government. State and local debt stands at an all-time high. World, national, and regional economic forces have produced sharp, diverse and sometimes disastrous dislocations on many state economies. Budgets in previously 'energy-rich' states have staggered under the turnabout in oil prices. States with agriculturally-based economies have also confronted unwelcome fiscal choices between significant tax increases and/or sharp budget cuts. Most local governments in these 'depressed' states have faced similar hard choices.

Federal aid cuts and changes. The problems precipitated by federal aid reductions and reorientations have been enormous. The 1981 omnibus legislation was significant in terms of policy shifts: reducing federal aid by $6 billion, consolidating nearly 60 categorical grants and eliminating about 60 other grant programs. These changes and the continued efforts, with selective success, by the Reagan Administration to alter the fundamental character of IGR, prompted a legal historian to use the term 'whiplash federalism' to describe the sudden rear-end policy impacts on federal aid recipients (Scheiber, 1985). Every budget submitted by former President Reagan in the 1980s proposed a significant cut (in actual dollars) in federal aid. Only one major reduction actually occurred (in 1981–82), but the regular rise in federal aid became a thing of the past. Equally significant have been new levels of unpredictability over federal aid funding. The vagaries of executive–legislative relations and of congressional political dynamics have produced one surprise after another. By the time general revenue sharing lapsed in 1986, state and local officials had experienced so many sudden shifts that its disappearance was not a surprise. It could be argued with some merit, of course, that these developments were probably healthy for the IGR system, which was overdue for adjustment.

The fiscal impacts of aid cuts varied significantly among the states and localities, as might be expected. But a significant non-fiscal theme emerged from studies of fourteen states and selected localities (Nathan & Doolittle, 1987). A major finding of that 1981–84 field research was the important *institutional* changes occurring at the state level. State governments significantly expanded their roles in the policy-making process in relation to *both* the national government and localities within each state. Roughly similar results emerged from studies of block grant implementation in the states (US General Accounting Office, 1985a, 1985b). More specifically, governors, state legislators and state administrators assumed more active and influential decision-making roles. This point confirms institutionally the statistical findings about the contraction (centralisation) of state–local relationships.

Juridical decision making. Who has an answer for the 'problem' that national (federal) court decisions pose for state and local governments? The 'problem,' of course, is that there is no one single problem. There are nearly as many 'problems' as there are cases at the federal bar. Three broad types of IGR legal issues were identified in the early 1980s (Carroll 1982): federal grants law, the liability of state and local officials and governments, and court-ordered remedies for constitutional and statutory wrongs committed by state and local actions. In all three areas the federal courts have become intensely involved, leading one analyst to conclude that juridical federalism represents the 'alienation of public policy' (Carroll, 1982:89). The courts have focused their high-resolution telescopes on decisions made by state and local officials and found numerous faults. In Carroll's view, they have singled out public administrators as 'the weakest' institutional actors and required them to serve as mediators to resolve IGR conflicts. Public administrators, according to Carroll and apparently the courts, are in the unique position of leading from weakness. As non-elected, non-constitutional actors, they are the least threatening, least legitimate and least powerful of several state and local institutions. These 'weak' administrators are obligated to convince popularly-elected officials and other actors into following the best courses of action in resolving disputes.

The administrator's role is, of course, strengthened when court proceedings or a court order are heavy-hanging threats over the heads of elected officials who are parties to an intergovernmental dispute. The amicable (or at least acceptable) settlement of IGR disputes is now approaching a high art. The National Institute of Dispute Resolution (in Washington, DC) has been active in stimulating research projects, conferences and courses that have important and direct relevance to resolving IGR disputes. The institute and many similarly oriented efforts are part of a growing search for the non-judicial settlement of conflicts in our increasingly litigious society (Huelsberg & Lincoln, 1985).

Managing mandates. Federal courts are not the only institutional source from which state and local officials receive obligations and requirements. Congressional statutes and administrative regulations continue to grow apace. Despite conscious and even vigorous deregulation efforts by the Reagan Administration, the scope, content and consequences of IGR mandates have, on balance, probably increased.

One close observer noted in an assessment of the Reagan New Federalism that 'federal mandates have by no means decreased and no fullscale legislative program for reducing federal intergovernmental regulations was ever formulated' (Walker, 1986). This point was carried further by the staff director of the Senate Subcommittee on Intergovernmental Relations (Wrightson, 1986). She commented from her strategic post (1986:5) that 'The Administration has been far less successful in reducing intergovernmental regulatory burdens and in some cases has actually increased them.' Examples of increases involved teenage drinking, large trucks on interstate highways and welfare assistance rules.

Even when the administration seemed to make a major breakthrough in reducing regulations, offsetting effects occurred. When the 1981 Omnibus Budget Reconciliation Act consolidated several human services categorical grants, the number of pages of regulations was reduced from 312 to 6! The states became responsible for administering these grants with broad discretionary authority. State apprehension, however, was great because of the uncertainty over how the Department of Health and Human Services, the Congress and national auditors might judge (and second-guess) the implementation of the programs. As a hedge against uncertainty, the states wrote extensive regulations and mandates binding on local recipients of the funds.

A systematic seven-state study of IGR mandates in the early 1980s concluded that 'the new block grants to the states do not necessarily mean less regulation or more flexibility (for) local governments since state regulations have replaced federal requirements' (Lovell, 1983:186). The research also found that there were conflicting purposes present in the changes made in several categorical grant programs under the Reagan Administration. This was particularly true in the public assistance field, where the substantive goals of reducing welfare costs and diminishing welfare dependency took precedence over the process aims of reduced regulations.

Participants' perceptions

Current IGR problems and conflicts, and the various means to resolve them, are closely tied to the perceptions and preferences of relevant participants. There is the risk of oversimplification in any attempt to summarise the views of national, state and local actors. The difficulty of the task and of potential distortions is compounded by the variety of the participants, the changing character of the issues and the varying intensity of the views expressed. Nevertheless, some general characterisations are possible.

National actors. Former President Reagan was aggressive, articulate and persistent in his efforts to reform or restore national–state relationships. One among several features of the Reagan New Federalism was its *state-*oriented focus (Nathan & Doolittle, 1987; Wright, 1982). Congress responded positively but selectively to a few of the former president's proposals, but generally adopted a cautious, often defensive posture in response to many Reagan 'restoration' efforts. Several studies disclosed the dampening effects that congressional actions had on the 1981 'shock' delivered by the omnibus legislation (Nathan & Doolittle, 1983; Nathan & Doolittle, 1987; Peterson, Rabe & Wong, 1986). A natural question arises at this point in the discussion of the contractive phase: How can the results induced by the Reagan New Federalism be classified? Are they revolutionary? Reactionary? Or reformist? Arguments could be marshalled for each of the three alternatives, just as a case could be made that the framers of the United States Constitution at the Philadelphia Convention were revolutionaries, reactionaries or reformers. The central point about the Reagan aims and results is that they do not fit neatly nor fully into any one of the three categories.

There is no doubt that significant changes occurred in IGR as a result of the Reagan 'era.' One group of writers describes it as 'the new direction in American politics' (Chubb & Peterson, 1985) while another refers to the changes as 'fundamental' (Nathan, 1982). But to call these changes 'revolutionary' is to stretch the meaning of that term beyond its normal bounds. It suggests that the shifts departed drastically or completely from past patterns, as in the case of a revolution. The Reagan-induced changes were a departure from trend, not a revolt from or a reversal of preceding IGR phases.

The reform and reaction aspects of the Reagan New Federalism commanded the attention of many students of IGR. The system had reached a stage where numerous reforms had been proposed to deal with significant problems. A reaction had set in against the system's size, complexity and calculations. The Reagan proposals had some reform markings on them, but they were also imprinted with strong and clear ideological branding irons. One social critic described those signs in essays on the social policies of the Reagan Administration (Glazer, 1984, 1986). He noted that the first and dominant ideological theme was a rejection of 'social engineering,' the use of governmental actions and institutions to affect human behavior and improve the human condition. The specific intent of this strategy was 'to reverse the course of social policy that had been set for almost 20 years' (Glazer, 1984:77). The second ideological theme, closely related to the first, was the New Federalism strategy, namely, 'returning programs to the states and restricting federal controls' (Glazer, 1984:91). The Reagan administration's reform intentions however greatly exceeded the actual results in these interconnected areas of social policy and federalism.

If the Reagan efforts do not fit the reformist, reactionary or revolutionary categories, how can we identify or designate the IGR changes during the decade? The word *redirection* probably best describes the policy shift that occurred. The 1980s, and perhaps beyond, are likely to be viewed as a departure from trend, a reorientation of IGR in fiscal and political terms. From the 1930s through the 1970s the long-term trend was, with only incidental exceptions, 'a bias for centralisation' toward the national government (Chubb, 1985a:273–306). That bias has been blunted in important ways in some significant policy areas, but it is too early to tell whether the fiscal, programmatic and political results of the Reagan era will, in the long run, achieve a reversal, a bias toward *de*centralisation.

State and local actors. How might the views of the numerous state and local participants be described in the current phase of IGR? Their views can be summarised as 'Don't look back!' 'Don't look up!' 'Look out!' 'Look around!' An ageless and legendary baseball player once expressed a motto that marked his lengthy and distinctive career: 'Don't look back, something may be gaining on you.' His observation is both a description of, and a prescription for, state and local officials' views in the contractive phase of IGR. It advises them not to look backward in time for the 'good old days' of the 1960s and 1970s. Those times of federal aid grantsmanship are past and, by and large, should be forgotten. Although lessons may be learned from prior IGR experiences, they should be used for forward oriented actions rather than as nostalgic reflections.

'Don't look up!' describes the apparent and dramatic shift away from Washington in the views of state and local officials generally, but most particularly among local actors. Looking 'up' to Washington for assistance in time of fiscal crisis was a common response in the 1960s and 1970s. This 'Potomac-pipeline' pattern has undergone a turnabout in the 1980s. Speaking in metaphoric and semi-jesting terms, one critic said, 'Mayors, managers, and other local folks have thrown away their airline schedules to Washington, DC and gotten out road maps to find their way to the state capitol.'

The 'Look out!' warning is subject to multiple interpretations, but mainly it describes how state and local officials feel in the wake of sudden, unanticipated actions by national actors. For local officials, it also describes their shock at precipitous state actions. This idea was partially captured by the term 'whiplash federalism,' but it is broader in scope than merely a pain in the neck, or in other parts of the anatomy. The outlook is one that expects an accident. It might be described as hoping for the best but (Look out!) preparing for the worst. A position of defensiveness is combined with an element of contentiousness. In other words, give in only grudgingly; don't give up without a fight.

A major avenue to pursue such strategies is, of course, the courts. The rise of federal grant law has been mentioned, but this is only a small and in some respects a minor part of IGR legal issues. The current legal dimensions of IGR are multiple, varied and complex. Tort liability, for example, has produced havoc in the insurance field, resulting in huge increases in insurance premiums for local governments (and their officials). The tendency to use the courts to settle differences (litigiousness) has received wide press coverage. It has probably been overemphasised by the media, but the problems exist.

One more viewpoint among state and local officials needs to be noted: 'Look around!' This view describes the lateral linkages and support that some state and many local officials strongly seek. These support networks based on mutual interests are not new, of course. The state and local 'public' interest groups constitute one long-standing example. But these networks have taken on new vigour and variety. Furthermore, they tend not to be restricted to fiscal issues. One illustration will suffice.

The State and Local Legal Center is an entity that is officially housed within the Academy for State and Local Government in Washington, DC (Academy, 1986). The Center has a brief history and, as Washington influence goes, is on the periphery of power. It is nevertheless emblematic of the novel and varied ways in which positive efforts are necessary for state and local officials to mount a better defence. The Center exists for one explicit purpose: to improve the content and calibre of legal advocacy before the federal (national) courts in cases of major significance in which the states or localities are a party to the suits.

The Center is the result of multiple forces and influences. The need for better state and local representation before the Supreme Court had been known informally for a considerable period of time. It surfaced explicitly, however, in a 1974 speech by Justice Lewis Powell to the Fifth Circuit Judicial Conference. He noted that some of the weakest briefs and arguments come from the state's lawyer (Baker & Asperger, 1982).

The need for improved legal representation becomes apparent when one considers the following:

1 In any one term of the Supreme Court, from one-third to one-half of the cases involve states or localities at bar.
2 Between 1970 and 1978 the Supreme Court held state and local laws unconstitutional in 180 cases (contrasted to 18 US statutes).
3 When state and local governments are parties to a suit before the Supreme Court and the United States solicitor-general argues in opposition, states and localities win less than a third of the cases.
4 When the solicitor-general sides with the state or local government, the state or local position prevails in over two-thirds of the cases.
5 Suits against state and local governments for alleged civil rights violations, especially under section 1983 (ch. 42) of the United States Code, have reached 'epic proportions': 15–20 000 cases filed each year.
6 The number of civil rights petitions filed in federal courts by state prisoners against correctional officials rose from 218 in 1966, to 2030 in 1970, and to 12 397 in 1980 (Howard, 1982).

The State and Local Legal Center may or may not produce the desired results in many (or even a few) federal court cases. It is, however, a noteworthy development in the way the state and local officials 'look around' for strength and support in a changing and uncertain IGR environment.

The main problems and the varied perspectives of participants reflect the distinctiveness of the contractive phase of IGR. The cluster of terms used to describe this period may be too broad and imprecise to capture its many specific nuances. The terms and the illustrations should, however, convey the existence of significant shifts in IGR.

IGR mechanisms

The contractive phase of IGR demonstrates not only new techniques but also similarities to previous IGR phases. Prominent mechanisms are congressional statutes; court decisions; information resources; dispute settlement techniques; and privatisation.

National statutes (laws) and court decisions are instruments that were important in a much earlier phase of IGR—the *conflict* phase which spanned a period from the founding of the Republic to the 1930s. The resurgence of 'legalism' in IGR is significant in serving as a reminder that some of the most crucial and difficult questions of American politics are often framed in legal terms and taken to legislative bodies or the courts for resolution. It is also not surprising—for at least two reasons. One is that certain participants' perceptions in the 1980s are contemporary analogs of perceptions prevailing in IGR before the 1930s. There seems to be a strong sense of 'us-against-them' among participants. This encourages recourse to the law more and more often. It also tends to emphasise, especially in a time of limited or declining resources, the intensive and strengthened attachment to a participant's 'turf,' jurisdiction or 'policy space' (Downs, 1967).

A second link between the 1980s and the 1930s is the Reagan 'restoration' theme. One view of Reagan's strategy is to see it aimed at repealing many of the features found in the phases intervening between the conflict and contractive periods. Historians have been intrigued by the links between Ronald Reagan and Franklin D. Roosevelt (Leuchtenberg, 1983). Some see Reagan's policies as an effort to repeal most social and domestic policy legislation passed since the new deal.

New techniques that appear to be distinctive and unique to the contractive phase of IGR are information (hardware/software) technology, dispute settlement (social) technology, and privatisation. Local and state governments have exploited new information technologies in numerous ways. By relying, knowingly or unknowingly, on Bacon's aphorism that 'knowledge is power,' hundreds and even thousands of sub-national governments have pooled information in data banks for analysis and decision-making purposes. Many of these locally-oriented information networks are limited to the confines of a single state, a factor that contributes further to 'state-oriented' federalism.

When one turns from computer hardware and software technology to the social technology of dispute settlement techniques, the challenges of coping with system contractions are both magnified and dramatised. The mediation of disputes between and among jurisdictions appears to be a long-practised but little-understood process. Research, writing and formal instruction in intergovernmental mediation has expanded considerably within the past decade (Huelsberg & Lincoln, 1985; Richman, White & Wilkinson, 1986). Privatisation has been mentioned previously, but an appreciation of its full IGR impact merits added comments (Savas, 1982, 1987; Kolderie, 1986; Moe, 1987). Another side of privatisation has become an important part of the 'look-around' strategy of state and local officials. At the state level the aim of attracting private industries, especially high-technology ones, has fostered interstate and even international competition. The *Wall Street Journal* a few years ago captured the core of this idea when it mentioned that 'state governments are increasingly acting like sovereign nations' in both domestic and international arenas (Ricklefs, 1979).

One example of the high-tech IGR 'wars' waged to attract commerce and industry appeared in December 1980 when the Governor of North Carolina, Governor James B. Hunt, Jr., went on an industrial recruitment excursion to the Bay Area of California. The Governor was visiting 'Silicon Valley' to encourage microelectronics firms to relocate in his state. He had placed top priority on economic growth and development, and this policy became more specific when he presented a budget to the legislature in January 1981. It included $24 million to establish a microelectronics research centre in a large research park near the state capital to attract out-of-state microchip firms.

The Governor's incursion into the west coast's microchip centre did not go unnoticed. California Governor Jerry Brown's budget to the legislature contained a response to the North Carolina overtures. It called for $10 million in funds for microelectronics research. According to one source, 'Brown explained the proposal as a measure designed to help a key California industry fend off competition from outside the state' (Knox, 1981; *Science*, 1981). A further episode in the tug-of-war over the 'industry of the future' occurred in late January. The North Carolina Department of Commerce recommended to the Governor that a full-time recruiter be hired and stationed permanently in Santa Clara County, California. This out-of-state recruiter would join three other 'remote' industry recruiters in Tokyo, Seoul and Brussels. Whether the competition is for exotic industries of the future or for the more conventional 'car wars' for huge auto plants, this type of IGR competition for private goods is likely to continue.

The other side of the coin is that instead of trying to be a leading or innovative state in a positive policy sense, state decision makers compete in a 'downward' direction. This pattern has been formalised as an IGR game called 'beggar thy neighbor' (Wright, 1980). Justice Louis Brandeis termed this 'competition in laxity,' a phrase to describe the frequent rivalry among the states to find the lowest common denominator (Scheiber, 1978).

Federalism metaphors

The contrasting and even contradictory aspects of the contractive phase make it unlikely that a single metaphor adequately conveys the nature of relationships in this period. Three metaphors have been used as simplified descriptors of the present phase: *de facto*, telescoped and whiplash federalism.

De facto federalism is, strictly speaking, not a metaphor but a way of denoting the presence of federalism in fact—the reality of a formal federal relationship. The term was used in 1984 by the ACIR-US's executive director to signify a degree of fiscal disengagement (or movement toward separation) between the national government and the state–local sectors (Howard, 1984). The Reagan redirection results are partial justification for indicating federalism-in-fact, but they are not the single nor complete basis for the term.

Another ACIR-US staff member, the assistant director for finance and taxation, was particularly convincing in arguing that a slow but steady secular shift was in process in IGR finances (Shannon, 1984; Calkins & Shannon, 1982). The trend is toward more state and local self-sufficiency in fiscal affairs. The other side of this coin is fiscal constraint at the national level. These constraints include the defence buildup, social security financing problems, reduced tax revenues from the 1981 tax cut, the ballooning federal deficits, and skyrocketing debt. The central point of *de facto* federalism is that national-level problems, especially fiscal ones, dominate the Washington, DC stage. That dominance is so pervasive that state and local concerns are unable or unlikely to get on the national stage, much less steal a small scene during the 'play' of national public policy. A close analysis of federal aid finances shows that the shift toward fiscal disengagement actually started *before* the onset of Reagan's New Federalism. The Reagan initiatives basically accentuated a trend shift that had already started (Nathan & Doolittle, 1987).

The *telescope* metaphor expresses the legal dimension of the contractive phase. The adjective *telescoped* describes a collapsed, condensed or compacted condition. This circumstance is roughly analogous to the present legal-juridical situation in IGR. Gaining 'standing to sue', identifying a federal question, invoking precedents, and finding responsive judges (in federal courts) have produced telescoped legal relationships. The 'telescope' also represents the magnifying power and resolution capacity of the federal courts in providing intense scrutiny of state and local activities. Two major eye-pieces employed in this scanning-oversight effort are the due process and equal protection clauses of the Fourteenth Amendment. There is a paradox in this court review process, however. The focus of the telescope and the critical eyes seem more intent on questioning state and local actions. National (congressional) actions impinging on IGR appear to enjoy less rigorous examination.

The *whiplash* term has been used previously. It comes from an essay by a highly regarded legal historian who noted the sudden IGR financial shifts (Scheiber, 1985). It applies more broadly, however, and that breadth leads to a concluding observation about the contractive phase.

The metaphors, mechanisms, perspectives, and problems are not restricted to nor centrally concerned with fiscal matters. This is an indication of the rise of non-monetary matters to greater prominence in IGR. Financial exchanges, especially national and state aid, were once *the* stuff of IGR. The ascendancy and primacy of fiscal issues have receded with the rise to prominence of non-fiscal concerns. Elazar's point made at the start of this discussion (Elazar, 1984:252), that 'federal grants...no longer set the tone in intergovernmental relations,' is congruent with the prominent non-fiscal aspects of the contractive phase of IGR. One major non-fiscal dimension, in addition to the legal arena, is that of management.

Intergovernmental management (IGM)

As a concept, IGR was coined in the 1930s and still today it remains a relatively new term that falls far short of standardised and universal usage.

If this is the case with IGR, then IGM surely belongs to the esoteric vocabularies of specialised participants in United States governmental processes. Reducing the mystery surrounding IGM is one of the purposes of this chapter. In the process, we explore the meaning, usage, and relevance of the concept.

Meaning and significance

It will be helpful to contrast and compare IGM with IGR and federalism (FED). Over a century ago, Woodrow Wilson, in his 1887 essay, launched and actively pursued broad-ranging and strategic solutions to questions of administrative responsibility *and* questions of federalism (Wilson, 1887). Indeed, the attention Wilson's noteworthy essay devoted to FED is often overlooked (Wright, 1987). Wilson's confidence in finding clear and constructive solutions to federalism issues may not have been justified, even in his day. Today, however, the complexity of interjurisdictional problems seems biased against major changes in different political jurisdictions. Many of the intergovernmental system changes are small, gradual shifts that occur incrementally.

The emergence of the concept of IGM seems indicative of this more modest approach to the resolution of intergovernmental issues. Some might even argue that IGM is indicative of the minimalism prevalent in American politics and administration. Research under the IGM rubric has blossomed in the past decade. Three of the defining concepts of IGM exemplify its more limited but nevertheless important focus. *Problem-solving, coping capabilities* and *networking* are three terms used in defining the concept that emphasises the essential implementation roles of policy administrators (Mandell, 1979; Agranoff & Lindsay, 1983; Wright, 1983; Agranoff, 1986).

Robert Agranoff focused on IGM in human service delivery programs in the early 1980s as 'an emerging concept in the study of affairs between governments, reflecting the increase in public officials who work at the margins between their governments' (Agranoff, 1986:1). The activities that constituted IGM in a metropolitan context, according to Agranoff, 'in no way lead to fundamental changes in the social structure or resolve complex problems within the metropolitan areas' (Agranoff, 1986:1). More broadly, Agranoff argued that the kinds of problems that IGM addresses 'are not the type of fundamental solutions that eliminate major social problems nor do they lead to any substantial realignment in the federal system' (Agranoff, 1986:2). The problem-solving focus and implementation emphasis of IGM have been extensively illustrated in articles, essays and monographs. The larger and more controversial aspects of IGM, however, remain to be explored. Only a clarification of the issues will be attempted here.

With its emphasis on *management*, IGM has not only gained moderate usage but has also generated a significant amount of controversy. This is particularly true when it is understood to imply a clear hierarchical ordering in the relationships among political jurisdictions (Elazar, 1981). The following observations address one political issue implicit in the term:

> The popular acceptance of intergovernmental management is not a historically discrete occurrence. The starting premise of this article is that 'intergovernmental management' (as that term has developed since 1974) is best understood not as a president's pipe dream but as the completion of the twentieth century revolution in public administration first enunciated by Woodrow Wilson. For its adherents, 'intergovernmental management' is more than merely compatible with federalism; it is both the natural extension and resuscitating element of the twin commitment to federalism and managerialism in a time of scarcity—both of resources and leadership. (Schechter, 1981:127–28)

The writer's concern is not that IGM is fundamentally incompatible with federalism 'but simply that the *constitutional* relationship between the two has been largely ignored' (Schechter, 1981:129). Elsewhere, Schechter sharply contrasts the different orientations of the terms *federalism* and *IGM*:

> The basic difference between federalism and managerialism, and hence the tension between them, has to do with ends and limits. The end of federalism, in the American system at least, is liberty; the end of managerialism is efficiency. In this sense, the challenge of *public* management consists largely in directing the 'gospel of efficiency' to the constitutional ends of limited government. (1981:136)

Broadly speaking, IGM might be construed as a major manifestation of two important and related organisational forces at work. One of these forces has been called 'the age of organization' (Wolin, 1960:260). Major social, political and administrative organisations, with associated large powers, must be managed. These organisations must be enticed or goaded into action toward some asserted goal. On the contemporary political scene large administrative organisations, both public and private, have become the primary institutions through which individuals increasingly secure political satisfaction and social and economic gratification. Such gratification was once obtained through traditional political participation—in political parties, clubs, and associations. One result has been the sublimination of politics, in which 'the problem is not one of apathy, or of the decline of the political, but the absorption of the political into non-political institutions and activities' (Wolin, 1960:353).

A second force associated with IGM is the rise in regulation, which might be traced to a dramatic decline in trust in and among public officials and plummeting legitimacy in the relations between citizens and administrative agencies (Carroll, 1982). Increased litigiousness compounds the operational aspects of IGM. It produces thousands of problems that can be solved only by courts, by newly-invented administrative appeals units, or by mediation and bargained compromises that emerge from specialised, boundary-spanning management skills.

With this as background let us turn more directly to a clarification of IGM as something that codifies a dimension of administrative activity that is politically significant.

Comparing FED, IGR and IGM: system features

One approach to a further understanding of IGM is to compare it with its sister concepts, FED and IGR. The comparison can be made on the basis of various system features. Table 4.2 identifies particular system features and then indicates the manner in which those features are manifested under each of the three contrasting concepts. The body of the table consists of brief characterisations of how these features find expression under FED, IGR and IGM. Space and other constraints limited the amount of attention given to the several descriptors contained in the body of Table 4.2, however, the table is followed by descriptive notes.

Table 4.2: Federalism, IGR and IGM compared

System features and illustrative contrasts between federalism (FED), intergovernmental relations (IGR) and intergovernmental management (IGM) (a framework for comparative analysis)

System features	FED	IGR	IGM
1 Units involved	National–state, Interstate	National-state–local, state–local, national–local, interlocal	IGR units plus: Politics-in-administration continuum, Public–private sector mix
2 Authority relations	National supremacy (contingent hierarchy)	Perceived hierarchy (asymmetric orientations)	Non-hierarchy networks (matrix management)
3 Means of conflict resolution	Laws Courts Elections	Markets Games Coalitions	Bargaining/negotiation Dispute settlement Coping
4 Values	Purposes (mission)	Perspectives (policy-in-administration)	Products program results (management)
5 Political quotient(s)	High politics (partisanship)	Policy making (co-ordination)	Implementation (problem solving)
6 Lead(ing) actors	Elected politicians	Administrative generalists	Policy professionals

1 The first system feature refers to the types of entities involved in boundary-spanning interactions. For FED and IGR these are commonly referred to, respectively, as national–state relations under FED and the several combinations of permutations of interjurisdictional exchanges under IGR. To the IGR combinations and permutations are added, under IGM, the politics–administration continuum and the blending of public–private sector relationships.

   The addition of these two continua to the formal governmental entities involved under IGR clearly adds to system complexity. That added complexity, however, reflects the reality of managing under conditions where there is no clear demarcation of political versus administrative activities and roles. The blending of roles and activities approximates a continuum. Thus, it is not happenstance that an appointed administrative official might be actively engaged in political support-building efforts.

   Furthermore, the involvement of private and non-profit sector organisations in the conduct of public programs may even be crucial to securing results. This produces a blurring of the distinctions between the public, private and non-profit sectors. Such a condition might be better described as a mix of these sectors.

2 The pattern of authority relations varies under the three different concepts. In the case of FED, while power may be dispersed and variably clustered, it is ultimately lodged in last-resort cases in the hands of the *national* government. In IGR the power distribution pattern is less hierarchical; asymmetric relations in terms of power are common. One keen observer (Lovell, 1979, 1980) has argued that it is not surprising to find IGR circumstances in which there is no one 'in charge.' Co-ordination or concerted action may come about in a variety of ways, sometimes more by accident and by informal links than by force or central direction.

   The nature of authority relations in IGM is preponderantly non-hierarchical. The pervasiveness of networks creates a presumption of widely if not evenly-shared power distribution patterns. There may be varying power patterns among specific entities in a network, but across the complete network there is no single source of guidance. The idea of matrix management as it has evolved in private-sector organis-ations is a rough analog for IGM public sector inter-jurisdictional relations.

3 One proposition that seems widely accepted in organisation theory is Downs' assertion about interorganisational conflict. One of Downs' 'laws' is that every organisation operates in an environment where it is in some degree of conflict with other organisations in that environment (Downs, 1967). The particular conflict-resolution mechanisms chiefly associated with FED, IGR and IGM are specified in Table 4.2.

The constitutional base of FED and the prominence of courts have been noted previously. The popular election of nearly 500 000 public officials in the United States makes elections an important means of conflict creation as well as resolution. Additionally, in many states and in most local governments, a variety of referenda elections are used to resolve specific-issue conflicts.

Markets, games and coalitions are three broad categories of structuring competition and resolving conflicts in an IGR context. The literature on IGR games is modest but noteworthy (Bardach, 1977; Wright, 1980). More extensively and rigorously developed in IGR is the concept of markets. Dating chiefly from the 1960s, the idea of governmental entities operating as firms in a market environment has taken numerous directions (Ostrom, Tiebout & Warren, 1961; Warren, 1964; Ostrom & Ostrom, 1965). We need not adopt one or another of the philosophical positions surrounding this public choice orientation to make use of a market perspective (Rosenthal & Hoefler, 1989). Recently a political market analysis of IGR has been pursued from the standpoint of 'benefit coalitions' (Anton, 1989).

Bargaining, negotiation and mediation serve as hallmarks for IGM conflict resolution strategies. Literature on these has expanded rapidly in the 1980s. The problem-solving thrust underlying IGM encourages movement toward agreement that involves continuous interaction between those in conflict. This contrasts with court cases under FED, which tend toward authoritative termination of inter-party contacts. It also differs from markets, games and coalitions under IGR, where contacts may be distant or non-existent and inter-party relations may focus chiefly on assuring that all players abide by some set of pre-specified rules.

4 The fourth system feature specified in Table 4.2 is the values component, referring to what guides the analysis underlying each of the three concepts. For FED the focus, as mentioned earlier, may be variously described as liberty, freedom, constitutional rights. These broad but fundamental values of an ordered society are widely noted as purposes fostered by FED.

By way of contrast, IGM's underlying value is achieving concrete program results. Earlier references were made to 'efficiency' and 'managerialism,' not necessarily in a favourable light, as the ends or aims of IGM. Clearly, the problem-solving thrust, used as one of the defining features of IGM, gives the term a results-oriented bias.

For IGR, neither the specific, programmatic, results-focused bent of IGM nor the global, system-wide values of liberty and freedom of FED appear appropriate. Indeed, one of the reasons why IGR as a term was coined in the 1930s was because of its lowered value content. IGR developed and appeared to gain greater usage because of its *denotative* nature. This descriptive feature in the origin and expanded use of IGR tended to avoid, in greater or lesser degree, the partisan and/or political 'weaponry' aspects that were associated with the use of FED. But the predominantly descriptive and analytic nature of the term is not adequate to convey the results-focused emphasis of IGM. Rather, IGR has emerged as a descriptive term that emphasises an understanding of the images, orientations or perspectives of the various actors operating between and among political jurisdictions.

5 The fifth feature used to explore contrasts among FED, IGR and IGM is indicated by the term 'political quotient.' The term is intended to convey the scope and public visibility of the issues covered under each of the three concepts.

The issues associated with FED tend to be 'high politics' in the United Kingdom (Bulpitt, 1983). Illustrative of such issues in the United States are those connected with the 'new federalism' proposals of both the Nixon and Reagan Administrations, the 'creative federalism' of the Johnson Administration and similar broad political initiatives. The level of partisanship linked to FED issues is substantial and the locus of decision making on these issues tends to be in Washington, DC, resulting in what might be called a 'politics of the centre'.

If high- and centrally-based politics dominates FED issues, then low-level, implementation-oriented politics characterise IGM activities. Note that politics is not *absent* from problem-solving and implementation efforts. IGM issues, and the strategies associated with their resolution, simply contain a lower visibility, scope and political quotient. IGR matters, on the other hand, are posited as representative of intermediate levels of politics and partisanship. Advocacy of substantive policy is present, but in a somewhat constrained and confined context. Furthermore, IGR, and to some extent IGM, involve state and local (peripheral) entities in the resolution of problems. The type of 'politics' present in these arenas might be termed the politics of implementation, or the politics of peripheral participation.

Two factors should be kept in mind when reflecting on the terms and relationships summarised in Table 4.2. First, they are a matter of analytic emphasis rather than behavioural exclusiveness. The patterns present under FED, for example, are matters of degree rather than neat or sharp separations from IGR and IGM. One example is the contrast between high and low politics. Furthermore, the uses to which Table 4.2 may be put are, at this stage, primarily heuristic. The contrasts and emphases are aimed at promoting a basic understanding of the different types of phenomena occurring in the United States political system. They are not advanced as an explanatory or predictive model. Neither is the framework intended to be normative. Nothing is implied about the desirable or undesirable qualities of FED, IGR or IGM.

This leads directly to a second important factor. The framework laid out in Table 4.2 is provisional, exploratory, and, in a sense, experimental. It is formally presented here to test its capability in helping understand and interpret the continuing evolution of interjurisdictional relationships in the United States. Its wider utility remains an open question.

Actor roles and FED, IGR, IGM

Pursuing these initial efforts one step further, we shall examine the respective roles of three different types of officials in relation to the three major concepts under discussion, but especially IGM. The sixth system featured in Table 4.2 refers to three types of leading actors: popularly-elected politicians; appointed administrative generalists; and program-professional managers. The three categories have been analysed in interjurisdictional literature over the past three or more decades. Perhaps the sharpest delineation has been by Samuel Beer who placed the first two positions in the same category and called them 'topocrats' (Beer, 1978). The last group, program managers, he identified as 'technocrats'. The position(s) occupied by these three types are arrayed (vertically) in Table 4.2 against a trio of subsidiary concepts under FED, IGR and IGM. The resulting matrix produces role relationships between types of actors and the several subsidiary concepts.

In contrast to Beer's classification, we have chosen to separate popularly-elected officials from appointed generalists such as city/county managers, central staff and non-program personnel. Both empirical and impressionistic observations suggest that there are differentiated interjurisdictional role patterns between officials of these two categories (Svara, 1985; Wright, 1973). Elected local officials, for example, tend to be the lead persons in making contacts with elected officials in other jurisdictions while appointed generalists tend to contact most often their counterparts in other entities. Similarly, the programmatic professionals or functional managers tend to establish strongest interjurisdictional linkages with like-minded program people in other entities. The concentration of these functional linkages, of course, has given rise to the 'picket-fence federalism' metaphor coined by a former state governor (Sanford, 1967).

The three categories of officials are cross-classified in relation to several process concepts associated with FED, IGR and IGM. Under each of the three general concepts we have added for clarification purposes some of the explicit or implicit components of each concept. These subsidiary components are based in part on the elaboration of system features discussed in conjunction with Table 4.2. Thus, politics, purposes and power are subsidiary components of FED; policy, perspectives and priorities are components of IGR; programs, projects and procedures are aspects of IGM.

The cells of the matrix in Table 4.3 are filled by indicators (symbols) of varying size. The large symbols in the upper left, for example, indicate the large and prominent roles played by elected officials in each component under FED. Likewise, in the lower right sector of the table, the large symbols indicate the major role played by program managers in implementation processes involving programs, projects and operational procedures. The middle cell of the table highlights the prominence of generalist administrators in the IGR arenas of activities that involve policy, perspectives and priorities.

The upper-left to lower-right diagonal cells could be interpreted in a normative or prescriptive sense to be 'proper' roles for each set of actors. Such an interpretation carries the scheme beyond its intended aim. Furthermore, the presence of role extensions, breadth or 'spillovers' is expected and is indicated by the use of lesser-graded symbols in other cells of each vertical column. That is, elected officials are not restricted to the elements listed under FED; they also participate, in a progressively lesser manner, in the elements noted under IGR and IGM. Program managers' roles and efforts similarly extend into the activities indicated under IGR and FED.

One further comment: this formulation is clearly linked to recent efforts to conceptualise and operationalise the links between politics, policy and administration (Svara, 1985; Browne, 1985). That research focused on city managers (generalist administrators) and their relationhips with city councils (elected politicians) in four areas of activity—mission, policy, administration and management. The underlying conceptual parallels between the city manager and city council relationships and the IGM framework elaborated in this essay should be evident. The chief contrast, of course, is the more complex and uncertain environment of interjurisdictional relationships.

Conclusion

This concluding section is in two parts. The first part offers a summary and surface-level set of observations about current patterns of FED, IGR and IGM in the United States. The second part identifies and interprets some less obvious issues associated with the concept of implementation, focusing on IGM.

Summary observations

Evolutionary change. The pluralistic patterns of power among thousands of political jurisdictions in the United States continues to undergo changes. The most distinctive shift appears to be a pause in a secular policy trend, a bias toward greater centralisation. The policy redirection partially implemented by the Reagan New Federalism has not, however, produced a bias toward *de*centralisation.

Table 4.3: FED, IGR and IGM: concepts, actors, roles

Concepts	Interjurisdictional actors		
Actors:	Elected politicians	Generalist administrators	Program managers
FED			
Politics (partisanship)	🧍 (large)	🧍 (medium)	🧍 (small)
Purposes (mission)	🧍 (large)	🧍 (medium)	🧍 (small)
Power (sanctions, rewards)	🧍 (large)	🧍 (medium)	🧍 (small)
IGR			
Policy (directionality)	🧍 (medium)	🧍 (large)	🧍 (medium)
Perspectives (images)	🧍 (medium)	🧍 (large)	🧍 (medium)
Priorities (tradeoffs)	🧍 (medium)	🧍 (large)	🧍 (medium)
IGM			
Program (functions)	🧍 (small)	🧍 (medium)	🧍 (large)
Projects (tasks)	🧍 (small)	🧍 (medium)	🧍 (large)
Procedures (methods)	🧍 (small)	🧍 (medium)	🧍 (large)

Multidimensional shifts. The multi-dimensional character of interjurisdictional relations has long been present but seldom more apparent than in contemporary features of 'contractive' IGR. There is a national-state *fiscal* 'sorting-out' or disengagement—a type of *de facto* federalism. From a *de jure* or legal (constitutional) standpoint, however, the scope and significance of national judicial authority over state and local entities remains pre-eminent. Other dimensions of IGR in the spheres of regulation, administration and political party patterns add to the diversity and often contradictory forces operating among the political systems in the United States. The multiple, conflicting and inconsistent character of IGR patterns is further illustrated by centralising trends in state–local relationships, especially in contrast to fiscal disengagement trends in national–state relations.

Altered attitudes. A marked change in the views of intergovernmental actors has emerged over the past decade. The reasons are diverse, but they have engendered more aggressive, litigious predispositions. Some analysts argue that this is traceable to increased zero-sum fiscal relationships (actual or perceived) among intergovernmental actors. Others questions the efficacy of such a strongly-based fiscal explanation. There is general concurrence, however, that state and local government officials have shifted much of their energy away from the national government as a source of policy initiatives, political innovations and especially fiscal resources.

Institutional equilibrium. Several writers on FED and IGR have identified the presence of compensatory forces at work among structures and institutions in the United States. Selective forces, particularly in the institutional realm, appear to be at work. National-level fiscal constraints and general domestic policy quiescence have left a substantial policy gap. This gap is being filled in various non-uniform ways by different state governments, sometimes supported by and sometimes in opposition to their respective local governments. The policy fields are tremendously varied, ranging from education and economic development to welfare and work release for prison inmates. In short, there has been an institutionally-based policy resurgence by the states which has, in no small measure, offset domestic policy exhaustion at the national level.

Management methods. More than a decade ago two writers on Australian federalism noted that 'In the day-to-day operations of government in a federation the subtleties of means are easy to overlook' (Peachment & Reid, 1977). This chapter's analysis of IGM is aimed at specifying not only the subtleties but also the significance of management means and administrator roles in the United States federation. The hypothesis states simply that management will be as instrumental in shaping federalism in the year 2000 as finance, constitutional law, presidential leadership, congressional entrepreneurship and party politics. This management or bureaucratic-based hypothesis is not only prospective; it is also retrospective. It suggests, in other words, that bureaucratically-grounded forces have exerted a significant and testable explanatory impact on interjurisdictional relations at least over the past ten to twenty years, and perhaps over several prior decades.

One specific policy initiative offers an operational base for examining this managerial-bureaucratic hypothesis. In 1987 a presidential executive order (EO 12612) on federalism was issued. This was in fact a presidential mandate to all executive agencies that the agencies take federalism into account when developing policy alternatives and in issuing of all implementing regulations. The order is, in short, a type of 'federalism impact statement' expected of executive agencies.

A second 'tracer' policy for following the impact of management on FED and IGR involves implementation of the Regulatory Flexibility Act of 1980. This particular piece of legislation, chiefly congressionally inspired, grants to administrative agencies a larger measure of flexibility in rule-making processes. It authorises a process that has, in the United States context, become known as negotiated rule making. Clearly, this gives program managers an even stronger hand or pull on the steering wheel (and perhaps the accelerator) of policy vehicles. It should also be emphasised that this statute applies not only to the negotiated flexibility of regulations affecting state/local governments; it also applies to processes involving private individuals and corporate entities.

Interpretations

The emphasis given management/administration in this chapter calls for a few final interpretive comments. It focuses on the origin and evolution of policy implementation research over the past two decades. There have been at least three generations of research and theorising about policy implementation since the subject was opened by a trail-blazing book (Pressman & Wildavsky, 1973). The first generation, both represented by and derived from that volume, documented the immense difficulty of successful implementation. This early literature uncovered the complexities and contingencies of implementation, specifically in an IGR context. On the negative side its moral was: most policies and programs are likely to fall far short of stated aims because of implementation difficulties.

The second generation of research was more positive and prescriptive. It suggested that implementation could best be understood as a 'game'. Successful implementation consisted of learning the 'rules' of the game, the names and roles of the players, the stakes, etc. (Bardach, 1977; Pressman, 1975). Special emphasis was placed on the strategic roles of a few specific players—'fixers', boundary-spanners and linking-pin actors.

The third and most recent generation of implementation research has been the 'critical variables' approach (Montjoy & O'Toole, 1979; Williams, 1982). This looks for the crucial factors (or actors) that are barriers to or facilitators of the intended result. A thoughtful and fairly formalised expression of this focus is the 'backward mapping' approach (Elmore, 1982). According to this strategy, the policy implementor focuses on the specific and precise result desired. He or she then moves backward in time organisational and system processes by asking, in effect, what must be changed to bring about the intended result.

The implementation-oriented import of this chapter suggests the emergence of a fourth generation of implementation literature. Only the broadest shape and selected concepts of such an approach can be mentioned. First, consistent with the positive findings of research about 'when federalism works,' this approach is normatively optimistic (Chubb, 1985b; Nathan & Doolittle, 1987; Peterson, Rabe, & Wong, 1986). Second, it explicitly takes into account different policy arenas, e.g., distributive, redistributive or regulatory policies (Lowi, 1964, 1972). Third, it examines, often comparatively, specific issue networks (sub-governments), policy communities, and organisational cultures. Finally, it is more specifically propositional. One sample hypothesis states: greater specificity in the roles of intergovernmental actors contributes to greater co-operation and more effective implementation of intergovernmental policies. This role-premised hypothesis might be tested on the basis of the comparative frameworks presented in Tables 4.2 and 4.3 with regard to FED, IGR and IGM.

Bibliography

Academy for State and Local Government, State and Local Legal Center, 1986. 'Memorandum (10 July): State and Local Legal Center,' Washington, DC.

Advisory Commission on Intergovernmental Relations (ACIR-US). 1989. *Significant Features of Fiscal Federalism: 1989 Edition*, Vol. 1, Washington, DC.

Agranoff, R., 1986. *Intergovernmental Management: Human Services Problem Solving in Six Metropolitan Areas*, State University of New York Press, Albany, New York.

Agranoff, R. & Lindsay, V.A., 1983. 'Intergovernmental Management: Perspectives on Human Service Problem Solving at the Local Level', *Public Administration Review*, 43, 227–37.

Anton, T.J., 1989. *American Federalism and Public Policy: How the System Works*, Random House, New York.

Baker, S. & Asperger, J.R., 1982. 'Foreword: Toward a Center for State–Local Legal Advocacy', *Catholic University Law Review*, 31, 367–73.

Bardach, E., 1977. *The Implementation Game: What Happens After a Bill Becomes a Law*, MIT Press, Cambridge, Massachusetts.

Beer, S.H., 1978. 'Federalism, Nationalism, and Democracy in America', *American Political Science Review*, 72, 9–21.

Browne, W.P., 1985. 'Municipal Managers and Policy: A Partial Test of the Svara Dichotomy–Duality Model', *Public Administration Review*, 45, 620–22.

Bulpitt, J., 1983. *Territory and Power in the United Kingdom: An Interpretation*, Manchester University Press, Manchester.

Calkins, S. & Shannon, J., 1982. 'The New Formula for Fiscal Federalism: Austerity Equals Decentralization,' *Intergovernmental Perspective*, 8, 23–29.

Carroll, J.D., 1982. The New Juridical Federalism and the Alienation of Public Policy,' *American Journal of Public Administration*, 16, 89–105.

Chubb, J.E., 1985a. 'Federalism and the Bias for Centralization', in *The New Direction in American Politics*, eds J.E. Chubb & P.E. Peterson, Brookings, Washington, DC, 273–306.

—— 1985b. 'The Political Economy of Federalism,' *American Political Science Review*, 79, 994–1015.

Chubb, J.E. & P.E. Peterson, eds., 1985. *The New Direction in American Politics*, Brookings, Washington, DC.

Downs, A., 1967. *Inside Bureaucracy*, Little Brown, Boston.

Elazar, D.J., 1965. 'The Shaping of Intergovernmental Relations in the Twentieth Century', *The Annals*, 359, 10–22.

—— 1981. 'Is Federalism Compatible with Prefectoral Administration?' *Publius: The Journal of Federalism*, 11, 3–22.

—— 1984. *American Federalism: A View from the States*, Harper & Row, New York.

Elmore, R.F., 1982. 'Backward Mapping: Implementation Research and Policy Decisions', in W. Williams and others, *Studying Implementation: Methodological and Administrative Issues,* Chatham House, Chatham, New Jersey, 18–35.

Glazer, N., 1984. 'Reagan's Social Policy—A Review', *Public Interest*, 75, 76–98.

—— 1986. 'The Social Agenda', in *Perspectives on the Reagan Years*, ed. J.L. Palmer, The Urban Institute Press, Washington, DC, 5–30.

Howard, A.E. D., 1982. 'The States and the Supreme Court', *Catholic University Law Review*, 31, 375–438.

Howard, S.K., 1984. 'DeFacto New Federalism', *Intergovernmental Perspective*, 10, 4.

Huelsberg, N.A. & Lincoln, W.F., eds, 1985. *Successful Negotiating in Local Government,* International City Management Association, Washington, DC.

Kettl, D.F., 1981. 'The Fourth Face of Federalism,' *Public Administration Review*, 41, 366–71.

Knox, M., 1981. 'Micros Could Get Us In The Chips', *The Leader: Research Triangle Newsweekly*, The Leader Publishing Co., North Carolina.

Kolderie, T., 1986. 'Two Different Concepts of Privatization', *Public Administration Review*, 46, 285–91.

Leuchtenberg, W.E., 1983. *In the Shadow of FDR: From Harry Truman to Ronald Reagan*, Cornell University Press, Ithaca, New York.

Lovell, C.H., 1979. 'Coordinating Grants from Below', *Public Administration Review*, 39, 432–9.

—— 1980. 'Where We are In Intergovernmental Relations and Some of the Implications', *Southern Review of Public Administration*, 3, 6–20.

—— 1983. 'The Effects of Regulatory Changes on States and Localities', in R.P. Nathan & F.C. Doolittle, *The Consequences of Cuts*, Princeton Urban and Regional Research Center, Princeton, New Jersey: 169–87.

Lowi, T., 1964. 'American Business, Public Policy, Case Studies, and Political Theory', *World Politics*, 16, 677–715.

—— 1972. 'Four Systems of Policy, Politics, and Choice' *Public Administration Review*, 32, 298–310.

Mandell, M., 1979. 'Letters to the Editor: Intergovernmental Management', *Public Administration Times*, 2 (15 December), 2, 6.

Moe, R.C., 1987. 'Exploring the Limits of Privatization', *Public Administration Review*, 47, 453–60.

Montjoy, R.S. & O'Toole, L.J., Jr., 1979. 'Toward a Theory of Policy Implementation: An Organizational Perspective', *Public Administration Review*, 39, 465–76.

Nathan, R.P., 1982. 'Fundamental Changes in the 1989s', *National Civic Review*, 71, 516–18.

——1986. 'Institutional Change Under Reagan', in *Perspectives on the Reagan Years*, ed. J.L. Palmer, Urban Institute Press, Washington, DC, 121–43.

Nathan, R.P. & Doolittle, F.C., eds., 1983. *The Consequences of Cuts: The Effects of the Reagan Domestic Program on State and Local Governments*, Princeton New Jersey.

—— 1987. *Reagan and the States*, Princeton University Press, Princeton, New Jersey.

Ostrom, V. & Ostrom, E., 1965. 'A Behavioral Approach to the Study of Intergovernmental Relations', *The Annals*, 359, 137–46.

Ostrom, V., Tiebout, C.M. & Warren, R., 1961. 'The Organization of Government in Metropolitan Areas: A Theoretical Inquiry', *American Political Science Review*, 55, 831–42.

Peachment, A. & Reid, G.S., 1977. *New Federalism in Australia: Rhetoric or Reality?* Australasian Political Studies Association, Adelaide.

Peterson, P.E., Rabe, B.G. & Wong, K.K., 1986. *When Federalism Works*, Brookings, Washington, DC.

Pressman, J.L., 1975. *Federal Programs and City Politics*, University of California Press, Berkeley, California.

Pressman, J.L. & Wildavsky, A.B., 1973. *Implementation: How Great Expectations in Washington Are Dashed in Oakland*, University of California Press, Berkeley, California.

Richman, R., White, O.F., Jr, & Wilkinson, M., 1986. *Intergovernmental Mediation: Negotiations in Local Government Disputes*, Westview Press, Boulder, Colorado.

Ricklefs, R., 1979. 'Manager's Journal—Early Warning System', *Wall Street Journal*, 30 April, 16.

Rosenthal, D.B. & Hoefler, J.M., 1989. 'Competing Approaches to the Study of American Federalism and Intergovernmental Relations', *Publius: The Journal of Federalism*, 19, 1–24.

Sanford, T., 1967. *Storm Over the States*, McGraw Hill, New York.

Savas, E.S., 1982. *Privatizing the Public Sector: How to Shrink Government*, Chatham House, Chatham, New Jersey.

—— 1987. *Privatization: The Key to Better Government*, Chatham House, Chatham, New Jersey.

Schechter, S.L., 1981. 'On the Compatibility of Federalism and Intergovernmental Management', *Publius: The Journal of Federalism*, 11, 127–41.

Scheiber, H.N., 1978. 'American Federalism and the Diffusion of Power: Historical and Contemporary Perspectives', *University of Toledo Law Review*, 9, 619–80.

—— 1985. 'Some Realism About Federalism: Historical Complexities and Current Challenges', in Advisory Commission on Intergovernmental Relations, *Emerging Issues in American Federalism*, Washington, DC, 41–63.

Science. 1981. 'Governor Brown Boosts Microelectronics', 211 (13 February), 688.

Shannon, J., 1984. 'Dealing with Deficits—Striking a New Fiscal Balance?' *Intergovernmental Perspective*, (Winter) 10, 5–9.

Shribman, D., 1989. 'Among the Generalizations, Bush Gives a Few Signals to the States and Localities', *Governing*, 2, 19–23.

Stephens, G.R., 1974. 'State Centralization and the Erosion of Local Autonomy', *Journal of Politics*, 36, 44–76.

—— 1985. 'State Centralization Revisited', Paper presented at the annual meeting of the American Political Science Association, New Orleans, Louisiana.

Svara, J.H., 1985. 'Dichotomy and Duality: Reconceptualizing the Relationship Between Policy and Administration in Council Manager Cities', *Public Administration Review*, 45, 221–32.

US General Accounting Office, 1985a. *Block Grants Brought Funding Changes and Adjustments to Program Priorities* (HRD-85-33), Washington, DC: 21pp.

—— 1985b. *State Rather Than Federal Policies Provided the Framework for Managing Block Grants* (HRD-85-36), Washington, DC, 55pp.

Walker, D.B., 1986. 'New Federalism: 1981–1986', *SIAM Intergovernmental News*, 9 (Winter), 1–4.

Warren, R., 1964. 'A Municipal Services Market Model of Metropolitan Organization', *Journal of the American Institute of Planners*, 30, 193–203.

Williams, W., et al., 1982. *Studying Implementation: Methodological and Administrative Issues*, Chatham House, Chatham, New Jersey.

Wilson, W., 1987, 'The Study of Administration', *Political Science Quarterly*, 1, 197–222.

Wolin, S.S., 1960. *Politics and Vision: Continuity and Innovation in Western Political Thought*, Little Brown, Boston.

Wright, D.S., 1973. 'Intergovernmental Relations in Large Council-Manager Cities', *American Politics Quarterly*, 1, 151–88.

—— 1974. 'Intergovernmental Relations: An Analytic Overview', *The Annals*, 416, 1–16.

—— 1980. 'Intergovernmental Games: An Approach to Understanding Intergovernmental Relations', *Southern Review of Public Administration*, 3, 383–403.

—— 1982. 'The New Federalism: Recent Varieties of an Older Species', *American Review of Public Administration*, 16, 56–74.

—— 1983. 'Managing the Intergovernmental Scene: The Changing Dramas of Federalism, Intergovernmental Relations and Intergovernmental Management', in *Handbook of Organization Management*, ed. W. Eddy, M. Dekker, New York, 417–54.

—— 1987. 'A Century of the Intergovernmental Administrative State: Wilson's Federalism, New Deal Intergovernmental Relations, and Contemporary Intergovernmental Management', in Ralph Clark Chandler, *A Centennial History of the American Administrative State*, Macmillan, New York, 219–60.

—— 1988. *Understanding Intergovernmental Relations*, Brooks/Cole, Pacific Grove, California.

Wrightson, M., 1986. 'From Cooperative to Regulatory Federalism', *SIAM Intergovernmental News*, 9 (Spring), 1–5.

5 Canada

Martin Painter

Canada is generally considered to be one of the more decentralised of federal systems. Regional conflicts are rife; there are major interprovincial cultural, political and economic differences; and the provincial governments possess substantial powers to block or modify many areas of federal policy and to take unilateral actions. But the federal government, too, possesses substantial powers and has exercised them effectively in many spheres, both through direct legislative and administrative action, and through exerting influence over provincial policies, in particular through financial grants.

As a federal system, the levels of government are parallel regimes with overlapping jurisdictions; that is, they are both constitutionally independent and functionally interdependent. The division of powers, which enumerates both provincial and federal powers (most of them discrete, but some concurrent), produces a *de facto* sharing of responsibility for all but a very small number of the activities of government. This 'entanglement' (Leslie, 1987) results in a complex system of intergovernmental relations in which both levels of government assert their constitutional prerogatives and pursue their distinct political objectives, while negotiating over the substance of public policy.

This overview of Canadian intergovernmental relations begins with a brief discussion of the salient features of the Canadian federal polity; moves on to look at varying 'images' or interpretations of the nature of intergovernmental relations; provides a brief account of the evolution of the system in recent years; and finally, turns to the question of its impact on both the processes of decision making and the outputs, or the performance, of Canadian governments.

The Canadian federal polity

Jurisdictional entanglement has been but one source of constitutional anxiety in Canadian political life. The provinces and the federal government have engaged in repeated conflicts over their respective jurisdictions, and over their capacity to exercise the powers that they claim to possess. In addition, the constitution has been subject to radically different interpretations by its constituent units, in particular the assertion by Quebec that the 'compact' embodied a fundamental safeguard of the 'distinct society' status of the francophone enclave. Quebec's claim for special status within the constitution, reinforced since the late 1960s by the assertiveness of the Parti Quebecois, has maintained a continuing sense of constitutional crisis. Over the last few decades, constitutional reform has been a recurring source of tension in Canadian political life, and has had a profound impact on the conduct of intergovernmental relations.

Meanwhile over the past 40 years, the increase in the scope of government, and the evolution of the respective roles of provincial and federal governments in pursuing a greatly expanded policy agenda, have resulted in significant changes in the relations between these governments. In 1950, federal government expenditure (excluding government grants) amounted to 11.5 per cent of GNP, compared with 5.7 per cent by the provinces; by 1980, the respective percentages were 16.2 and 13.5 (Leslie, 1988:24). Such data provide support for the commonly used expression 'province-building' to describe the changing status of provincial governments in the federation. Caution needs to be exercised in seeing this as either new (in 1939, prior to the impact of World War II, the provinces spent 7.8 per cent of GNP compared with Ottawa's 7.2 per cent) or carrying all the implications often attributed (Young et al., 1984). For instance, part of the increase in provincial expenditures arose from the growth in federal grants. But it is certainly the case that provincial governments, particularly from the 1960s on, have reasserted themselves as independent actors, and vigorously advanced the interests of their electorates, their status as governments and their concerns for regional and provincial economic prosperity.

Linguistic duality and regional conflicts are the two central cleavages of Canadian politics. Quebec's assertiveness in defence of francophone cultural and communal integrity has not been markedly out of step with the assertiveness of some other provinces in defending regional economic interests. There are deep-seated provincial rivalries and jealousies, notably the overwhelming sense that the industrial and commercial heartlands of Ontario and, to a lesser extent, Quebec have prospered at the expense of the rest of the country. The regional economies of provinces such as Alberta, Saskatchewan and Newfoundland are distinctive, being based to a large extent on particular natural resources or primary products. Regional economic interests have often been defined in quasi-mercantilist terms, focusing on regional imbalances in economic prosperity and security.

Indeed, federation itself is often viewed outside central Canada as a device to entrench that region's economic dominance, for instance through the tariff and through national transportation and energy policies that ensured central Canada's access to natural resources and primary products. This perception gains plausibility when we note that, due to the concentration of population in Ontario and Quebec, any federal government relies on support from those provinces to win office. The 'party of government' for most of this century, the Liberal Party, has had a close, intimate relation with the region's business and commercial interests, as well as a strong electoral base in Quebec. Time and again, Ottawa's attempts to present its programs as part of a 'national policy' have foundered on the perception that their underlying rationale is to protect the 'privileged position' or special interests of central Canada. One of the roots of heightened intergovernmental conflict in recent decades has been a shift in the imbalance of economic power as other provinces have acquired new sources of wealth. The resource rents that Alberta, for instance, extracted in the 1970s allowed it to undertake the highest provincial levels of expenditure with the lowest personal tax rates, and provided it with a new sense of confidence and new levers of power. However, its sense of marginality in terms of federal politics remains (Gibbins, 1985a).

The party system is a further indication of the regional basis of political cleavages. Neither the Liberals nor the Progressive Conservatives have been able, for much of their history, to lay claim to being truly 'national' mass parties, and have continually faced challenges in the federal sphere from regional protest parties, particularly in the west. In their efforts to build a pan-Canadian base of support and legitimacy, the major parties have had to rely on the personal appeal and political acumen of particular leaders (Smith, 1985). Moreover, provincial party systems are, in many provinces, distinctive. This asymmetry between provincial and federal party systems (Smiley, 1987) is a major factor underlying the deep-seated basis of provincial–federal conflict and interprovincial rivalry.

The distinctive political traditions of provincial polities, their economic and social dissimilarities and their conflicting views of the aims and benefits of federation and the role of national governments add up to a heady brew of intergovernmental ferment. The provinces have been remarkably successful in exploiting their political advantages and reaping benefits from federation. Ottawa has had to play a delicate balancing act in attempting to satisfy the disparate and contradictory demands of Canada's regions and provinces. The independence and assertiveness of Alberta, for instance, stands in stark contrast to the 'pensioner' status of the poorer Atlantic provinces—'the Maritimes' blustering subordination, and Newfoundland's desperate optimism' (Young et al., 1984:814). The interdependencies, the 'special relationships' and the political deals are complex, and are often province-specific and issue-specific.

In sum, intergovernmental relations are multi-faceted and hard to capture in simple, universal categories. For this reason, it is possible to identify a variety of images that have been put forward as characterisations of different facets of intergovernmental relations. Some describe what appear to be dominant trends in a particular historical period; each has been presented with a view to evaluate and prescribe, as well as describe; and they are not mutually exclusive. In the recent literature, four such images of federalism recur: 'executive', 'collaborative', 'competitive' and 'co-operative'.

Executive federalism

This image depicts intergovernmental relations as political contests between ambitious, self-aggrandising 'whole governments' (Smiley, 1980; Cairns, 1979). It draws on the image of 'province building' and emphasises the growing sophistication of provincial bureaucracies. It links a particular style of intergovernmental relations with a common set of intragovernmental administrative reforms and changes that began in the 1960s, resulting in greatly strengthened central agencies and political executives, with a heightened consciousness of their collective capabilities and their sense of strategic direction (Woolstencroft, 1982). Relations are conducted under the umbrella of 'summit meetings' between provincial and federal ministers, with officials playing vital roles in laying the groundwork for negotiations. These arenas are depicted as being secretive and exclusive. Political executives monopolise the conduct of intergovernmental affairs, and public access and influence are limited.

The image of executive federalism emphasises conflict, and a common outcome of such conflict is paralysis: '(l)ike lumbering mastodons in tireless competition these governments are possessed of an infinity of weapons capable of wreaking deliberate and inadvertent harm on each other, but incapable of delivering a knockout blow' (Cairns, 1979:191). There is a close parallel between this view of intergovernmental relations in the federal system and the deadlocks of 'intergovernmentalism' in international organisations, such as the European Community (Wallace, Wallace & Webb, 1983:11–15; 21–27). However, some point to the instances in which mutual interdependencies between provincial and federal executives and agencies contain incentives to co-operate (Fletcher & Wallace, 1985:167–74). Bargaining and negotiation, or 'diplomacy', can result in the avoidance of deadlocks and the forging of joint solutions by agreement.

Collaborative federalism

Like executive federalism, this image focuses on political executives as the central actors, emphasising collaboration rather than conflict. There are two quite distinct models within this image. The first calls on a model of federalism in which the levels of government are co-equal, but distinct. It points to such agreements as the 1977 Established Program Funding (EPF) arrangements (under which the federal government withdrew from specific-purpose shared cost program funding in favour of block grants) as cases of collaborative 'disentanglement', and it applauds attempts at clarifying jurisdictions so as to remove sources of conflict.

This image has a strong programmatic emphasis, and has much in common with the Mulroney Government's avowed program of 'reconciliation' with the provinces when elected in 1984. However, it embodies a basic contradiction between 'provincialist' and 'centralist' versions. The former tends to view the source of destructive conflict as lying mainly in federal intrusions, and emphasises the need for federal 'disengagement'. The latter stresses the need for intergovernmental collaboration to achieve national goals, for instance in economic policy. Both versions have a 'managerialist' bias, in the sense that the institutions of federal–provincial relations are conceived as occasions for problem solving rather than political conflict (Dupre, 1987), and in the sense that the role of the federal government is linked with a general program of economic rationality and, in recent times in particular, fiscal responsibility.

The second model is more pessimistic, and stems from public choice theory. Collaboration amounts to a 'tyranny of harmony', to borrow Simeon's phrase (Simeon, 1988:519). Governments get together in a cartel-like collusion to raid the public purse for political purposes, leading to fiscal irresponsibility and the expansion of bureaucratic and jurisdictional empires (Sproule-Jones, 1975). This view has developed as a critique of executive federalism, but its normative prescriptions differ markedly from those who propose managerialist solutions. Competitive federalism is advocated as the preferred image.

Competitive federalism

Again, this image has distinct empirical and normative elements. Descriptively, it is a further variant of executive federalism, emphasising the independent, competing actions of provincial and federal governments. Federal and provincial governments compete for political support and are responsive to different sets of interests and different publics. This image allows for greater access by outside interests, who are able to play one level of government off against the other. Policy making often proceeds by unilateral action and counteraction, or 'thrust and riposte' (Leslie, 1987). Direct bargaining does occur via 'summitry', but just as important is co-ordination by mutual adjustment and initiative and response.

For the managerialist school of collaborative federalists, this process is chaotic. Others, however, emphasise the scope for innovation, experimentation and a mix of diversity and uniformity. For the public choice school, competitive federalism is the closest thing to the market place to be hoped for, providing choice and promoting efficiency through competition (Breton, 1985). However, from this perspective—despite the competitive dynamic—executive dominance severely limits the responsiveness of the system to the diversity of preferences and tastes that exist in the community. Competition is very far from perfect, and tends, in the intergovernmental arenas of executive federalism, towards collusion. In an 'ideal world', competition for support from overlapping electorates would breed administrative co-operation if public demands required a joint solution, but executive dominance and jurisdictional jealousies inhibit this, and collaboration occurs only for the mutual advantage of the cartel of executives.

Co-operative federalism

This image lays stress on the administrative dimensions of joint action between federal and provincial governments. Its model of federalism, in contrast to the collaborative image, is more hierarchical, seeing the provinces, in so far as they engage in joint action, as administrative agents implementing agreed national policies, for instance via shared cost programs. Alternatively, the axes of co-operation are depicted as professional communities overlapping provincial and federal governments and agencies. Rather than being merely administrative agents, officials are seen as program initiators, and engaged in exercising discretion within agreed guidelines.

Not all who focus on the administrative dimensions of Canadian federalism view them in this light. Some stress the importance of bureaucratic politics as a source of conflict (Schultz, 1980), and depict the policy communities within which officials interrelate as riven with disputes, resulting in the importation of group conflict, via different patterns of agency–client relations at provincial and federal levels (Pross & McCorquodale, 1987). Such views of the process have more in common with the competitive than the co-operative image.

The images and the issues: recent developments

In a limited sense, the images correspond to different phases in the recent history of Canadian intergovernmental relations. Co-operative federalism is a label most commonly applied to the 1950s, when the federal government entered into agreements with the provinces on the basis of shared cost funding of specific 'national' programs. Subsequently, executive federalism came to be employed as a description of a phase of growing assertiveness by the provinces, when bones of increasing contention were the distorting effects of federal grants on provincial priorities, and federal jurisdictional 'intrusions'. But even in the 1950s, there was a notable exception from the general pattern in the shape of Quebec, which often refused federal largesse rather than compromise its autonomy. Moreover, in spheres of interaction other than shared cost programs, provincial assertiveness and jurisdictional strife were not uncommon.

Nevertheless, it is accurate to say that during the 1960s and 1970s intergovernmental relations went through a phase of heightened tension, in which provincial and federal politicians engaged in repeated public clashes, and negotiations sometimes ended in deadlock. The growing bureaucratic resources of some provincial governments, which enhanced their confidence and skills in negotiation, may have been one factor, as was the increasing power of provincial and federal central agency officials, whose perspectives tended to focus on non-negotiable 'whole government' issues such as jurisdictional integrity. But perhaps more important were the increasing size and scope of government and the nature of the issues that were now prominent on the enlarged agenda of both provincial and federal governments. As governments became more active and interventionist in a wider range of economic and social affairs, the tensions over jurisdictional entanglement grew.

Meanwhile, Quebec's 'quiet revolution' brought a new kind of assertiveness, involving a heightened level of state intervention in provincial economic and social affairs, driven by a modernising impulse. No longer was Quebec content merely to opt out of federally-sponsored social programs; it wanted to substitute its own. For instance, in framing the Canada Pension Plan in 1964, Ottawa had to accept Quebec's insistence on instituting its separate, parallel scheme. On cultural and linguistic matters, Quebec fiercely asserted its right to go its own way. The emergence of the Parti Quebecois as a potent political force, and its election to office in 1976, brought Quebec's radical demands for constitutional reform to the fore. To some extent, the other provinces rode the wave of Quebec's political campaigns against Ottawa, gaining in confidence and exploiting Ottawa's increasingly embattled state.

Ottawa's response on many issues in the 1960s and 1970s was accommodative. The opting out provisions of the Canada Pension Plan, the EPF arrangements of 1977, and a succession of agreements with Alberta over oil prices and revenues were examples of this approach. Indeed, behind the scenes of federal–provincial conflicts there continued to operate an ever-expanding array of administrative joint programs and agreements, in which mutually beneficial co-operation was evident.

However, the Trudeau government, elected in 1980 after a very brief period in opposition, adopted a new stance of aggressive unilateralism, embroiling intergovernmental relations in a period of intense, rancorous conflict. Trudeau had presided over a protracted series of negotiations on his treasured agenda of constitutional reform, which ended in stalemate. The provinces, in this and in other spheres, had become increasingly adept at blocking federal moves and taking the initiative. During the repeated rounds of intergovernmental summitry, the provinces had learned to thwart federal moves by building coalitions combining their disparate interests in common positions against Ottawa. Trudeau decided to fight fire with fire. In a series of initiatives, the government introduced an interventionist energy policy that directly invaded a provincial preserve and brought it into confrontation with Alberta (Doern & Toner, 1985); commenced unilateral moves to amend the British North America Act (Romanow et al., 1984); and moved to reassert its power over social programs, notably health, where it claimed that the provinces had departed from guidelines established before Ottawa relaxed its direct control with the EPF arrangements (Milne, 1986).

These three years of sometimes frenetic intergovernmental conflict brought their share of both successes and failures for Ottawa: the constitution was patriated, and now incorporated a Charter of Rights as the result of events set in train by Trudeau's unilateral strategy; but, on the other hand, the New Energy Policy (NEP) ran into a series of difficulties and reverses. In a classic case of thrust and riposte, Alberta responded to federal plans to take a larger slice of revenues from its treasured oil reserves by turning the taps off, and by refusing to approve new developments. A compromise was finally agreed on after tough bargaining (Meekison, 1986). But most of the elements of the NEP fell apart in the face of changing conditions in the world oil market. In the field of social expenditures, however, the government unilaterally passed new legislation that succeeded in forcing the provinces to move against hospital charges and over billing by doctors, on pain of withholding federal health care grants, despite a series of fruitless appeals by the provinces to the Supreme Court.

In some senses, this period showed competitive federalism at work. One of the strategies pursued by Trudeau was to appeal directly to the Canadian electorate and to a growing array of public interest and minority groups to assert federal power against the provinces. The unilateral approach to constitutional reform rested heavily on Trudeau's advocacy of the popular Charter of Rights, and he succeeded in isolating the provinces who opposed it by providing opportunities for these groups to exert pressure. Similarly, he paved the way for the 1983 Health Act by setting up a parliamentary inquiry that provided a forum for welfare groups to catalogue a litany of complaints about provincial policy and administration (Milne, 1986:178–84). Conversely, the heightened confrontation was a godsend to some provincial premiers who mobilised provincial anti-Ottawa sentiments on the strength of Trudeau's incursions on provincial jurisdiction. And yet, amidst this rancour and controversy, in 1982 in Alberta—one of the principle protagonists—there were 124 federal–provincial programs and agreements in effect (Gibbins, 1985a:223). Beneath the surface, co-operative federalism was alive and well.

Trudeau retired in 1983 and the Liberal government lost the 1984 election. Mulroney's platform of 'reconciliation', and his party's success in making inroads into the traditional Liberal stronghold of Quebec, prompted him to re-open the constitutional issue, to assuage the bitterness left after most of Quebec's demands had been rejected in the final round of bargaining over constitutional reform in 1981. Ottawa dismantled what was left of the NEP and effectively vacated the field of energy policy, at least in so far as such a policy had previously been conceived in interventionist terms (Hawkes & Pollard, 1986). And a new set of constitutional amendments, making major concessions to Quebec was put together as the 'Meech Lake Accord' (Simeon, 1988).

Some commentators saw this accord as the finest hour of executive federalism, in that it was reached at a country retreat behind closed doors, by provincial and federal first ministers. It contained provisions that cemented the constitutional status and jurisdictional power of provincial governments. It clarified and limited the federal spending power, provided for involvement, by the provinces, in appointments of judges of the Supreme Court and of senators, and would have entrenched the power of the provinces in the constitutional amending formula. Not only was unanimity required on many key issues, but, on those relating to provincial powers, a province had the right to 'opt out' of any amendment extending federal powers, and receive full financial compensation. A qualified majority rule was to apply to most amendments, but no role was provided for popular participation in constitutional amendments. Other measures included a constitutionally entrenched permanent first ministers' conference. In sum, the image that some saw best exemplified by the Accord was the collaborative version of executive federalism.

This interpretation was also put on the 'distinct society' clause, which would have entrenched in the constitution the special claims and status of Quebec. It has been argued that this clause would place further limits on the universality of the rights guaranteed by the 1982 Charter—limits that already exist in any case due to the 'notwithstanding clause' in the Charter, which permits a provincial legislature to declare that some sections do not apply to that province. Quebec had made use of this provision to pass legislation to overturn a Supreme Court judgment that its language laws prohibiting English language signs on commercial premises denied the freedom of expression guarantees of the charter.

Public objections to the accord, from many quarters, gave the opportunity for some provincial governments to reopen the issue on the basis of demands for special treatment to match the special treatment given to Quebec. In the event, the Accord failed to be ratified by all of the legislatures of the provinces by the required deadline of 23 June 1990, once again raising the possibility of Quebec's secession.

Processes

Clearly, Canadian intergovernmental relations are multi-dimensional. The institutions of co-operative federalism—joint agreements and regular official level contacts, both formal and informal—are well established and ongoing, regardless of the degree of heat generated by political conflicts. However, where such institutions and processes of co-operation exist, they mostly rely on the prior establishment of a set of political agreements between the governments concerned over priorities, principles, jurisdictional responsibilities and the allocation of costs. On these matters, conflict is common, although mutual dependencies provide common ground for setting in train processes of conflict resolution. Indeed, perceptions of mutual benefits to be achieved by reaching intergovernmental agreements can produce strong incentives to co-operate and to submerge potential conflicts. Depending on the nature of the issue, the intergovernmental arena is quite capable of producing either intractable deadlocks or harmony. Simultaneously, in other spheres of policy, federal and provincial governments may be proceeding unilaterally in areas of overlapping responsibility, with co-ordination occurring as the result of mutual adjustment, or not at all. Moreover, administrative co-ordination can proceed in such cases without formal, joint agreements, as attempts are made to 'mop up' some of the adverse consequences of parallel, unilateral programs and activities (Fletcher & Wallace, 1985:132, 195).

As a general rule, conflict and deadlock are most likely in intergovernmental relations under two conditions: first, where a joint agreement is either necessary or is seen to be desirable; and second, where there are intense inter-regional conflicts, or major differences in preferences and demands from province to province (Fletcher & Wallace, 1985:150). To some extent, the first is a matter of federal political strategy—how far is the goal of uniformity under the banner of 'national policy' to be pressed? Likewise, the second is partly a matter of *provincial* political strategies. But as well, the nature of different issues is an important factor. Interprovincial and provincial–federal conflict will be more intractable where issues are defined in zero sum terms, that is, where gains for some entail losses for others.

Mintz and Simeon (1982) distinguish between regional 'conflicts of taste' and 'conflicts of claim', the former arising from differences in preferences due to cultural or other factors peculiar to different regions, the latter arising when regions share values (e.g., welfare goals) but clash over the distribution of goods between different regions. It is conflicts of claim that give rise to zero sum situations. However, in addition, there is an important sub-set of regional conflicts of taste, involving *indivisible* goods, that also give rise to severe conflicts, because uniformity is necessary and conflict resolution through decentralised solutions impossible. The rights and duties of citizens (so long as 'citizenship' is conceived of in national terms) provide cases of such issues (Leslie, 1987:124).

Conflicts of claim also often arise between the provinces and Ottawa over the distribution of costs and over access to revenue (for instance, disputes over the share of resource rents). Those who argue that intergovernmental bargaining is conducted in a cartel-like setting in the context of executive federalism stress the importance of purely *governmental* interests. For instance, equalisation is about topping up the budgets of governments as much as redistributing resources among citizens in different regions. Grounds for co-operation or conflict arise from interdependencies or mutually irreconcilable interests that relate to the 'survival needs' of governments. This dimension of conflict may cut across that which arises from the conflicts of taste or claim between different regional groups or communities—a 'win-win' situation may be found in terms of governmental interests by redefining an issue in such terms, even though apparently irreconcilable regional conflicts appear to exist; conversely, an issue that may be capable of being resolved through decentralised policies and programs may be resisted by the federal government because it compromises its claims to jurisdiction and its assertion of 'national' priorities.

Nevertheless, where there are, potentially, zero sum regional conflicts of claim, there may be ways of avoiding intractable conflict. Such conflicts are often over the distribution of the costs of welfare improvements, and a solution is often to be found in absorbing these costs in the federal budget, thereby masking their differential inter-regional impact. Equalisation payments and other federal grants to poorer provinces are paid for in this way—a 'no losers' pay-off rule applies for the provinces. The deflection of regional conflicts of claim onto the federal budget, under the condition of such a pay-off rule, is just the kind of outcome predicted by those pointing to the dangers of collusion among governments in the intergovernmental system. Similarly, provincial governments can be 'bribed' through specific-purpose grants, even though the 'strings' attached to those grants distribute benefits differentially to the detriment of some regional interests. Indeed, the terms and conditions, especially where they require matching contributions, can effectively turn such discriminatory policies on their head, because only the better-off provinces may have the resources to take full advantage of such offers. Moreover, such terms and conditions are notoriously difficult to enforce by the federal government, so that grants become merely an addition to the provincial budget to be expended according to provincial rather than 'national' priorities. Only when the federal government comes under political pressure from 'non-regional' citizens' or producers' groups, or sees electoral advantage in making an issue out of provincial 'diversion' of federal funds, is it likely to take the risk of confronting the provinces jurisdictionally. Such, indeed, was the case in Trudeau's assault on provincial health policies in 1983. One interpretation of this episode is to see it as a case of the dynamics of competitive federalism interrupting a cosy *status quo* of intergovernmental collusion.

In recent years, a further dimension has been added due to fiscal scarcity. With the federal government focusing increasingly on cutting the budget deficit, deflection of intergovernmental conflict via federal largesse is less likely to occur, producing a situation where zero-sum conflicts over a finite cake will exacerbate regional conflicts.

In cases where provinces possess the powers and the resources to satisfy regional tastes and claims without joint action, policy making in the intergovernmental system will proceed by parallel action, perhaps followed by co-ordination through mutual adjustment. But for some policies and programs, unilateral actions leading to considerable variation between provinces can result in counter-productive effects, creating the need for joint, uniform agreements. These are cases where there are inescapable negative 'spillover effects' arising from provincial policies to satisfy regional conflicts of taste. An example would be provincial pension schemes that were incompatible and 'non-portable'.

The Canada Pension Plan was established in 1965 following a constitutional amendment that permitted federal action to introduce a uniform scheme (Banting, 1984, 1985). Part of the price of provincial agreement was to build in a complicated amending formula for the federal legislation that required the agreement of two-thirds of the provinces representing at least two-thirds of the population. No amendments will occur without the federal government agreeing to submit a Bill to federal parliament, while any four provinces in concert enjoy a blocking power. In addition, the larger provinces have greater weight than the smaller, while Ontario (so long as it retains at least two-thirds of the population) enjoys a veto power. Amendments are thus feasible, but rely on the building of a coalition of provinces to support them.

The formalisation of these voting rules in this case draws attention to an important aspect of the institutional structures of intergovernmental relations: the 'aggregation rules' (Ostrom, 1986). A sure recipe for dead-lock is a unanimity rule, as was shown in the long drawn out, abortive efforts to amend the constitution in the 1970s (Cairns, 1983). Indeed, the deadlock was broken only after the Supreme Court ruled in 1981 that provincial agreement to constitutional changes did not require unanimity. The federal government's attempts to implement a national energy policy were also inhibited by the inability of the producing provinces (notably

Alberta) to find any common ground with the consuming provinces (especially Ontario) (Meekison, 1986); for each, the issues at stake, such as pricing and taxation, were inescapably zero sum in character.

Unanimity, of course, gives a hold-out disproportionate power, and its debilitating effects would be likely to block many attempts at joint agreement in cases where there were significant regional conflicts, whether of taste or claim. In the pensions case, a less strict aggregation rule (but one that still gave provinces substantial power) was instituted once the provinces had agreed unanimously that the proposed national pensions scheme was acceptable. Such agreement was conditional on the ability of individual provinces to continue to sponsor private pension schemes; provincial government having access to, and control of, pension funds for public authority borrowing purposes; and the possibility of 'opting out' of the national scheme if a province decided to introduce its own public scheme. Quebec insisted on this provision, and was the only province to take advantage of it. Uniformity and portability have subsequently been ensured through administrative co-operation.

Thus, the debilitating effects of a unanimity rule are avoided not only by adopting other aggregation rules, but also by reaching agreements that incorporate the possibility of provincial variations to an otherwise uniform measure. Deliberate opting out provisions are one route, and have been applied frequently to accommodate Quebec's demands. Another is to frame guidelines that are sufficiently flexible to permit provincial administrative discretion, or to allow for separate, parallel provincial measures. This can go so far as specific bilateral agreements (Fletcher & Wallace, 1985:170–71), with the federal government negotiating separately with each province within a general framework of a 'national' policy. Such 'multiple bilateral accords' (McRoberts, 1985) were a feature of federal–provincial relations in drawing up provincial economic development strategies. In effect, such measures change the aggregation rule from unanimity to an 'any two...any three...etc.' rule.

In the case of energy policy, the federal government in the 1970s was driven to making bilateral deals with Alberta over oil and gas pricing and taxes, because Ontario asserted its hold-out power against any common agreements at federal–provincial summits (Meekison, 1986). Ontario, in effect, overplayed its hand, because both Alberta and Ottawa possessed the capacity to take unilateral actions without Ontario's consent. Here, attention is drawn to other kinds of rules, in this case 'authority rules' that prescribe what actions the participants can take unilaterally. These, in turn, are related to 'boundary rules' that prescribe the number of participants among whom agreement is necessary (Ostrom, 1986).

Unilateralism, bilateralism and opting out are ways of resolving intergovernmental conflicts, or of avoiding deadlocks, in circumstances where there are sharp inter-regional conflicts and where the provinces are in a position to defend and advance them effectively in the intergovernmental arena. The prevalence of these devices in the history of Canadian intergovernmental relations provides support for the 'competitive federalism' image.

At the same time, where interdependencies are perceived and the provinces and Ottawa see mutual benefits arising from joint action, co-operative arrangements will evolve for joint problem solving and negotiation, and for program formulation and implementation. A number of studies have described cases where successful joint decision making systems have evolved, many of them involving official level, 'in camera' processes of continuing, face to face discussion (Fletcher & Wallace, 1985:169–70, 173–74). Such processes 'encourage the development of common vocabulary and perspectives, thereby facilitating agreement', and 'promote mutual understanding and trust' (Fletcher & Wallace, 1985:170). Once major jurisdictional problems and issues of principle have been settled, joint federal–provincial task forces have been shown to operate successfully in producing detailed, workable agreements (Murray, 1983; Savoie, 1981).

As a result of intergovernmental agreements among ministers and among officials, a bewildering array of joint administrative arrangements has evolved. Wiltshire (1986:142–43) provides figures that show there were nearly 200 such agreements between 1979 and 1983, but warns that this data is, in all likelihood, incomplete. While 76 of these agreements involved Ottawa and all ten provinces, 48 were bilateral; the rest were multilateral, but did not involve all provinces. In drawing up and administering these agreements, there is a continual round of meetings and negotiations. According to Veilleux (1979), in 1957 there were five ministerial and 59 official level intergovernmental bodies, rising to 31 and 127 respectively in 1977. The 31 ministerial bodies met a total of 39 times, but the 127 official committees met 296 times. In these figures, there is clear evidence of the increasing entanglement, through joint action, of federal and provincial governments, and circumstantial evidence that much of this entanglement gives rise to attempts at co-operative, mutually beneficial discussion by officials, to whom are delegated the more routine tasks of working out the details of joint action.

This 'other face' of Canadian federalism is not inconsistent with a continuing level of conflict over many matters of jurisdiction and policy. As well as occurring over matters where conflict is not acute, co-operation occurs, in many cases, to resolve mutually damaging conflicts, or to draw up the 'fine print' after confrontations have been resolved in the context of intergovernmental political competition. The 'collaborationists' often hanker after a more orderly, uniform system in which joint agreements based on a rational ordering of provincial and national priorities are arrived at cordially and in a spirit of co-operative problem solving at the *political* level. For instance, institutional reforms are suggested to improve the procedures of 'summitry', such as more regular, institutionalised summits (Dupre, 1987) that are supported by permanent secretariats (Jenkin, 1983).

However, insofar as such measures inhibit the dynamics of competitive federalism and the resolution of severe conflict by bilateralism and opting out, they may lead intergovernmental relations down the paths of deadlock. Institutionalised summits reinforce an 'all in or none in' boundary rule and may restrict the capacity of governments to take unilateral actions to break such deadlocks, which are sure to arise when conflicts between regions and between provincial and national priorities are encountered. Scharpf 's analysis of the 'joint-decision trap' in West German federal–Lander joint programs, where intergovernmental relations had exactly these characteristics, is an object lesson in the dangers of collaborative federalism (Scharpf, 1988).

Outcomes and impact

Not surprisingly, the findings of a large number of studies that attempt to assess the impact of intergovernmental relations on policy outcomes are contradictory. In some cases (for example, health care) the existence of multiple jurisdictions has led to innovation and experimentation, but in others (for example, social welfare) the same cannot be said (Fletcher & Wallace, 1985:136–37). Evidence exists in the social welfare field that the provinces have exercised a conservative influence because of their blocking and delaying powers, but not to the extent of preventing major reforms in the long run (Banting, 1982). However, in defending their jurisdiction against unilateral initiatives by an expansionist federal government, the provinces are unlikely to succeed merely by digging their heels in; they must counter the federal government's appeals for electoral support by announcing initiatives of their own (Banting, 1982; Fletcher & Wallace, 1985:151).

In the field of economic policy, provincial power will inevitably be viewed as a constraint on the development of so-called 'rational' national policies. Provincial assertiveness has been highlighted as a major source of interprovincial competition for development, leading to inefficient industry and 'market distortions'; it has also been said to weaken the capacity of the federal government to plan effectively: 'an unrelenting pursuit of "national efficiency" is not a viable policy option for Canada' (Savoie, 1984:193) because the federal government cannot ignore competing conceptions of regional versus national interests. More specifically, divided jurisdiction and provincial power have 'limited provincial tax rates; weakened laws protecting labour; restricted environmental protection laws; (and) hampered federal efforts to reduce regional disparities...however the effects do not appear to be drastic, and the jurisdictional factor has only been one among many' (Fletcher & Wallace, 1985:194).

There are also conflicting interpretations of the impact of Canada's federal system of intergovernmental relations on interest group access and governments' responsiveness to public opinion. Simeon's conclusion based on three cases of intergovernmental negotiations in the 1960s was that the machinery of intergovernmental relations limited the participation of interest groups in the policy process (Simeon, 1973:144). In the case of highway transportation regulation, however, Schultz (1980) shows that interest groups can critically affect this process by entering into exchange relations with provincial and/or federal departments, and playing one level of government off against the other. However, when governments become concerned first and foremost with jurisdictional matters, all other concerns and interests tend to be subordinated (Fletcher & Wallace, 1985:185). But even here, governments may present their jurisdictional claims in public so as to win support from particular groups. For instance, the federal government's advocacy of the Charter of Rights was accompanied by a deliberate strategy to generate support from women's groups, minority groups and other supporters.

Responsiveness to public opinion is a virtue that those who subscribe to the image of competitive federalism claim for the system. Banting (1982) found that where the federal government and the provinces competed for the credit of introducing or expanding a popular joint social program, this competition enhanced responsiveness and introduced a 'competitive dynamic'. However, shared jurisdiction was often accompanied by conflicting policies and responsiveness to different interests, in which case those interests supporting a more limited role for public welfare provision had an advantage because of the blocking and delaying potential of intergovernmental negotiations. But where either federal or provincial unilateral action is possible, there seem to be no institutional barriers to the normal workings of electoral competition and responsiveness within each level of government, and there may even be a degree of 'out-bidding' between the levels.

Regional conflicts are fundamental characteristics of Canadian political life. The federal system has institutionalised these cleavages to the point that some would argue that regional interests, as interpreted by provincial governments, are blown up out of proportion to their true significance. Cairns' seminal critique of executive federalism homes in on the extent to which provincial assertiveness is based primarily on considerations of jurisdictional and institutional status and power (Cairns, 1979). Support for the view that the 'regional dimension' is in part, at least, an artifact of provincial self-aggrandisement is drawn from findings that, despite regional variations in some dimensions of political culture, there are basic underlying commonalities across most of Canada on many other measures (Simeon & Elkins, 1980). Moreover, at various times, many Canadians have responded enthusiastically to unifying, 'nation-building' appeals by federal governments, most notably, recently, in relation to human rights and cultural policy (where 'Americanisation' is a constant source of anxiety).

However, the regional factor in Canadian politics is evident in patterns of support and mobilisation in the 'national' political arena, as well as in the sphere of intergovernmental relations. As pointed out earlier, there is often some plausibility in claims that so-called 'national policies' are often, in fact, political stratagems directed at harvesting support in particular electorally crucial regions. In addition, ardent provincialists have plausibly argued that federal unilateralism, like provincial assertiveness, is as much motivated by institutional and jurisdictional expansionism for its own sake as by the attainment of substantive, ineluctably 'national' goals (Milne, 1986).

One is tempted to depict the Canadian version of federation as a loosely-knit voluntary association of mutually hostile provinces whose main reason for remaining associated is a common suspicion of the imperial ambitions of the Canadian and American governments (in that order). Canadian federalism and intergovernmental relations are a source of continual introspection by its citizens and by official bodies. But the sense of continual crisis is, at least, a sign of life. Moreover, the federal system has shown a remarkable capacity to evolve constructive institutional and political solutions to seemingly intractable problems of political order. Particularly where federal–provincial relations are conducted in a climate of competitive political interaction, rather than under the banner of a managerially-inspired model of rational, collaborative planning, then some of the potential costs of intergovernmentalism may be avoided. If the problems lie, in part, in some of the institutions and working rules of executive federalism, then so, too, do the solutions, which will continue to draw on the experience and habits of a tradition of competitive federalism.

Bibliography

Banting, K., 1982. *The Welfare State and Canadian Federalism*, Montreal, McGill-Queens University Press.
—— 1984. 'The Decision Rules: Federalism and Pension Reform', in *Pensions Today and Tomorrow*, Toronto, Ontario Economic Council.
—— 1985. 'Institutional Conservatism: Federalism and Pension Reform', in *Canadian Social Welfare Policy: Federal and Provincial Dimensions*, ed. J. Ismael, Montreal, McGill-Queens University Press.
Breton, A., 1985. 'Supplementary Statement', in Royal Commission on the Economic Union and Development Prospects for Canada, *Report Volume Three*, Ottawa, Minister of Supply and Services, 486–526.

Cairns, A.C., 1979. 'The Other Crisis of Canadian Federalism', *Canadian Public Administration*, 22, 175–95.

—— 1983. 'The Politics of Constitutional Conservatism', in *And No One Cheered: Federalism, Democracy and the Constitution Act*, eds K. Banting & R. Simeon, Toronto, Methuen.

Doern, G.B. & Toner, G., 1985. *The Politics of Energy: The Development and Implementation of the NEP*, Toronto, Methuen.

Dupré, J.S., 1987. 'The Workability of Executive Federalism in Canada', in *Federalism and the Role of the State*, eds H. Bakvis & W. Chandler, Toronto, University of Toronto Press.

Fletcher, F.J. & Wallace, D.C., 1985. 'Federal–Provincial Relations and the Making of Public Policy in Canada: A Review of Case Studies', in R. Simeon (research co-ordinator), *Division of Powers and Public Policy*, Toronto, University of Toronto Press.

Gibbins, R., 1985a. 'Alberta: Looking Back, Looking Forward', in *Canada: The State of the Federation 1905*, ed. P.M. Leslie, Kingston, Institute of Intergovernmental Relations.

—— 1985b. *Conflict and Unity: An Introduction to Canadian Political Life*, Scarborough, Ontario, Nelson.

Hawkes, D.C. & Pollard, B.G., 1986. 'The Evolution of Canada's New Energy Policy', in *Canada: The State of the Federation 1986*, ed. P.M. Leslie, Kingston, Institute of Intergovernmental Relations.

Jenkin, M., 1983. *The Challenge of Diversity: Industrial Policy in the Canadian Federation*, Ottawa, Science Council of Canada.

Leslie, P.M., 1987. *Federal State, National Economy*, Toronto, University of Toronto Press.

—— 1988. *National Citizenship and Provincial Communities: A Review of Canadian Fiscal Federalism*, Kingston, Institute of Intergovernmental Relations.

McRoberts, K.M., 1985. 'Unilateralism, Bilateralism and Multilateralism: Approaches to Canadian Federalism', in R. Simeon (research co-ordinator), *Intergovernmental Relations*, Toronto, University of Toronto Press.

Meekison, J.P., 1986. 'Negotiating the Revenue-Sharing Agreements', in *Managing Natural Resources in a Federal State*, ed. J.O. Saunders, Toronto, Carswell.

Milne, D., 1986. *Tug of War: Ottawa and the Provinces Under Trudeau and Mulroney*, Toronto, James Lorimer.

Mintz, J. & Simeon, R., 1982. 'Conflict of Taste and Conflict of Claim in Federal Countries', Institute Discussion Paper 13, Kingston, Institute of Intergovernmental Relations.

Murray, C., 1983. *Managing Diversity: Federal–Provincial Collaboration and the Committee on Extension of Services to Northern and Remote Communities*, Kingston, Institute of Intergovernmental Relations.

Ostrom, E., 1986. 'A Method of Institutional Analysis', in *Guidance, Control and Evaluation in the Public Sector*, eds F.X. Kaufmann, G. Majone & V. Ostrom, Berlin, Walter de Gruyter.

Pross, A. P. & McCorquodale, S., 1987. *Economic Resurgence and the Constitutional Agenda: The Case of the East Coast Fisheries*, Kingston, Institute of Intergovernmental Relations.

Romanow, R., Whyte, J. & Leeson, H., 1984. *Canada Notwithtanding: The Making of the Canadian Constitution 1976–82*, Toronto, Carswell/Methuen.

Savoie, D.J., 1981. *Federal–Provincial Co-operation: The Canada New Brunswick General Development Agreement*, Montreal, McGill-Queens University Press.

—— 1984. 'The Toppling of DREE and Prospects for Regional Economic Development', *Canadian Public Policy*, 10, 328–37.

Scharpf, F.W., 1988. 'The Joint-Decision Trap: Lessons from German Federalism and European Integration', *Public Administration*, 66, 239–78.

Schultz, R.J., 1980. *Federalism, Bureaucracy and Public Policy: The Politics of Highway Transport Regulation*, Montreal, McGill-Queens University Press.

Simeon, R., 1973. *Federal-Provincial Diplomacy: The Making of Recent Public Policy in Canada*, Toronto, University of Toronto Press.

—— 1988. 'Meech Lake and Shifting Conceptions of Canadian Federalism', *Canadian Public Policy*, 14, S7–24.

Simeon, R. & Elkins, D.J., 1980. 'Conclusion: Province, Nation, Country and Confederation', in D.J. Elkins & R. Simeon, *Small Worlds: Provinces and Parties in Canadian Political Life*, Toronto: Methuen.

Smiley, D.V., 1980. *Canada in Question: Federalism in the Seventies*, 3rd edn, Toronto, McGraw-Hill Ryerson.

—— 1987. *The Federal Condition in Canada*, Toronto, McGraw-Hill Ryerson.

Smith, D.E., 1985. 'Party Government, Representation and National Integration in Canada', in P. Aucoin (research co-ordinator), *Party Government and Regional Representation in Canada*, Toronto, University of Toronto Press.

Sproule-Jones, M.H., 1975. *Public Choice and Federalism in Australia and Canada*, Canberra, Centre for Research on Federal Financial Relations, Australian National University.

Veilleux, G., 1979. 'L'évolution des Mecanismes de Liaison Intergov-ernmentale', in *Confrontation and Collaboration—Intergovernmental Relations in Canada Today*, ed. R. Simeon, Toronto, Institute of Public Administration of Canada.

Wallace, H., Wallace, W. & Webb, C., 1983. *Policy-Making in the European Community*, 2nd edn, London, John Wiley.

Wiltshire, K., 1986. *Planning and Federalism: Australian and Canadian Experience*, St. Lucia, University of Queensland Press.

Woolstencroft, T.B., 1982. *Organizing Intergovernmental Relations*, Kingston, Institute of Intergovernmental Relations.

Young, R.A., Faucher, P. & Blais, A., 1984. 'The Concept of Province-Building: A Critique', *Canadian Journal of Political Science*, XVII, 783–818.

Part 3: Intergovernmental relations in select policy areas

6   The offshore

Marcus Haward

It is clear from earlier chapters that the *intergovernmental* is an important determinant of Australian political or policy responses. The development, and formalising, of intergovernmental practices, institutions, or agreements may be more important in determining outcomes than the constitutional or legal framework. The significance of these elements on policy outcomes is most clearly shown in the development of Australian intergovernmental relations offshore. The struggle over offshore jurisdiction, reaching its zenith in the 1970s, led to the High Court upholding commonwealth jurisdiction from low-water mark. The development of an accommodation between the commonwealth and the states which circumvented the High Court's decision illustrates the significance of intergovernmental relations in determing policy outcomes.

A simple view of Australian intergovernmental relations offshore is to highlight the increasing commonwealth involvement in the period following World War II. This perspective, highlighting the importance of the question of jurisdiction *vis-à-vis* the commonwealth and the states, downplays the influence of the states and the influence of intergovernmental interactions on policy making. Limiting analysis to a consideration of commonwealth power or influence ignores the legislative and regulatory measures adopted by the state parliaments or the importance of state politicians and administrators in influencing offshore policy. The states retain considerable expertise in specific policy areas, for example fisheries administration, and have long established links with resource users. Intergovernmental relations offshore highlights the balance between commonwealth jurisdiction and the presence of state interests in the policy area and the states' ability to maximise these interests and influence outcomes.

This influence is reflected in the states' membership of institutions such as 'inter-jurisdictional ministerial councils' and their advisory committees. These institutions, mediating the demands from commonwealth or state governments, are significant elements in the federal system (Chapman, 1985, 1988; Wettenhall, 1985). The existence of numerous ministerial councils with an interest in offshore policy, including the Standing Committee of Attorneys-General, the Australian Fisheries Council, the Australian Minerals and Energy Council, the Australian Ports and Harbours Council, and the Council of Nature Conservation Ministers provide several (and sometimes cross-cutting) intergovernmental contact points. As intergovernmental relations are often more appropriately viewed as interactions between 'individuals', rather than 'governments' (Warhurst, 1987), the linkages made by membership of these councils by politicians or officials have great influence in the policy process.

Intergovernmental agreements dealing with the offshore, most notably the offshore petroleum agreement of 1967, and the rather curiously named Offshore Constitutional Settlement (OCS) of 1979, emphasise the role of interjurisdictional ministerial councils in contentious policy areas. The OCS, arguably the most complex intergovernmental agreement in Australia, arose from a desire by the commonwealth and *all states* to sidestep the decision of the High Court in the *Seas and Submerged Lands* case (1975), which resolved the question of offshore jurisdiction in favour of the commonwealth. The OCS, returning power and title to the states from low-water mark, illustrates that the High Court's role in arbitrating intergovernmental jurisdictional disputes may be overshadowed by the impact of political bargaining, the process of 'high intergovernmental politics' (see chapter 1). This bargaining, carried out in the institutions of 'executive federalism', enabled the state premiers to gain through negotiation what had been 'lost' through constitutional adjudication.

The development of offshore intergovernmental relations

Although colonial parliaments enacted legislation governing fisheries prior to federation, maritime matters were administered under United Kingdom law. The nexus between Australian and British law continued to be an important influence on subsequent debates over offshore jurisdiction. At federation the commonwealth government gained limited powers in relation to offshore resources, the major head being the 'fisheries power', section 51(x) of the Australian constitution. This specified commonwealth power over fisheries 'in Australian waters beyond territorial limits'. Australia followed international convention in establishing a three-mile territorial sea, a claim that has its basis in seventeenth-century notions of maritime law. A coastal state was considered to control that part of the sea that it could defend from shore, a three-mile limit arising from the range of shore-based batteries. Since most Australian fisheries were based on inshore resource stocks, and both the commonwealth and states accepted the states' competence within the three-mile limit, there was little need for commonwealth involvement. Until the first intergovernmental skirmishes in the late 1940s, the states retained responsibility for fisheries matters, including licensing and regulation previously undertaken by the colonial parliaments.

There would be infrequent meetings between commonwealth and state fisheries officers (Harrison, 1982). Then, in 1946, a decision of the Premiers' Conference established a commonwealth fisheries agency and, in 1947, a conference of commonwealth and state fisheries officers was convened. Here commonwealth representatives foreshadowed increasing their involvement in fisheries matters, with the likelihood of specific commonwealth legislation being enacted (Harrison, 1982). Two related arguments were used to justify the commonwealth's involvement; the first was a response to the growing international interest in high sea resources after the World War II, in particular the United States' declaration of national jurisdiction over the continental shelf, and the second the development of deep-sea trawl fisheries (Haward, 1989). The commonwealth argued that, due to the particular wording of sec. 51(x), these fisheries were outside the competence of state fisheries legislation. While there was some resistance from the states to the passage of this legislation, the proclamation of the Australian Fisheries Act 1952 (Cth) in 1955 provided the first legislative base for formal intergovernmental relations offshore. It is interesting that, although there were regular meetings between state and commonwealth ministers and fisheries officers following the proclamation of the fisheries Act, formal establishment of a ministerial council (the Australian Fisheries Council) and associated standing committee (officials from state and common-wealth fisheries agencies) did not take place until 1968.

It was interest in offshore oil and gas exploration in Bass Strait that provided an impetus for broadening the discussion of intergovernmental relations. The lack of specific commonwealth legislation for the granting of offshore permits and legal doubts over the validity of permits granted under state legislation encouraged the development of an *intergovern-mental* regime for the admininstration of petroleum exploration (Wilkinson, 1983). Negotiations over this regime took place as the first offshore permits were allocated in Bass Strait. The original exploration permit area (much of it later revoked) covered the whole Bass Strait region, with exploration permits granted under South Australian, Victorian and Tasmanian legislation.

The immediate success of the first 'wildcat' well in the summer of 1965 gave impetus to conclude the commonwealth–state agreement. The agreement, the responsibility of the Standing Committee of Attorneys-General, aimed to 'facilitate and encourage the exploration of, and production from, offshore leases'. Neither the commonwealth nor the states wished to consider the issue of offshore jurisdiction, hence the offshore petroleum agreement was established without derogating the constitutional claims of either government.

The 1967 intergovernmental agreement on offshore petroleum

The Petroleum Agreement involved five years of negotiations prior to its release in 1967, and went to considerable lengths to avoid raising the questions of sovereignty or jurisdiction (Cullen, 1985). In order to achieve this the agreement was based on 'mirror' commonwealth and state legislation, the Petroleum (Submerged Lands) Acts, which ensured that granting of exploration permits or production licences would not be disrupted (Stevenson, 1975). If either commonwealth or state Act was challenged, rights conferred on exploration companies, either in terms of title to permit areas or production licences awarded as of right of discovery (Lang & Crommelin, 1979:248), would be retained as they would be validated by the alternative Act.

A feature of the intergovernmental administrative arrangements of the 1967 Petroleum Agreement was the establishment of 'designated authorities', state ministers, who would implement and oversee *both* commonwealth and state 'mirror' Acts. The 'designated authority' would award exploration permits and production licences for the 'adjacent area' offshore from a particular state. The Petroleum Agreement formalised both the procedures under which permits and licences would be awarded and established intergovernmental consultation at both minister and state officer level through the Australian Minerals and Energy Council.

The most contentious part of the 1967 Petroleum Agreement concerned arrangements for royalty payments. Although the royalty arrangements only directly affected Victoria—the sole state with potential commercial oil and gas production at the time (Cullen, 1988:28)—the issue had concerned all states. Disputes over royalties evolved into a major intergovernmental issue in the 1970s and 1980s. The commonwealth's claim of a 50/50 share led to a compromise with the states, embodied in the 1967 agreement, where a basic royalty of 10 per cent 'well head value' would be divided 60/40 between the state and commonwealth governments (Cullen, 1988:28). Although this royalty arrangement has remained in place, the states have had their share of potential royalty revenues reduced in real terms. The oil companies, locked into a fixed pricing structure for five years after the first Bass Strait production came on line, lobbied hard for a change to 'world parity pricing' for local production. The introduction of parity pricing in September 1975 provided increased revenues, although the return to Victoria was reduced by the subsequent introduction of a commonwealth excise on 'downstream production' by the Fraser Government. This excise resulted in

> [m]ost of the revenue levied by governments on Bass Strait oil production go[ing] to the Commonwealth, which collects about $3.5 billion in royalties or excise under the world parity pricing arrangements and the Commonwealth *Petroleum (Submerged Lands) Act*, while Victoria receives only about $170 million. (Galligan, Kellow & O'Faircheallaigh, 1988:222)

In response, the Victorian government attempted to increase revenue by charging a licence fee on production passing through pipelines within the state's jurisdiction. This scheme was overturned by the High Court in the *Pipelines* case (1983). The attempts by the Victorian government to increase its share of offshore revenues reflects state frustration at the existing system although since 1981 all states have shared, to a limited extent, the revenues raised by the downstream excise. The revenue raised by this levy contributes to the tax pool from which general revenue grants are made to the states (Cullen, 1988).

Challenges to the 1967 agreement

Several factors led to doubts being expressed over the robustness of the 1967 Petroleum Agreement. The 1967 accommodation depended on the acquiescence of the commonwealth, which became less likely to be sustained with the 1958 United Nations' Convention on the Continental Shelf entering into force in 1964. The precedent of increasing federal involvement in offshore management in the United States (Cullen, 1985; Lumb, 1978) was seen as lending support to greater commonwealth involvement. Further support was given by a minority of the High Court bench, including Barwick CJ, in judgments expressed in *Bonser* v. *La Macchia* (1968–69). This case, which concerned the prosecution of a fisherman under the commonwealth Fisheries Act, was defended on the argument 'that the provisions of the Commonwealth Act were beyond the power of the Commonwealth parliament'. While the unanimous view of the Court in Bonser was that relevant provisions of the Act were within the power of the commonwealth parliament, Sir Garfield Barwick argued that he 'regarded as a "misconception" the view...that the colonies and the states had territorial seas of their own' (Waugh, 1988:21–2).

Intergovernmental tensions increased when the Gorton Government, arguing for a greater role for the commonwealth, introduced the Territorial Sea and Continental Shelf Bill into parliament in 1970. This Bill claimed commonwealth sovereignty over the territorial sea from low-water mark to the edge of the continental shelf although it 'claimed a general saving provision for existing and future State laws' (Bailey, 1972:236). The states, not surprisingly, opposed what became known as the 'Gorton Bill' and this opposition was reflected in backbench dissent over the Bill. The turmoil caused by the Territorial Sea and Continental Shelf Bill, given as contributing to Gorton's defeat, meant that the new Prime Minister, McMahon, showed little interest in pursuing the legislation. Although the McMahon Government held meetings with the states over the issue of offshore jurisdiction in August 1972, the Territorial Sea and Continental Shelf Bill lapsed with the proroguing of parliament before the federal election in December 1972. The Australian Labor Party (ALP) supported the 'Gorton Bill', with opposition leader Whitlam foreshadowing legislation to assert commonwealth sovereignty in the territorial sea when the ALP achieved government. This resulted in 'the offshore' becoming *the* focus of intergovernmental relations in the 1970s.

The seas and submerged lands case

The Whitlam Government quickly asserted its view of the commonwealth's constitutional primacy in relation to offshore resources. The Seas and Submerged Lands Act, introduced in May 1973, declared commonwealth sovereignty and jurisdiction from low-water mark. The declaration of commonwealth sovereignty was deliberate as this would provoke a challenge from the states to the High Court over the validity of the legislation (Crommelin, 1977). This challenge would, indirectly, resolve the question of jurisdiction in the territorial sea. The states attacked the Seas and Submerged Lands legislation on several fronts. The opposition, with a majority in the Senate, ensured major amendments were made to the Bill before it completed its passage through parliament. The Tasmanian and Queensland parliaments attempted to refer the case to the Privy Council, even dispatching the Tasmanian solicitor-general to London. The Privy Council refused to intervene, leaving the states to mount a High Court challenge to the validity of the legislation. All states, including the Labor governed states of South Australia and Tasmania, intervened in the subsequent High Court challenge.

The *Seas and Submerged Lands* case (*New South Wales* v. *The Commonwealth* 1975), was a major, if awkward, victory for the commonwealth. The High Court's decision upholding the commonwealth's Seas and Submerged Lands legislation was released four days after the Whitlam Government had been defeated in the federal election of 13 December 1975. The case provided the Fraser Government with an early test of its commitment to enhancing intergovernmental relations. This commitment, embodied in 'new federalism', was that the commonwealth would reduce its influence in policy areas considered to be the responsibility of the states. The new federalism promoted intergovernmental co-operation and negotiation and a maintenance of the states' role in policy areas with overlapping responsibility (Peachment & Reid, 1980; Saunders & Wiltshire, 1981).

As the new federalism promised a means of resolving the states' concern over the High Court decision, the state premiers lobbied Prime Minister Fraser to implement the new federalism in the offshore. The premiers requested the Standing Committee of Attorneys-General to report on the implications of the High Court's decision. In April 1976, Prime Minister Fraser sent a letter to the premiers agreeing to 'consult the states on matters of principle arising from the *Seas and Submerged Lands* Case'. The reponsibility for examining the 'offshore problem' was given to the state solicitors-general who 'agreed to explore areas of co-operation in relation to the legal aspects of offshore matters' (Cullen, 1985:63) and to report back to the attorneys-general prior to a special Premiers' Conference in October 1977. This conference was held 'to deal specifically with the offshore issue' (Cullen, 1985:64).

The Premiers' Conference dealt with the challenge posed by the *Seas and Submerged Lands* case in a particularly innovative manner. The premiers and prime minister, following their earlier correspondence, reached agreement over a more co-operative approach to offshore issues. The conference resolved that 'the [three mile] territorial sea should be the responsibility of the states'. In order to implement this resolution the Premiers' Conference agreed that the 'limits and powers of the states should be extended', and that the attorneys-general provide advice on how this could be achieved. This resolution provided the basis for what was to be later termed the Offshore Constitutional Settlement.

Several avenues were investigated in order to extend the 'limits' and 'powers' of the states. These included provisions available under sections 128, 123 or 51(xxxviii) of the Australian constitution, the Colonial Boundaries Act, or possible specific commonwealth or United Kingdom legislation. The solicitors-general resolved that, given problems with both sections 123 and 128, section 51(xxxviii) provided the most appropriate means to implement the resolution of the Premiers' Conference. Placitum xxxviii required unanimous support from the states, a factor which encouraged intergovernmental agreement and which reduced the possibility of constitutional challenges to the agreement.

The Offshore Constitutional Settlement (OCS)

Following discussion at the 1978 Premiers' Conference, negotiations over the offshore settlement concluded at the Premiers' Conference of 29 June 1979. The OCS arose as 'a reordering and readjustment of powers and responsibilities—as between the Commonwealth and the States—was clearly required to take account of the 1975 [*Seas and Submerged Lands* case] decision' (*Offshore Australia*, 1980:4). It was claimed that the OCS 'marked the solution of a fundamental problem that had bedevilled Commonwealth-State relations and represents a major achievement of the policy of co-operative federalism' (*Offshore Australia*, 1980:1).

Senator Durack, then attorney-general, stated that the settlement 'will ensure that the States will have adequate powers to deal with matters in the territorial sea. History, commonsense and the sheer practicalities make these matters for State administration, rather than central control, in the absence of overriding national or international considerations' (*Offshore Australia*, 1980:11). The principles underpinning the OCS embodied the essence of the 'new federalism's' intergovernmental co-operation. A decade later it is clear that the OCS has been the most lasting element of this policy (Galligan, 1987; Haward, 1989).

One major difference between the OCS and the earlier 1967 Petroleum Agreement is that 'the actual agreement between the parties resulting from the offshore negotiations has not been published' (Cullen, 1985:141). The commonwealth government, under the auspices of the Attorney-General's Department, published a kit entitled *Offshore Australia* explaining the origins, aims and mechanics of the OCS. This kit included what were known as the OCS 'agreed arrangements', which are summarised in appendix I. The key elements of the OCS were the Coastal Waters (State Powers) Act, and its companion legislation, the Coastal Waters (State Titles) Act. Following Bills passed by the states (to fulfil the 'request clause' of pl. xxxviii), the commonwealth would introduce the 'powers' and 'titles' legislation. 'Complementary', rather than 'mirror' legislation was then to be enacted by the states to retain state jurisdiction within a boundary drawn three nautical miles from low-water mark. Outside three miles, to the edge of Australian jurisiction, the commonwealth's legislation would apply. Although there was some pressure from the states to retain flexibility in the boundary of the state legislation, the OCS arrangements stated '[t]he...legislation and also the petroleum and fisheries arrangements...will be limited to a territorial sea of 3 miles, irrespective of whether Australia subsequently moves to a territorial sea of 12 miles' (*Offshore Australia*, 1980:7).

The Coastal Waters (State Powers) Act and the Coastal Waters (State Title) Act, in conjunction with the amendments to ten existing acts (necessary to avoid invalidating the settlement), were introduced into the commonwealth parliament in May 1980. The settlement then required complementary 'powers' and 'titles' legislation to be enacted by the states and the Northern Territory to complete the legislative design. Unlike the earlier 'mirror' legislation adopted in the 1967 Agreement, the Coastal Waters (State Powers) Act and Coastal Waters (State Title) Acts drawn up by the states contained some minor differences (Cullen, 1985). This legislation was enacted by the various parliaments between 1980 and 1982 and the OCS was proclaimed on 14 February 1983. It is ironic that the Fraser Government was defeated at the polls within three weeks of the OCS being proclaimed. The ALP had bitterly opposed the OCS during parliamentary debate and had threatened to overturn the agreement and return to the sovereignty established by the High Court. Legal opinion on the Coastal Waters Acts differed over the extent to which the arrangement could be repealed, given the return of title to the seabed to the states (Crommelin, 1983; Cullen, 1985). The election of the Hawke Government provided the first test of the strength of the arrangement. As Cullen commented, 'it will be interesting to monitor the Settlement's progress over the next few years in the face of judicial review and the attitude of a federal government with an official policy of dismantling the settlement' (1985:141). The states—with the most to lose from an overturn of the OCS—waited for the government's response. A major issue was whether the Hawke Government would dismantle the entire OCS or just the elements concerned with offshore petroleum and minerals (Herr & Davis, 1986:689). It was expected that some form of modification of the OCS would take place, given the ALP's opposition to the arrangements: notwithstanding the interesting legal problems of unravelling the 'settlement' (Crommelin, 1983).

Although the states exerted considerable pressure on the commonwealth to implement areas of the OCS where substantive agreement had been reached, particularly in fisheries matters, the Hawke Government established a wide ranging internal review of the OCS arrangements. The review arose from a resolution at the 1984 Biennial ALP Conference endorsing the restoration of commonwealth power and title in the three-mile zone. The review examined the legal basis to the OCS and the extent to which it could be altered. The commonwealth government's concern over a reduction in commonwealth power in the offshore was weighed against the success of the intergovernmental arrangements operating under the OCS framework. The result of the review into the OCS was that while

> the Government is of the view that title over the territorial sea should not have been transferred from the Commonwealth by the previous government...the arrangements which were entered into as part of the Offshore Constitutional Settlement have been working satisfactorily and for this reason the government does not intend to take action at the present time to regain title to the territorial sea. Nor does the Government intend to alter the current powers legislation. (CPD (H), 20 March 1986:1781)

The commonwealth warned that this approach would depend on the 'satisfactory operation' of the existing arrangements. Commonwealth intervention was foreshadowed if a state or the Northern Territory failed to act 'in a manner compatible with the national interest'.

The review of the OCS arrangements led to criticisms from the states that this process delayed implementing arrangements over fisheries. The adoption of the OCS arrangements for fisheries was promoted as the 'one law' approach and was seen as a way of resolving problems arising from awarding commonwealth and state fisheries licences for the same fishery (Haward, 1986b). One effect of the lengthy period taken to implement the

OCS was the enhancement of a sectoral approach to offshore intergovernmental relations. Commonwealth–state interaction moved towards specific offshore policy areas that involved less input from executive institutions. While increasing the possibility of dispute this approach enabled areas outside the original agreed arrangements (such as the management of floating hotels) to come under OCS style arrangements.

IGR and the implementation of the OCS packages

Offshore oil and gas

The administrative regime for offshore petroleum established under the OCS did little more in practical terms than to update the arrangements of the earlier 1967 agreement. This regime

> provides for Joint Authorities, comprising the Commonwealth
> Minister and the relevant State Minister, [to] decide the major issues
> under the legislation including the award, renewal, variation, suspen-
> sion and cancellation of titles and conditions of titles. Day to day
> matters are handled by the State Ministers and their Departments.
> (Starkey, 1987:25)

The regime involves close consultation between departmental officials from the commonwealth and the states through the the Standing Committees of the Australian Minerals and Energy Council and consultation between these officials and industry.

The arrangements enabled the commonwealth to retain its major influence over oil and gas exploration and production policy, although the states and corporate interests had significant inputs into this policy area. The Hawke Government's attempt to implement changes to the method of awarding exploration permits and the system of royalty payments illustrates the impact of the states and corporate interests on the policy process and the importance of this interaction on policy outcomes. The traditional method of awarding permits involved competing interests submitting their proposed exploration programs with the 'best' work program gaining the permit. A system of 'cash bidding', a competitive auction system, was proposed by the Hawke Government to remove the dissipation of rent caused by over-ambitious work programs (Haward, 1986b). Opposition to cash bidding by the non-Labor state governments and the industry was concerned with possible reductions in level of returns and a slackening of interest in exploration as a result of this 'up front impost'. After negotiations with industry groups the commonwealth government agreed to abandon cash bidding for existing permit areas and accepted suggestions to modify the existing work program system. Cash bidding was eventually restricted to permits in highly prospective areas in the Timor Sea.

To replace the existing complex amalgam of well-head *ad valorem* royalties and downstream excise arrangements, the Hawke Government proposed the introduction a profits-based Resource Rent Tax (RRT). The states, and many of the exploration companies, objected to the RRT as they felt that it would be a disincentive for exploration and they would not gain any increased benefits. These objections led to its modification to apply only to 'greenfields' projects, that is new wells discovered after 1 July 1984, excluding existing fields in Bass Strait and the North-West Shelf.

The issue of royalties from offshore petroleum production has continued to be a major focus of intergovernmental consultation. Negotiations with the states over royalties are continuing, with the states arguing for a larger proportion of 'well-head' royalties as the imposition of a downstream excise by the commonwealth has effectively reduced their share of revenues. A model for a future royalty system may be the agreement reached between the Western Australian and commonwealth governments over what has been termed the Resource Rent Royalty or RRR (Cullen, 1988:35–36). The RRR, introduced for Barrow Island production, replaced the commonwealth's crude oil excise and the state's *ad valorem* royalty. On a similar basis to the RRT, the RRR established a royalty of 40 per cent 'well-head value' once returns had passed a particular threshold. Payment of the RRR is split 75/25 between the commonwealth and Western Australia.

Marine parks

The regime governing the administration of the Great Barrier Reef Marine Park, established by the Great Barrier Reef Marine Park Act 1975 (Cth), was reinforced by the OCS agreed arrangements. Joh Bjelke-Petersen, then Queensland premier, had opposed the commonwealth legislation and argued that this infringed the rights of Queensland to determine the management of the area. Conflicts between the commonwealth and Queensland had risen earlier, with proposals to drill for oil in the early 1970s raising intergovernmental tensions. Attempts to increase commonwealth involvement by establishing the Great Barrier Reef marine park heightened hostilities between Queensland and the commonwealth. Bjelke-Petersen opposed the duplication of a major activity of the state government and the involvement of the commonwealth in a large percentage of Queensland's coastline (1983:64). This opposition was tempered as commonwealth involvement in offshore Queensland became firmly entrenched following the High Court's decision in the *Seas and Submerged Lands* case, the signing (and later ratification) of the Torres Strait Treaty, and the listing of the Great Barrier Reef under the World Heritage Convention.

The reality of commonwealth involvement enhanced the adoption of the OCS arrangements for the Reef. The Great Barrier Reef Marine Park

Authority (GBRMPA), a joint commonwealth and state authority established by the commonwealth legislation, was given formal responsibility for the management of the Park. It is interesting that, considering the earlier hostilities over its establishment, the GBRMPA is regarded as a model organisation for management of marine parks (Kriwoken, 1989). The success of GBRMPA illustrates that such institutions can reach agreement over policy even in areas characterised by intergovernmental disputes.

The OCS agreement led to the proclamation of the first zone of the Great Barrier Reef Marine Park. Consultation between GBRMPA and the commonwealth and Queensland governments has led to almost all the reef area being proclaimed within the Great Barrier Reef Marine Park. Apart from the establishment of GBRMPA the OCS agreement over the Barrier Reef led to the establishment of the Great Barrier Reef Ministerial Council. This ministerial council has served an important role in maintaining intergovernmental co-operation and has had a major role in developing policy since its first meeting in 1979 (Kriwoken, 1989). Like other ministerial councils the Great Barrier Reef Ministerial Council is able to routinise intergovernmental relations and formalise interaction between governments. It is the ability of the ministerial council and GBRMPA to mediate the policy demands of the Queensland and commonwealth governments which illustrates the 'institutionalising' of intergovernmental relations in Australia.

The Great Barrier Reef Marine Park comprises 94.2 per cent of the total declared area of Australian marine parks and protected areas (Ivanovici, 1987). The remaining marine and estuarine protected areas range from proclaimed marine parks or aquatic reserves to marine extensions to terrestrial national parks. Although the OCS arrangements have allowed for joint commonwealth–state management only the Ningaloo Marine Park in Western Australia has been established under joint commonwealth and state legislation (Ivanovici, 1987). It is interesting that the Ningaloo Reef working party emphasised 'that the management of a joint Commonwealth–State Marine Park is the prerogative of the State. The agreement [over the proclamation of the park] does not provide for Commonwealth involvement without the concurrence of the State' (May, Lenanton & Berry, 1983:ix).

Ship-sourced marine pollution

The OCS retained arrangements established in 1960 for the management of ship-sourced marine pollution which implemented the 1954 international Convention for the Prevention of Pollution of the Sea by Oil. The states failed to establish complementary legislation following the proclamation of the commonwealth's Protection of the Sea (Prevention of Pollution from Ships) Act in 1983, as there seemed no pressing need to do so. The 'roll back' provisions in the agreed arrangements allow the states to enact their own legislation while the commonwealth still retains responsibility for fulfilling the international convention.

Offshore dumping

Australia signed the London Dumping Convention in 1973. This treaty came into force in 1975, although 'it was applied in Australia on a voluntary basis in co-operation with the states and industry until the Environmental Protection (Sea Dumping) Act 1981 (Cth), was passed to give legislative effect to the Convention' (Burmester, 1984:443). This legislation was enacted within the OCS framework. The issue of the dumping of radioactive wastes now has to conform with Australian responsibilities under recent South Pacific regional agreements: the South Pacific Regional Environmental Protection Convention and the South Pacific Nuclear Free Zone Treaty, or, more correctly, the Treaty of Raratonga. Ratification of these agreements has meant that the states will no longer be able to legislate for the loading, dumping or incinerating at sea of radioactive waste (Brown, 1988:60).

Fisheries

The fisheries package of the OCS remains incomplete, although the state ministers had readily agreed to the OCS provisions in the early phases of the negotiation of the settlement (Chatterton & Arnold, 1977). The delay in concluding the fisheries component of the settlement resulted from several factors, including the length of time taken to complete negotiations between the commonwealth and the states over the classification of fisheries. The attempt to administer Australian fisheries under 'one law' was bound to involve lengthly negotiation (and disputation) between the commonwealth and the states, and also ensured that the fisheries package could only proceed at the pace set by the slowest participant (Herr, 1987).

A further complication in the development of the OCS fisheries regime was a High Court decision upholding the validity of particular state fisheries legislation within the territorial sea after the 1975 Seas and Submerged Lands case. The decision in Pearce v. Florenca (1976) ratified the power of the states to enforce fisheries laws within the territorial sea and reinforced the position of the states in developing fisheries policy.

Intergovernmental negotiations were crucial where fisheries involved vessels from different states or where they were based on grounds which transcended the offshore extensions of state boundaries. Adopting a 'single law' was further complicated where different regulations and management governed each state's fishery. Originally, the OCS agreed arrangements proposed a three-tiered structure of fisheries administration. Fisheries would be administered by either a state, the commonwealth or by a joint authority. It was envisaged that the commonwealth would retain control over foreign fisheries within the Australian (Extended) Fishing Zone (AFZ) and retain control of migratory species, such as the blue fin tuna, which could provide problems that any one state may not be able to manage adequately. The commonwealth's position on the tuna fishery was reinforced by 'a transcendent international obligation through the membership of a regional regulatory organisation' (Herr & Davis, 1986:690). Under the OCS arrangements, where agreement was reached with the commonwealth, fisheries administered by a state could extend to the boundary of the AFZ. A fourth possibility was to retain the status quo, that is licensing and management under overlapping state and commonwealth legislation and regulations.

There has been limited progress towards the establishment of joint authorities. Disputes over their functions , including whether licences could be issued by joint authorities, revived long-standing tensions between the state and commonwealth fisheries agencies. The states' lack of enthusiasm for the joint-authority system is perhaps understandable, as under the 'agreed arrangements' the commonwealth's view will prevail (*Offshore Australia*, 1980). The only examples of such formal arrangements are within Torres Strait, where the commonwealth administers the fisheries on behalf of the Queensland government, and in the newly-created joint authority in Western Australia for the shark fishery. The establishment of the Western Australian joint authority may reflect a change in the states' attitude towards these intergovernmental authorities, where it is seen that such arrangements increase the state's ability to manage particular fisheries.

Agreement was reached on management of the first fishery under the provisions of the OCS in June 1986. Following further negotiations between the commonwealth and the states, arrangements were gazetted on 1 June 1987 implementing the OCS fisheries package for fisheries in waters off Queensland, South Australia, Western Australia and Tasmania. The management of the tuna fishery and the fishery within the area of Australian jurisdiction in the Torres Strait Protected Zone were agreed to be commonwealth responsibility. The Torres Strait resolution involved extensive negotiations with the Queensland government and reflected the states concern over the implication of the Torres Strait Treaty. The remaining fisheries were to be managed under state law. The commonwealth has yet to gain an agreement with New South Wales or the Northern Territory over the classification of fisheries, a major parameter of the OCS fisheries agreement. New South Wales' failure to enter negotiations reflected the state Fisheries Department's concern over possible loss of influence. Key New South Wales officials regarded fisheries as solely a state matter (Francois, 1984).

Arrangements which continued to be gazetted in 1987 and 1988 included the rock lobster fishery in South Australia, the focus of a High

Court challenge to the validity of the Coastal Waters (State Powers) Act 1980 in the *Port Macdonnell* case (1989). In the *Port Macdonnell* case (brought down in October 1989) the High Court upheld the validity of the section 51(xxxviii) 'request' power as an anchor for the Coastal Waters (State Powers) Act 1980 (Cth). The Court also held that the arrangements entered into between the commonwealth and South Australia over the rock lobster fishery were valid. It did, however, provide a specific definition of the concept of 'adjacent waters' in Port Macdonnell, which will lead to better intergovernmental consultation in OCS fisheries arrangements. In the second OCS-related case decided in 1989 (*Harper v. Tasmania*) the High Court held that the license fee levied by the Tasmanian government for the abalone fishery was valid, and rejected the challenge to the Coastal Waters State Titles Act 1980 (Cth).

Offshore installations

The development of commonwealth legislation to control offshore installations such as floating hotels, although strictly not part of the 'agreed arrangements', reflects the importance of the OCS framework for marine policy making. The 1987 Sea Installations legislation was initiated in response to the establishment of a floating hotel on part of the Great Barrier Reef, 73 kilometres offshore, and Queensland attempts to regulate such installations. The legislation followed the arrangements of the Petroleum (Submerged Lands) Act, with the commonwealth retaining its legal power over developments on the continental shelf, but delegating day-to-day administration of the Bill to the appropriate state government. Licences or permit fees to operate such installations accrued to the commonwealth, although the costs to the state for administering the Act would be reimbursed by the commonwealth.

Conclusion

It is clear that the introduction of the OCS was a significant achievement in intergovernmental relations. Several interesting issues arise when looking at the 'intergovernmental' in offshore federalism. The question of jurisdiction or constitutional power *vis-à-vis* the commonwealth and the states was a fundamental element in it, although the resolution of constitutional questions provided an unpalatable policy framework for a newly-elected commonwealth government. The Fraser Government, promoting a return to a more co-operative pattern of intergovernmental relations, found the upholding of commonwealth power by the High Court conflicted with its new federalism proposals. The opposition from the states to the High Court's decision hastened the search for an intergovernmental, or political, solution to the problems provided by the *Seas and Submerged Lands* case.

The OCS, in circumventing the High Court's decision, illustrates the significance of the political and administrative elements of Australian federalism, even in a policy area where commonwealth power has been reinforced. The development of the OCS emphasises the significance of the intergovernmental 'moderating institutions' (Chapman, 1985). It is clear that the OCS, like the earlier Petroleum Agreement, owes much to the work of intergovernmental councils of legal officers and attorneys-general. That the offshore was considered important enough for a specific Premiers' Conference in 1977 underlines the 'high intergovernmental politics' involved.

Examining the implementation of the OCS arrangements illustrates that the agreement, while extending and formalising the role of the states, did not diminish the role or influence of the commonwealth. Several examples can be drawn from this chapter to illustrate this point. Although the states are involved in administration of petroleum legislation, the commonwealth retains control of permit allocation and licensing. The dominance of the commonwealth's share of offshore petroleum royalties is due to its 'excise powers', with the return from petroleum giving the commonwealth a major financial incentive to retain such arrangements. In other policy areas, such as fisheries, the commonwealth has to approve an increase in state activity, even where the OCS arrangements make provision for state participation. This gives further evidence of the commonwealth's considerable influence in the development of marine resource policy.

The commonwealth's power to influence final policy outcomes is perhaps a paradox in the light of the original commitment to intergovernmental co-operation, although it explains some of the tensions experienced during the implementation of the agreement. The implementation emphasises, however, that offshore policy relies upon negotiation with the states (Haward, 1989). The OCS has ensured that states retained a major role in the offshore, particularly in fisheries management, extending and developing legislative, administrative and resource management functions. The states' extensive experience in offshore resource management is an important bargaining point, and explains their reluctance to lose any autonomy in this area. In addition, the OCS acknowledged that the states are important actors with key responsibilities in offshore policy areas.

It is the need for state involvement in offshore policy which explains the complex intergovernmental arrangements that led to the OCS. Although the OCS implied a major re-ordering and settlement of constitutional issues, it should properly be seen as an attempt to provide a political settlement to a contentious policy area. The success of the offshore settlement shows the significance of the interaction between the political and administrative elements of intergovernmental relations. The OCS is a unique intergovernmental agreement, and, in many ways, solely the product of several timely yet coincident factors, although it highlights the importance of negotiation and bargaining between the commonwealth and the states. The accommodation reached in the offshore 'settlement' demonstrates that intergovernmental relations are crucial in resolving tensions arising from the legal, political and administrative overlays of Australian federalism.

Case references

Bonser's case: *Bonser* v. *La Macchia* (1968–69) 122 CLR 177.
Harper v. *The Minister of Sea Fisheries* (1989) 63 ALJR 687.
Pearce v. *Florenca* (1976) 135 CLR 507.
Pipelines' case: *Hematite Petroleum Pty. Ltd.* v. *State of Victoria* (1983) 57 ALJR 591.
Port Macdonnell case: *The Port Macdonnell Professional Fishermen's Association and Ronald Olerich* v. *South Australia and The Commonwealth* (1989) 63 ALJR 617.
Seas and Submerged Lands case: *New South Wales* v. *The Commonwealth* (1975) 135 CLR 337.

Bibliography

Attorney-General's Department, 1980. *Offshore Australia*, AGPS, Canberra.

Bailey, K., 1972. 'The Constitutional and Legal Framework', in *The Natural Resources of Australia: Prospects and Problems for Development*, ed. J.A. Sinden, Angus & Robertson in association with ANZAAS, Sydney.

Bjelke-Petersen, J., 1983. 'Australian Federalism: A Queensland View', in *Australian Federalism: Future Tense,* eds A. Patience & J. Scott, Melbourne University Press, Melbourne.

Brown, J., 1988. *Australian Practice in International Law 1986–87*, Public International Law Seminar, ANU, 20–22 May.

Burmester, H., 1984. 'Australia and the Law of the Sea—The Protection of the Marine Environment', in *International Law in Australia*, 2nd edn, ed. K. Ryan, The Australian Institute of International Affairs/Law Book Company, Sydney.

Chapman, R.J.K., 1985. 'Federalism as Interdependence: The Role of Moderating Institutions', Paper Presented to the Comparative Federalism Study Group, IPSA Congress, 15–22 July.

—— 1988. 'Inter-governmental Forums and the Policy Process', in *Comparative States Policies*, ed. B. Galligan, Longman Cheshire, Melbourne.

Chatterton, B. & Arnold, L., 1977. 'Fisheries Management and the New Federalism', in *The Politics of New Federalism*, ed. D. Jaensch, APSA Adelaide.

CPD(H): Commonwealth Parliamentary Debates (House of Representatives).

Crommelin, M., 1977. 'National Development', in *Labor and the Constitution 1972–75: Essays and Commentaries on Controversies of the Whitlam Years*, ed. G. Evans, Heineman, Richmond.

—— 1983. *Offshore Mining and Petroleum: Constitutional Issues*, Papers on Federalism, 3, Intergovernmental Relations in Victoria Programme, Law School, University of Melbourne.

—— 1987. 'Commonwealth Involvement in Environment Policy: Past Present and Future', *Environment and Planning Law Journal*, 4, 101–12.

Cullen, R., 1985. *Australian Federalism Offshore*, Intergovernmental Relations in Victoria Programme, Law School, University of Melbourne.

—— 1988. *Australian Federalism Offshore*, 2nd rev. edn, Intergovernmental Relations in Victoria Programme, Law School, University of Melbourne.

Francois, D., 1984. 'Lessons for the Future—A Look at Commonwealth–State Relations in Fisheries', Paper presented to Australian Fishing Industry Seminar, Australian Maritime College, Launceston, July.

Galligan, B., 1987. *The Politics of the High Court: A Study of the Judicial Branch of Government in Australia*, University of Queensland Press, St Lucia.

Galligan, B., Kellow, A. & O'Faircheallaigh, C., 1988. 'Minerals and Energy Policy', in *Comparative State Policies* ed. B. Galligan, Longman Cheshire, Melbourne.

Harrison, A.J., 1982. 'Marine Living Resources Policy in Tasmania', in *Issues in Australian Marine and Antarctic Policy*, eds R.A. Herr, R. Hall & B.W. Davis, Public Policy Monograph, Department of Political Science, University of Tasmania.

Haward, M., 1986a. Institutions, Interest Groups and Marine Resources Policy', unpublished MA thesis, Department of Political Science, University of Tasmania.

—— 1986b. 'Marine Resource Policy In Australia; The Policy Environment, The Policy Process and the Issue Community', *Maritime Studies*, 26, 12–16.

—— 1989. 'The Australian Offshore Constitutional Settlement', *Marine Policy*, 13(4), 334–48.

Herr, R.A., 1987. 'Federalism and Fisheries', Paper presented to National Fisheries Officers Course, Australian Maritime College November.

Herr, R.A. & Davis, B.W., 1986. 'The Impact of UNCLOS III on Australian Federalism', *International Journal*, XLI. 3, 674–93

Ivanovici, I., 1987. 'Marine and Estuarine Protected Areas (MEPAs): A National Perspective', *Maritime Studies*, 32, 11–15.

Kriwoken, L.K.K., 1989. *Great Barrier Reef Marine Park Intergovernmental Relations: Report of Augmentative Research Grant*, Great Barrier Reef Marine Park Authority, mimeo.

Lang, A.G. & Crommelin, M., 1979. *Australian Mining and Petroleum Laws: An Introduction*, Butterworths, Sydney.

Leigh, C.H., 1970. 'Oil and Natural Gas Developments in the Bass Strait Area, Australia', *Geography*, 55, 221–23.

Lumb, R.D., 1978. *The Law of the Sea and Australia's Offshore Areas*, 2nd edn, University of Queensland Press, St Lucia.

Macdonald, D., 1982. 'Fishermen and the Offshore Constitutional Settlement', *Australian Fisheries*, Feb. 2–3.

May, R.F., Lenanton, R.C.J. & Berry, P.F., 1983. *Ningaloo Marine Park: Report and Recommendations by the Marine Park Working Group*, West Australian National Parks Authority.

Offshore Australia, see Attorney-General's Department, 1980. *Offshore Australia*, AGPS, Canberra.

Peachment, A. & Reid, G.S., 1980. 'New Federalism in Australia', in *Government, Politics and Power in Australia: An Introductory Reader*, 2nd edn, eds A. Parkin, J. Summers & D. Woodward, Longman-Cheshire, Melbourne.

Quick, J. & Garran, R.R., 1901. *The Annotated Constitution of The Australian Commonwealth*, Angus and Robertson, Sydney.

Saunders, C. & Wiltshire, K., 1981. 'Fraser's New Federalism 1975–1980: An Evaluation', *Australian Journal of Politics and History*, 26(3), 355–71.

Sharman, C., 1985. 'The Commonwealth, the States and Federalism', in *Government, Politics and Power in Australia*, 3rd edn, eds D. Woodward, A. Parkin, & J. Summers, Longman-Cheshire, Melbourne.

Starkey, J.C., 1987. 'Australia's Offshore Petroleum Legal and Administrative Regime', *Maritime Studies* 37, 24–31.

Stevenson, G., 1975. *Mineral Resources and Australian Federalism*, Research Monograph 17, Centre for Research on Federal Financial Relations, ANU, Canberra.

Warhurst, J., 1987. 'Managing Intergovernmental Relations', in *Federalism and the Role of the State*, eds H. Bakvis & W. Chandler, University of Toronto Press, Toronto.

Waugh, J., 1988. *Australian Fisheries Law*, Intergovernmental Relations in Victoria Programme, Law School, University of Melbourne.

Wettenhall, R.,1985. 'Intergovernmental Agencies: Lubricating a Federal System', *Current Affairs Bulletin*, April.

Wilkinson, R., 1983. *A Thirst For Burning: The Story of Australia's Oil Industry*, David Ell Press, Sydney

Appendix I

The Offshore Constitutional Settlement 'agreed arrangements'

1 A legislative package—using section 51 (xxxviii) of the constitution to (i) extend the legislative power of the states with regard to the adjacent territorial sea, and (ii) vest title of the seabed beneath the territorial sea to the states. Amending applicable legislation such as the Seas and Submerged Lands Act was also foreshadowed. This legislative design also treated the Northern Territory as a state.

2 An offshore petroleum regime—established that operations outside the three-mile boundary would be regulated by commonwealth legislation with day-to-day administration to continue, as with the 1967 Agreement, to be undertaken by the states. The legislation established a joint authority for each state's adjacent area (comprising the commonwealth and state minister).

3 Offshore mining for minerals other than petroleum—a commitment was made to develop such a regime. This regime would include complementary commonwealth and state legislation embodying a common mining code.

4 An offshore fisheries regime which aimed to introduce a more flexible approach to fisheries administration. As far as possible a fishery would be managed by a single law. Fisheries joint authorities, consisting of the commonwealth minister and the appropriate state ministers would be set up to regulate fisheries where the fishery involved more than one state. Four joint authorities were included in the 'agreed arrangements'; a South-Eastern Fisheries Joint Authority (the Commonwealth and NSW, Victorian, Tasmanian and South Australian ministers), a Northern Australian Fisheries Joint Authority (Commonwealth and Queensland and Northern Territory ministers), a Western Australian Fisheries Joint Authority (Commonwealth and Western Australian ministers) and a Northern Territory Fishery Joint Authority (Commonwealth and Northern Territory ministers). In the event of disagreement within a fisheries joint authority, the views of the commonwealth minister would prevail.

5 Arrangements to administer historic shipwrecks—the amendment of the commonwealth's Historic Shipwrecks Act 1976 to apply to waters adjacent to a state or the Northern Territory with the consent of that state or territory.

6 Agreement over the Great Barrier Reef Marine Park—the Great Barrier Reef Marine Park Act 1975 was to continue to apply to the whole of the Great Barrier Reef, as defined by that Act. Joint consultative arrangements were to be established between the commonwealth and Queensland.

7 Arrangements for other marine parks—established that, under the agreed arrangements, these areas were to be under state or commonwealth responsibility depending whether they were inside or outside the three-mile boundary.

8 Legislation covering crimes at sea, shipping and navigation and ship-sourced marine pollution (the lattter also including offshore dumping) would include 'roll back' provisions to avoid the problems of inconsistency between state and commonwealth laws, and maintain commitments under existing international conventions or agreements to which Australia was a party (*Offshore Australia*, 1980:6–16).

7 The Murray-Darling Basin

Aynsley Kellow

On 15 and 16 November 1985 a meeting was held in Adelaide of state and government ministers whose portfolios included some responsibility for the Murray-Darling Basin.[1] What emerged from this meeting was the establishment of a Murray-Darling Basin Ministerial Council, a move that ushered in a period of change in the administration of the Basin, which, in the light of the previous history of the Basin, can only be called extremely rapid. Not only has a new administrative body, the Murray-Darling Basin Commission, been established to take over from the River Murray Commission, which suffered from having rather restricted jurisdiction over water only in the main stem of the Murray, but also the four governments involved have reached substantial agreement on the most pressing problem which afflicts the Basin: saline water flows.

This chapter examines the intergovernmental politics that produced this rapid change in the regime governing Australia's most important river system (Young, 1982), which has been the focus of much interstate suspicion and argument. It seeks to explain the factors which facilitated this change, and more particularly to explain why change became possible from 1985 onwards. A much-touted explanation of this change (and one referred to in the communique issued at the end of the ministerial meeting) is the alignment of Labor governments in all three states and the commonwealth during this period. While this explanation has some validity, this chapter will argue that other factors were probably more decisive. In particular, the changed stance of Victoria must be seen as crucial, stemming not only from emerging awareness of salinity problems within Victoria, but also from the reform of agencies with responsibilities for the administration of water and land resources within that state and, to a lesser extent, within New South Wales. In addition, it will be stressed that the involvement of entrepreneurial politicians was crucial in overcoming the forces favouring inertia; this finding is important because it goes against the established view that intergovernmental politics increases the involvement of bureaucrats at the expense of politicians (Holmes & Sharman, 1977:122) and suggests that such bureaucratic dominance is likely to yield stability even when change is overdue. This conclusion suggests that, if substantial advances to intergovernmental conflict are to be made, the politicians must be involved, and involved in a very active role.

Background to the ministerial meeting

There is no space—nor little need—to go into the background of the politics and administration of the Murray-Darling Basin in any great detail, as it has been covered elsewhere (Clark, 1983; Kellow, 1985). The Murray River question played an important part in the debates of the Constitutional Convention in the period leading up to federation. The compromise adopted in the constitution was to hand power over navigation (South Australia's concern, in the light of an even then declining river trade) to the commonwealth, but this power was tempered by the need to protect the reasonable use of water by other states (see sections 98 & 100).

This compromise failed to assuage those concerned for the fate of the Murray, and a conference was convened at Corowa by the Murray River Main Canal League. This resulted in the establishment in May 1904 of an Interstate Royal Commission which failed to reach a workable agreement in response to the demands for commonwealth control and construction of storages to protect irrigation in times of drought. The problem was referred to a conference of three engineers in 1911, and they produced a report in November 1913. As a result, the River Murray Waters Agreement was concluded, with parallel legislation being ratified by the commonwealth parliament and those of the states of New South Wales, Victoria and South Australia in 1915. The Agreement, and the River Murray Commission it established, came into force on 31 January 1917. The political background to these moves was the introduction of Bills for the Interstate Commission in the first session of the commonwealth parliament, and again in 1909, and motions (in 1910 and 1912) to amend the constitution to place the Murray and its tributaries under commonwealth control (Clark 1984:10). Only when the Interstate Commission Bill passed the house was this motion withdrawn, indicating that it was expected the Interstate Commission would have power to settle the Murray question. This was the hope, therefore, when the agreement was concluded, but, before the agreement came into effect, the Interstate Commission was 'annihilated' by the High Court in the *Wheat* case in 1915 (Clark, 1984:1).

The Agreement proved to be a reasonably successful and extremely resilient instrument for governing the Murray. It did not encompass the Darling nor any other tributaries, and it required unanimity among the four commissioners who represented each government, but it operated quite successfully by guaranteeing South Australia a fixed allocation of water and allowing the upstream states to share the balance. It resulted in the construction of a number of works including some locks and weirs (a concession to the vestigial river trade, but more important in providing regulation for irrigation) and the Hume Weir at Albury. The capital costs of these works were shared equally by the four governments, with operating and maintenance costs shared equally by the three states. The operation of the Commission was not always without controversy, and the squabbling over whether the Dartmouth Dam in Victoria or the Chowilla Dam in South Australia should be constructed led to the unseating of a government in South Australia.

The Agreement and the River Murray Commission could not, however, cope with the problems resulting from their success in providing a regime which allowed the development of the irrigation potential of the Basin. A number of water quality problems began to emerge in the 1960s and one of these—salinity—was on the table as an issue requiring attention from the early 1970s. The agreement was incapable of addressing these water quality problems but some early moves were made. The Commission engaged consulting engineers in 1967 to investigate salinity and their report was produced in 1970.

In March 1973, following an initiative from the Premier of South Australia, Prime Minister Whitlam convened a meeting of heads of government to discuss the future of the Murray with particular emphasis on salinity (South Australia, 1981). This resulted in a working party of officials from the various governments, the recommendations of which were accepted by a steering committee of ministers in October 1975. In October 1976, the four governments agreed that the report of the working party should serve as the basis for a new agreement, the working party was disbanded and the River Murray Commission was charged with the task of drawing up instructions for parliamentary counsel. The Commission put recommendations to the governments in July 1978, but no consensus emerged at ministerial meetings held in October 1979 and February 1981, largely because of the reservations of the upstream states (most particularly New South Wales), which had most to lose from paying for salinity mitigation measures seen as largely benefitting South Australia. A new Agreement was finally concluded in 1982, after some hard negotiation and interesting legal actions which saw South Australia intervening in the New South Wales legal process to appeal against water allocations for further irrigation and New South Wales responding with legislation to deny South Australia standing to sue.

The Agreement finally concluded was seen as a failure as it allowed the upstream states their veto, denied the Commission access to tributaries for water quality monitoring and (thanks to an eleventh-hour amendment inserted at the insistence of New South Wales) did not require states to notify the Commission of planned actions within their states which might affect water quality. There were, however, some portents for cautious optimism for greater co-operation despite the limited nature of the new agreement (Kellow, 1985). The new-found, if limited, co-operation was a start to the process of dealing with salinity, but it is doubtful whether much real progress would have been achieved without political intervention—either by the commonwealth using conditional grants or by its funding salinity mitigation works, or perhaps by some other means. The problem was that commonwealth funding of mitigation works could address only the symptoms of salinity problems, and what was really needed was some means of addressing both the acute symptoms and the chronic causes. The legalistic nature of the Agreement gave such stability to the regime governing the Basin that the prospect of fundamental change was remote indeed, especially given the time it took to negotiate the 1982 agreement.

The process of regime change

In many ways the seeds for change were sown by the River Murray Commission itself. In September 1984 it had published a report entitled *The River Murray Salinity Problem,* on which it conducted a number of public meetings along the river and sought to provoke public discussion and submissions. Then, in May 1985, the River Murray Commission submitted to the governments for endorsement a program of investigation and design works to tackle the salinity problem. It also sought approval for the River Murray Commission to become involved in developing land management strategies and research priorities.

In response to this proposal, South Australian Premier John Bannon sought a heads of government meeting to clarify funding and institutional arrangements the four governments had in place to bring about improved land management and research. Simultaneously—and the letters literally crossed in the mail—Victorian Premier John Cain suggested a meeting of ministers whose portfolios included water resources, environment, land protection and agriculture to review intergovernmental arrangements in the Basin. Cain was particularly concerned at the absence of a mechanism for integrating land and water management within the Basin.

There are suggestions that the South Australian initiative itself came in response to the Victorian initiative. The investigations of the Victorian Parliamentary Salinity Committee had helped the Victorian government conclude that the River Murray Commission was no longer adequate. The task force of ministers established in Victoria to oversee the salinity program recommended changing the regime, but there was a delay of about two weeks between the letter being drafted and the Premier signing it. It would be interesting to know whether, in the intervening period, word of the initiative reached the Chief Engineer of the South Australian Engineering and Water Supply Department, Mr Keith Lewis, through the River Murray Commission network. Lewis might then have suggested to the South Australian Premier, John Bannon, that the time was ripe to seek action.

At a meeting of the Australian Water Resources Council in Darwin in June, the ministers involved in the River Murray Waters Agreement agreed in principle to such a meeting and in July the Prime Minister agreed to convene it. The meeting was announced on 19 August 1985 in a joint statement issued by the Prime Minister and three premiers. South Australia was charged with preparing a discussion paper which would assist a meeting of officials to draft the agenda for the ministerial meeting (South Australia, 1985). This paper identified a number of deficiencies within the existing regime. Among these were:

1 there was no single agency with responsibility for the management of the Basin;
2 the River Murray Commission was empowered only to make recommendations;
3 the unanimity provisions of the River Murray Waters Agreement could be used to prevent the River Murray Commission from making recommendations;
4 the River Murray Commission had limited opportunity to influence land-use management and had only indirect influence over the tributaries of the Murray;
5 there were no effective institutional arrangements to bring about effective intergovernmental co-ordination on land management matters;
6 no single agency within a state had responsibility for the management of that part of the Basin which lay in the state;
7 the intragovernmental institutions for co-ordinating land and water management were generally inadequate;
8 institutional complexity inhibited the integration of water and land-use planning and management;
9 the current cost sharing arrangements for salinity interception works could be inequitable (South Australia, 1985:40–1).

The paper canvassed three options for institutional reform. The first was a Basin authority with comprehensive powers (which was quickly dismissed).[2] The second was an expression of intention to co-operate by means of exchanges of letters and meetings of ministers on an *ad hoc* basis. This was seen to be unsuitable as it lacked any formal arrangements to resolve conflicts. The option recommended was labelled a 'systems approach', which would involve the governments agreeing on a joint management statement and the individual states then establishing consistent state management statements for each portion. This was seen as providing a reasonable basis for integration while retaining state sovereignty.

The report recognised that a new interstate agreement would be necessary and that 'Since it is unlikely that the Governments will perceive a community of interest in all issues the maintenance of effective cooperation and coordination requires the involvement of Governments at the highest level in order to commit Governments to the chosen course of action' (South Australia, 1985:47). The report recommended against the establishment of an ongoing ministerial council, although it did support the establishment of one as an interim measure to develop the interstate agreement necessary to give force to the preferred institutional arrangement. This was a Murray Darling Basin Commission which would have the prime minister and three premiers as members. It would also have commissioners from the River Murray Commission as its commissioners. The members would meet only every one or two years, while the commissioners would meet monthly. Each government would service the Commission with its own cabinet committee and an interdepartmental 'coordinating and advisory committee'. This proposal was similar to that which had been proposed by the Chief Executive of the Delaware Basin Commission, Mr G.M. Hansler, in a report to the Department of Resources and Energy (Hansler, 1985).

The proposal emerging from the committee of officials which prepared the agenda for the ministerial meeting differed from this proposal. The agenda suggested that a ministerial council be established 'to provide the necessary focus and political commitment for enhanced intergovernmental cooperation' (Ministerial Council, 1986). It was proposed that the Council would be advised by the River Murray Commission on all matters relating to the River Murray Waters Agreement and by a Murray-Darling Basin Standing Committee on the development of consistent natural resource policies in the Basin. Provision was also to be made for community consultation at all levels of proceedings. To some extent, these proposals reflect a continuation of the reluctance of officials to alter, in any significant way, the operation of the River Murray Commission; as it was, the ministerial meeting exceeded these recommendations and not only took up the officials' suggestion of a ministerial council (dismissed in the earlier discussion paper as unnecessary), but also set in train events which resulted in the River Murray Commission being completely restructured into a Basin commission.

The recommended structure for the ministerial council was for it to consist of one minister from each government, with other ministers attending when the agenda warranted. The participation of ministers rather than heads of government was seen as providing sufficient political

commitment and authority to bring about the necessary intergovernmental collaboration. This was probably another attempt to limit change,
since the most obvious minister to attend on behalf of the state
governments would have been the minister in charge of water resources
in each case; the policy community effectively would have remained
much the same as under the RMWA. The ministerial meeting opted
instead for a larger council membership with members from the water,
lands/agriculture, and planning/environment areas of each government.

To service the Ministerial Council, a Murray-Darling Basin Standing
Committee was established. Although there was to be representation for
the River Murray Commission on the Standing Committee, its creation
was a clear acknowledgement that the River Murray Commission was
too narrow in scope to address the problems confronting the Basin,
although the agenda papers diplomatically acknowledged that the
Commission was meeting its responsibilities under the Agreement
efficiently. The need for a standing committee was to be reviewed after
the future of the River Murray Commission had been decided. The
question of where the secretariat servicing the Murray-Darling Basin
Ministerial Council was to be located could not be agreed upon by the
officials preparing the agenda, and the matter was referred to the
ministerial meeting for decision. The meeting decided to attach it to the
Department of Resources and Energy in the interim.

All this suggests that the River Murray Commission had lost its pre-
eminent position in the field. While this was true to an extent, the
previous work of the Commission served as the basis for the decisions of
the meeting on water-quality parameters. It was recommended that the
meeting agree to adopt the 1983 policy of the River Murray Commission
on water-quality objectives and note the interim salinity objective adopted
in 1985. The latter called for a reduction in salinity so that water passing
Morgan in South Australia would have a reading of 800 EC units
(electrical conductivity units) or less for 95 per cent of daily observations
by 1995. New South Wales still had reservations about this objective,
which would mean spending $55 million over five years to achieve a 20
per cent reduction.

There was a clear determination that the meeting should also establish
a suitable framework for public participation in the future administration
of the Basin. To achieve this end a number of organisations were invited
to attend the ministerial meeting for the introductory remarks before the
meeting proper commenced. Those groups attending included the Murray
Valley League, the New South Wales Irrigators' Council, the Victorian
Irrigation Research and Promotion Organisation, other irrigation interest
groups, the Victorian Farmers' and Graziers' Association, the Australian
Conservation Foundation, the National Trust, the South Australian
Tourism Industry Council, the South Australian Conservation Council,
and local government interest groups.

To bring about community consultation, the meeting established a working group to report to the first meeting of the Murray-Darling Basin Ministerial Council. Working groups were also established on environmental resources, on-farm water use, the status of irrigation infrastructure, and proposals for salt interception works. The meeting also decided that each government should prepare a paper setting out the current status of intragovernmental arrangements for co-ordinated land and water management, and that each government should prepare a paper on possible future institutional arrangements (including the future role of the River Murray Commission) to be considered at a meeting of lead ministers in February 1986.

The meeting of lead ministers did not take place until 2 April 1986 in Melbourne. Gareth Evans represented the commonwealth as Minister of Resources and Energy, with Don Hopgood from South Australia, John Aquilina from New South Wales and Evan Walker from Victoria. It was significant that Walker, Minister of Agriculture and Rural Affairs in the Cain Government, was not from a water-resources portfolio; his selection as lead minister stemmed from his chairing the Victorian Ministerial Task Force on Salinity. This task force was established in 1985 to follow up the work of the Parliamentary Salinity Committee, which had been set up because of concern over proposals to establish evaporation basins to dispose of saline drainage. These activities had highlighted a significant problem in Victoria with both dryland salinity and saline waterlogging and, together with the political reaction against the Mineral Reserves Basin Scheme, they helped change the stance of Victoria from being simply an upstream state with little interest in water quality in the lower river to being a state which also saw itself as a victim of salinity problems. Added to that, many of the saline drainage problems in the irrigation districts could only be solved by the disposal of highly saline water and there was a realisation that South Australia would not stand for that—at least not quietly.

Given that New South Wales continued throughout to be the state most reluctant to change and to suffer costs, this change in the position of Victoria and the participation of Walker were probably crucial elements in the process of regime change. Walker has a reputation for combining fine political instincts with a 'hands-on' approach; he appears to have been personally committed to doing something about the salinity problem and to have injected both the enthusiasm and the political commitment which were necessary to ensure that change occurred.

The meeting of lead ministers took a significant decision in the process of institutional reform: it established a 'high-level working group' to consider future institutional arrangements for the administration of the Basin. The ministers were able to achieve considerable progress on the question, but identified a number of other issues which required more detailed consideration. They were able to reach broad agreement for the establishment of a new organisation similar to the River Murray Commission, but encompassing land, water and environmental concerns. It had been intended at the ministerial meeting that the first meeting of the Murray-Darling Basin Ministerial Council would take place in May. The first meeting, in Sydney, did not occur until 27 August 1986. It was preceded by a meeting of the standing committee in Canberra on 4 June at which the draft reports of the working groups were discussed. The rescheduled meeting was first postponed until 2 July, but, with it further postponed until August, Senator Evans took the opportunity presented by the 3 July meeting of the Australian Water Resources Council to discuss with Messrs Hopgood and McCutcheon (the Victorian Water Resources Minister) ways of progressing the work of the Council in the period until the meeting took place. To this end, an Integration Steering Committee was established under the chairmanship of Mr Keith Lewis, Chief Engineer of the South Australian Engineering and Water Supply Department. The aim was for this Committee to commence work immediately on integrating the reports of the on-farm water use, irrigation infrastructure and salinity reduction options working groups with a view to establishing priorities. It would present a progress report to the inaugural Council meeting, at which the Council would confirm the establishment of the Committee and its terms of reference.

At the July meeting of the Water Resources Council, the Queensland Minister for Water Resources, Mr Tenni, apparently expressed an interest on Queensland's part in having observer status on the Ministerial Council. With the agreement of the ministers comprising the Council such an invitation was extended. This appeared to represent no more than a watching brief on the part of Queensland, as a representative was not sent to subsequent meetings of the Council. (At the second meeting of the Council it was decided that provision should be made, however, for the future participation of Queensland in the revised agreement.)

The decision to establish a basin commission required political rather than bureaucratic action, particularly on the part of New South Wales, which had demonstrated an unwillingness in the July meeting of Standing Committee to proceed beyond the establishment of the Ministerial Council until there had been an opportunity to review the operation of that arrangement (after at least one year). New South Wales was understandably concerned at the speed with which change was occurring; it was, after all, a contributor to problems in the river without being a significant victim of those problems and it had most to lose from a change in the *status quo*. It was, however, undergoing reform within its own water sector, with the Water Resources Commission being changed into a Department of Water Resources in 1986. This structural change was probably not crucial in the process of New South Wales agreeing to change, but neither was it completely without significance as it signalled the re-establishment of political control over the water agency.

Interestingly, this change came a couple of years after a review of the water industry in that state which had been conducted by Dr John Paterson, who had then been Chief Executive of the Hunter Valley Water Board, but who by 1986 was Director-General of Water Resources in Victoria. As we shall see, Paterson played a crucial role in making progress on the salinity problem possible. Another interesting point relating to personalities was that the Acting-Director of Water Resources in Victoria for the year preceding the establishment of the Department of Water Resources and Dr Paterson's appointment, was John Shepherd, who was seconded from the Engineering and Water Supply Department in South Australia. This interpenetration of agencies in the participating states can only have helped develop shared understanding of the problems of each.

There was not sufficient agreement at the first meeting of the Ministerial Council to move to establish the Murray-Darling Basin Commission. However, many of the features of the Commission eventually established were spelled out by then, thanks to the High Level Working Group on Future Institutional Arrangements, which had reported to the June meeting of the Standing Committee. It was proposed that the Basin commission would encompass the statutory responsibilities currently discharged by the River Murray Commission, but would be given an additional role in advising the Ministerial Council on land and environmental issues not covered by the River Murray Waters Agreement. In the former role, the requirement for unanimity in its decision making would remain, but in the latter there would be majority voting (with one vote per government), with provision for minority reporting. Membership would consist of commissioners from the land, water, and environmental management agencies in each government, with a quorum being one commissioner from each government, and the chair being appointed by Council. Funding arrangements would be those under the River Murray Waters Agreement: administration and capital costs would be shared by the four governments, but operating and maintenance costs would be shared by the three states.

If agreement had been reached at the first meeting of the Ministerial Council, it had been anticipated that the Council would meet again in November 1986 to discuss the necessary amendments to the agreement, with the governments to sign the new agreement and have it ratified by parallel legislation passed through all parliaments by June 1987. While the next meeting of the Council did not take place until 27 March 1987 in Melbourne, the conclusion of a new agreement was not delayed by long, especially given the intervention of a federal election. The process by which agreement was reached was significant. Most of the details had been agreed to at the ministerial dinner which occurred the evening before this second meeting. Evan Walker apparently had a clear understanding that little progress was to be expected in full sessions of the Council where the presence of ministers and officials together would encourage

posturing on the part of ministers, who would be reluctant to be seen by
their own officials as yielding to the pressures brought to bear by other
states. Each meeting of the Council was preceded by such a ministerial
dinner from which officials were excluded. Officials had their own
separate dinner, but the two groups often shared pre-dinner drinks. At the
third meeting (in Albury on 11 December 1987), the officials were
banished to the local Commercial Club, while their ministers supped at
the Albury Travelodge. It is not clear from this case study how common
this process of intergovernmental politics is at ministerial councils, but
one suspects that it will be used often in those councils were there are
substantial disagreements and the stakes are high. As the need for
political activity waned, it was apparent in this case that this epicurean
isolation diminished. At the fourth meeting of the Council (in Adelaide
on 11 August 1988), by which time most of the important decisions had
been made, there was a joint dinner for ministers and officials, but with a
separate table for the ministers.

In the period between the first and second Council meetings there were
negotiations which had to be authorised by the New South Wales
cabinet. There are no details available of the nature of this process, but
one significant change to the structure agreed to at the second meeting
was that the number of commissioners was reduced from three to two,
with the agencies to be given representation being those responsible for
land, water and environmental management. There was a danger that
environmental interests might be squeezed out and this might appear as a
concession to New South Wales, but it is not unambiguously so because
South Australia had tended to send only two ministers to Council
(Hopgood was Minister for both Water Resources and Environment and
Planning) and much of the concerns of land degradation and conservation
had been combined in Victoria in the Department of Conservation,
Forests and Lands.

The new institutional structure agreed to was that there would be a
Murray-Darling Basin Ministerial Council, a Murray-Darling Basin
Standing Committee would continue in existence (but be subjected to
future review), a Murray-Darling Basin Commission, and a
Murray-Darling Basin Community Advisory Council. The secretariat
servicing the Ministerial Council would now be moved from the
Department of Primary Industry and Energy to the Commission. Day-to-
day resource management responsibilities would continue to reside with
the individual governments so the Agreement would not threaten the
sovereignty of any state.

The timetable set was for the parallel legislation to be passed by
September 1987, with proclamation from 1 January 1988. This timetable
might have been regarded as extremely optimistic in the light of the
history of earlier revisions of the Agreement, but it was very nearly
adhered to. By 30 October, the Agreement had been signed by the Prime

Minister and all three premiers, and legislation had been introduced into all parliaments. The final form of the new Agreement was dealt with by out-of-session endorsement of a draft worked out after protracted negotiations. This form of decision was often used during the change process, with subsequent ratification at the next Council meeting, and the subjects dealt with (as this example shows) were by no means minor. The Victorian Bill had been passed by both houses by 14 November, and, by the time of the third meeting of the Ministerial Council, Bills had been passed by all state parliaments and the commonwealth House of Representatives.

Within a little more than two years since the ministerial meeting, therefore, there had been a change in the regime governing the Murray-Darling Basin which few would have anticipated. It had been achieved with much hard negotiating, and some reluctance on the part of New South Wales, but a spirit of consensus was emerging. It did not go as far as it might have—there is, for example, some evidence that provisions for the incorporation of environmental values were watered down (and this might have been due in part to the replacement of Gareth Evans by John Kerin as lead commonwealth minister). The Agreement, nevertheless, represented a substantial achievement, and one which was an enormous advance over the faltering steps towards reforming the Agreement and the River Murray Commission through the 1970s and early 1980s. If the minor advances made in the 1982 revision were seen by some as an opportunity lost, the formation of the Ministerial Council and the establishment of the Murray-Darling Basin Commission must be seen as an opportunity created, and—once created—an opportunity seized.

The act of creation was one in which political actors played a vital role; it is unlikely this progress would have been made without the involvement of politicians who were committed to the outcome and prepared to work long and hard to achieve it. Evan Walker and his Victorian colleagues were probably crucial in this respect because the changed position of Victoria, which now saw itself as a victim of salinity rather than just an upstream state causing problems for South Australia, was close to being the *sine qua non* of the process of regime change. The alignment of Labor governments cannot be entirely dismissed, but the issues were not those likely to result in much unity among previously divided states. The alignment most certainly helped to create a policy community marked by a reasonable level of trust.

What will be awaited with interest is how well the new machinery will run when it is put on autopilot—or when at least the political enthusiasm wanes, as seems inevitable. There were signs that the replacement of Gareth Evans by John Kerin might have led to a slight loss of the political head of steam, but the machinery will eventually have to be capable of performing with a reasonable degree of autonomy. Unlike the River Murray Commission, the Murray-Darling Basin

Commission will report to a Ministerial Council which (by statutory requirement) will have to meet at least annually, so the political hand will never be far from the controls. But rotation among political actors has changed the faces at the Council table, with Don Hopgood, the last survivor of those who attended the ministerial meeting in 1985, losing the South Australian portfolio two weeks before the fifth meeting at Moree on 27 and 28 April 1989. The defeat of the Labor government in New South Wales has caused some hiccups in the negotiation of a suitable salinity and drainage strategy (the development of which is discussed below), but probably as much because a new set of ministers became members of the policy community as because it ended the Labor axis.

The ultimate test for the new regime will come when it is controlled by ministers who lack the enthusiasm for the Agreement that was evident among its creators: can the regime survive the passing of its creators? There are hopeful signs in the development of the Salinity and Drainage Strategy, to which we shall now turn. The signs for optimism stem mostly from the fact that there have been marked changes in the water and land resources regimes within the states, which have resulted in the salinity problem being approached very positively and very creatively, making agreement possible. In brief, the engineers are giving way to those whose skills lie in resolving policy questions, as the water economies of the states have moved from a developmental to a more mature phase of their evolution.

The Salinity and Drainage Strategy

It is all very well to look at changes to structures, but the ultimate test of the reforms is whether they deliver satisfactory resolutions to problems confronting the Basin. For this reason it is worth examining briefly the development of the Salinity and Drainage Strategy because this constitutes the attempt by the new regime to deal with the most important problem. It also allows us an insight into the creation of a climate for consensus which underlay the creation of the Murray-Darling Basin Commission, and a hint into how officials might perform in future if the political rudder is eased.

The problem of saline water in the river and saline waterlogging in some irrigation areas in New South Wales and Victoria was a matter in which substantial progress was made even before the changed regime was in place. Indeed, it can be argued that the progress on the strategy helped bring about consensus on the institutional arrangements because it showed that, with co-operation, there were positive gains to be had for all parties in dealing with Basin problems. The emerging consensus over the strategy made the proposal for a new Agreement much less threatening to New South Wales. Of crucial significance in this process was the way in which the salinity problem was redefined as a positive-sum game, with gains for all states, whereas the prevailing perception up to this point had been that the problem was zero-sum, with any action (and expenditure) by New South Wales and Victoria being seen as acts of pure altruism, for the benefit of South Australia. The chief architect of this problem redefinition was the Victorian Director-General of Water Resources, Dr John Paterson, who chaired a high-level working group which had been constituted not by agreement at a Council meeting, but by out-of-session agreement sought by Senator Evans in July 1986. This was probably Paterson's suggestion, because he seems to have taken to the task with gusto and would have recognised that action was necessary if the resolution of the ministerial meeting that a broad strategy was to be developed within one year was to be implemented. Paterson had demonstrated a previous interest in the Basin and a clear understanding of the nature of the salinity and drainage problem (Paterson, 1985), and is also reputed to have enjoyed a close understanding with Evans. Whatever the origins of the Strategy Working Group, Paterson must be given the lion's share of the credit for its output—a report issued in time for the first meeting of the Council (Strategy Working Group, 1986).

Paterson's paper set out a number of trade-offs, which included:

1 Stream vs land salinisation: here the trade-off was between improving drainage in areas with saline waterlogging and resultant increased stream salinity. There was need to provide maximum freedom for the states by specifying global export limits and compensation criteria in terms of either dollars or dilution flows.

2 Salinity objective for the River Murray: here it was seen as necessary that politicians explicitly sanctioned the '800 EC at Morgan 95 per cent of the time' (or some alternative) criterion, which had been chosen only by officials in the past. One problem was that this criterion bore no clear relationship to the economic costs and benefits of salinity. It was seen that a political solution to the problem required that a way be found whereby all states could share in the benefits of water quality improvement.

3 Flow regulation and water allocations: changes in the operation of Lake Victoria and the Menindee Lakes could produce a 50 EC improvement at Morgan, but this would affect the security of supply enjoyed by the upstream states in periods of drought. There was also a need to move towards continuous water-accounting rules for Victoria and New South Wales, since the existing rules encouraged waste because any savings made by either state would be shared between them, rather than accruing to the frugal state. In addition, water-quality accounting rules needed to be adopted as provided for in the 1982 Act.

Other issues were cost sharing, investment, and institutional arrangements, but these have either been dealt with above or are not of great relevance here. This redefinition of the problem so that all states could share in the benefits was an important advance. There is not space here to detail either the process or the outcome, but the strategy developed involved the use of linear programing techniques to find a mix of salt interception works (to be funded by the states and the commonwealth equally), changes to the operation of some storages, and rights for the upstream states to dispose of saline drainage flows which would yield positive net benefits for all states involved. At the same time the question was dealt with in a way that was optimum from the national viewpoint. The salt interception works were mostly in South Australia, and the only (minor) losers will be those using river water for irrigation between the points of the increased saline discharge in New South Wales and Victoria and the salt interception works.

An immediate substantial improvement in river salinity will result and the longer-term causes of increasing salinity can now be tackled by the Ministerial Council and the revivified and expanded Murray-Darling Basin Commission. Neither the Agreement nor the Strategy is perfect (Queensland is still absent, and the regime depends upon the co-operation of state agencies for detailed land-use management within state borders), but both represent improvements which were not thought possible five years ago. A formal agreement ratifying the Strategy was adopted at the meeting of the Ministerial Council held in Moree in April 1989. The next test of the new arrangements will come as the level of political involvement inevitably diminishes.

Conclusion

This chapter shows quite clearly that politicians rather than bureaucrats played a crucial part in bringing about change in the Murray-Darling Basin. The problems in the Basin were intergovernmental in nature because of a lack of coincidence between jurisdictional and biophysical boundaries, which had not been addressed adequately by the constitution. The *ad hoc* arrangement of the original River Murray Waters Agreement had sufficed while the role of the state in the Basin was essentially developmental, guaranteeing water quantity adequate for the needs of each of the three states. Once the need was not for development but for regulation of quality, the existing regime was inadequate—but far too durable to allow change to take place readily. The legalistic nature of the Agreement, which made it a success, locked the parties into positions that they were intent on defending at all costs. A way forward could only be found by those with sufficient authority to commit their governments.

Crucial in the process of achieving change were changes within the upstream states—particularly Victoria. The Victorian Parliamentary Salinity Committee redefined that state's perception of itself from that of causative agent to that of victim, which changed its external stance and motivated key political actors such as Evan Walker. But reform at the intragovernmental level was also of vital significance, most particularly the establishment of the Victorian Department of Water Resources and the critical role of its Director-General in redefining the policy problem as positive-sum rather than zero-sum. These reforms have been echoed to some extent with the move from a Commission to a Department in New South Wales, which was, throughout the process of regime reform, the most reluctant state.

These factors were probably more important than the 'alignment' of Labor governments in the states and at the commonwealth level. While this 'alignment' contributed to a stable policy community during the crucial stages of the negotitations, there was minimal change of personnel until later in the process. Of as much importance as the presence of Labor governments was the absence of coalition Liberal–National governments in which the National Party, sensitive to farmer interests along the Murray, could exert considerable veto power.

There are many aspects of this issue which make it atypical of intergovernmental politics in Australia. It provides, however, an insight into the formation and operation of a ministerial council and an insight into how effective such a council can be. The achievements of the Murray-Darling Basin Council in effecting change which (in the light of the history of intergovernmental politics in the Basin) must be characterised as rapid should not be underestimated. Such an astute observer of the Murray as Professor Sandford Clark remarked rather pessimistically in 1984 'my firm conviction is that...a Ministerial Council will only work where there is a perceived community of interest on the part of each participating government. *Ex hypothesi*, this is not the case with the Murray-Darling Basin' (Clark, 1984). This view from a legal observer twelve months before the ministerial meeting shows the dangers of underestimating the political factor in intergovernmental relations—especially the ability of politicians and entrepreneurial bureaucrats to create at least a fruitful policy community, if not a community of interest, where none was previously apparent.

Endnotes

1 Throughout the period under discussion here there is considerable uncertainty over whether there should be a hyphen in 'Murray-Darling'; many
   of the early papers omit it, but as the new Murray-Darling Basin
   Commission includes it, so shall this paper, except where reference is
   made to earlier papers which omitted the hyphen.
2 The report stated: 'This option is not considered to be desirable or
   realistic' (South Australia, 1985:41).

Bibliography

Clark, S.D., 1983. 'Inter-governmental Quangos: The River Murray Commission', *Australian Journal of Public Administration*, 42, 154–72.

—— 1984. 'Other Models for Administration; The Intergovernmental Experience and Opportunities', Paper presented to the AIPS Conference, 'Governing the Murray-Darling Basin', Canberra, September.

Hansler, G.M., 1985. 'Observations, Conclusions and Recommendations on Management of Water and Related Resources of the Murray Basin', unpublished report to the Department of Resources and Energy.

Holmes, J. & Sharman, C., 1977. *The Australian Federal System*, Sydney, Allen & Unwin.

Kellow, A., 1985. 'Managing an Ecological System: the Politics and Administration', *Australian Quarterly*, 57, 107–27.

Ministerial Council, *see* Murray Darling Basin Ministerial Council, various.

Murray Darling Basin Management Strategy Working Group, 1986. *Framework for the Development of the Resource Management Strategy, Progress Report*, August.

Murray Darling Basin Ministerial Council, various. *Minutes of Council Meetings*.

Paterson, J., 1985. 'Managing an Ecological System: Reforming the Tariff', *Australian Quarterly*, 56, 139–47.

South Australia, 1981. *A Permanent Solution to the River Murray Salinity Problem*, Engineering & Water Supply Department, June 1981.

——1985. *Management of the Murray Darling Basin: A Discussion Paper*, Engineering and Water Supply Department, August 1985.

Strategy Working Group, *see* Murray Darling Basin Management Strategy Working Group, 1986.

Young, O., 1982. *Resource Regimes*, Berkeley, University of California Press.

8   Environmental management

Bruce Davis

Conceptual models of intergovernmental relations tend to take two forms: *conflict studies*, based upon an assumption that debates about jurisdiction and resources will be resolved through the exercise of political power and/or judicial (constitutional) interpretation; and *bargaining paradigms*, focusing upon interdependency, diplomacy and mutual accommodation, accomplished through the actions of intergovernmental officials and mediating institutions. In practice, both co-operation and conflict may simultaneously exist, even within a particular functional area of government. There is often a fundamental difference in rhetoric, ethos and style dependent upon whether issues are being treated at the political, as distinct from administrative, level of government.

If one examines Australian environmental management during the past two decades, some of these characteristics are clearly identifiable (Crommelin, 1985; Davis, 1985), but this presupposes that the perspective is largely focused upon commonwealth–state relations, i.e., a 'vertical' jurisdictional orientation. A slightly different view emerges, if state comparisons are attempted. This chapter provides an initial overview of both levels of government, noting major commonwealth–state tensions in environmental management, but arguing that some convergence of practice is emerging, subject only to variations reflecting the ideologies of the particular parties in power. The focus is principally upon nature conservation in rural or wilderness situations, although some parallels exist with urban environmental issues. The paradox is that more than 80 per cent of Australians live in eight conurbations at or near the coastal fringe, but most battles about 'wilderness' or scenic amenity relate to areas that few Australians may have seen.

More specifically, this chapter deals with important aspects of the following issues:

1 Given that the states and territories are in direct competition for economic development, why have similarities and differences in environmental management emerged in recent years?

2 What are the reasons why an enlarged commonwealth role has evolved?

3 To what degree has the debate about land rights or international treaties and conventions (e.g., the World Heritage issue) resulted in a shift in the constitutional balance favouring the commonwealth?

4 To what degree is environmental management in Australia influenced by interest-group activity (e.g., the voluntary conservation movement and/or mining or forestry lobbies)?

5 What mediating institutions have been established to handle and resolve such issues?

6 What are some of the current issues likely to provide the focus of policy debate in the early 1990s?

Jurisdictional issues and administrative problems

The Australian constitution does not make any specific reference to the 'environment', but this has not precluded both commonwealth and state legislation on environmental protection. In general, natural resources utilisation, land use planning and nature conservation programs are the prerogatives of the states and territories, with the federal role limited to providing common standards, research assistance and funds for some resource conservation activities (Fisher, 1980; Bates, 1983). In addition, the commonwealth jurisdiction includes federal sites and buildings within states and all federal territories, including some offshore islands and Antarctica (Ward, 1982). But during the 1970s widespread public concern about the environment, new resource development and conservation needs, plus various international obligations forced the federal government to intervene more directly and take an active role in environmental policy. Many decisions involving resource development projects, foreign investment and ownership, export licensing and nature conservation activities result in commonwealth actions cutting across state jurisdictions, engendering intergovernmental conflict in the process of trading off regional objectives and priorities relative to the national interest (Crommelin, 1983).

The cornerstones of national environmental policy are four statutes enacted between 1974 and 1976 during the Whitlam Labor regime. These are:

1 The Environmental Protection (Impact of Proposals Act), 1974, which ensures that matters affecting the environment to a significant extent are taken into account in all plans and actions of federal agencies;

2 The Australian Heritage Commision Act, 1975, which provides for identification, registration and protection at a federal level, of sites and structures constituting important elements of the built, cultural and natural environment, which have enduring national significance;

3 The Australian National Parks and Wildlife Conservation Act, 1975, which provides for the establishment and management of parks and reserves in federal territories as well as the protection of some other nature conservation sites and meeting various obligations under international treaties and conventions; and

4 The Great Barrier Reef Marine Park Act, 1975, which provides for the establishment and management of a major national park encompassing the Greater Reef off Queensland.

In addition to the above, other legislation deals with safeguards in uranium mining and exports, grants to the states for nature conservation purposes and, more recently, a World Heritage Properties Conservation Act 1983, aimed at the implementation of obligations incurred under international treaties (Australian Information Service, 1980; Zines, 1985). In general, these statutes and associated institutional arrangements and procedures seem to have worked reasonably well, although claims have been made that federal legislation represents an erosion of state rights. Also it has been claimed by Formby (1987) and Haward (see chapter 6) among others that too much discretion is permitted the Minister under the Environmental Protection (Impact of Proposals) Act, with the result that environmental inquiries are rarely properly conducted, nor is protection adequately enforced.

Paralleling these provisions at the commonwealth level, all of the Australian states and the Northern Territory have introduced land-use management reforms, environmental impact assessment procedures, enlarged national park systems, air and water quality controls and some coastal and marine conservation guidelines (Gilpin, 1980b). Yet the overall performance has been patchy, with many deficiencies in ecological sustainability and administrative regulation readily apparent (Hall, 1988; Solomon, 1988). Despite all the statutes, regulations, and political rhetoric about concern for the Australian environment, the past two decades have witnessed a series of major conservation controversies of unparalleled duration, intensity and costliness in national history (Davis, 1989b). Disputes concerning issues such as mineral sands mining on Fraser Island, destruction of rainforest in Queensland and New South Wales, threats to the Great Barrier Reef, uranium mining and land rights in the Northern Territory, hydroelectric development in south-west

Tasmania and bauxite mining in the jarrah forests of Western Australia have aroused much public comment and debate, occupied considerable time and effort within government and caused some frustration and delay to the plans of private corporations (Burton, 1980; Gilpin, 1980a,b; Tighe & Taplin, 1985).

Two questions arise: what is the role of the federal government in attempting to resolve environmental conflict? Why have extant legislation and procedures singularly failed to result in environmental mediation? Additional queries arise about individual values and the nature of politics. Are conservation disputes an inevitable consequence of divergent community values about the relationship of people to their natural environment? Or are such disputes more a manifestation of political and administrative failures in public policy? In this chapter it will be argued that both factors are present.

It can be persuasively argued that three reasons exist why Australian environmental management has been characterised by substantial disputation in recent years. The first reason is that historically there has been little comprehension of the fragility and complexity of many Australian ecosystems and biota. This has been compounded by considerable political expediency in natural resources management, resulting from competition between the states and Northern Territory for economic development (Powell, 1976; Head, 1986). The net result has been environmental attrition and land-use degradation, now causing considerable community concern and conflict, evident in social protest and attitudes revealed in public opinion polls (Chisholm & Dumsday, 1987).

Secondly, the forestry, engineering, economics and planning professions have sometimes exhibited elitist and conservative attitudes, failing to address diversity of values and recent advances in techniques for evaluating projects (Burton, 1980; Shrader-Frechette, 1985; Davis, 1986). This has been coupled with administrative failure within government to get functionally-specialised resource agencies (water, land, forestry, mining, etc.) to deal with overarching environmental problems where interdependency is of crucial importance (Feiveson et al., 1976; Birkeland-Corro, 1988).

Third, the rise of powerful interest groups, both pro-conservation and pro-development, has increased the complexity of political and administrative action and shown the lack of arrangements for resolving environmental disputes (Bradsen, 1987; Morris, 1987; Craig, 1988; Jeffery, 1986, 1987). Above all else, there appears to be a need to move towards what Yudelman (1986) has called 'maturity management' of natural resources, embracing sustainable development of the kind enunciated by Caldwell (1984), but further clarified in the *World Conservation Strategy* 1980, *A National Conservation Strategy for Australia* 1983 and the World Commission on Environment and Development Report, *Our Common Future*, 1987.

Without carrying out a detailed analysis of Australian environmental management during the past two decades, we can comment on achievements and failures at political and administrative levels. There are considerable variations in practice between the states, arising less from statutory differences than the personalities of premiers and the ideology of the party in power. There are also some variations *within* states, arising from the relative strengths and influence of development-orientated agencies and interests, *vis-à-vis* their conservation counterparts. Given the immense variation of climate, terrain, resource endowment and population distribution across Australia, it is a moot point as to whether one should accept some regional variation in environmental quality or expect that broad national standards will be set and enforced. Opinion polls suggest that the expectations of most Australians is that we should pursue the latter option (Figgis, 1979; Wendt, 1979).

Although some attempts have been made within the states to co-ordinate environmental policy through mega-ministries of conservation or various interdepartmental committees, the standard of performance does not appear significantly different from those jurisdictions where functional fragmentation occurs. (This is a personal judgement based on the severity of conservation controversies in various Australian states during the past twenty years). Nor can one argue that particular political ideologies guarantee environmental care; while Labor regimes have a more consistent record of nature conservation legislation and funding environmental programs, all political regimes permit major environmental attrition from time to time.

One antidote to variation amongst states has been the establishment of ministerial councils at the federal level, consisting of commonwealth ministers and their state counterparts. Examples are the AEC (Australian Environment Council) and CONCOM (the Council of Nature Conservation Ministers). The councils themselves deal with broad policy issues, attempts to standardise practice and the airing of grievances, but they work on a consensus basis, so an individual state or the commonwealth can veto proceedings. The really valuable exchange of ideas and information occurs mainly at the support group level, amongst task forces and working parties of professional officers preparing background documents and guidelines. (Information about the operations of bodies such as CONCOM is somewhat restricted. Discussions with national park officers in several states indicates that a wide range of issues is canvassed in such meetings). It is this full and frank exchange of views which has resulted in some convergence of practice at operational levels in land-use management and nature conservation, but once issues drift up to the political level, rationality decreases and expedient politics as well as 'states rights' rhetoric becomes the order of the day.

Contrasting experience exists in respect of trans-state problems. Considerable concern exists about water quality, irrigation and salinity problems in the Murray-Darling Rivers system, one of Australia's principle drainage and water supply catchments (see chapter 7). Three states are principally involved: New South Wales, Victoria and South Australia, hence the commonwealth has tended to play a limited role, attempting to facilitate discourse, research and organisational reform, without much direct intervention. Many Australians would prefer national action, but there are constitutional and political dangers involved (Crabb, 1984). This situation may be contrasted with the Great Barrier Reef, where despite intergovernmental friction, but with overwhelming public support, a federal agency, the Great Barrier Reef Marine Park Authority, has achieved a broad protective framework and effective management planning in the past decade (Kelleher, 1986).

One other case situation is worthy of contemplation. In July 1983 the High Court of Australia ruled by a 4:3 majority that the federal World Heritage Properties Conservation Act 1983 was valid. This permitted the commonwealth government to prevent the Tasmanian government proceeding with construction of a hydro-electric project in the Gordon-Franklin Rivers wilderness area of south-west Tasmania. The judgement (commonly known as the 'Dams' case) implied that Australia's adherence to international treaties and conventions would permit federal intervention in regional jurisdictions, if actions were deemed detrimental to environmental quality or heritage conservation (Sornarajah, 1983). Both levels of government were initially cautious about longer-term implications of this case, which seemingly signalled a considerable constitutional extension of commonwealth powers, arising from exercise of the external affairs power cited in the constitution (Coper, 1983; Lipman, 1985; Davis, 1988).

More recently, the intransigence of the Tasmanian and Queensland governments in forestry matters, coupled with pressure from the voluntary conservation movement, plus some temptation to apply leverage at times of potential electoral gain, has resulted in more frequent intervention by the commonwealth government in state environmental issues. This poses some dangers to state rights and has resulted in a number of High Court challenges which thus far have reinforced federal powers. The only countervailing factor has been the high level of financial compensation found necessary to appease outraged regional interests (e.g., $277 million in the Tasmanian Dams case).

There would appear to be a significant failure in environmental policy where ritualised conflict is the prevailing mode of settling disputes. Surely environmental mediation is a superior route, but as yet appropriate administrative machinery has not been devised and where quasi-judicial public inquiries have been substituted, highly variable performance has been the experience (James & Boer, 1988). But note the Australian government's intention to establish a Resource Assessment Commission, assigned the task of bringing economic and ecological factors into conjunction when contentious environmental issues must be dealt with in the future. It is by no means clear as yet how the Resources Assessment Commission will attempt to quantify and tradeoff a variety of social, ecological and economic variables, some of intergenerational character: nonetheless, it is clearly intended to present rounded judgments and options to Cabinet for consideration. The Commission itself will not pursue a quasi-judicial function, but merely provide overview assessment advice.

Perhaps the most substantial failure in recent years has been in application of the EIS (environmental impact assessment) technique. The deficiencies of this approach are already well recorded in a variety of texts (O'Riordan & Sewell, 1981; Porter, 1985; Formby, 1987), but in Australia such weaknesses have been further exacerbated by discretion permitted ministers to decide whether an EIS will be required, the terms of reference for such investigations and whether prescribed safeguards will actually be enforced (Hawkins, 1984). What little ex-post environmental assessment has been carried out reveals that many key issues have been omitted or glossed over, such as happened in the Tasmanian woodchips case (Dargavel, 1985). Here the forestry industry was supposed to examine whether feasible alternatives existed to logging forest of heritage value, as recorded on the Register of the National Estate. In practice the EIS merely attempted to justify extant logging practices and urged an increase in production quota. Environmental impact assessments often fail to take into account the social implications of projects, and where SIA (Social Impact Assessment) techniques have been substituted the studies have been fairly rudimentary in character and heavily slanted in favour of proponents (Dillon, 1985).

Enough is recorded, therefore, to conclude reluctantly that although there have been some important developments in natural resources management in the past two decades, considerable political tokenism and administrative failures have occurred. Indeed some commentators would claim that without the activism of a substantial voluntary conservation movement in Australia, few advances would have been achieved.

The Australian conservation movement

Throughout European settlement in Australia there have been concerned individuals and conscientious public servants actively promoting care of the environment, often in the face of much community apathy and destructiveness (Powell, 1976). Nevertheless in recent times a strong voluntary conservation movement has emerged and become a scientific-ally expert and politically active influence. The word 'environmentalism' can take on a variety of connotations, but here is taken to mean 'a social and political movement involving specific sets of beliefs about the relationship of Man and Nature, generally opposed to existing modes of technology and natural resources utilisation' (Davis, 1982).

Classification and labelling of interest groups within the community is complex. Diversities of motivations and values as well as variety of organisational forms may be masked by attempts to bundle individuals and groups into neat categorisations (Berry, 1977). When we speak of the Australian conservation movement, we are basically talking about a collection of community organisations using education, political lobbying, media publicity and activism to achieve new modes of natural resources management, the preservation of ecological diversity and what they believe to be improved standards of environmental protection. The Australian Conservation Foundation's *Green Book* (1978) lists some 1198 institutions scattered across the nation and the total number of groups appears to be increasing each year. Membership is difficult to calculate, given the ebb and flow of participation in particular causes, cases of multiple membership and much covert support, but calculations of overall numbers range from 150 000 to 300 000 people—remarkably high for a nation with a population of approximately 17 million (Davis, 1982).

The rise of a conservation movement from a series of isolated and somewhat naive participants in the early 1960s to a well organised, funded and politically astute coalition in the 1980s, has been partially, but not comprehensively, recorded by a number of authors (Figgis, 1979; Green, 1981; Thompson, 1984), but perhaps what is more pertinent here is the tactics employed. These have taken the following forms:

1 general lobbying activities aimed at the introduction or amendment of legislation, the modification of administrative procedures, or to prevent particular actions from taking place;

2 challenges to project-evaluation methodologies, seeking to influence key decision makers when resource exploitation programs are being contemplated;

3 recourse to environmental law, usually as a last resort, claiming that amenity rights are being threatened or that the public interest is ill-served by particular actions; and

4 using intergovernmental relations as a lever to force one level of government to act against another. Examples are the Fraser Island, Tasmanian dams and Daintree rainforest disputes (Davis, 1982).

The central problem of the eco-activists is to gain and hold public support, throughout the period of a conservation controversy, in a situation where their own organisation has limited resources and cohesiveness and is opposed by legitimate bureaucratic, political and private sector forces. The situation is not one-sided, however; since justice must appear to be done, politicians recognise the need to pay lip service to conservation, and official information is an Achilles heel, as much of it is suspect or open to challenge from alternative sources. The situation has been likened to guerilla warfare, in which voluntary groups harry the flanks of the established order, seeking not only to change resource management practices, but also to amend social values through educative processes aimed at winning 'the hearts and minds' of the people. One cannot take the warfare analogy too far, nevertheless conservation controversies do involve opposing forces with deeply-felt convictions. A wide array of tactics are employed, including strategic withdrawals, and battles of attrition, not to mention smokescreens and the blackening of opponents' names, but all protagonists are ultimately forced to recognise that in a democratic society solutions must be found which are roughly acceptable to the lay public. This is a dilemma for eco-activists and their opponents alike, since environmental policy involves both ethical choices and political compromise, a balance not easily achieved (Peres, 1970).

What *are* some of the lessons of past experience? In the *Lake Pedder* case (1967–1976) bureaucratic secrecy and the myth of hydro-industrialisation as an economic development strategy for Tasmania were exposed, but the conservationists were initially naive and idealistic, without the detailed technical expertise to challenge project evaluations prepared by the Hydro-Electric Commission of Tasmania and backed by a major industry lobby (Davis, 1980). The ensuing Commonwealth Committee of Enquiry 1973–74 identified amended procedures intended to avoid future confrontation, but these recommendations were virtually ignored by the Tasmanian government. Conflict erupted when plans for the Gordon-belowFranklin Power Scheme were announced in 1979. By now the environmentalists were better organised and more conscious of the need to mobilise community political support; moreover they possessed a charismatic leader in Dr Bob Brown, capable of articulating wilderness values to the media and attracting general support from particular sections of Australian society hitherto not motivated by conservation issues. Using intergovernmental relations as leverage, initially much against the federal will but ultimately through electoral pressure and a site blockade, the Tasmanian Wilderness Society and associated groups achieved a substantial victory when the High Court of Australia made its judicial determination on 1 July 1983 that the federal government could prevent construction of the Gordon River Dam (Coper, 1983; Bates, 1984).

On other fronts the environmentalists achieved only limited success in the late 1970s and early 1980s. In the *Precipitous Bluff* case, the Tasmanian Conservation Trust used the courts to thwart a proposed quarrying operation in a wilderness area of south-west Tasmania. Although the Trust eventually lost its High Court battle and had substantial legal costs awarded against it, the intervening time delay and vigorous lobbying led to incorporation of the Precipitous Bluff region into the South-West National Park, an area which subsequently achieved World Heritage status. In New South Wales protracted campaigns were required before mineral sands extraction in coastal areas were prohibited and remnant rainforests were protected by the Wran Labor Government (Tighe & Taplin, 1985). In Queensland, the commonwealth government attempted for several years to avoid confrontation with the state over attrition of rainforest in the Daintree-Cape Tribulation area, only to gradually lose patience and in June 1987 nominate almost the entire resource for World Heritage listing (Davis, 1989a). In the Northern Territory debates about uranium mining, aboriginal land rights and Stages I, II and III of the Kakadu National Park have extended over more than a decade without final resolution in sight.

Individuals such as the Routleys (1974), who opposed clearfell woodchip extraction from the hardwood forests of south-east Australia in the early 1970s were sometimes accused of being luddites threatening the economic development of the nation. Scientific complexities and investment factors were difficult for the general public to grasp and the gradual transformation of the forests gave little hint of impending crisis (French, 1980; Dargavel, 1985, 1987). It was only when the *Tasmanian Dams* case was finally resolved in 1983 that the environmental lobby could redirect its attention to other conservation issues, such as forestry operations. As yet, this battle remains unresolved, although recent agreements concluded between environmental groups, the forest industry and the commonwealth and Tasmanian governments now bring some prospect of a forest accord.

It is important to recognise that each of the above cases entails a number of intergovernmental dimensions. Apart from debate about the degree to which the *Dams* case judgement may have implied a constitutional shift in favour of the commonwealth (Zines, 1985), there is also the question of financial compensation to the states and territories if federal intervention occurs. Both the commonwealth Treasury and Department of Finance have expressed concern to federal cabinet about the budgetary implications of involvement in state development issues, but even in managing newly-protected areas and World Heritage sites, some federal assistance grants are normally required (Davis, 1985). The commonwealth is also willing to offer technical assistance and scientific expertise, where relevant, to assist with management planning of key sites.

Whatever the fiscal realities of conservation measures, politicians appear more concerned about electoral impacts, gauging environmental issues largely on media reportage and construed public opinion, rather than hard scientific evidence or economic data. By the early 1980s there was widespread recognition by the major political parties that the 'green movement' now possessed some political clout and the Australian community appeared to have some sympathy with its cause. The real issue was whether this would be transformed into votes. The election of the Hawke Labor Government in 1983 largely settled that issue and the Prime Minister's more recent July 1989 environmental statement, *Our Country, Our Future*, appears to confirm the continued electoral importance of conservation initiatives. However, in recent times a discernible backlash against the conservation movement has resurfaced, largely as a result of commonwealth delay in approving the proposed Coronation Hill mining venture in Stage III of Kakadu National Park, plus a variety of concerns about exclusion of forestry areas from woodchip operations. The principal opposition to the environmental cause stems mainly from the mining and forestry lobbies, some elements of the trade union movement and at least one federal minister.

On the face of it, it is difficult to tell whether environmentalism is a passing phase or an enduring social movement, although three factors favour the latter interpretation. In recent times an increasing number of 'green' candidates have been standing at state and federal elections in Australia. While a number of little-known individuals are rejected by the voters, a few of the more prominent green candidates have been elected on the basis of their environmental ideology. Some Australian Democrat senators fit this prescription, as do the five green independents now holding the balance of power in the Tasmanian parliament. An additional factor is growing community acceptance of the concept of 'sustainable development', first promulgated in the Brundtland Report of 1987, but now espoused by the Australian government. A third factor is the realisation that some conservation policies, such as waste recycling and appropriate technology, may make economic sense, if scale effects and attitudinal change can be achieved. A final reason is the enhanced internationalisation of environmental issues, such as concern for Antarctica, attempts to save tropical rainforest and the desire for administrative reforms to handle the greenhouse effect, acid rain, marine pollution and other trans-jurisdictional problems.

Counterveiling forces

The existence of one or more community groups devoted to a particular cause is usually the signal for counterveiling forces to emerge, either to oppose new ideas or preserve the status quo. In some instances governments attempt to absorb or deflect criticism by co-aptation, i.e., granting limited representation to particular interests (Scott, 1980). But sometimes long wars of attrition are pursued, in the hope of deterrence or that existing practice will survive. Cutting across such scenarios are supplementary factors, such as the existence of opposing factors within the bureaucracy or the paradox that governments are often pursuing divergent policies simultaneously.

Without doubt the most entrenched opposition to Australian environmentalism is to be found within the ranks of the mining and forestry industries, who feel threatened by the 'locking up' of resources in national parks and other nature reserves. The Australian Mining Industry Council and the National Association of Forest Industries are well organised and funded, with ready access to key politicians and public servants. With respect to the latter, it is not uncommon for a form of clientelism to develop between public sector agencies and relevant industries, with some state and federal departments openly adopting a pro-development stance, while others adopt a more neutral posture. The tendency of critics of the conservation movement is to pursue the rhetoric of 'balanced' development, in situations where decision processes are already heavily weighted in favour of resource exploitation. The environmentalists are sometimes equally selective in publicity, making extravagent claims about 'pristineness' or possible impacts on wildlife. The great danger of such over-simplification is that it can soon degenerate into unreason, rendering political mediation extremely difficult.

The propaganda war over woodchip operations in the forests of south-east Australia has had one unanticipated benefit for the pro-development lobby: it has so frightened some trade union representatives about prospective job losses, that they have sided with management against the conservation lobby. In reality, structural employment losses in forestry industries have arisen from new technology and clearfell practices, rather than the creation of new national parks, but this inconvenient fact is slid over by the industry as a whole. In one respect, however, the critics are correct; with the possible exception of the Australian Conservation Foundation, few environmental groups have demonstrated much sympathy for, or dialogue with, blue-collar workers. Fortunately the situation is now changing with more environmentalists focusing on the link between ecological and economic factors, as Australia undergoes major industrial and rural structural change.

Governments cannot so easily slide away, which explains why the commonwealth government is concerned its new Resource Assessment Commission should attempt a more rounded perspective on major natural resource allocation referrals. If democracy is to prevail, all potential stakeholders must have an opportunity to state their case (O'Riordan & Sewell, 1981). It is proper that economic realities, as articulated by their respective adherents, should be juxtaposed against the claims of ecologically-orientated groups. How such information becomes incorporated or neglected in decision processes is a matter of collective concern for all levels of government. Various interests will attempt to use intergovernmental relations as leverage to further their aims, but fortunately the checks and balances of the federal system will limit such impacts. All policy decisions are made against the background of harsh political realities and while in recent years the pendulum may have swung a little in favour of an extension of commonwealth powers and jurisdiction, there are many reasons why co-operative ventures also have to be pursued (Crommelin, 1985).

Local government

Missing in current studies of Australian environmental management is the role that municipalities play. While it is commonly claimed that local government is a creature of the states, enjoying no constitutional recognition, the reality is that many of the day-to-day planning decisions of local authorities, their siting of facilities and amenities, their role in road construction and provision of water or sewerage infrastructure and their concern for adjacent parks and reserves does have an ecological impact. While local government may possess few tangible means of enforcing environmental standards, the degree of co-operation or conflict with state and commonwealth agencies can have a marked influence on local amenity. It would be an interesting exercise to trace the funds from state and commonwealth sources that directly and indirectly contribute to environmental management at regional and municipal levels, but thus far in Australia no attempt has been made to gauge such impacts.

In recent times a number of federal initiatives have emerged, aimed at reafforestation, salinity prevention, total catchment management, soil conservation and land rehabilitation. Additional programs are likely in coastal and marine estuary management, agroforestry and regional climatic variation assessment, as part of international attempts to assess the likely impact of the greenhouse effect. More of the planning and management of regionally-orientated programs may well occur at the grassroots level, but the role of municipal authorities in such environmental initiatives is by no means clear. It is important to recognise the diversity and major geographical scale of continental Australia. The tendency in environmental federalism is often to seek uniformity, and while this may have some statutory and administrative advantages, perhaps a greater challenge lies in recognising different needs and opportunities in various parts of the nation. Innovative approaches and some experimentation need to be encouraged at the local level, while focus on national objectives is retained.

Conclusion

The principal evidence in this chapter is that intergovernmental relations in Australian environmental management are gradually shifting in favour of an increased federal role, perhaps in response to deficiencies in state administration as articulated through community concerns and the voluntary conservation movement. In part it reflects the growth of international environmental diplomacy, concerned with global ecological issues transcending the boundaries of nation states. But having made this point, it is clear that the Australian states and territories still carry the principal burden of natural resources management and this appears likely to continue into the foreseeable future.

There have been significant improvements in environmental protection and nature conservation during the past two decades, but only at the cost of protracted and at times acrimonious conservation controversies, which have cost the community a great deal of time, money and value modification. We need to move from the contemplation of past follies towards bolder experiments in environmental mediation. If Planet Earth is to be safeguarded and continue to yield its benefits, there is more than enough hard work ahead for all levels of government.

Bibliography

Australian Conservation Foundation, 1988. *Green Book* (Directory of Environmental Groups), Melbourne,.

Bates, G., 1983. *Environmental Law in Australia*, Butterworths, Sydney
—— 1984. 'The Tasmanian Dams Case and its Significance in Environmental Law', *Environmental and Planning Law Journal*, 1(4), 325–45.

Berry, J., 1977. *Lobbying for the People*, Princeton University Press, Princeton NJ.

Birkeland-Corro, J., 1988. 'Redefining the Environmental Problem', *Environmental and Planning Law Journal*, 5(1), 109–33.

Bradsen, J., 1987. 'Land Degradation: Current and Proposed Legal Controls', *Environmental and Planning Law Journal*, 4(1), 113–33.

Burton, J., 1980. 'Conservation Issues of the Last Decade', *BHP Journal*, 1, 40–47,

Caldwell, L., 1984. 'Political Aspects of Ecologically Sustainable Development', *Environmental Conservation*, 11(4), 299–308.

Chisholm, A. & Dumsday, R., eds, 1987. *Land Degradation: Problems and Policies*, Cambridge University Press, Cambridge.

Commonwealth of Australia, 1984. *A National Conservation Strategy for Australia*, AGPS, Canberra.

Coper, M., 1983. *The Franklin Dam Case: Commentary and Text*, Butterworths, Sydney.

Crabb, P., 1984. 'Whither the Murray? Politics and the Management of Australia's Water Resources', *Search*, 15(1–2), 36–41.

Craig, D., 1988. 'SIA and Policy-Making: The Relationship between SIA, EIA and the Decision Process', Faculty of Law, Macquarie University.

Crommelin, M., 1983. 'Resources Law and Public Policy', Reprint Paper No. 59, Centre for Research on Federal Financial Relations, ANU.

—— 1985. Federal–Provincial Cooperation on Natural Resources: A *Comparative Discussion of Problems and Solutions*, Intergovernmental Relations in Victoria Programme, Law School, University of Melbourne.

Dargavel, J., 1985. 'Allocating Forest Resources to Woodchip Exports: Articulated Impacts and Public Policy', Working Paper, Centre for Resource and Environmental Studies, ANU.

—— 1987. 'Problems in Australia's Mixed Forest Economy', *Journal of Australian Political Economy*, 21, 36–48.

Davis, B.W., 1980. 'The Struggle for South-West Tasmania', in *Interest Groups and Public Policy: Case-Studies from the Australian States*, ed. Scott R., Macmillan Co. of Australia, Melbourne, 152–69.

—— 1982. *Characteristics and Influence of the Australian Conservation Movement An Examination of Selected Conservation Controversies*, PhD thesis, University of Tasmania.

—— 1985a. 'Aftermath of the Tasmanian Dam Case: Protecting the World Heritage Area', *Environmental and Planning Law Journal*, 2(2), 167–268.

—— 1985b. 'Federalism and Environmental Politics—An Australian Overview', *The Environmentalist*, 5(4), 269–78.

—— 1986. 'Beyond Cost-Benefit Analysis: Project Evaluation in the Caring Society', Paper presented at National Environmental Engineering Conference, Institution of Engineers Australia, Melbourne.

—— 1988. 'Heritage Conservation in Australia: Some Issues and Dilemmas', *Australian Journal of Public Administration*, XLVII(1), 49–57

—— 1989a. 'Federal–State Tensions in Australian Environmental Management: The World Heritage Issue', *Environmental and Planning Law Bulletin*, 6, 66–78.

—— 1989b. 'Wilderness Conservation in Australia: Eight Governments in Search of a Policy', Seminar Paper, School of Social Sciences, Murdoch University 1988 (Reprinted in Special Edition, 'Wilderness: Past, Present and Future', *Natural Resources Journal* (USA) 29(1), 103–14).

Department of Foreign Affairs, Australian Information Service, 1980. *Flora and Fauna Conservation in Australia*, Canberra.

Dillon, M., 1985. 'Social Impact Assessment and Public Policy-Making', Working Paper No 5/1985, Centre for Resource and Environmental Studies, ANU.

Feiveson, H., Sinden F, Socolow R., eds, 1976. *Boundaries of Analysis: The Tocks Island Dam Controversy*, Ballinger Publishing Co, Cambridge, Mass.

Figgis, P., 1979. *The Politics of Wilderness Conservation in Australia: The Movement and the Issue*, Honours thesis, Department of Government, University of Sydney.

Fisher, D., 1980. *Environmental Law in Australia*, University of Queensland Press, St Lucia.

Formby, J., 1987. 'Environmental Impact Assessment: Where Has it Gone Wrong? EIA and the Tasmanian Woodchip Controversy', *Environmental and Planning Law Journal*, 4(1), 191–203.

French, J., 1980. 'Australian Forestry Policy: A Critical Review', *Current Affairs Bulletin*, 57(5), 4–16.

Gilpin, A. 1980a. *The Australian Environment: Twelve Controversial Issues*, Sun Books, Melbourne.
—— 1980b. *Environment Policy in Australia*, University of Queensland Press, St Lucia.
Green, R., 1981. *Battle for the Franklin*, Fontana/Australian Conservation Foundation, Melbourne.
Hall., C.M., 1988. *The Geography of Hope: The History, Identification and Preservation of Wilderness in Australia*, PhD thesis, University of Western Australia.
Hawke, R.J., 1989. *Our Country. Our Future*, Statement on the Environment by the Prime Minister of Australia, Canberra, July.
Hawkins, K., 1984. *Environment and Enforcement*, Clarendon Press, Oxford.
Head, B. ed., 1986. *The Politics of Development in Australia*, Allen & Unwin, Sydney.
International Union for the Conservation of Nature, 1980. *World Conservation Strategy*, A report prepared in collaboration with the United Nations Environmental Program and World Wildlife Fund, Gland, Switzerland.
James, D. & Boer, B., 1988. *Application of Economic Techniques in Environmental Impact Assessment* (Monograph), Macquarie University.
Jeffery, M., 1986. 'The Appropriateness of Dealing with Scientific Evidence in the Adversarial Arena', *Environmental and Planning Law Journal*, 3(1) 313–19.
—— 1987. 'Accommodating Negotiation in Environmental Impact Assessment and Project Approval Processes', *Environmental and Planning Law Journal*, 4(1), 244–52.
Kelleher, G., 1986. 'Australia's Great Barrier Reef Marine Park: A Conservation Strategy in Action', Paper presented to the Conference on Conservation and Development: Implementing the World Conservation Strategy, Ottawa, Canada, May–June.
Lipman, Z.M., 1985. 'The Cape Tribulation: The Legal Issues' (2 parts), *Environmental and Planning Law Journal*, 2, 131–42 & 206–14.
Morris, M., 1987. 'In the Evolution of Environmental Impact Assessment and Project Approval Processes', *Environmental and Planning Law Journal*, 4(1), 295–303.
O'Riordan, T. & Sewell, G., eds, 1981. *Project Appraisal and Policv Review*, John Wiley & Sons, Chichester.
Peres L, 1970. 'Ecology, Conservation and Politics', in *The Processes and Problems of Seeking Conservation*, Centre for Continuing Education, Australian National University, Canberra, 1–10.
Porter, M., 1985. *Environmental Impact Assessment: A Practical Guide*, University of Queensland Press, St Lucia.
Powell, J., 1976. *Environmental Management in Australia, 1788–1914*, Oxford University Press, Melbourne.
Routley, R. & Routley, V., 1974. *The Fight for the Forests*, Research School of Social Sciences, Australian National University, Canberra.
Scott, R., ed., 1980. *Interest Groups and Public Policy: Cases from the Australian States*, MacMillan Co. of Australia, Melbourne.
Shrader-Frechette, K.S., 1985. *Science Policy, Ethics and Economic Methodology*, D. Reidl Publishing Company, Dordrecht.

Solomon, D., 1988. 'The High Court's Present View of the Federal Balance', Paper presented at Eighth Federalism Project Conference, ANU, February.

Sornarajah, M., ed., 1983. *The South-West Dam Dispute: The Legal and Political Issue*, Faculty of Law, University of Tasmania.

Thompson, P., 1981. *Power in Tasmania*, Australian Conservation Foundation, Melbourne.

—— 1984. *Bob Brown of the Franklin River*, Allen & Unwin, Sydney.

Tighe, P. & Taplin, R., 1985. 'Lessons from Recent Environmental Decisions: The Franklin Dam Case and Rainforest in New South Wales', Paper presented at 27th Conference of Australasian Political Studies Association, Adelaide, August.

Ward, E., 1982. 'The Constitutional Basis for Commonwealth Involvement in Environmental Matters, Basic Paper No. 10, Legislative Research Service, Department of Parliamentary Library, Canberra.

Wendt, N., 1979. *Who has Power in Australia? An Examination of the Public's Ability to Participate in Government Decisions*, Honours thesis in Sociology, University of Sydney.

World Commission on Environment and Development, 1987. *Our Common Future* (The Brundtland Report) Oxford University Press, Oxford.

Yudelman, D., 1986. 'Maturity Management: A New Mineral Policy for Canada', *Resources Policy*, 1986, 29-39.

Zines, L., 1985. 'The Environment and The Constitution', in *Federalism and the Environment*, ed. R.L. Mathews, Centre for Research on Federal Financial Relations, Australian National University, Canberra.

9 Health care

Jim Butler

Intergovernmental relations have played an important part in the design and conduct of policy in the health sector, especially in more recent times. From having a rather limited role at the time of federation, the commonwealth has extended its influence in this field, primarily as a result of events in the 1940s and the 1970s. Its increasing role in the financing of health services, the provision of which lies in the domain of the states, has brought the financial aspects of intergovernmental relations in this area to the fore, particularly since 1975 when the commonwealth's policy of providing universal hospital insurance was achieved by the use of intergovernmental grants.

Although the politics of intergovernmental relations in health are undoubtedly of importance and have been examined from the perspective of theories of federalism (Gray, 1987), the emphasis in this chapter is largely, but not exclusively, on the economic dimensions of the problem. Given the large intergovernmental grant programs which have developed over the last decade or so, it is time to assess the way these programs are designed and whether there is any economic rationale in the assignment of functions in health care between the commonwealth and the states. This is particularly so given that the economic debates have centred upon whether, and to what extent, government intervention in health service financing and/or provision is justified rather than on the allocation of any set of responsibilities between levels of government.[1]

Accordingly, the section following outlines the analytical framework provided by the economic theory of fiscal federalism. This is followed by a discussion of intergovernmental relations in health in an Australian context and an appraisal of the assignment of functions and other aspects in terms of this framework. The importance of the health sector in the deliberations of the Commonwealth Grants Commission is examined, and the administrative arrangements for the conduct of intergovernmental relations are briefly reviewed.

Analytical framework

The conventional normative theory of public finance suggests that the economic case for a federal system of government arises out of efficiency considerations or the allocation branch of the multi-branch budget (Musgrave, 1959). This argument, formalised by Oates (1972) in what he called the decentralisation theorem, indicates that sub-sets of citizens within a country should be able to vote for themselves different levels of provision of public goods as long as the benefits are confined to the relevant sub-sets of citizens. On efficiency grounds, then, the role of the national government should be confined to the provision of national public goods (i.e., public goods whose geographic spread of benefits encompasses the entire population). This provides a basis for 'states rights' with respect to the provision of sub-national public goods.[2]

The pursuit of equity objectives—the distribution branch in Musgrave's schema—is argued to be properly a function of the national government. The problem with redistribution policies implemented at the sub-national level is that they may distort individuals' choices with respect to location. For example, suppose a particular region is pursuing a policy aimed at redistributing income from the rich to the poor. Wealthy residents who are not beneficiaries of the redistribution will have an incentive to emigrate to another region to avoid the tax burden. Conversely, poor non-residents who would qualify for benefits under the redistribution policy have an incentive to immigrate to the region. Such population movements would have the effect of eroding the tax base as wealthier residents departed and poorer residents arrived, thus frustrating the achievement of the redistribution objective.[3]

Separation of the efficiency and equity aspects of public goods provision in this way implies that the funding of public goods, whether at the national or sub-national level, should be through benefit taxation, i.e., taxation of individuals according to the benefits they receive from the public goods. The use of ability-to-pay taxation is confined to the national government and is to be used for distributional purposes only, as any departure from benefit taxation at the sub-national level indicates that redistribution is taking place.[4]

The translation of this theory into practice encounters a number of difficulties. Foremost among these are an imperfect correspondence between the geographic boundaries of jurisdictions and the geographic spread of the benefits of public goods (resulting in interjurisdictional spillovers), and the financing of public goods other than through benefit taxation at the sub-national level. In general, though, the model establishes a *prima facie* case for the provision of public goods at the state or local level unless their benefits are national in scope, and for the pursuit of distributional objectives being left with the national government.

Public-good aspects of health care

In order to discuss the assignment problem specifically in the context of health care, it is necessary to define what characteristics of health care qualify it as being a public good. The possible geographic spread of the benefits can then be indicated.[5]

There are few health care services which are 'pure' public goods either in the sense that one person's consumption does not detract from the amount available for others to consume, or in the sense that all consumers must consume an equal amount of the good. Quarantine services are an example of this polar case—by preventing certain diseases from entering the country the probability of catching the disease for each citizen, and therefore for all citizens, is virtually reduced to zero. Medical research also possesses 'pure' public good characteristics. For both these examples there is no spatial limitation on the spread of benefits. Accordingly they can be regarded as national public goods.

Of more importance in the field of health care services are external effects or spillovers, i.e., unintended, unpriced side effects or by-products of a transaction affecting those who are not a party to it. Such effects can be either physical (or tangible) or psychic. An example of the former would be the effect on residents of the pollutants emitted by a factory in a certain area. A psychic spillover arises when individuals not directly involved in a transaction are affected in an emotional or intangible way because of, for example, altruism or envy.

With regard to tangible spillovers, the most important example is the prevention or treatment of infectious diseases. The vaccination (treatment) of a person at risk reduces the probability of that person catching (spreading) the disease to zero and also reduces the probability of others catching the disease. The geographic distribution of this external effect is widespread, and provides a strong case for subsidisation of an immunisation program by the national government.[6]

Turning to psychic spillovers, these give rise to what Culyer (1971:202) regards as the 'key problems in health economics'. Altruistic spillovers may manifest themselves either as a concern for the general level of well being of fellow citizens (so-called general welfare interdependence) or as a concern for the level of consumption of specific commodities, such as food or housing, by fellow citizens (specific commodity interdependence). The existence of general welfare interdependence provides a case for redistributing income in favour of those whose circumstances give rise to the spillover. In the case of specific commodity interdependence, subsidising the relevant commodities may be sufficient (but not necessary) to eliminate the spillover.[7]

With regard to health care, specific commodity interdependence would justify the subsidisation of health care or health insurance, assuming it is the commodity health care and not health itself which is the focus of the spillover (Culyer & Simpson, 1980). Further, depending on the extent of the geographical distribution of these spillovers and whether or not they are reciprocal (citizens in each state are concerned about the level of consumption of citizens in each other state), national rather than sub-national government intervention may be required for their correction.[8]

Intergovernmental relations and intergovernmental grants

If an optimal or first-best assignment of functions was attainable in a federal system with the national and sub-national governments each providing the relevant public goods with a perfect correspondence between the geographic spread of benefits and the boundary of the jurisdiction, what scope would exist for any specifically *intergovernmental* relations? In general, there are at least two reasons why such interrelationships may emerge.

First, even in this rarefied world, the national government may wish to engineer grants between lower-level jurisdictions to correct for horizontal imbalance—a situation where some states would have to levy taxes at higher rates than others in order to raise the same amount of revenue (Buchanan, 1950). Second, even though there may be little or no intergovernmental financial relations, there may be administrative relations between various levels of government for purposes of information dissemination and co-ordination of activities, e.g., with respect to law enforcement activities. In reality, of course, 'existing fiscal structures do not conform with the normative model' (Musgrave & Musgrave, 1973:609). Imperfect correspondences resulting in interjurisdictional spillovers are likely to arise. In addition vertical imbalance—a mismatch between a state's revenue sources and expenditure responsibilities—may be a problem. These imperfections also suggest a role for intergovernmental grants.

The economic analysis of intergovernmental grants classifies them along three dimensions: first, according to whether the grant is conditional (specific-purpose) or unconditional (general revenue); second, whether the grant is matching (requires a matching contribution from the recipient) or non-matching; and third, whether the grant is open-ended (no limit on the total amount) or closed-ended (limited in amount).

The types of grants required to move the system towards an efficient outcome will depend upon the underlying imperfection to be corrected. If the grant is aimed at correcting vertical imbalance, then general revenue, non-matching, closed-ended grants are called for, and similarly for the correction of horizontal imbalance. If the objective is the correction of beneficial spillovers, intergovernmental grants to the spillover-generating jurisdiction are required, this being the analogue of a subsidy paid to individuals whose activities give rise to external benefits. Such grants should be conditional, matching and open-ended, and tied to the activities generating the spillover.

Intergovernmental relations

Under the original constitution, the commonwealth's role in health matters was restricted to quarantine with the Quarantine Act being passed in 1908. Increased commonwealth participation resulted from an outbreak of smallpox in 1913 and an influenza epidemic in 1918–19. A commonwealth Department of Health was formed in 1921

> to administer the *Quarantine Act*; investigate the causes of disease and death, establish and control laboratories for this purpose and assume control of the Commonwealth Serum Laboratories; collect sanitary data and investigate methods of preventing disease and factors affecting health in industry; administer subsidies to the States for the eradica-tion, prevention or control of any disease; conduct campaigns of prevention of disease in which more than one State was interested; administer the Australian Institute of Tropical Medicine; administer the control of infectious disease among discharged members of the Australian Imperial Forces; generally to inspire and coordinate public health measures; and carry out other functions which might be assigned (Sax, 1972:121–22).

The grounds for a major increase in commonwealth involvement in health care were laid with the passing of an amendment to the constitution in 1946. In common with various other countries, access to health care was increasingly being viewed as one part of a more comprehensive social security system and was consequently being used as an instrument to pursue more general redistributional objectives.[9] The commonwealth's first initiative in this area was by way of the National Health and Pensions Insurance Act 1938, establishing a scheme which included health insurance for the employed and pensions for the sick and unemployed (Kewley, 1973:159–65; Thame, 1974:311–18). However, with mounting international problems and the opposition of the medical profession to the scheme, it was never implemented.

Another important commonwealth foray into this area was the Pharmaceutical Benefits Act 1944, which established a scheme for the provision of prescribed drugs to all at no charge. While this scheme would certainly have been implemented, the declaration of the Act as unconstitutional by the High Court in 1945 thwarted this initiative. The High Court's decision motivated the commonwealth to seek to broaden its powers under the constitution via a referendum in 1946, a move which resulted in the addition of section 51 (xxiiiA) to the constitution.

This expanded the powers of the commonwealth to include 'The provision of maternity allowances, widows' pensions, child endowment, unemployment, pharmaceutical, sickness and hospital benefits, medical and dental services (but not so as to authorise any form of civil conscription), benefits to students and family allowances.'[10]

The constitutional amendments paved the way for increased direct commonwealth involvement in health care by way of 'sickness and hospital benefits' which could be paid to individuals and organisations. But the commonwealth had already undertaken another funding initiative with respect to hospitals by entering into agreements with the states. The Hospital Benefits Act 1945 authorised the payment of funds to states which agreed to provide public ward treatment in public hospitals at no charge and without means test. This intergovernmental initiative was, of course, also in pursuit of the objective of reducing the financial barriers to the use of health care.

The intergovernmental arrangements which arose out of the Hospital Benefits Act lasted only until 1949, when they were reviewed following the defeat of the Chifley Labor Government. The subsequent development of a commonwealth-subsidised voluntary health insurance scheme for medical and hospital benefits resulted in rewritten commonwealth/state agreements 'which involved the reimposition of both means tests and fees for public patients' (Scotton, 1974:68).[11] The new agreements, however, did not result in any direct intergovernmental financial relations (except for Queensland). Public ward hospital charges were set by the states (and did vary between the states)[12] with the commonwealth hospital benefits being paid to registered hospital benefits organisations. An analogous system operated for medical benefits based on fee-for-service medicine.

While the late 1940s and early 1950s saw an increased commonwealth role in the financing of health services, this did not result in an increase in intergovernmental activity in health care. While there were some intergovernmental programs, e.g., the national anti-tuberculosis scheme and funding of mental hospitals, the major commonwealth funding initiative relating to hospital and medical benefits did not actually include a large intergovernmental component.[13]

Following the above changes, the proportion of total recurrent health expenditures borne by the commonwealth remained relatively stable until 1975, at around 28 to 32 per cent, as illustrated by Figure 9.1. It was in this year that the national health insurance scheme (medibank) commenced, with the result that, in 1975–76, the commonwealth sourced just under 50 per cent of all recurrent health expenditure. The increase in commonwealth involvement in 1975, however, is not as dramatic if estimates of tax expenditures by the commonwealth are included with commonwealth direct expenditures. Including tax expenditures adds around 10 to 12 percentage points to the commonwealth's share from

1967 to 1975, with the result that its share then fluctuates from 39 to 42 per cent over this period. This is also illustrated in Figure 9.1.

Figure 9.1: Percentage of recurrent health expenditures borne by commonwealth and state/local governments, selected years, 1960–61 to 1985–86

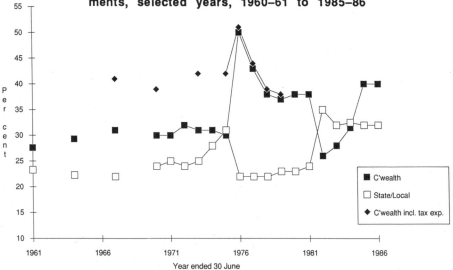

Year ended 30 June

Note: Data for several years in the 1960s are unavailable. The data series for the commonwealth including tax expenditures includes estimates of the value of tax expenditures by way of deductions for health insurance contributions and net medical expenses.

Sources: Deeble (1970:Table 3.10); Deeble (1982:Table 4); Australian Institute of Health (1988a:Table 3.03); and Australian Institute of Health (1988b:Table 9).

The medibank scheme provided medical benefits for the entire population through national health insurance based on private practice fee-for-service medicine. Now while it would have been possible for hospital benefits to be provided in an analogous fashion with the benefit being paid to the public (or private) hospital of the individual's choice, this method of providing hospital cover was not employed. The way in which hospital cover was arranged resulted in a major expansion in intergovernmental financial relations in health care provision.

Like its predecessor—the Chifley Labor Government of the 1940s— the Whitlam Labor Government had a policy of ensuring universal access to public ward treatment free of charge and without means test. This objective was achieved by means of a commonwealth/state agreement, *viz.* in return for the states agreeing to provide treatment on this basis through their public hospital systems, the commonwealth agreed to pay the states either 50 per cent of the net operating costs of all recognised public hospitals or the amount of such costs met by each state from its own sources, whichever was the lesser. These agreements, which came into effect during the latter half of 1975, were known as the hospital cost-sharing agreements.[14]

While various other commonwealth programs involving assistance to the states had been introduced by the Whitlam Labor Government over the 1973–75 period (e.g., the school dental scheme and the community health program), the hospital cost-sharing agreements accounted for most of the increases in specific-purpose payments to the states for health care in the latter half of the 1970s.[15] This increase is graphically illustrated in Figure 9.2, which shows the real value of such payments each financial year over the period 1961–62 to 1988–89.

The hospital cost-sharing agreements remained in place up to and including 1980–81, although they were modified to limit the commonwealth's contribution to 50 per cent of approved net operating costs by the Fraser Government in 1976 (Scotton, 1980:183–85).

Following consideration of the report by the Jamison Committee of Inquiry into the Efficiency and Administration of Hospitals, the commonwealth announced in April 1981 that the hospital cost-sharing agreements with States (other than South Australia and Tasmania) and the Northern Territory would not be renewed. These agreements were to expire on 30 June 1981 (Australian Treasury, 1982:22).

The cost-sharing grants were effectively absorbed into general revenue grants, although an allocation of funds continued to be identified as 'a commonwealth contribution towards the cost of health programs in the states and the Northern Territory' (Australian Treasury, 1982:22). Hence the term 'identified health grants' was used to describe this allocation. This arrangement was viewed as a transitional one, the ultimate objective being full absorption of the health grants into the tax sharing grants.[16] The only condition attaching to the identified health grant was that the recipient states and the Northern Territory continue to provide public ward treatment to eligible pensioners, people in special need and their dependents at no charge. States had a financial incentive to reintroduce charges for all other public patients as the grant to each state was reduced by the commonwealth's assessment of each state's revenue-raising capacity in this regard.

The reduction in specific-purpose payments occasioned by the move to identified health grants in 1981–82 is evident in Figure 9.2, while the extent of the substitution of identified health grants for specific-purpose payments is illustrated in Figure 9.3. This latter figure shows the commonwealth's payments to the states and Northern Territory for hospital funding from 1972–73 to 1988–89 as a percentage of GDP, with the specific-purpose/identified health grant distribution incorporated from

1981–82.[17] Both Figures 9.2 and 9.3 indicate a reduced commonwealth presence in the health care sector from 1981–82, given the nature of the identified health grants outlined above.[18]

These intergovernmental arrangements remained in place until 1984 when the medicare national health insurance scheme was introduced by the Hawke Labor Government. The identified health grants were continued, but a new specific-purpose payment—the medicare compensation grant—was introduced. This new grant was conditional upon the states providing universal access to public ward treatment free of charge, and was designed to compensate the states for the subsequent loss in fee revenue and any additional hospital costs imposed as a result of medicare.

Figure 9.2: Specific-purpose payments to the state/local government sector for health, 1961–62 to 1988–89 ($, constant 1980–81 prices)

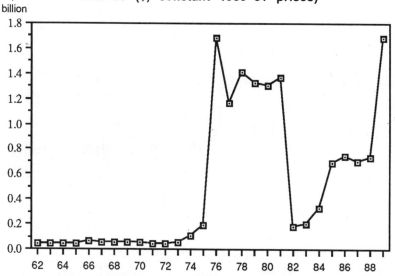

Notes: Figure for 1975–76 is affected by early payment of assistance for hospital running costs. From 1981–82 to 1987–88, identified health grants are treated as general revenue grants. For 1988–89 the CPI change has been taken as twice the June–December 1988 change, with the eight capital city weighted average being used from 1986–87 onwards.

Sources: Specific-purpose payments: Australian Treasury Budget Papers, various years. Consumer Price Index supplied by ABS.

This 'dual' system continued until the end of 1987–88 (see Figure 9.3), at which time both grants were replaced by a single specific-purpose payment—the hospital funding grant. The initial (i.e., 1988–89) distribution of these grants among the states and the Northern Territory is on a per capita basis weighted by age and sex. Future grants are indexed for award wage and CPI changes and weighted by age and sex. The hospital funding grants also include: an incentives package to encourage day surgery, post-acute care and the development of hospital cost accounting systems which attribute costs to the different types of cases treated by a hospital (i.e., case-mix sensitive hospital cost systems); a public provision adjustment to penalise per capita in-patient medicare benefit payments above a prescribed maximum and reduction in public patient access below a prescribed minimum; and additional support for the treatment of AIDS cases (Australian Treasury, 1988:60–62).

Figure 9.3: Commonwealth hospital funding for the states and Northern Territory, 1972–73 to 1988–89

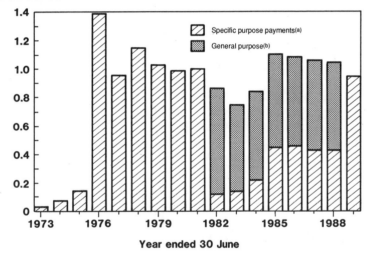

Per cent of GDP–

Year ended 30 June

Notes: a   Includes hospital cost-sharing grants (1975–76 to 1983–84), medicare compensation grants (1983–84 to 1987–88) and hospital funding grants (1988–89).

   b   Identified health grants.

Source: Australian Treasury (1988:58).

In concluding this historical overview, the particular position of Queensland warrants mention. Since 1944, this state has operated a public hospital system which provides universal access to both in-patient and out-patient treatment to all the state's residents at no charge, employing salaried medical staff.[19] This system has been retained regardless of the policy changes outlined above and as a consequence has given rise to some difficulties in intergovernmental relations. These have arisen because the commonwealth's policies have been designed for the most part with the other states in mind, and have not always been tailored to encompass Queensland's quite different policy. Two examples will be cited. The first relates to the commonwealth's health insurance policy introduced in the 1950s (the Page plan) which paid a higher rate of hospital benefits for insured as opposed to uninsured patients. Since the public hospital systems in all states other than Queensland imposed charges on public patients, the commonwealth's policy provided a financial incentive for such patients to buy cover. But public patients in Queensland had no need for insurance cover because of the 'free' public hospital system, so hospital cover was much less widespread. The Queensland government then received the considerably lower rate for uninsured patients for a much larger proportion of its hospital bed-days.[20]

The second example relates to the introduction of the medicare compensation grants in 1984. As already mentioned, fee revenue forgone as a result of eliminating public ward charges was an important determinant of the compensation grant. But Queensland had no fee revenue to lose so its grant, in per capita terms, was considerably less than those for the other states (see Table 9.2). 'This situation lies at the crux of the argument that ensued between the commonwealth and the Queensland government before the latter signed the Heads of Agreement' (Marshall & Mason, 1984:36). Queensland's lower per capita medicare compensation grant has, however, since been compensated by a higher per capita general revenue grant on that account as a result of the Commonwealth Grants Commission's relativities inquiry (Commonwealth Grants Commission, 1988a; Butler, 1988b). This matter will be raised again later.[21]

The assignment of functions

In terms of the analytical framework outlined earlier the division of functions with respect to health care in Australia does, in broad respects, conform with the assignment of allocative functions in the normative model. At least prior to the 1940s the commonwealth's role was limited to functions which could be viewed as national public goods, such as quarantine and medical research. In the late 1940s it became involved in the funding of an anti-tuberculosis program, combating an infectious disease of national concern. Health service provision has resided with the states which, except in more recent times, have levied charges for many services in the vein of 'benefit taxation'.[22]

An economic justification for the expansion of the role of the commonwealth which occurred in the 1950s and again in the 1970s and 1980s can also be sought in terms of psychic spillovers. If individuals gain from increased consumption of health services by others and this interdependence is sufficiently widespread, commonwealth involvement to internalise the spillover may be necessary. This does not justify commonwealth provision of services, but then the commonwealth's actual involvement in service provision has always been minimal, as the Australian Institute of Health has recently stated: 'The Commonwealth Government provides very few services itself. Its main involvement is in subsidising the provision of services by state and territory governments and the private sector' (Australian Institute of Health, 1988c:129). For example, commonwealth ownership of hospitals is confined to a small number of armed services and Department of Veterans' Affairs institutions.

Apart from any logic which may be found in the present arrangements in an efficiency context, the commonwealth does seem to have been motivated by more general equity considerations. To the extent that this is so, it is again appropriate that the redistributive policies be pursued at the commonwealth level, as indicated in the analytical framework.

The concurrence of the broad features of Australian federalism in the health sector with normative economic theory may, of course, be entirely fortuitous, being caused by accident rather than by design. Indeed, given the importance attached by some to 'basic political realities' (Scotton, 1982:20) as an explanation of the federal structure, economic factors may have been of minor importance in framing the assignment of functions. Nevertheless, the resulting assignment does have some measure of economic rationality associated with it. This is not to imply, though, that the specific policies adopted within this broad assignment also have this characteristic. This point will be amplified in the following discussion of the use of intergovernmental grants.

Table 9.1: An economic typology of hospital funding grants from 1975 to present

Year	Grants	Economic characteristics
1975	Hospital cost-sharing grants	Specific-purpose Matching (50/50) Open-ended
1976	Modified hospital cost-sharing grants	Specific-purpose Matching (50/50) Closed-ended
1981	Identified health grants (replaced hospital cost-sharing grants)	General revenue Non-matching Closed-ended
1984	Medicare compensation grants (paid in addition to identified health grants)	Specific-purpose Non-matching Closed-ended
1988	Hospital funding grants (replaced both identified health grants and medicare compensation grants).	Specific-purpose Non-matching Closed-ended

The use of intergovernmental grants

Attention here will be focused on the hospital funding grants, for these constitute the great bulk of intergovernmental grants for health care. First, an economic categorisation of the grants actually employed will be presented and the grants evaluated in terms of their possible policy objectives. Second, the use of intergovernmental grants *per se* compared to other possible policy instruments will be considered briefly.

As already documented, intergovernmental activities with respect to hospital funding commenced on a substantial scale in 1975. The types of intergovernmental grants which have been used since then, classified according to the criteria presented earlier, are listed in Table 9.1. The five major schemes which have been implemented over the period 1975 to the present encompass four different types of intergovernmental grant with the fifth (the 1984 grants) being an amalgam of two of the other types.

From a normative perspective, the specific-purpose, matching, open-ended hospital cost-sharing grants introduced in 1975 are an appropriate instrument for internalising interjurisdictional spillovers, subject to two qualifications. First, the provision of such grants to all states presumes that whatever spillovers do exist are reciprocal, but under these circumstances 'the determination of the efficient set of subsidies becomes quite complicated...because the subsidy to one economic unit depends on the subsidies provided for others' (Oates, 1972:71). The second qualification is that the dollar-for-dollar matching requirement may not be the most efficient matching rate. Nevertheless, this grant is the type of grant required if correction of spillovers is the policy objective.

The 1976 amendments to the hospital cost-sharing agreements were intended to impose a ceiling on the grants by requiring that the net operating costs be approved by the commonwealth for the purpose of cost sharing. If the commonwealth was concerned about the original cost-sharing grants leading to an over-expansion of hospital services, a more appropriate response would have been to change the matching ratio and retain open-endedness as indicated by the economic theory of spillovers.

The identified health grants were effectively lump-sum general revenue grants or block grants, as indicated earlier. Given that they were not required to be spent on health care services, states were free to use the funds for whatever purpose they saw fit. The medicare compensation grants and the hospital funding grants are also block grants without matching provisions, but are specific-purpose payments.

The absence of any matching provisions in the hospital grants since 1981 suggests that internalising spillovers may not have been the policy objective, for if it was, these instruments were certainly not those prescribed by economic theory. Another possible objective is the achievement of uniform national standards 'when regional governments undertake fiscal activities competitive with a national government's responsibilities' (Brown, 1984:8). If this is the case, the national government may need to provide economic incentives to the sub-national governments to expand their programs up to the desired national standard. Specific-purpose block grants are suitable for this purpose, but an objective of attaining national minimum standards would suggest that a systematic effort be undertaken to determine the extent to which each state was below the national minimum. There is no evidence of such considerations entering into the determination of the grant for each state.

If it is argued that the earlier hospital cost-sharing grants are motivated by the pursuit of national minimum standards, then application of the same cost-sharing ratio to all state governments would have been justified if either all states were 'equally below' the national standard and had the same expenditure elasticity with respect to the commonwealth subsidy, or the differing relativities of the states with respect to the national standard and the differing expenditure elasticities were such that they resulted in each state arriving at the national standard.[23]

In summary, it is not difficult to agree with Lane's assessment of specific-purpose payments in general:

> There is little evidence that the conditions incorporated in the various specific purpose grants in Australia have been framed in accordance with the economic theory of spillovers. In most cases it would seem that the rationale does not go beyond recognition that there is a national interest in the expenditure in question which justifies some action to increase it. Where matching ratios have been used, they seem to have been based on crude notions of "fair sharing" (such as dollar for dollar matching), rather than an analysis of the extent of spillovers or national interest. They have been uniform for all States, rather than differentiated according to different proportions of spillovers generated by the expenditures of different States. In most cases, the matching has not been open-ended, but cut out suddenly at some upper limit (Lane, 1975:61).

Before moving on to the second aspect of this discussion on the use of intergovernmental grants, it should be pointed out that little work of a positivistic kind analysing how the states have actually responded to the various grants listed in Table 9.1 has been done. An exploratory analysis of the hospital cost-sharing agreements was undertaken by Weier (1981), who found some evidence suggesting a leakage of funds into other expenditure areas by states following the introduction of the cost-sharing agreements. This issue, however, warrants more intensive investigation to determine whether or not a flypaper effect is at work.[24]

The second aspect of this discussion of the hospital grants concerns the decision by both the Whitlam and Hawke Labor Governments to secure universal hospital coverage by the use of intergovernmental grants. It is this policy which has accounted for the two major upsurges in specific-purpose payments in 1975–76 and 1983–84 evident in Figure 9.2. Why choose the intergovernmental route to securing public ward treatment free of charge in every state? Alternative policies based on direct payment of hospital benefits to individuals could have been implemented that would also have achieved universal coverage. Part of the answer lies in the government's belief 'that the best care for "hospital patients" would be provided through a system of salaried, sessional or contract services' (Sax, 1984:113). Implementing a hospital benefits scheme analogous to the medical benefits scheme would have meant reimbursing doctors on a fee-for-service basis for treatment provided in hospitals, a scheme which both Labor Governments wished to avoid. The intergovernmental route afforded the opportunity to secure access by all to public ward treatment through the states' hospitals, where doctors would be paid on a salaried, sessional or contract basis. Another part of the answer lies in the government's desire to protect patients against any extra-billing, i.e., charging above the schedule fee. This has been achieved by making hospitals responsible for the full cost of medical treatment.

The health sector and the Commonwealth Grants Commission

Although it is impossible here to do justice to the complexity of the issues surrounding the role of the health sector in the Commission's deliberations, no discussion of intergovernmental relations and health would be complete without at least a brief discussion of this matter.

The health sector figures prominently in the Commission's work for two reasons. First, in assessing each state's revenue and expenditure needs, the Commission has to estimate the extent to which interstate differences in revenue and expenditure are attributable to differences in government policy or efficiency in service provision as distinct from differences in fiscal capacity and the costs of providing services. The size of the health care sector makes it imperative that this be done carefully, but it is also an area bedevilled by conceptual problems and shortcomings in available data. Difficulties of this kind are particularly well illustrated in the 1981 and 1982 relativities inquiries (Commonwealth Grants Commission, 1981, esp. Vol. 1, 178–87; 1982, esp. Vol. 1, 112–43).

The second reason the health sector is prominent in the Commission's work is because of the large intergovernmental health grants. The Commission's assessments relate to the distribution of general revenue grants to the states. In making such assessments it has to decide whether and to what extent it will take into account assistance made available to the states by way of specific-purpose payments. The Commission has decided to treat the health grants by what it calls the 'inclusion approach', the result of which is that any horizontally unequalising effects of the actual distribution of the grants are over-ridden through a compensating variation in the assessed general revenue grants.[25] The effect of this on the distribution of medicare compensation grants is illustrated in Table 9.2. Column 1 in that table shows the actual per capita distribution of the grants among the states in 1986–87. Column 2 shows what the distribution would have been if the same grant total had been distributed in a horizontally equalising manner. The inclusion approach results in the differences between these columns being reflected in the Commission's assessed general revenue grants for the states.[26]

Table 9.2: Changes in per capita medicare compensation payments implied by CGC relative health needs factors, states and Northern Territory, 1986–87

	Actual distribution[a] ($ per capita) (1)	Distribution based on relative health needs factors[b] ($ per capita) (2)	Change (%) (3)= ((2)-(1))/(1)
NSW	74.53	60.44	-18.9
Vic.	63.78	60.09	-5.8
Qld	29.65	65.01	+119.3
WA	58.15	68.06	+17.0
SA	78.51	68.12	-13.2
Tas.	78.18	68.94	-11.8
NT	79.14	105.59	+33.4
States and NT	63.18	63.18	

Sources: [a] Commonwealth Grants Commission (1988a:Vol. II, Table C–12, 259).

[b] Calculated using three-year average relative health needs factors for states and Northern Territory in Commonwealth Grants Commission (1988a:Vol. I, Table 1–3, 8), population data in Commonwealth Grants Commission (1988b:Vol. 3, 359), and total medicare grants for 1986–87 of $1003m as per Commonwealth Grants Commission (1988a:Vol. II, Table C–11, 258).

As mentioned earlier, the medicare compensation grants and the identified health grants have been replaced by the hospital funding grants as from 1988–89. Any unequalising differences in the interstate distribution of the new grants are again likely to be overridden by the Grants Commission, with the exception of the AIDS funding, which has been legislatively excluded (or 'quarantined') from the Commission's equalisation procedures. From 1989–90 the incentives package and the public provision adjustment are also quarantined (Australian Treasury, 1989:66). The interstate distribution of the new hospital funding grants, however, is not likely to be overridden by the Commission to anything like the extent shown for the medicare compensation grants in Table 9.2. The new distribution, which is essentially on a weighted per capita basis, can be expected to approximate a horizontally equalising distribution.[27]

Administrative aspects

The emphasis of this chapter has been on the financial aspects of intergovernmental relations in the health sector, but this should not obscure the complexity of the administrative machinery which underlies the conduct of intergovernmental relations in this area.

The main forum for co-operation between the commonwealth and state/territory health ministers is the long-standing Australian Health Ministers' Conference (AHMC), which 'provides a mechanism for commonwealth, state and territory governments to discuss matters of mutual interest concerning health policy, services and programs' (Commonwealth Department of Health, 1987:75). Established in the 1940s, it originally included only the state health ministers but was expanded in the late 1960s to include the commonwealth minister. The Conference established the Hospital and Allied Services Advisory Council in the early 1960s, this council remaining in operation until 1980, when it was replaced by the Standing Committee of the Health Ministers' Conference (SCOHM). With the introduction of medicare in 1984 the commonwealth formed another advisory council—the Australian Health Services Council (AHSC)—which in many respects duplicated the functions of SCOHM. Consequently, in 1986, both SCOHM and the AHSC were abolished and replaced by the Australian Health Ministers' Advisory Council (AHMAC), comprising the permanent heads of each health authority (state/territory and commonwealth) and their associates. The AHMC and its advisory body AHMAC work on a purely co-operative basis and are not binding on any commonwealth or state minister.

Another important forum closely allied to the AHMC is the Ministerial Council on Drug Strategy. This comprises the health ministers (as does the AHMC) and an additional minister from each of the six states and the commonwealth. This council works closely with the National Campaign Against Drug Abuse (NCADA) and has endorsed several commonwealth/state cost-shared programs as part of the campaign.

The longest-standing advisory committee in the health sector with explicit intergovernmental representation is the National Health and Medical Research Council (NH&MRC). From its inception in 1936 it has included, among others, nominees from the commonwealth, state and territory health authorities. Currently it has four principal committees on medical research, health care, public health, and public health research and development. At any time these principal committees have a number of other committees, sub-committees, working parties and expert advisory panels examining a wide range of issues relating to health.

The multiplicity of committees which have been and are in existence as part of the administrative conduct of intergovernmental relations in health cannot be covered completely here. The AHMC sets up advisory committees on specific issues from time to time, e.g., the

Commonwealth/State Advisory Committee on Nursing Issues. This committee, in turn, has two sub-committees—the Nursing Education Subcommittee and the Nurse Laborforce Subcommittee. The AHMC also set up the Health Targets and Implementation Committee in April 1987 to build on the recommendations of the Better Health Commission. This Committee includes representatives from commonwealth, state and territory governments.

The National Therapeutic Goods Committee is an AHMAC committee which provides recommendations on the co-ordination and administration of controls on therapeutic goods. This Committee in turn has several sub-committees concerned with, among other things, codes of good manufacturing practice and advertising of therapeutic goods.

When the hospital cost-sharing agreements were implemented in 1975, a series of state standing committees (one for each state) and a national standing committee were formed to administer the agreements. These committees were disbanded with the termination of the agreements in 1981.

Other examples of commonwealth/state co-ordinating committees are the National Pathology Accreditation Advisory Council and the National Specialist Qualification Advisory Committee. The National Health Technology Advisory Panel (NHTAP) provides an example of an advisory committee to the commonwealth minister that allows membership of two state representatives.

This brief discussion gives some feel for the breadth of intergovernmental co-ordination which takes place in matters of health policy. It is evident that a plethora of committees have existed and continue to exist in order to co-ordinate policy, even in areas where no intergovernmental financial relations are involved.

Some issues for the future

While there are several possible health issues which may have implications for intergovernmental relations in the future, two which might be of particular importance are the problems of AIDS and organ transplantation.

From the first diagnosed case of AIDS in Australia in 1982, a total of 1187 cases had been reported by the end of 1988, of which 580 had died (Solomon, Doust & Wilson, 1989:Table 1). Given the steep increase in the number of cases detected and the substantial costs involved in treating people with the disease (Whyte, Evans, Schreurs & Cooper, 1987; Scitovsky, 1988), increasing budget allocations to the treatment of AIDS can be expected.

Being an infectious disease of national concern, the commonwealth clearly has a role in addressing this problem and has proceeded to do so through health education, research funding and the support of state-based programs. In 1984, the commonwealth established a 'scientific' committee (the AIDS Task Force) and a 'social' committee (the National Advisory Committee on AIDS—NACAIDS) to provide advice to health ministers on the disease. The functions of these committees have since been subsumed under the National Council on AIDS and the Intergovernmental Committee on AIDS.[28] By late 1984, all states and the Northern Territory had enacted mandatory notification of AIDS cases to their health departments, and subsequently to the NH&MRC Special Unit in AIDS Epidemiology and Clinical Research at the University of New South Wales. Combating the disease has given rise to small but rapidly growing recurrent grants to the states—$3.7 million in 1984–85 rising to an estimated $21.7 million in 1989–90 (Australian Treasury, 1987:Table 31; 1989:66). There will be increasing scope for intergovernmental relations surrounding this disease as the epidemic develops, both financially and administratively, e.g. with regard to the question of testing.

Organ transplantation is an area where advances in medical technology can be increasingly expected to expand the market for organs beyond state boundaries. If the ability to transport organs interstate is enhanced then the problem of levelling out the geographical variations in demand for and supply of organs arises. Informal arrangements have already developed between transplant co-ordinators in the states for the interstate transfer of organs, but as yet there has been no formal public policy on the matter. Again the situation would be one where the states are providing the services but commonwealth involvement may be necessary to assist in establishing a national database of potential recipients and in equilibrating the market for organs if, as will probably be the case, price is not used as a rationing device.

The role of federalism in organ sharing has been the subject of a report compiled by the Ethics and Social Impact Committee of the Transplant Policy Center at the University of Michigan (Ethics and Social Impact Committee, 1987). The report argues against complete reliance on either a purely national system or a pure state system for the organisation of organ distribution. The case against a state-based system is clear enough—the interstate flow of organs may be impeded resulting in a failure to match an available organ with a potential recipient. The case against a purely national system is made on the grounds of efficiency, justice, flexibility and research, and greater depersonalisation of completely centralised networks. One can only speculate on how long it will be before Australian federalism has to confront these challenges.

Endnotes

The advice, comments and assistance of J. Barker, J.S. Deeble, R.F.G. Hart, R.B. Scotton and C. Walsh are gratefully acknowledged. They do not, of course, necessarily agree with the views put forward here. The responsibilty for any remaining errors rests solely with the author.

1   Some examples are Doman (1986), Logan (1988) and Butler (1988a). An exception is the set of papers contained in Mathews (1983).

2   This conclusion holds under the following assumptions: first, that the costs of providing any level of output of the good are the same for the national and sub-national governments; and second, that national government provision of the good requires equal quantities of the good to be provided to all sub-sets of the population. With respect to the latter, Tresch (1981:569) points out that constraining the national government to provide equal service levels to all constituents makes the decentralisation theorem 'an exercise in the theory of second best'. He develops a first best justification for federalism based on 'misperceived preferences' in which sub-national governments know the preferences of their constituents with certainty but the national government's perception of their preferences is subject to a random error.

3   The third branch of Musgrave's multi-branch budget is the stabilisation branch concerned with macroeconomic policy formation. This can also be argued to be a function of the national government (Oates, 1972:ch. 1), but this argument is of minor significance to this chapter. While health policy in Australia has apparently been formulated at times with macroeconomic objectives in mind (Scotton, 1980), this has not generally been the case.

4   For a criticism of the conventional view that sub-national governments should not pursue distributional objectives, see Tresch (1981:ch. 30).

5   The concern throughout this paper is with the commodity 'health care' as opposed to 'health'. While the former is an input into the latter, health is also affected by a range of other factors, including diet, exercise, motor vehicle safety legislation and exogenous influences.

6   See Weisbrod (1961). It is not always the case that infectious diseases will be nationally transmitted. In less developed countries, for instance, outbreaks of such diseases can occur within well-defined geographic areas, in which case the argument for national government intervention, or any government intervention, may be considerably weakened (Perlman, 1964).

7   On the distinction between necessary and sufficient conditions in this context, see Brennan and Walsh (1977). The policy relevance of psychic externalities is not accepted by all, e.g., Mishan (1972:336) asserts: 'They play no part in economic policy and are ignored in all cost-benefit studies'.

8   The concept of psychic externalities is taken here as being quite distinct from the concept of merit goods, the latter having had quite a turbulent history in the theory of public finance with no sign of that turbulence receding. See Walsh (1987) and Head (1988).

9 Of the health insurance system which developed in Australia in the early 1950s, Sax (1972:126) asserts that it 'can be regarded as a social security scheme. Its administration by the Department of Health rather than the Department of Social Security is an accident of history which should not conceal what it really is'. An example of the combination of health and social security administration is provided by France where, in 1977, the ministries of health and social security were combined although they were separated again in 1981 (Lacronique, 1984).

10 Interestingly, the commonwealth's attempt to reintroduce the pharmaceutical benefits scheme in 1947, following this amendment, was again declared unconstitutional. For a discussion, see Galligan (1987:148–57) and Sax (1984:47–56).

11 Queensland was the only state which did not reintroduce public ward charges.

12 A list of public hospital charges levied in each state over the period 1952 to 1970 can be found in Senate Select Committee on Medical and Hospital Costs (1970:137).

13 'The commonwealth has been providing assistance to the states for health services and facilities since 1949–50, when it began providing grants for the control of tuberculosis. Grants of relatively minor amounts have also been made for blood transfusion services since 1953–54, for the disposal of ships' garbage since 1966–67 and for nursing homes and certain health education services since 1970–71' (Australian Treasury, 1978:46).

14 Private hospitals were not covered by these arrangements but received a subsidy of $16 per occupied bed-day.

15 In 1975–76, for instance, they accounted for $870 million, or 80 per cent of the total specific-purpose payments to the states for health of $1164 million. See Australian Treasury (1978:Tables 2, 21).

16 The specific-purpose payments for the community health program and the school dental scheme were also discontinued upon the introduction of the identified health grants.

17 The figures for 1975–76 include an estimated $216 million prepayment for services that would normally have been paid for in 1976–77.

18 The reduced commonwealth presence as a result of these changes has been discussed by Palmer (1982). See also the discussion by Scotton (1982).

19 Interestingly enough, it has also had the lowest cost per capita and/or per case treated of all the Australian states for some time (Butler, 1987).

20 The commonwealth benefit was 80 cents per day for uninsured patients and $1.20 per day for insured patients, with the latter increasing to $2.00 per day in 1958. In 1968, the proportion of bed-days provided to uninsured patients was 41.1 per cent in Queensland compared with a weighted mean of 15.9 per cent in the remaining states. See Senate Select Committee on Medical and Hospital Costs (1970:Tables 27, 36, 37).

21 Some other examples where Queensland's different position produced a different result include the 1975 hospital cost-sharing grants by which half its hospital operating costs were met by the commonwealth without any loss in fee revenue, and the reversal of this situation with the termination of these grants as discussed earlier.

22 The exceptional situation in Queensland has already been discussed.

23 The second assumption would mean that the further a state is below the national standard, the higher its expenditure elasticity would have to be, given a particular cost-sharing ratio. On the general question of grants to achieve minimum standards, see Oates (1972:91–93) and King (1984:132–33).

24 For an explanation and critique of the flypaper theory see Barnett (1985).

25 'The Commission does this because the allocations of specific-purpose grants among states and Territories tends to be arbitrary, seldom being related to expenditure needs or the capacity of governments to raise funds from their own sources' (Mathews, 1986:35).

26 For a more extensive discussion of this issue, see Butler (1988b).

27 Given that the incentives package is now quarantined, it will be interesting to see if, in future, a larger proportion of the hospital funding grants is channelled through this package to avoid the Commission's equalisation procedures.

28 For an examination and evaluation of the impact of federalism on AIDS policy development in Australia, see Ballard (1988). A more general discussion of the politics of AIDS can be found in Ballard (1989).

Bibliography

Australian Institute of Health, 1988a. *Australian Health Expenditure 1970–71 to 1984–85*, AGPS, Canberra.

—— 1988b. *Australian Health Expenditure 1982–83 to 1985–86*, Information Bulletin No. 3, Australian Institute of Health, Canberra.

—— 1988c. *Australia's Health*, AGPS, Canberra.

Australian Treasury, 1978. *Payments to or for the States, the Northern Territory and Local Government Authorities 1978–79*, AGPS, Canberra.

—— 1982. *Payments to or for the States, the Northern Territory and Local Government Authorities 1982–83*, AGPS, Canberra.

—— 1987. *Commonwealth Financial Relations with other levels of Government 1987–88*, AGPS, Canberra.

—— 1988. *Commonwealth Financial Relations with other levels of Government 1988–89*, AGPS, Canberra.

—— 1989. *Commonwealth Financial Relations with other levels of Government 1989–90*, AGPS, Canberra.

Ballard, J., 1988. 'The Impact of Federalism on AIDS', in Department of Community Services and Health, *Living with AIDS: Toward the Year 2000. Report of the 3rd National Conference on AIDS*, AGPS, Canberra.

—— 1989. 'The Politics of AIDS', in *The Politics of Health: The Australian Experience*, ed. H. Gardner, Churchill Livingstone, Melbourne.

Barnett, R.R., 1985. 'On the Flypaper Theory of Local Government Response to Grants-in-Aid', *Environment and Planning C: Government and Policy*, 3(3).

Brennan, G. & Walsh, C., 1977. 'Pareto-Desirable Redistribution in Kind: An Impossibility Theorem', *American Economic Review*, 67(5).

Brown, M.C., 1984. *Established Program Financing: Evolution or Regression in Canadian Fiscal Federalism?*, Research Monograph No. 38, Centre for Research on Federal Financial Relations, Australian National University, Canberra.

Buchanan, J.M., 1950. 'Federalism and Fiscal Equity', *American Economic Review*, 40(4).

Butler, J.R.G., 1987. 'The Queensland Public Hospital System—An Economic Perspective', *Australian Health Review*, 10(2).

—— 1988a. 'Issues in Hospital Funding', *Growth 36: The Economics of Health Care*, October.

—— 1988b. 'Specific Purpose Payments and the Commonwealth Grants Commission', in *Economics and Health: 1988 Proceedings of the Tenth Australian Conference of Health Economists*, ed. C. Selby Smith, Public Sector Management Institute, Monash University, Melbourne.

Commonwealth Department of Health, 1987. *Annual Report 1986–87*, AGPS, Canberra.

Commonwealth Grants Commission, 1981. *Report on Tax Sharing Entitlements 1981*, 3 Volumes, AGPS, Canberra.

—— 1982. *Report on Tax Sharing and Health Grants 1982*, 2 Volumes, AGPS, Canberra.

—— 1988a. *Report on General Revenue Grant Relativities 1988*, 2 Volumes, AGPS, Canberra.

—— 1988b. *Report on General Revenue Grant Relativities 1988: Working Papers 1984–85 to 1986–87*, 7 Volumes, Commonwealth Grants Commission, Canberra.

Culyer, A.J., 1971. 'The Nature of the Commodity "Health Care" and its Efficient Allocation', *Oxford Economic Papers*, 23(2).

Culyer, A.J. & Simpson, H., 1980. 'Externality Models and Health: A Ruckblick over the last Twenty Years', *Economic Record*, 56(154).

Deeble, J.S., 1970. *Health Expenditures in Australia 1960–61 to 1966–67*, PhD thesis, University of Melbourne.

—— 1982. 'Financing Health Care in a Static Economy', *Social Science and Medicine*, 16(6).

Doman, A.S., 1986. 'Health Insurance and Efficient Service Delivery', in C.M. Lindsay, et al., *Policies and Prescriptions: Current Directions in Health Policy*, Centre for Independent Studies, Sydney.

Ethics and Social Impact Committee, 1987. 'The Case for Federalism in Organ Sharing', Transplant Policy Center, University of Michigan, Ann Arbor.

Galligan, B., 1987. *Politics of the High Court*, University of Queensland Press, Brisbane.

Gray, G., 1987. 'Health Policy in Two Federations', PhD thesis, Australian National University, Canberra.

Head, J.G., 1988. 'On Merit Wants: Reflections on the Evolution, Normative Status and Policy Relevance of a Controversial Public Finance Concept', *Finanzarchiv*, 46.

Kewley, T.H., 1973. *Social Security in Australia 1900–72*, Sydney University Press, Sydney.

King, D.N., 1984. *Fiscal Tiers: The Economics of Multi-level Government*, Allen & Unwin, London.

Lacronique, J.F., 1984. 'Health Services in France', in *Comparative Health Systems*, ed. M.W. Raffel, Pennsylvania State University Press, Pennsylvania.

Lane, W.R., 1975. 'Financial Relationships and Section 96', *Public Administration*, 34(1).

Logan, J., 1988. 'Australian Health Policy: A Case of Government Failure', *Growth 36: The Economics of Health Care*, October.

Marshall, J.V. & Mason, C.A., 1984. *Financing Health Care and the Australian Health Insurance Experiment*, Health Planning Studies No.19, Planning and Development Unit, Queensland Department of Health.

Mathews, R.L., ed., 1983. *Hospital Funding*, Centre for Research on Federal Financial Relations, Australian National University, Canberra.

—— 1986. 'Fiscal Federalism in Australia: Past and Future Tense', Reprint Series No.74, Centre for Research on Federal Financial Relations, Australian National University, Canberra.

Mishan, E.J., 1972. 'The Relationship between Joint Products, Collective Goods, and External Effects', in *Externalities: Theoretical Dimensions of Political Economy*, eds R. Staaf & F. Tannian Dunellen, New York.

Musgrave, R.A., 1959. *The Theory of Public Finance*, McGraw-Hill, New York.

Musgrave, R.A. & Musgrave, P.B., 1973. *Public Finance in Theory and Practice*, McGraw-Hill, New York.

Oates, W.E., 1972. *Fiscal Federalism*, Harcourt Brace Jovanovich, New York.

Palmer, G., 1982. 'Commonwealth/State Fiscal Relationships and the Financing and Provision of Health Services', in *Economics and Health: 1981 Proceedings of the Third Australian Conference of Health Economists*, ed. P.M. Tatchell, Health Research Project, Australian National University Canberra.

Perlman, M., 1964. 'Some Economic Aspects of Public Health Programs in Underdeveloped Areas', in *The Economics of Health and Medical Care*, ed. S.J. Axelrod, University of Michigan Press, Michigan.

Sax, S., 1972. *Medical Care in the Melting Pot*, Angus & Robertson, Sydney.

—— 1984. *A Strife of Interests*, George Allen & Unwin, Sydney.

Scitovsky, A.A., 1988. 'The Economic Impact of AIDS', *Health Affairs*, 7(4).

Scotton, R.B., 1974. *Medical Care in Australia: An Economic Diagnosis*, Sun Books, Melbourne.

—— 1980. 'Health Insurance: Medibank and After', in *Public Expenditures and Social Policy in Australia. Volume II: The First Fraser Years 1976–78*, eds R.B. Scotton & H. Ferber, Longman Cheshire, Melbourne.

—— 1982. 'Discussion', in *Economics and Health: 1981 Proceedings of the Third Australian Conference of Health Economists*, ed. P.M. Tatchell, Health Research Project, Australian National University, Canberra.

Senate Select Committee on Medical and Hospital Costs, 1970. *Part 1. Report*, Commonwealth Government Printing Office, Canberra.

Solomon, P.J., Doust, J.A. & Wilson, S.R., 1989. 'Predicting the Course of AIDS in Australia and Evaluating the Effect of AZT: A First Report', Working Paper No. 3, National Centre for Epidemiology and Population Health, Australian National University, Canberra.

Thame, C., 1974. *Health and the State: The Development of Collective Responsibility for Health Care in Australia in the First Half of the Twentieth Century*, PhD thesis, Australian National University.

Tresch, R.W., 1981. *Public Finance: A Normative Theory*, Business Publications Inc., Texas.

Walsh, C., 1987. 'Individual Irrationality and Public Policy: In Search of Merit/Demerit Policies', *Journal of Public Policy*, 7(2).

Weier, A.M., 1981. *Commonwealth/State Funding Arrangements for Hospitals*, BEcon (Hons) thesis, University of Queensland.

Weisbrod, B.A., 1961. *The Economics of Public Health*, University of Pennsylvania Press, Philadelphia.

Whyte, B.M., Evans, D.B., Schreurs, E.J. & Cooper, D.A., 1987. 'The Costs of Hospital-Based Medical Care for Patients with the Acquired Immunodeficiency Syndrome', *Medical Journal of Australia*, 147(6).

10 Community services programs

Judith Healy

Making intergovernmental programs work

This chapter examines two community service areas: emergency accommodation and related services for homeless people, and domiciliary and community care for the aged and the disabled. In 1985, the commonwealth consolidated various subsidies into two intergovernmental programs: the Supported Accommmodation Assistance Program (SAAP), and Home and Community Care (HACC)—hereafter referred to by their not very euphonious acronyms. SAAP and HACC are chosen for analysis rather than other community services programs (for example, the Children's Services Program which mainly funds child care), because they illustrate key issues in intergovernmental relations as well as the implementation difficulties experienced by new programs. Controversies abound in SAAP and HACC, but I concentrate in this chapter upon the intergovernmental issues.

A characteristic of community services is that the commonwealth and the states are generally the funders rather than the service providers. As the 'community services' label implies, the services are mainly delivered by the voluntary rather than the government sector, that is, by a multitude of non-government agencies, some local governments and by community groups, and they are intended for people living in the community rather than in institutions. The community services field is, therefore, a complex mix of commonwealth, state and local governments, the voluntary sector, the informal sector (family, friends and neighbours), and the private 'for profit' sector. A second characteristic is that the commonwealth depends upon the states to implement joint policies, as the human services are traditionally a state responsibility.

The intergovernmental relations area includes the study of program implementation and intergovernmental management. Much discussion in the HACC and SAAP programs revolves around defining respective commonwealth and state management responsibilities in a federal system. This chapter does not discuss issues in service delivery, as the delivery network is better analysed from an interorganisational relations perspective, which places the commonwealth and state government agencies among the many other players in the network.

This chapter supports intergovernmental human services programs on equity grounds. Further, the pragmatic argument is that intergovernmental programs are well entrenched in modern government as there is no simple way to divide respective government responsibilities for complex social and economic matters. But there are important efficiency objections to intergovernmental programs, usually couched in terms of economic rationalism. Efficiency and effectiveness are frequently coupled terms in the public administration lexicon, but in practice there is often a trade-off. Intergovernmental programs are often criticised upon grounds of inefficiency and conflict:

> Joint commonwealth–state funding through specific purpose grants creates clumsy, sluggish, bureaucratic machinery...The two bureaucracies, federal and state, argue, each blaming the other for the failures that occur. The whole system flouts the most basic axioms of management. Services should be either commonwealth or state (Henderson, 1981:8).

Some recent studies take the view that intergovernmental conflict, although inevitable, is not pathological (see, for example, Buntz & Radin, 1983). Intergovernmental management should adopt a developmental perspective in dealing with conflict: productive intergovernmental relations develop as programs mature. More sophisticated management philosophies and techniques have facilitated better programs and reduced intergovernmental conflict in the USA (see, for example, Agranoff, 1986). Further, the political and bureaucratic climate has changed. Wright, (1982:43, & ch. 3) describes the recent phases in USA intergovernmental relations: competition between spheres of government and vested interests in the 1970s; a calculated phase of weighing up the costs and benefits in achieving mutual program goals in the 1980s; and currently a contractive phase involving shrinking federal aid, more state government power, and increasing legal and procedural program specifications.

Recent studies of USA grant-in-aid programs argue that the intergovernmental conflict perspective has been exaggerated. This more optimistic stance and emphasis upon interdependence is particularly relevant to community service programs:

> Our findings concerning the federal role are more optimistic than has been typical in previous studies...Instead of conflict, we found

cooperation...Instead of federal coercion, we found mutual accommodation...Mutually accommodating intergovernmental relationships are founded on the reality that each participant needs the other. Federal agencies have crucial legal and fiscal resources; locals have the operational capacity without which nothing can be achieved. (Peterson, Rabe & Wong, 1986:6)

I do not intend to paint quite so harmonious a picture of SAAP and HACC, partly because these programs are still young and are experiencing considerable teething difficulties. Further, they are primarily redistributive programs with specific requirements as to their target populations and service activities, and such programs are much more difficult to administer than developmental programs, which allow more discretion to the states and to the service providers (Peterson, Rabe & Wong, 1986) .

Packaging programs

The commonwealth has consolidated a range of separate subdsidies into broad-based cost-shared programs, in line with both the administrative trend in the USA and public sector amalgamations in Australia. The intention is to exert greater commonwealth policy control, to extract greater financial effort from the states, and to achieve greater managerial efficiency. The functions of these programs have been restructured in terms of broad social purposes, for example, providing transitional emergency shelter for the homeless, and keeping the aged and disabled at home rather than in institutions. This is a shift away from the separate program packages which were a response to specific population groups— the aged, battered women, youth; or which were based upon a specific activity—home help, home nursing, child care (Healy, 1988b). This move away from the clientele-based policies of the 1970s is justifiably viewed with suspicion by the lobby groups whose interests are now submerged in the larger programs.

The grouping of various subsidies into SAAP and HACC was a convenient rather than the only possible arrangement. Social programs are imbued with multiple social purposes and the perception of whose purposes are served changes over time. For example, the purpose of another commonwealth community service program, child care, has been variously portrayed as part of a health program for disadvantaged children, as an employment program to enable mothers to remain in the workforce, as compensatory child development and education, as a welfare program for 'at risk' children, and as contributing to equal opportunity for women.

Table 10.1 shows commonwealth expenditure and staff numbers organised in program budgeting categories. The SAAP and HACC programs are administered by the Department of Community Services and Health (DCS&H). The community services programs are small compared to both the health programs and residential care. The SAAP and HACC outlays amounted to 2.6 per cent of the department's budget in 1987–88, and directly involved around 2.0 per cent of department staff. The community service components are dwarfed by the large common-wealth health budget, for example, over $5 billion for 'health care access' which mainly comprises the medicare and pharmaceutical benefits schemes. The commonwealth specific-purpose payments, however, are important in terms of state government health and welfare budgets. In South Australia, both the SAAP and HACC programs are administered by the Department for Community Welfare (DCW), and in 1987–88 this commonwealth money amounted to 18 per cent of the state department's recurrent budget (DCW, 1988:150).

The following account of the background to the SAAP and HACC programs illustrates several points. First, the voluntary sector is a major participant. Second, commonwealth funding was sought by community lobby groups. Third, the commonwealth announcements of new programs were often hastily timed for elections, which caused considerable implementation problems. Fourth, the states remain wary about changing commonwealth priorities and funds.

Table 10.1: Annual expenditure and number of staff, DCS&H 1987–88.

Program	Outlays		Staff	
	$'000	%	Number	%
Health advancement	179 600	2.0	397	6.0
Home and community care	202 754	2.2	113	1.7
Residential care for elderly	1 366 289	15.3	478	7.2
Assistance for the disabled	299 998	3.4	1512	22.8
Therapeutic goods	13 088	0.1	318	4.8
Health care access	5 529 871	62.0	1752	26.4
Housing programs [a]	1 005 408	11.3	457	6.8
Families and children	231 692	2.6	192	2.9
Corporate management	91 910	1.0	1421	21.4
Total	8 920 608	100	6640	100

Source: DCS&H, 1988:94, 100–101.

Note: [a] Includes the Supported Accommodation Assistance Program constituting 0.4 per cent of the budget at $31 697 ($'000)

Supported Accommodation Assistance Program (SAAP)

Shelters for the homeless were run by voluntary-sector organisations with some help from state funds. However, in July 1984, the commonwealth announced the Supported Accommodation Assistance

Program under a five-year agreement with the states and territories to run until 30 June 1989. The program funds eligible organisations in the voluntary and local government sectors. SAAP was intended 'to provide a range of supported accommodation and related support services to assist people who are either permanently or temporarily homeless as a result of a crisis' (DCS&H, 1988:56). Seven different commonwealth and state arrangements were grouped into three sub-programs: general, youth and women (Chesterman, 1988:7). The history of this somewhat uneasy grouping is now reviewed.

The general sub-program mainly consisted of the overnight and short-term shelters providing beds for alcoholic and itinerant men, run by church agencies such as the Salvation Army and St Vincent de Paul. The commonwealth began to fund these in 1974 under the Homeless Persons' Assistance Program, through capital grants and beds and meals subsidies. Despite occasional bursts of publicity, this 'skid row'-labelled population does not rate high as a public issue and cannot mount photogenic public funding appeals. These general shelters have been the major winner under SAAP, as their funds more than doubled over the first three years of the program (Chesterman, 1988:20). In effect, the very inadequately funded men's shelters moved forward on the slip-stream of the higher profile social issues of domestic violence and homeless youth.

The youth sub-program evolved from the small Youth Services Scheme begun in 1979 within the Children's Services Program (Chesterman, 1988:7). This was prompted by the increase in the number of both homeless and unemployed youth and the growth of a disparate collection of youth shelters. The original intention of the Child Care Act 1972 was stretched somewhat by the inclusion of this commonwealth–state cost-shared program aimed at under eighteens.

The women's sub-program funded the refuges which opened in Australia from the early 1970s, mainly for the victims of domestic violence. Upon election in 1972, the Whitlam Labor Government appointed the first women's advisor and domestic violence was put on the agenda as a major social issue. The problem of how to obtain funds for women's refuges was solved by linking domestic violence with women's health, and funds were allocated in International Women's Year 1975 from the new Community Health Program (Dowse, 1984). The generous commonwealth funding formula was later reduced by the Fraser Government, nevertheless 97 women's refuges were being funded under this program when it ended (Department of Health, 1981).

After seven years of commonwealth project grants, in line with its stated policy of devolving health and welfare responsibilities, the Fraser Government transferred the responsibility for women's shelters to the states' health block grants in July 1981. The women's refuge movement strongly protested both its loss of national recognition and its abandonment to the variable state governments, and the protest culminated in a vociferous demonstration in Kings Hall, Parliament House. In July 1983, the newly-elected Hawke Labor Government announced the resumption of commonwealth involvement with a new Women's Emergency Services Program on a cost-shared basis with the states over and above their 1982–83 expenditures. However, the states maintained that they were unable to find the funds to match the extra $4 million for women's shelters, and the commonwealth finally waived the requirement and released the money in February 1984.

Meanwhile, a commonwealth review released in November 1983 proposed the consolidation of the piecemeal subsidy programs under the umbrella of crisis accommodation. The men's and the youth shelters favoured the more secure funding arrangement, but the women's shelters were strongly opposed: they wanted to maintain national visibility in a separate program; they feared that matched state funding would constrain expansion; and they believed that they offered a skilled range of intervention on domestic violence, not just crisis accommodation.

Nevertheless, the SAAP program went ahead and has now entered a second stage. The Supported Accommodation Assistance Act 1989 authorises the commonwealth to enter into another five-year agreement with the states and territories to run until 30 June 1994. The vicissitudes of the first five years and the import of the changes in the new act will be discussed later in this chapter.

Home and Community Care (HACC)

Commonwealth aged care policies have been fundamentally reassessed during the 1980s. The impetus for the new HACC program was the *House of Representatives Inquiry* (McLeay Report, 1982) which criticised the concentration of commonwealth funds upon institutional care and urged that funds be redirected to community services to keep people out of institutions. The *Nursing Homes and Hostels Review* (Department of Community Services, 1986) later pointed out that the provision of nursing home beds was high in comparison to other OECD countries, and recommended a ceiling upon the rate of institutional growth.

These reviews were prompted by the growing number of elderly people (a projected doubling of those aged 75 years and over by the end of this century), and by the rapid growth and cost of institutional care. The commonwealth now wishes to harness community services to a comprehensive policy on long-term care for the aged and the disabled for both humanitarian and financial reasons. The three-pronged commonwealth strategy is to limit institutional places, to require assessment before entry to nursing homes, and to expand the community services to target the 'at risk' population (Healy, 1990).

The HACC program was announced by the Hawke Labor Government before the December 1984 election. Unlike SAAP, the eligible providers include state governments, which deliver some services. This has shaped the HACC program by introducing an extra dimension for intergovernmental negotiation. HACC is intended 'to provide a range of home and community based support services...[to] people living in the community who, in the absence of basic maintenance and support services, might otherwise be admitted to nursing homes and hostels before they need such an intensive level of care' (DCS&H, 1988:23). It is directed at three main groups: the frail elderly, younger people with disabilities, and their carers. The funded services include: home help and personal care, home maintenance and modification, food services, community respite care, transport services, community paramedical services, community nursing, assessment and referral, education and training for service providers and users, and information and co-ordination.

HACC subsumes four commonwealth acts which had never operated as one coherent program (Brennan, 1984). The Home Nursing Subsidy Act 1956 was primarily a health policy which subsidised the salaries of registered nurses in the district nursing services. The next three initiatives, prompted by the state health ministers, were announced during the 1969 election campaign, with the Gorton Liberal Government envisaging considerable political mileage in assisting the elderly and bolstering the voluntary sector with a scatter of small subsidies to popular local projects.

The States Grants (Home Care) Act 1969, administered by the Department of Social Security, offered cost-shared home help, cost-shared aged care welfare officer salaries, and 2:1 construction costs for senior citizen's centres. The States Grants (Paramedical) Services Act 1969, administered by the Department of Health, matched the salaries for paramedical staff. The Delivered Meals Subsidy Act 1970 bypassed the states and directly subsidised the meals delivered by voluntary agencies such as Meals on Wheels and by local government.

As provided for in the HACC agreement, the commonwealth and states reviewed the program and subsequently agreed to continue after the first triennium ended in mid-1988. The implementation and management of the HACC program has been accompanied by considerable intergovernmental tension.

Commonwealth policy dominance?

Constitutional and fiscal powers in federal systems are assumed to confer central power, but is the commonwealth entitled to overriding policy dominance? Bakvis and Chandler (1987:4) point out that as federal systems are designed to divide power, it is harder for a central government to exert control in a federal than in a unitary system, and that hierarchical control mechanisms tend to be relatively weak. The study of policy implementation illuminates intergovernmental relations, and community services are a good example of an area where 'policy implementation is not the concern of a single hierarchically integrated organisation, but depends rather on the collaboration of a number of independent organisational units from the public and private sectors' (Hanf & Toonen, 1985:vi).

Constitutional power

As the commonwealth government has no specific constitutional power for welfare services (apart from social security), it has no constitutional mandate to flourish, which paradoxically can be a source of power in intergovernmental negotiations, as the commonwealth can withdraw from programs. The funds (usually reduced) are then included either in general-purpose or block grants to the states in the Commonwealth Grants Commission allocations.

The constitution originally assigned only very limited social security powers to the commonwealth (Kewley, 1980). Section 51 gave the power to enact legislation on old age pensions and invalid pensions. It was not until a post war 1946 amendment that the range of other social security pensions, benefits and allowances was validated and extended under section 51 (xxiiia). The specific-purpose payments to the states for welfare programs are made under section 96, although the state governments (or at least their treasuries) prefer money with fewer strings attached. There was considerable intergovernmental tension during the Whitlam era when specific-purpose payments rose from 7 per cent to nearly 18 per cent of all government public expenditures for social purposes (Scotton & Ferber, 1980:8).

The most controversial federal funds are those under the general purpose section 81 power, which bypass the states and are paid directly to local government, voluntary-sector agencies or community groups. The state of Victoria challenged the commonwealth's use of section 81 in directly funding community organisations under the Whitlam Government Australian Assistance Plan. The Plan survived the challenge in the High Court by a narrow margin, but the ruling did not establish conclusively the power of the commonwealth to intervene directly in welfare services in each state (Graycar, 1981). This is one of the few examples of judicial intervention in resolving intergovernmental welfare program disputes in Australia, although the courts frequently arbitrate in the United States.

Table 10.2 shows the acts under which funds for the various community service programs are appropriated, the year enacted, and the relevant constitutional power. The funds for the earlier programs were mainly appropriated through the broad section 81 power, whereas the 1985 acts set up cost-shared programs with the states under the section 96 power. The Hawke Government thus no longer operates these programs under shaky constitutional powers, nor exerts central power by bypassing the states. However, the commonwealth motivation for these changes was more fiscal than constitutional, as the operative principle in both the SAAP and HACC programs is cost sharing.

Table 10.2: Commonwealth community services legislation, year enacted, and the relevant section of the constitution.

Program	Act	Year	Section
Supported Accommodation Assistance (SAAP)	Supported Accommodation Assistance Act	1985	96
SAAP subsumes the following:			
Family Services Support Scheme accommodation;			
Child Care in Women's Refuges; Youth Services Scheme:	Child Care Act	1972	81
	Homeless Persons Assistance Act	1974	81
Women's Emergency Service Program		1984	96
Home and Community Care (HACC)	Home and Community Care	1985	96
HACC subsumes the following:			
	Home Nursing Subsidy Act	1956	81
	States Grants (Home Care) Act	1969	96
	States Grants (Paramedical Services) Act	1969	96
	Delivered Meals Subsidy Act	1970	81

Fiscal power

The Australian literature on federalism assumes central dominance because of the commonwealth's monopoly over income tax. The financing of welfare received little analysis until the late 1970s (see, for example, Mendelsohn, 1983), then the research concentrated upon fiscal federalism (see, for example, Scott & Graycar, 1983). This direction was sign-posted by the ANU Centre for Research on Federal Financial Relations, and reinforced for the pragmatic reason that expenditure data is available from the commonwealth but is otherwise hard to gather. Further, the commonwealth wants the money trail traced, ostensibly in the pursuit of greater financial accountability in welfare (see, for example, Baume Report, 1979; Auditor-General, 1988).

The argument runs that the government that controls the purse controls policy. The first question to ask about the community services area is whether the commonwealth is fiscally dominant, that is, does the commonwealth contribute most of the program funds? The second question addressed throughout this chapter is, to what extent does financial power confer policy power?

Table 10.3 shows that both commonwealth and state governments significantly increased their contributions over the first funding cycle in both programs. The commonwealth contribution to SAAP now hovers at around 60 per cent. In HACC, the commonwealth share rose from 51 per cent prior to the program in 1984–85 to 58 per cent in 1987–88. The funding formula and the respective shares were keenly negotiated. A cost-shared program implies equal shares, but the states managed to negotiate several favourable modifications to the HACC agreement, while in the first SAAP agreement the commonwealth allowed the states to count some 'SAAP like' projects (Chesterman, 1988:153).

Table 10.3: Expenditure by the commonwealth and the states–territories on SAAP and HACC

Program	Commonwealth		States		Total	
	$m	%	$m	%	$m	%
SAAP [a]						
1984–85					43.2	
1985–86					55.4	
1986–87					68.7	100
1987–88	55.2	62	34.4	38	89.6	100
1988–89 (est.)	62.2	61	40.0	39	102.0	100
HACC [b]						
1984–85	78.5	51	75.5	49	154.0	100
1985–86	90.8	53	81.3	47	172.1	100
1986–87	135.7	56	105.1	46	240.8	100
1987–88	169.4	58	123.0	42	292.4	100
1988–89 (est.)	209.0	59	147.7	41	355.7	100

Notes: [a] SAAP Review, 1988:1, 33, 148; DCS&H, 1988:57.

[b] HACC Review, 1989:3; DCS&H, 1988:24.

Therefore, the commonwealth does fund the larger share (around 60 per cent) and does claim the stronger policy voice. The auditor-general holds that the high level of commonwealth funding in joint programs warrants commonwealth policy domination, and castigated the DCS&H for not more actively pursuing commonwealth objectives in the HACC program (Auditor-General, 1988:4, 30). This is a commonwealth 'top-down' perspective, but the fiscal picture looks very different to the service providers. Many of the SAAP and HACC services are provided by voluntary-sector agencies, but beyond asserting that their contribution is substantial, there is no cost estimate. Very little is known about the large voluntary sector contribution to health and welfare, and although voluntary agencies receive perhaps 40 per cent of their revenue from government, there is considerable variation (Milligan et al., 1984). Local government, especially in Victoria, also contributes a substantial amount to the HACC area (Bowman & Healy, 1988:191).

A striking example of the voluntary-sector contribution is Meals on Wheels, where the meals are cooked and delivered to frail and disabled people in their own homes by unpaid volunteers. For example, government money comprises less than one-quarter of the annual revenue of Meals on Wheels SA Inc. (Leahy, 1987). The service operates in South Australia mainly through the efforts of 8000 volunteers who cook and deliver 3700 meals per day (Meals on Wheels, 1986). The scale and cheapness underlines why government wishes to bolster the voluntary sector in delivering community services, and why the celebration of such 'community care' is an important part of the government devolution rhetoric.

The federal rationale

The rationale for commonwealth involvement in social programs is based upon the following grounds: the need for a national policy on some social issues; the commonwealth role in promoting innovation; and the pursuit of equity.

A national policy

The SAAP and HACC community service areas attracted enough public recognition to gain a place on the national agenda. The aged have traditionally been a strong political claimant group on the basis of 'age' as much as 'need', and the commonwealth views the condition of the aged as a national responsibility. The national claim of the homeless is argued more on redistributive grounds. This claim was pushed higher on the national agenda by the women's movement, which achieved public recognition for the problem of domestic violence. The national spotlight now includes youth, as the second reading speech for the amended SAAP program promised 'major improvements to the government's response to the problem of homeless young people' (Parliamentary Debates, 1989:2007).

The formulation of a national policy raises vexed questions as to whether the commonwealth can impose one policy upon each state, and whether unity is more desirable than diversity. A unified policy implies a normative view despite the fact that there is no agreement as to the best service model. The unity versus diversity debate also invokes public choice theory, which supports diversity and competition, although few of the clients in these social programs resemble the consumers in a perfect market who can shop around or move to where the best services are on offer. Nevertheless, the diversity argument is an important objection to a unified program.

The community service structures differ in each state, which militates against the operation of a national program. For example, home care services are delivered mainly by local government in Victoria, local voluntary groups in New South Wales, regional state authorities in South Australia, central voluntary associations in Western Australia, and local groups with state health department administration in Queensland and Tasmania (Shannon & Foster, 1987:106). However, despite the different service structures the domiciliary service outputs have been very similiar (Healy, 1988a). A decade of commonwealth funding has shaped similar service patterns, which lends support to the thesis that central programs exert a unifying influence over time. There is also a trend to increasing state government responsibility and funding in community services for the aged and the disabled.

Innovation

Central governments claim a key role in promoting social experimentation (Rivlin, 1971), although state governments have convincingly demonstrated that innovation is not the sole preserve of central government (see, for example, Parkin & Patience, 1981). Nevertheless, innovation is regarded as inherently desirable, and the commonwealth is keen to encourage innovation in the HACC program as part of the process of restructuring long-term care for the aged and disabled. From 1987–88, the commonwealth earmarked $94 million over four years in unmatched funds for innovative projects (the project funding to be later incorporated in the HACC funds). The Supported Accommodation Assistance Act 1989 also calls for 'a range of innovative accommodation and non-accommodation service models'.

The intergovernmental challenge is to agree upon mutually acceptable directions and new projects. In some instances the commonwealth is dissatisfied with the state system or the traditional service providers, while the states regard the demonstration projects as interference in their domain. For example, in South Australia, the state government domiciliary services regard some of the projects as commonwealth meddling and a waste of scarce resources. Futher, the other states accuse Canberra of accepting New South Wales and Victoria as the norm. Mutual agreement is desirable because centrally funded innovation has a history of lapsing with the earmarked funds.

Equity

The pursuit of equity is the main rationale for central intervention, that is, a redistribution between states and between population groups. The HACC program calls for the allocation of services upon the basis of 'needs' rather than 'age'. 'Need' is a slippery concept and is defined in the HACC program as an incapacity to carry out the tasks of daily living, leading to premature institutional care. In addition, various priority groups are listed as warranting improved access. Equity considerations also enter the debate over the importance of preventive 'quality of life' goals versus the commonwealth goal of concentrating maintenance services upon people 'at risk' of entering commonwealth-subsidised nursing homes. There are also equity implications in the extension of HACC services to the young disabled as well as the aged, which greatly increases the number of potential clients (ABS, 1989), and the number of lobby groups.

Equity issues are important as these community services programs include both developmental and redistributive goals. Peterson, Rabe and Wong (1986, 15) define developmental policies as those broadly intended 'to improve the economic position of a community in its competition with other areas'; whereas redistributive policies are those 'that benefit low-income or otherwise especially needy groups in the community'. The equity implications and the ensuing dynamics of intergovernmental relations are now discussed.

Developmental policies

The SAAP and HACC programs have achieved developmental aims in that the funds have expanded. This is a major achievement in an era of budgetary restraint. Table 10.3 shows that total commonwealth and state expenditures upon SAAP rose from $43.2 million in 1984–85 to $89.6 million in 1987–88. In addition, commonwealth grants for capital purchases and upgrading are available to the states on a per capita basis under the Crisis Accommodation Program. These specific-purpose grants paid to state housing authorities totalled $40.79 million in the three years to June 1987 (Chesterman, 1988:23). In the HACC program, commonwealth and state expenditure more than doubled in the first full three years, rising from $172.1 million in the first year of the program in 1985–86 to an estimated $355.7 in 1988–89.

The scope and scale of the services have increased significantly. However, the details are unknown as the central data collection systems are still being developed. In the SAAP program, some 800 services currently operate from about 1200 outlets, which on any one day assist more than 11 000 people (Commonwealth of Australia Parliamentary Debates, 1989:2006). However, service expansion under SAAP was modest, with only a one-third increase in the number of new projects over three years (Chesterman, 1988:1, 29). Both commonwealth and state governments accepted that the existing service providers were severely under-resourced, and concentrated upon consolidation by increasing staffing levels, raising salaries, and improving working conditions. This was reinforced because the service providers on the state-level advisory committees were reluctant to recommend new services when their own were under-funded (Chesterman, 1988:28).

Aggregate figures are not yet available on HACC, partly because the more varied services are harder to count. HACC began with 2380 projects and claims considerable expansion since then, for example, 450 new or expanded services were approved in New South Wales, and home help hours were increased by nearly one-third in Victoria (Saunders, 1989:5, 63).

The commonwealth devised complicated fiscal strategies to extract greater financial effort from the states. To encourage the states to participate, a one-off unmatched $10 million was offered in the HACC program in 1984–85, followed by tapering commonwealth subsidies. The commonwealth–state ratio for the new money tapered from 3:1 in 1985–86, to 2:1 in 1986–87, to 1:1 in 1987–88. An expansionary clause requires the states to thereafter expand their annual outlay by 20 per cent unless otherwise negotiated. (A less ambitious expansionary clause has also been included in the new SAAP agreement.) Extra unmatched funds are available to those states who exert this 'maximum effort'. Despite these inducements the states have been slow to gear up, given the complexities of the HACC program, the dependence upon the voluntary sector for service provision, and the cost to the states. In the first triennium, the commonwealth spent far less than its appropriation, which was difficult for the minister to justify to cabinet annually whilst also claiming increasing community need.

Redistributive policies

Redistributive achievements are more difficult to assess as very little information is as yet available on the clientele of either program. The commonwealth is attempting to equalise the states' financial outcomes by offering matched funds on a population basis to the states in order to promote per capita equity. However, from a state budgetary perspective this appears inequitable as it disadvantages the high-spending states who have to support the recurrent costs of earlier expansions in their service infrastructure. Generally speaking, the economic rationale of the commonwealth is to take the national average. This pulls up the low-spending states, but pulls down the high-spending states and perhaps the quantity and quality of their services. More complicated funding clauses provoke more intergovernmental negotiations, as each state wants the most advantageous formula. For example, South Australia with the oldest state demographic structure unsuccessfully proposed a share of the HACC funds based on the elderly population rather than the total population.

Commonwealth expenditure on community services for the aged in each state has varied greatly over the years both in aggregate and in each subsidy program (ACIR, 1983; Howe, 1987). The total commonwealth and state expenditure in each state on age services cannot be explained by predictive factors such as the number of elderly or the number of nursing home beds. The variable pattern is in part due to the earlier confusing programs and to the different service structures. Some states did not 'participate', for example, in the paramedical program which required services to visit people at home rather than be offered from hospital sites, which suited the system in South Australia but not in the other states. Some states, such as Queensland, lagged in finding the funds to match the commonwealth; others, such as South Australia, encouraged commonwealth subsidised services such as meals rather than commonwealth–state cost-shared services such as home help.

Table 10.4 shows the per capita commonwealth expenditure on community services for the population aged 65 years and over, in the states by selected years. In 1974–75, four years after commonwealth funding began, the per capita expenditure varied from a high of $24.20 in Tasmania to a low of $11.70 in New South Wales. The differences between the states have persisted in the HACC funds, which are in large part governed by the allocations made under the previous acts. In 1987–88 the estimated commonwealth per capita expenditure on the population aged 65 years and over ranged from $69.6 in Queensland to $136.2 in Western Australia, an over 90 per cent range of variation.

Table 10.4: Commonwealth outlays on community care, $ per capita 65 and over, selected years (state rank order in brackets)

	NSW/ACT	Vic.	Qld	SA/NT	WA	Tas.	Range
1974–75	11.7	12.8	20.4	20.3	20.3	24.2	90%
	(6)	(5)	(2)	(3)	(3)	(1)	
1985–86	78.2	93.0	72.3	80.0	120.5	104.8	67%
	(5)	(3)	(6)	(4)	(1)	(2)	
1987–88	100.1	126.7	69.6	88.0	136.2	75.8	96%
	(3)	(2)	(6)	(4)	(1)	(5)	

Source: Shannon & Foster, 1987:117; *DCS&H*, 1988:24; ABS, 1987.

The considerable variation in SAAP expenditure between the states also results partly from historical differences. For example, South Australia had a well established state program for women's shelters prior to SAAP (Chesterman, 1988:30). In 1986–87 the commonwealth–state per capita expenditure upon SAAP was lowest in the three most populous states (New South Wales, Victoria and Queensland). A more complicated funding formula in the second five-year agreement is intended to reduce these state variations (Chesterman, 1988:ch. 9).

The SAAP program is inherently redistributive. As the minister pointed out in the second reading speech, the program provides assistance 'to the most disadvantaged people in Australia—people who are poor with insecure housing, many of whom having suffered physical abuse, addiction or institutionalisation' (Commonwealth of Australia Parliamentary Debates, 1989:2006). The program initially concentrated upon developmental goals, and redistributive debates revolved around allocations between the three sub-groups. The commonwealth did not specify internal priorities, and given the controversy surrounding the establishment of SAAP, was happy to leave these recommendations to the states. Therefore, SAAP experienced much less intergovernmental tension in the implementation stage than HACC.

The commonwealth now proposes more specific redistributive aims, which will increase intergovernmental negotiations and change the program advisory structure. The new act identifies a broader range of target groups and includes other service models besides shelters. It also requires equitable access for Aboriginal people and people from non-English-speaking backgrounds.

The 1985 HACC agreement set out detailed redistributive aims, in terms of preventing institutional admission, extending coverage to the younger disabled, and promoting equity for geographic regions and groups such as migrants, Aborigines and the financially disadvantaged. The HACC agreement left the quantification of these priorities to the states, which provoked considerable competition between the various interest groups. Current redistributive issues are the extent to which additional funds and existing services will be offered to the young disabled in addition to the aged, and to support and respite services for the carers of the aged and the disabled.

Intergovernmental agreements

The main instrument for regulating intergovernmental relations in these programs is the commonwealth–state agreement. This is given effect by the legislative branch of government in a parliamentary Act, which authorises the commonwealth to enter into an agreement with each state and territory. These agreements give considerable rein to executive federalism. The HACC agreement is a complex document with 35 clauses and a plethora of sub-clauses. Under clauses 31 and 32, the commonwealth and the states can continue the agreement or change it without recourse to parliament so long as both parties agree, although any funding variation must be 'insignificant' (clause 22.3). The new SAAP Act 1989 is more complex than the old, and gives the parties power to agree upon changes which are 'substantially in accordance' with the Act. The Bill was endorsed by the social welfare ministers at their meeting in March 1989 before being presented to parliament.

These agreements are negotiated and administered by administrative units and interdepartmental committees, rather than by formal intergovernmental bodies. The agreements were signed after a hectic round of negotiations, characterised as 'fly-in, fly-out' consultation (Chesterman, 1988:9). The time frame between the program announcements and the advertised start was short, both for electoral reasons and because the arrangements were due to expire on some of the subsumed programs. The state negotiating teams comprised senior managers from the state operating departments and the intergovernmental experts located in premiers' departments (on the latter, see Warhurst, 1987). After the establishment of these programs, the intergovernmental negotiations have been conducted by the program professionals. State treasury officers, however, are key players in each budget cycle. Some states also set up large steering committees during the initial negotiations in order to involve the organisations which actually delivered the services, as both local government and the voluntary sector objected to their exclusion from the discussions. A sore point for local government, as the third tier of government, is that they were not a party to the agreements, being regarded as a service-delivery sector.

The commencement of the SAAP program was delayed by the lengthy negotiations and the opposition from the women's movement. The announced July 1984 start was shifted to January 1985 so that in practice the agreement ran for less than five years. The HACC program was also delayed while the states challenged the complex agreement: in particular, their level of cost sharing and lack of policy control, the administrative arrangements, and the areas under the old acts now designated as state responsibilities. HACC began operating from July 1985, but the last state, Queensland, did not sign the agreement until April 1986. This slow start contributed to the initial underspending in both programs.

Intergovernmental management

SAAP and HACC involve various intergovernmental forums. Negotiations are conducted at the ministerial level through the regular commonwealth and state health and welfare ministers' conferences, and at occasional special meetings such as those held by the HACC ministers. Ministerial negotiations have been important in intergovernmental management. For example, the HACC ministers at their meetings during 1988 and 1989 agreed upon numerous measures to simplify the decision-making process (Saunders Report, 1989:Appendix C).

Negotiations are conducted at the departmental executive level, and at regular meetings such as the Standing Committee of Social Welfare Administrators. Formal reviews include representatives from both levels of government and program administrators from each state. The professional program administrators meet at state level in joint officers groups (JOGs), which are interdepartmental and intergovernmental committees comprising both the state-based commonwealth project officers and officers from the state administering departments. Public service administrators have a vested interest in intergovernmental programs as they have a policy commitment to the area, and because these programs increase career opportunities and facilitiate job mobility (see Wright, 1982:ch. 3). The career trajectories of program professionals versus generalist administrators have implications for social policy commitment versus managerialism.

Ministerial decision making was pervasive in the early stages of both new programs, but especially in HACC. First, new programs require considerable policy interpretation, which was lacking as both sets of national guidelines were not ratified for two years. Second, the funding is on the basis of individual project approvals by the joint ministers. Compared to the fiscal weight of their other portfolio responsibilities, these programs take up a disproportionate amount of ministerial time. From July 1987, the Hawke Government appointed assistant ministers to the large portfolios, which increased the opportunity for ministerial intervention.

The chain of decision making is particularly lengthy in HACC. Funding recommendations wind their way up from local and regional advisory committees (in some states), to a state level committee, thence to JOG, then (sometimes) to their respective department heads, to the state minister, and lastly to the commonwealth minister, with the usual loops for more information and resubmissions. This cumbersome chain typically impedes decision making (see, for example, Pressman & Wildavsky, 1974). The process was shortened somewhat in the HACC in March 1988, when the commonwealth minister agreed to clear the bottleneck by guaranteeing a decision within seven days on projects which accorded with the recommendations (Saunders Report, 1989:76). Intergovernmental programs also have different funding cycles. The commonwealth initially worked on a triennial basis in HACC, but state treasuries are not prepared to commit funds beyond their one-year budget cycle, especially as that might lock the states into commonwealth rather than state budgetary priorities.

Differing departmental philosophies and practices have complicated the management of HACC. The program was consolidated at the commonwealth level under the new welfare-oriented Department of Community Services, which was subsequently amalgamated with Health, but the locations of the HACC state administrative units vary. At the meeting of the HACC ministers in May 1988, HACC came under a welfare portfolio in Victoria, New South Wales and Western Australia; health in Queensland and Tasmania; a combined welfare and health portfolio in South Australia and the Northern Territory; and territories in the case of the Australian Capital Territory.

New managerialism

The commonwealth capacity to manage intergovernmental community service programs was enhanced with the establishment of a new department. Subsidy programs were removed from the Department of Social Security and the Department of Health, where they had always been peripheral, to form the new Department of Community Services in December 1984. The fledgling Department was then amalgamated with Health after the July 1987 election to form the Department of Community Services and Health (DCS&H). Thus both the administering department and its programs were restructured at the same time, which undoubtedly exacerbated management difficulties.

The mandate for the new Department was to bring order into the confusing subsidy field. The Fraser Government had initiated reviews of the health and welfare subsidy programs in the late 1970s, which criticised their fragmentation and lack of accountability. For example, the Bailey Report (1979) recommended setting up four block grant programs, while a Senate report concluded that:

> One sees in health and welfare in Australia a system out of control—
> part of a larger crisis in administration; certainly out of the control of
> the individuals it is supposed to serve and of the institutions and
> political agencies to which we look for national management. It is also
> probably out of the control of the public servants immediately
> responsible for its management and of the agencies actually delivering
> the services (Baume Report, 1979:1).

The new Department was therefore primed to embrace the 'new managerialism', now an influential philosophy in the upper echelons of the commonwealth and state bureaucracies (see, for example, Painter, 1988). The Department was keen to overhaul old-fashioned practices in the fragmented community services system, and to install such rational planning techniques as output measures and performance indicators.

The Department championed needs-based planning as one manifestation of a rational planning approach, with professional rather than political judgments in accordance with a formula based upon an agreed measure of individual and aggregate 'need'. The new Department was mindful that the Department of Social Security had been severely criticised by a Senate committee for admitting that subsidies were allocated to the most vocal lobby groups (Baume Report, 1979:57). The Department was therefore keen to depoliticise decisions and to reduce its reliance upon the inequitable submission model of funding, although a consultancy report on needs-based planning warned that there was no magic objective formula (Lee, 1987).

In order to institute needs-based planning and trace the money trail, the Department needed information on what services were being provided and who was getting them. Detailed data collection schemes were proposed for SAAP and HACC, which foundered after protests from the service agencies. There were three major difficulties. First, central planning cannot be imposed upon a fragmented collection of separate agencies accustomed to considerable autonomy. Second, the agencies are mostly small and do not have the capacity to undertake sophisticated procedures. Third, the service providers operate from a different value base. For example, many of the SAAP-funded agencies and their clientele are opposed to intrusive official questions, and many of the HACC-funded services are delivered by volunteers who are more interested in putting hot meals on the table before grateful elderly people than in filling out government forms. The extent of such differences is illustrated by the story of the women's refuge in Victoria which refused to divulge to the government bureaucrats any more than a post office box number (in order to receive its funds), citing an instance when a woman's address at a refuge had been betrayed to her homicidal husband.

A serious consequence of the stalled information systems was the lack of data for the reviews required in the HACC program after three years (Saunders Report, 1989) and in the SAAP program after five years (Chesterman, 1988). Despite the short life of the HACC program, the DCS&H was reprimanded for its lack of knowledge about the program beneficiaries (Auditor-General, 1988:1). Modified information requirements and annual collections have now been negotiated. Information confers power and the states might emerge from this exercise with more power as they control the information collection and initial processing.

Peterson, Rabe and Wong (1986) differentiate between professional and political decision making, claiming that developmental programs work best with political decision making, and redistributive programs work best with professional decision making. The SAAP and HACC decision structures have largely been professional and have not been devolved, as is the case in some USA grant-in-aid programs, to locally elected politicians and local lobby groups. However, the principle of community participation is accepted and required in the SAAP and HACC advisory committees, which introduces a more political element.

Lobby groups

Binstock et al. (1985:598) suggest that federal governments in their social development legislation apply a 'circuit breaker' strategy. This copes with an overload of lobby groups by sweeping them together into a broad program which passes on the onus of response to lower administrative levels. The expectations of these lobby groups are high because the legislation is passed using the common political strategy of promising vague and ambitious goals in order to win acceptance. The crucial implementation issues are postponed for resolution at state level. Thus the lobby groups turn to the state level rather than the national level.

The state advisory committees and administrators in the HACC program had the unpalatable task of dampening down the expectations which were raised by the somewhat premature announcement during the 1984 federal election campaign. For example, in the first year, 85 per cent of the money was already committed under the previous acts, and much of the new money went on extensions to existing projects (Auditor-General, 1988:1).

The commonwealth switched much of the focus for lobby-group politics in SAAP and HACC to the state level by requiring state advisory committees with service provider and consumer representation. Typically, more power is exerted by service providers than by consumers, and by established provider agencies rather than by agencies trying to break into the program. The diffusion of lobbying to the state level was challenged by the national community consultation on HACC, which recommended a national policy advisory committee with representatives from the peak organisations (Saunders Report, 1989:57). The commonwealth is unlikely to want such a committee, but an increased number of access points for lobby group influence is a feature of federal programs (Coleman, 1987). These lobby groups are now more influential with the political emergence of 'grey power', 'the women's vote', better organised disability groups, and youth issues.

Intergovernmental issues

The following intergovernmental issues have emerged as particularly controversial in the SAAP and HACC programs: administrative duplication, the assignment of respective governmental responsibilities, and conflicting policy purposes.

Administrative duplication is a perennial issue in intergovernmental programs. South Australia has raised this issue at Premiers' Conferences, charging that the salaries of commonwealth project officers would be better spent on services, leaving administration to the state officers (Bannon, 1987). This duplication of tasks also means that it is essential for the commonwealth and state officers to establish good personal working relations. At the 1988 HACC ministers' conference, the state ministers successfully pushed for administrative streamlining and less commonwealth oversight. The commonwealth conceded that its project officers would not initiate contact with service agencies and would instead work through the state officers (Saunders Report, 1989:77). Much of the duplication arises from commonwealth insistence upon individual project approvals, as much for political as for accountability purposes. The SAAP and HACC agreements both require joint press releases on new projects by commonwealth and state ministers, as the commonwealth is determined to achieve more program recognition in the electorate than in the past.

The 'Queensland factor' is informally given as a major reason for close commonwealth oversight. However, the presence of commonwealth officers did not make any difference in the Queensland examples cited by the Auditor-General (1988:19), where HACC purposes were ignored but the commonwealth still paid. Dealings with a commonwealth agency are also complicated by the occasional uncertainty as to whether the regional office represents the thinking of the Canberra executive and minister.

The second problem is the assignment of respective governmental responsibilities for intergovernmental program management. The division of powers in a federal system is controversial as there is little agreement on the appropriate division of functions, and no clear economic or administrative criteria for permanently assigning different functions to the different levels of government (Simeon, 1985; Galligan, 1989). In SAAP and HACC, both commonwealth and state governments are involved in policy formulation, planning, funding decisions, administration, monitoring and evaluation. The responsibility issue has therefore consumed considerable time, but some protocols have now been established.

The states' general preference in joint programs is for the commonwealth to limit its involvement to policy formulation—a common recommendation for intergovernmental programs in federal systems (see, for example, Rivlin, 1971). However, the commonwealth has written in a considerable administrative role for itself in the SAAP and HACC agreements. Although the state governments are said to have the administrative responsibility, commonwealth as well as state officers attend the state-level advisory committees on an *ex officio* basis, and are members of JOGs, which make the final detailed funding recommendations. The SAAP Act 1989 attempts to clarify the issue by setting out in detail the respective roles and tasks of the commonwealth and the states. The device of an annual state strategic plan has also been seized upon in both programs which the commonwealth, after endorsing, will theoretically leave to the states to administer.

A common issue in intergovernmental programs is the conflict of policy purposes. A basic conflict is that the commonwealth hopes that HACC services will keep people out of commonwealth-subsidised nursing homes; while the states hope that HACC services will keep people out of the overloaded state hospitals. One example is clause 7(4) in the HACC agreement, which designates 'no growth' areas which the commonwealth will not fund above the 1985 level. The commonwealth regards rehabilitation, treatment for acute illness, and post-acute and convalescent care as state health budget responsibilities. However, in the rush to commence the HACC program the states avoided an estimate of the 1985 level, and the commonwealth suspects that over half the HACC funds are being diverted to such state purposes (Auditor-General, 1988:67). These conflicts were allayed somewhat with the allocation of some medicare funds for post-acute care and for palliative care for people who are dying. Also, in view of the frequent overlap between HACC and health system clients, the agreed focus is now upon the purpose of the service intervention rather than the circumstance of its occurrence (Saunders Report, 1989:19).

A second example is the clause in the proposed SAAP Act 1989, which excludes projects exclusively for children under sixteen years. Previously there had been no sharp distinction of commonwealth and state responsibilities on the basis of age. The minister made clear the intent of this clause in the second-reading speech:

> It is important that SAAP not be used as a substitute for other programs
> of assistance by state governments for homeless youth. State
> governments have responsibility for children under 16 years and the
> commonwealth is concerned to ensure that SAAP does not become the
> easy way out for states...SAAP will not be used to replace or duplicate
> services and assistance already provided by, or which are the responsi-
> bility of, other government programs or services (Commonwealth of
> Australia Parliamentary Debates, 1989:2007–2008).

Program phases

Peterson, Rabe and Wong (1986) chart maturation phases in which the intergovernmental participants modify their respective interests over time. In redistributive programs, the first phase is characterised by high expectations and vague guidelines; the second phase by the elaboration of requirements; and the third by mutual compromise based upon a commitment to common purposes. The SAAP and HACC programs are both moving from an implementation to a consolidation phase in a second round of program agreements. SAAP is following the path charted by Peterson, Rabe and Wong (1986) in that the program is being elaborated in its second phase by tighter redistributive aims and more structured administration. In contrast, the initially elaborate HACC program exhibits some of the characteristics of the later maturation phase in which intergovernmental compromise and simpler administrative procedures are agreed upon.

While intergovernmental policy aims require mutual agreement, administration should be left to the states. Some of the early implementation problems in SAAP and HACC have been resolved, but program administration could be further streamlined in the interests of efficiency and better intergovernmental and interorganisational relations. Greater commonwealth managerial emphasis and exertion of central policy control provokes tension between governments and with the service providers. A national policy does not require a unified program which ignores the existence of diverse state delivery systems. Such state diversity calls for more state discretion on service development and funding. The state central agencies prefer general rather than specific-purpose grants, but the program professionals prefer earmarked money which protects their programs. If state commitment is to be maintained and extended, the programs must pursue state as well as commonwealth goals. These increasingly important community services are still underfunded. However, given tighter state budgets, the states are wary of taking on more responsibility and expanding a service structure in which they might inherit high future recurrent costs.

SAAP and HACC have succeeded in attracting public attention, and have stimulated forward planning and some restructuring of the fragmented largely voluntary-sector services. Client demand will continue to rise and the agencies will be hard pressed to respond. Government funds more than doubled in the first phases of both programs, which is a major achievement in a time of fiscal austerity. Equity purposes have been enunciated, but the achievements in terms of equity for individual clients have yet to be evaluated.

Bibliography

ACIR (Advisory Council for Inter-government Relations), 1983. *The Provision of Services for the Aged: A Report on Relations among Governments in Australia*, Report 6, AGPS, Canberra.

Agranoff, R.J., 1986. *Intergovernmental Management: Human Services Problem-Solving in Six Metropolitan Areas*, State University of New York Press, Albany.

Auditor-General, 1988. *Efficiency Audit Report: Department of Community Services and Health, Home and Community Care Program* AGPS, Canberra.

Australian Bureau of Statistics, 1987. *Age and Sex of Persons in Statistical Local Areas and Statistical Divisions*, ABS, Canberra (catalogue number for each state).

—— 1989. *Disabled and Aged Persons Australia, 1988, Preliminary Results*, ABS, Canberra, Cat. No. 4118.0.

Bailey Report (Task Force on Coordination in Welfare and Health), 1979. *Report*, AGPS, Canberra.

Bakvis, H. & Chandler, W.M., eds, 1987. *Federalism and the Role of the State*, University of Toronto Press, Toronto.

Bannon, J.C., 1987. 'Overcoming the Unintended Consequences of Federation', *Australian Journal of Public Administration*, XLVI(1).

Baume Report (Senate Standing Committee on Social Welfare), 1979. *Through Glass Darkly: Evaluation in Australian Health and Welfare Services*, Vol. 1, AGPS, Canberra.

Binstock, R.H., Levin, M.A. & Weatherly, R., 1985. 'Political Dilemmas of Social Intervention', in *Handbook of Aging and the Social Sciences*, 2nd edn, eds R.H. Binstock & E. Shanas, Von Nostrand Reinhold, New York.

Bowman, M. & Healy, J., 1988. 'Human Services in South Australia and Victoria', in *Comparative State Policies*, ed. B. Galligan, Longman Cheshire, Melbourne.

Brennan, A., 1984. 'Home Care: The Origins and Implementation of the National Home Care Program', *Proceedings of the 19th Annual Conference of the Australian Association of Gerontology*, Sydney.

Buntz, C.G. & Radin, B.A., 1983. 'Managing Intergovernmental Conflict: The Case of Human Services', *Public Administration Review*, 43(6).

Chesterman Report (National Review of the Supported Accommodation Assistance Program), 1988. *Homes Away From Home*, Department of Community Services and Health, Canberra.

Coleman, W.D., 1987. 'Federalism and Interest Group Organisations', in *Federalism and the Role of the State*, eds H. Bakvis & W.M. Chandler, University of Toronto Press, Toronto.

Commonwealth of Australia, Parliamentary Debates, House of Representatives, 1989. *Daily Hansard*, Thursday, 4 May 1989, Canberra.

Department for Community Welfare, 1988. *Annual Report 1987–88*, DCW, Adelaide.

Department of Community Services and Health, 1986. *Nursing Homes and Hostels Review*, AGPS, Canberra.

—— 1988. *Annual Report 1987–1988*, AGPS, Canberra.

Department of Health, 1981. *Annual Report 1980–81*, AGPS, Canberra.

Dowse, S., 1984 . 'The Bureaucrat as Usurer', in *Unfinished Business: Social Justice for Women in Australia*, ed. D. Broom, Allen & Unwin, Sydney.

Galligan, B., 1989. 'Australian Federalism: Perceptions and Issues', in *Australian Federalism*, ed. B. Galligan, Longman Cheshire, Melbourne.

Graycar, A., 1981. 'The Australian Assistance Plan', in *Decisions: Case Studies in Australian Public Policy*, eds S. Encel & P. Wilenski, Longman Cheshire, Melbourne.

Hanf, K. & Toonen, T.A.J. eds, 1985. *Policy Implementation in Federal and Unitary Systems: Questions of Analysis and Design*, Martinus Nijhoff Publishers, Dordrecht.

Healy, J., 1988a. 'Home Care Before HACC: Interstate Comparisons', *Australian Journal on the Ageing* 7(4).

—— 1988b. 'Packaging the Human Services', *Australian Journal of Public Administration*, XLVII(4).

—— 1990. 'Community Services: Long Term Care at Home?', in *Grey Policy: Australian Policies for an Ageing Society*, eds H.L. Kendig & J. McCallum, Allen & Unwin, Sydney.

Henderson, R.F., 1981. 'Policies for the Poor', in *The Welfare Stakes: Strategies for Australian Social Policy*, ed. R.F. Henderson, Institute of Applied Economic and Social Research, Melbourne.

Howe, A.L., 1987. 'Interstate Variations in Commonwealth Financing of Services for Older People', in *Who Pays? Financing Services for Older People*, eds C. Foster & H.L. Kendig, ANUTECH, Canberra.

Kewley, T.H., 1980. *Australian Social Security Today*, Sydney University Press, Sydney.

Leahy, R., 1987. 'Ongoing Plans for Funding Meals Services', *Proceedings of the Second National Meals On Wheels Conference*, Meals on Wheels SA Inc., Adelaide.

Lee, T., 1987. 'Needs Based Planning and Services for Older People', in *Who Pays? Financing Services for Older People*, eds C. Foster & H.L. Kendig, ANUTECH, Canberra.

McLeay Report (House of Representatives Standing Committee on Expenditure), 1982. *In A Home Or At Home*, AGPS, Canberra.

Meals on Wheels SA Inc., 1986. *Annual Report 1986*, MOW, Adelaide.

Mendelsohn, R., ed., 1983. *Australian Social Welfare Finance*, Allen & Unwin, Sydney.

Milligan, V., Hardwick, J. & Graycar, A., 1984. 'Non-Government Welfare Organisations in Australia: A National Classification', *SWRC Reports and Proceedings*, No. 51, Social Welfare Research Centre, University of New South Wales.

Painter, M., 1988. 'Editorial: Public Management: Fad or Fallacy?' *Australian Journal of Public Administration*, XLVII(1).

Parkin, A. & Patience, A., eds, 1981. *The Dunstan Decade: Social Democracy at the State Level*, Longman Cheshire, Melbourne.

Peterson, P.E., Rabe, B.G. & Wong, K.K., 1986. *When Federalism Works*, The Brookings Institution, Washington, D.C.

Pressman, J. & Wildavsky, A., 1974. *Implementation: How Great Expectations in Washington are Dashed in Oakland*, Jossey Bass, Berkeley.

Rivlin, A., 1971. *Systematic Thinking For Social Action*, The Brookings Institution, Washington, D.C.

Saunders Report (Home and Community Care Review Working Group), 1989. *First Triennial Review of the Home and Community Care Program*, AGPS, Canberra.

Scotton, R.B. & Ferber, H., 1980, *Public Expenditures and Social Policy in Australia, Vol. II, The First Fraser Years, 1976–78*, Longman Cheshire, Melbourne.

Scott, I. & Graycar, A., 1983. 'Aspects of Fiscal Federalism', *SWRC Reports and Proceedings* No. 33, Social Welfare Research Centre, University of New South Wales.

Shannon, P. & Foster, C., 1987. 'Interstate Comparisons of State Outlays on Services for Older People', in *Who Pays? Financing Services for Older People*, eds C. Foster & H.L. Kendig, ANUTECH, Canberra.

Simeon, R. ed., 1985. *Division of Powers and Public Policy*, Vol. 61, University of Toronto Press, Toronto.

Warhurst, J., 1987. 'Managing Intergovernmental Relations', in *Federalism and the Role of the State*, eds H. Bakvis & W.M. Chandler, University of Toronto Press, Toronto.

Wright, D.S., 1982. *Understanding Intergovernmental Relations*, 2nd edn, Brooks/Cole Publishing Company, Monterey, California.

11 Tertiary education

Neil Marshall

Over the last twenty or so years, the commonwealth and state governments have often been depicted as adversaries in the tertiary education policy arena. This view arose largely because of the division between the legal and fiscal responsibilities of the two levels of government. Constitutional authority for universities, colleges of advanced education (CAEs) and colleges of technical and further education (TAFE) rests entirely with the states. Since World War II, however, the commonwealth has used its powers under section 96, and to a lesser extent section 51 (xxiiia), of the constitution to become increasingly involved in the funding of institutions. From 1974 onwards, universities and CAEs have been supported almost completely by federal monies. The financial assistance provided by the commonwealth has placed it in a strong position to influence the development of tertiary education policy. The effect of this dominance, a number of scholars suggest, has been to impose national direction on the country's campuses. State administrative autonomy has been infringed and regional priorities distorted. As a consequence, relations between state and federal authorities have frequently been under strain.

It is argued here that interaction between the levels of government has been characterised by co-operation rather than conflict. Disagreements have tended to be occasional and temporary occurrences. Until recently, tertiary education never entered the arena of 'high politics' described by Galligan et al. in chapter 1. This situation prevailed as a result of the nature of intergovernmental mechanisms used to administer colleges and universities. Between 1959 and 1987, independent statutory commissions, or intergovernmental boards (Chapman, 1988), were mainly responsible for the formulation and implementation of policy.

These commissions were successful in accommodating and reconciling commonwealth and state expectations. At the end of 1987, the statutory commission structure was largely dismantled when the Hawke cabinet introduced a completely revised framework of governance. Though these reforms have resulted in a substantially different approach to policy making (and injected a new element of friction into the intergovernmental arena), they nevertheless involve an evolutionary development of past procedures and practices.

The formative years, 1959–74

Two statutory education commissions were established during this period; the Australian Universities Commission (AUC) and the Commonwealth Advisory Commission on Advanced Education (CACAE).[1] The terms of reference and operating procedures of the bodies were almost identical. Both were given regulatory as well as advisory functions. They were to make recommendations to the federal government on the amount and conditions of financial assistance to be made available to universities and CAEs, to 'promote the balanced development' of institutions so that their resources 'can be used to the greatest possible advantage of Australia', and to administer monies provided by the commonwealth (AUC, 1960:Appendix 3; CACAE, 1966:Appendix B). Funding took place in terms of a triennial cycle with the commonwealth matching state grants on a 1:1.85 basis for recurrent expenditure and 1:1 for capital programs (tuition fees were a third source of funds and accounted for about 15 per cent of institutional income). The commissions were required to consult with the states before submitting final recommendations to the federal government. The two bodies functioned until 1977, when they were absorbed into the Commonwealth Tertiary Education Commission (CTEC).

The AUC was the product of the Murray Report (1957), set up by Prime Minister Menzies to inquire into the financial needs of universities and to suggest means of assistance. Menzies had been concerned that, despite substantial injections of commonwealth funds into the country's campuses from the early 1940s to the mid-1950s, their condition had continued to deteriorate. Scott remembers them as being in a state of 'rampant decay' with 'crimped facilities' and 'dingy Gothic buildings' (1985:120). The Murray Report's subsequent proposal for the establishment of a grants committee and shared commonwealth/state funding received strong support from Menzies as well as the 'unanimous' approval of the states (Gallagher, 1982:56). The states felt that such measures were necessary, partly because they were unable to fund the expected growth in student numbers, and partly because an independent expert body was seen as vital to evaluate needs and preserve institutional autonomy. Much the same views were forthcoming following the publication of the Martin Report (1964) and Menzies' establishment of the CACAE.

The achievements of the two commissions were considerable. By 1975, there were nineteen universities enrolling 150 000 students and 62 CAEs with 126 000 students. Facilities were generally good and a number of new areas of study and research had blossomed. The reason underlying the commissions' success was that they became astute managers of the intergovernmental arena and won the strong support of both federal and state authorities. Over the years the great majority of the commissions' triennial recommendations were accepted without dispute by the two levels of government.

From the outset, the commissions established elaborate consultative procedures with institutions and state authorities. The AUC built up a close relationship with each university and attempted to engender a sense of national identity for the sector as a whole. Initiatives proposed by campuses were often incorporated into the commission's plans. The CACAE functioned in a somewhat different environment in so far as it dealt mainly with state co-ordinating authorities. These authorities had been set up after the Martin Report and possessed varying degrees of control over the activities of the state's CAEs. After discussions with universities and co-ordinating authorities, the commissions approached state treasuries and education ministers to ascertain which new projects were acceptable and the extent of financial commitment state governments were prepared to give. The commissions' triennial reports to the federal government were always couched in terms of what the states were likely to support. Overall, interaction between the commonwealth and the states was characterised by persuasion and negotiation rather than hard bargaining. Over time, they honed their political skills and on occasions were able to play governments off against each other (Gallagher, 1982:116). Coercive tactics were not employed. The CACAE 'rarely if ever' used finance as a weapon (Wark, 1977:159); the 'big stick' approach to policy was simply 'not on' (Wark, 1977:156).

Though the commissions were highly successful in securing state support for their recommendations, they nevertheless made substantial concessions to accommodate state priorities. The terms of reference of the two bodies charged them with promoting 'balanced development' in the national interest. This concept, one federal minister suggested, involved 'an equal standard of opportunity' in tertiary education wherever the student might live (quoted in Gallagher, 1982:110). Clearly there was an expectation that the commissions would reduce the considerable disparities in participation rates, disciplinary spread, and levels of finance that existed between states. In their various reports, however, the AUC and CACAE largely ignored these questions as they could not be seriously confronted without upsetting relations with the states. The commissions also went to considerable lengths to ensure particular state demands were met. Both bodies, Anderson noted, 'demonstrated an extreme reluctance to oppose major developments proposed by the states, and it is difficult to think of any state-backed proposal for a new university or CAE which did not receive Commonwealth government support between 1960 and 1975.' Many of these proposals, he added, were 'based on flimsy evidence and evaluation' (Anderson, 1982:116). In the long run, balanced development really boiled down to mean reasonably balanced development within individual states and in terms of that state's resources and priorities. The CACAE especially was forced to substantially compromise its goals. As a result of pressure from the states, teachers' colleges were allowed to become CAEs and colleges permitted to upgrade their diploma courses to degree status. The CACAE could have prevented these occurring, but only at considerable cost in terms of state co-operation. Clearly such developments succeeded in changing the whole character of the advanced education sector.

The overall outcome of the interaction between the commissions and the states was the accommodation of state priorities and aspirations within the general development of the university and CAE sectors. In 1975 there remained significant differences between the states in terms of the extent of the provision of tertiary education. This is not to downplay the significant achievements of the AUC and the CACAE, which undoubtedly exerted the major influence over the broad direction of policy. Rather it indicates that trade-offs were necessary to ensure continued co-operation between the two levels of government. Certainly this arrangement appears to have been mutually satisfactory, for serious conflict rarely, if ever, surfaced. It is significant that throughout the 1960s and early 1970s meetings of the Australian Education Council—an inter-jurisdictional ministerial council consisting of commonwealth and state ministers of education—only occasionally discussed matters relating to universities and CAEs (Spaull, 1987).

From about 1970 onwards, the substance of tertiary education policy seems to have been increasingly left in the hands of the two commissions and, to a lesser extent, state co-ordinating bodies. State and commonwealth ministers presided over broad levels of expenditure, but the question of the allocation of funds was generally left to the AUC and CACAE. State ministerial involvement was usually restricted to issues with immediate electoral consequences, such as the procurement and siting of new institutions. In Peterson et al.'s terms, political interest was confined largely to matters of an overtly developmental nature (Peterson et al., 1986:ch. 1). There were a number of reasons for this approach. First, both commissions were viewed as genuinely independent and impartial organisations possessing considerable expertise. Second, tertiary education was not a politically salient issue as only a very small percentage of the population was affected. It was an area that could be safely left to specialist bodies. Third, state ministers and departments had become preoccupied with the problems of secondary schooling and had neither the time nor the energy to immerse themselves in the relatively arcane affairs of universities and CAEs.

Total federal funding and the CTEC era, 1974–87

At the beginning of 1974, the Whitlam Government abolished fees in all tertiary institutions and assumed full responsibility for the funding of universities and CAEs. Such a move, Labor envisaged, would make post-secondary education more accessible to a wider cross-section of the community. The states were 'attracted to the idea of being relieved, in the long term, from a considerable financial burden' and had 'readily agreed' to the Whitlam proposals at the June 1974 Premiers' Conference (Harman, 1982:93). The campuses, for their part, appeared happy to be free from the spending constraints imposed by state governments. Such a significant shift in the federal funding equation did not result in the complete imposition of commonwealth direction over tertiary education policy, as has sometimes been suggested. Nor did it lead to the distortion of state priorities or irresponsible actions by state governments. This was because the format of the intergovernmental commissions developed during the 1950s and 1960s was successfully adapted to the changed fiscal and administrative environment. A new statutory body—the Commonwealth Tertiary Education Commission (CTEC)—was created to co-ordinate the activities of all tertiary sectors.[2] Its modus operandi was subsequently shaped by the Australian Education Council to ensure responsiveness to state as well as commonwealth requirements. Until the mid-1980s, CTEC more than met initial political expectations and was allowed to develop a very high degree of functional independence.

The immediate catalyst leading to the formation of CTEC was probably the setting up of the Technical and Further Education Commission in July 1975 to inject financial assistance into the nation's technical colleges. Unlike the universities and CAEs, commonwealth TAFE funding was intended to supplement state expenditure. Federal monies accounted for only about 15 per cent of total recurrent grants and were directed at particular programs. In relation to capital expenditure, TAFE provided general-purpose grants which funded about two-thirds of new buildings and equipment.

The existence of three separate commissions created problems for the newly-elected Fraser Government. There was 'wasteful duplication and overlap' (TEC, 1979:115), they competed against each other for funds and, most importantly, it became increasingly difficult for federal cabinet to determine policy priorities within the tertiary education arena as a whole. It was with these considerations in mind that CTEC was established in 1977 with terms of reference similar to those of the AUC and CACAE. Specifically, it was charged with ensuring 'the balanced and co-ordinated development' of all the nation's tertiary institutions and the 'diversifying of opportunities' by encouraging the close involvement between campuses in relation to teaching activities (CTEC Act, 1977:5). The new body consisted of a chairman and seven commissioners. Following strong representations from the universities, it was decided to preserve sectoral identities. Three subordinate advisory councils—the Universities Council, the Advanced Education Council and the Technical and Further Education Council—were appointed to provide assistance on the particular needs of their clientele. Personnel and resources from the three disbanded commissions were absorbed into CTEC, thus providing the new body with continuity of expertise and access to an established communications network. At its peak, the Commission possessed an overall staffing contingent of about 120.

CTEC's enacting legislation had emphasised the importance of consultation with the states but did not spell out the format it should take. During 1977/78, the Commission and its councils developed upon past practices in conducting negotiations with state authorities. The states, however, were unhappy with the informality of these procedures and concerned at the potential power of the commonwealth to dictate on the direction of tertiary education policy. Consequently, at the June 1979 meeting of the Australian Education Council, a framework of regularised 'consultative arrangements' was agreed upon that ensured the close involvement of states' interests in policy formation and implementation. The new arrangements were worked into a triennial planning cycle (TEC, 1979:29).

In addition to the development of these consultative mechanisms, four of the six states (Victoria, Tasmania, Western Australia and South Australia) created new co-ordinating authorities which mirrored CTEC's functions at the state level. These authorities evolved from the bodies established in the wake of the Martin Report and were given broad powers to monitor institutional and course development across the three sectors within the state. The setting up of such authorities, along with the institutionalisation of CTEC's decision making mechanisms, contained the Commission's functions to a considerable extent, and ensured that the states maintained an effective voice in the processing of new initiatives. As Williams commented in 1979, 'all states have made it clear that their agreement to the Commonwealth's proposal to assume full financial responsibility [for universities and CAEs] did not carry with it agreement to transfer issues of policy and administration' (Williams, 1979:705). The outcome of the states' actions was to reinforce vertical differentiation within the tertiary education sector; that is, between commonwealth and state authorities, and state authorities and institutions. When this was combined with existing horizontal differences—between universities, CAEs and TAFE colleges—it meant that CTEC was forced to preside over an unwieldy structure that consisted of a large number of disparate organisational interests, each pursuing its own goals. The inbuilt 'tensions' within the system, though low key, were very real. The three subordinate advisory councils viewed each other with some suspicion (Fensham, 1981), as did their constituent campuses, while state authorities saw themselves, with varying degrees of commitment, as defenders of the regional bailiwick (for example, Howse, 1982). In addition to this collection of participants was the involvement of pressure groups such as academic unions and employer associations and other bodies whose objectives were related to tertiary education outcomes. Such entities had matured and proliferated during the 1970s and their involvement in the system constituted a vital contribution to the policy process. CTEC possessed limited resources and relied on interest groups for both the provision of information and substantive policy advice. In this regard, the Australian Vice-Chancellors' Committee and the Australian Committee of Directors and Principals were the most salient actors.

Despite the inherent conflict within the system, it was incumbent upon all participants to work together if policy proposals were to be formulated and implemented. Certainly CTEC was in no position to 'run' tertiary education, as the chairman acknowledged (TEC, 1979:26). Rather, there was a clear recognition that 'the Commission's objectives of balanced development can be achieved only in co-operation...with the state authorities and institutions responsible for tertiary education' (TEC, 1979:27). Such co-operation in fact emerged from the beginning of the CTEC era and continued to work 'remarkably well' for a number of years (Harman, 1984:514). This was due largely to the fact that desirable modes of interaction were well understood as a result of the previous sixteen years' experience with the AUC and CACAE. It was very much a matter of adjusting long-accepted procedures to a broader, more complicated systems environment.

There were two basic dimensions underlying these interactive procedures. The first was recognition of the need for compromise both in the course of negotiation and the exercise of formal authority. The state co-ordinating bodies respected the autonomy of the universities, for example, and were reluctant to involve themselves too deeply in the affairs of the CAEs, even though they were clearly empowered to do so (Hall & Willett, 1979:34–35). Similarly, the Advanced Education Council made a point of being responsive to the recommendations of state authorities in its distribution of financial allocations to institutions (TEC, 1979:212). Second, there was a shared commitment to academic values (though to a lesser extent in TAFE). This attribute manifested itself in the way issues were generated and conflicting concerns resolved. Encounters between groups were characterised by openness of discussion, the presentation of hard facts and sound analysis. Outcomes were the consequence more of good argument than bargaining. Indicative of this style of decision making were CTEC's voluminous triennial reports, which ran to many hundreds of pages and canvassed all matters exhaustively.

The system's lengthy consultative procedures, in conjunction with the willingness to compromise and the particular negotiating characteristics adopted by participants, resulted in a policy process that was classically incremental in format. Issues were discussed in depth at each level of the structure and widespread agreement from all groups was required before a final decision was taken. Though CTEC undoubtedly wielded the greatest influence over the course of events, the taking of major decisions was essentially a shared exercise. The process was a time-consuming and demanding business with the eventual output usually amounting to a marginal shift in policy. Significant changes in direction were rare.

CTEC's final recommendations to cabinet, however, had been thoroughly researched and considered, and constituted, by and large, very sound advice. As Harman observed, the Commission's triennial reports achieved 'a standard reached by relatively few similar agencies anywhere in the world' (Harman, 1984:514). Moreover, because the recommendations had received system-wide support, CTEC could assure the minister and cabinet of certainty of implementation in proposed courses of action. Another benefit that accrued from this style of policy making was reasonable flexibility in operation over time and an ability to adapt to changing circumstances. For example, along with other welfare sectors during the mid-1970s and early 1980s, tertiary education was subjected to a shrinking funding base. Grants were cut by 8 per cent between 1975 and 1984. Yet the system succeeded in accommodating a 25 per cent increase in student numbers. The country's institutions, CTEC tersely reported in 1986, had managed to do quite a lot more with considerably less (CTEC, 1986a:5).

Such attributes held considerable appeal for governments. This was perhaps the major reason why successive commonwealth ministers were prepared to allow the system relatively free rein to develop and carry out policy. Indeed, almost all sectoral initiatives emanated from CTEC or its subordinate groups from 1977 until the mid-1980s. The minister might reject or amend particular matters, but the policy agenda was effectively set by the Commission. The quality of CTEC's performance, however, was not the only reason underlying this state of affairs. A further contributing factor was that the Commission enjoyed a monopoly of expertise, authority and communications in the tertiary education arena. Other commonwealth agencies were not in a position to provide substantive alternative advice to cabinet. In part this was because the functions of colleges and universities were seen to be of only peripheral relevance to the furtherance of bureaucratic interests. Nevertheless, the fact that the tertiary education system was allowed to exercise such a high degree of control over its own affairs suggests that political actors were more than satisfied with the nature of the Commission's activities.

State governments appear to have been equally content with CTEC's role. Though state ministers maintained a close involvement with the TAFE sector, they seem to have delegated most responsibility for the affairs of universities and CAEs to their co-ordinating bodies. The withdrawal of state ministers from the higher education arena was due partly to the fact that CTEC's system was seen as being reasonably responsive to particular state needs and partly because the overall direction of higher education policy was largely congruent with state objectives. Anderson perhaps best summed up the situation:

> There are no grounds for believing that if a state were fully responsible for higher education, it would develop radically different policies... There is a general consensus among governments—state and federal, Labor and Liberal—with respect to post-secondary education, particularly higher education...[the states] believe they get the best deal under the present arrangements and have no objectives which are frustrated. (Anderson, 1982:120)

Perhaps a further reason for lack of state government interest, Petersen et al. would suggest, was that during these years tertiary education was in a retractionary phase and the system's functions were predominantly regulatory and administrative. Very few high-profile developmental projects which might have had broader political implications—such as new institutions—were forthcoming. By and large, the states were happy to leave decision making to the 'policy professionals' (Peterson et al., 1986:ch. 7. See Sharman, 1988, for a discussion of the nature of one state government's interaction with the tertiary education sector).

Though CTEC's policy process contained many strengths, there was, nonetheless, a serious weakness. This was a variation of what Chapman has referred to as the 'minimum tolerable consensus' (1988:117). In this instance, the incremental style adopted and the need to achieve agreement meant that the 'big' issues were never really confronted. The hoary old question of 'balanced development', which had been problematic with the CACAE and the AUC, continued to plague their successor. The Commission was criticised for having 'failed to produce a satisfactory national plan' (Williams, 1979:716). The reason for this, the chairman of CTEC later conceded, was that balanced development 'has too often...been interpreted to mean resolution of the competing claims of sectors and their institutions' (Hudson, 1985:18). For similar reasons the Commission's responsibility for 'diversifying opportunities' was not achieved. This term of reference had alluded to the importance of closer sectoral co-ordination of coursework and the introduction of credit transfers between campuses. Though the matter was discussed repeatedly in successive reports, by 1987 very little real progress had been made.

A further drawback was the system's lack of formal accountability. In 1979 one critic suggested that such mechanisms were 'virtually non-existent' (Chippendale, 1979:17). The use of commonwealth funds for TAFE was of particular concern. There were very few evaluative procedures. Objectives for programs 'were consistently cast in the most general of terms' (CTEC, 1986b:37). Moreover, CTEC could 'never be sure' that earmarked grants were being employed to complement state projects or as a substitute for other state commitments (CTEC, 1986b:37). Higher education presented less of a problem. The system's ability to absorb consistent funding cuts suggested at least reasonably efficient use of public monies. Nevertheless, there were difficulties in ascertaining the actual performance of individual institutions. In its last report, CTEC took steps to counteract this situation by proposing requirements for staff appraisal, strategic planning, discipline reviews, and measurement of program goals. These initiatives, however, came too late to offset the growing criticism in federal cabinet that CTEC's structure was deficient in terms of both accountability and effectiveness.

The disintegration of CTEC

During 1986–87 CTEC's policy-making structure began to disintegrate quite dramatically. Actions taken by several commonwealth agencies and by state governments effectively undermined the coherence and authority of the system. Developments at the commonwealth level were largely a consequence of the market-liberal economic policies introduced by the incoming Labor Government after 1983. These policies were directed at enhancing competitiveness and productivity, encouraging an export orientation on the part of the manufacturing sector, creating new high-tech enterprises, and cutting back on public-sector spending. In the course of implementing the Hawke cabinet's measures, a number of federal departments came to view tertiary education as a vital infrastructure resource that could be utilised in the pursuit of national objectives. In particular, it was thought that universities and colleges could produce larger numbers of technological and business graduates, gear their research capacities more closely to manufacturing needs, and carry out their functions on a more cost-efficient basis. The result was that several agencies entered the tertiary education arena either by way of initiating new fields of activity or through gaining control of existing programs (Marshall, 1988). The effect of these moves was to disperse authority for tertiary education policy amongst a number of departments and weaken the integrated approach that had previously prevailed. Perhaps the agency initiatives which had the greatest impact were the Department of Trade's introduction of full-fee-paying overseas students and the Department of Industry, Technology and Commerce's mounting of a 150 per cent tax concession scheme for private-sector organisations which contracted research projects to campuses. Both initiatives added an entrepreneurial dimension to the role of institutions over which CTEC possessed little control.

In addition to the fragmentary influence of these developments, the Commission's previously secure position in the commonwealth bureaucratic environment was shaken by the substance of the public service reforms introduced by the government during 1984-85. The new managerialism, with its emphasis on corporate planning, measurable goals and evaluation of outcomes, inevitably highlighted the deficiencies of CTEC's operational network. The Commission was depicted as ineffective in its functions and lacking in adequate accountability. Such criticism, moreover, served to justify intrusions made by departments into the tertiary education sector.

The initiatives taken by departments in the federal arena had an immediate impact on the states. Governments quickly perceived that large influxes of overseas students and the ability of institutions to obtain lucrative research contracts would reap significant benefits for local economies. It was very much with this consideration in mind that the Western Australian and New South Wales governments moved unilaterally to upgrade their biggest CAEs to university status. A university, it was argued, would be more attractive to both foreign students and corporations seeking R&D facilities. Though CTEC pointed out disconsolately that such moves had a 'destabilising effect' on the system as a whole, and 'disturbed' balanced development within regions (CTEC, 1987:43), other states soon announced that they had similar measures in the pipeline. These actions were not entirely opportunistic, however. There was a growing realisation that the resources of campuses could be harnessed to the particular commercial requirements of the state. To this end governments began supporting the development of industry research parks adjacent to universities and colleges, and a number of state departments began funding research projects in institutions. The Victorian government went so far as to establish the Victorian Education Foundation. This body is financed jointly by the government and the private sector and its objective is to provide additional places in universities, CAEs and TAFE colleges 'identified by business as high priority and essential to economic development' (Hannan, 1987). The contributions of companies can be claimed as a payroll tax deduction. New South Wales was to follow suit less than a year later with a similar scheme. Such political involvement inevitably disrupted the conventions and processes upon which CTEC's structure was based.

By mid-1987, much of CTEC's policy-making authority had been whittled away and its control over planning procedures seriously compromised. Participants were less committed to adhering to system expectations and willing to make departures when it suited them. Furthermore, the Commission lacked credibility in the eyes of political and bureaucratic actors. One observer noted sadly that the difficulties facing CTEC 'are so vast that it is impossible that they can be dealt with using existing policy arrangements' (Anwyl, 1987). The Hawke

Government seems to have shared this view, for shortly after the 1987 federal election an entirely new administrative framework for tertiary education was created that made provision for a much greater degree of political control and system accountability.

The Hawke Government's reforms

The Department of Employment, Education and Training (DEET), one of the 'super departments' created by the Hawke Government in July 1987, formed the cornerstone of the new framework. The minister appointed to preside over DEET was John Dawkins, previously Minister of Trade and principal architect of the 1984–85 public service reforms. Many of the disparate policy elements that had sprouted in various commonwealth agencies were relocated under DEET. CTEC was disbanded and its administrative functions transferred to the Department. Corporate management procedures were introduced from the outset and by early 1988 DEET's affairs had been arranged into a coherent program format. The outcome was a single integrated body responsible for the great bulk of tertiary education activity.

It was on this bureaucratic foundation that a detailed governing framework was built. The framework was outlined in the course of three major documents. The first, tabled in September 1987, was *Skills for Australia* (Dawkins & Holding, 1987), which focused on the TAFE sector. This was followed by the green paper, *Higher Education: A Policy Discussion Paper* (Dawkins, 1987), released in December, which dealt with universities and colleges. Campuses were given a period of seven months for discussion and to submit recommendations before final proposals were put forward in the white paper. The thrust of the white paper—*Higher Education: A Policy Statement* (Dawkins, 1988a)—published in July 1988, confirmed the substance of the green paper with relatively few modifications.

There were three broad dimensions to Dawkins' governing structure. The first was the utilisation of the managerialist approach introduced into the Australian Public Service. Though procedures differ between TAFE and higher education institutions, the underlying principles are the same. In relation to TAFE, commonwealth funding is made available under two broad categories of expenditure: the General Recurrent Program and the TAFE Infrastructure Program. Recurrent finance is provided after DEET has reached a resource agreement with individual state authorities. This involves the negotiation of mutually acceptable educational objectives in terms of college activities. Actual outcomes 'will be subject to regular monitoring and evaluation' by DEET (Dawkins & Holding, 1987:36). The infrastructure program covers capital works and equipment with grants being produced 'on the basis of competitive bidding' (Dawkins &

Holding, 1987:34). Commonwealth–state funding ratios remain much the same as they were under CTEC.

The contractual approach is also adopted with regard to CAEs and universities, except that negotiations are conducted directly with campuses. For institutions to be eligible for commonwealth funding they first have to join the Unified National System. The binary format has been removed and all colleges and universities are treated on an equal footing. A precondition for joining the national system is that institutions must have a minimum enrolment of 2000 students. However, in order to receive funding for a broad range of teaching and research activities, campuses are required to have a minimum enrolment of 8000 students. The intention here is to force amalgamations between smaller institutions on the understanding that large institutions permit ease of transfer between levels of study, encourage more efficient use of facilities, and promote concentration of resources. Having become a part of the national system, campuses are entitled to draw up a contract with DEET. Monies are provided on the basis of institutions agreeing to meet a range of mutually determined objectives. These objectives are subject to evaluation and actual performance is taken into account when new discussions are opened at the beginning of the next triennium. All campuses must negotiate an 'educational profile' with DEET which sets out the aims of the institution in such areas as the projected number of students, scope of research activities, equity arrangements, and participation and graduation rates (Dawkins, 1987:29). The profile for each campus is different, reflecting individual resource constraints, regional requirements and particular aspirations. In addition to these measures, a proportion of research monies is made available on a competitive basis.

The second dimension of Dawkins' governing structure was the creation of a new statutory body—the National Board of Employment, Education and Training (NBEET)—to act in an advisory capacity to the minister and his department. NBEET replaces CTEC, but is quite different in scope and orientation. The purpose of this body is very much wider in so far as it is charged with reporting not only on the development of tertiary education, but also employment programs, schooling, skills training, research, and the promotion of greater industry involvement (EET ACT, 1988). Despite the salience of the Board's role, however, its power and potential influence have been limited to the submission of proposals. The actual determination of policy and its subsequent implementation is the responsibility of the minister and DEET. The Board's function, it seems, is to identify overall trends in the area of employment and education and let DEET get on with the detailed substance of policy making. The government appears determined that the Board will not emerge with the same status and independence that CTEC possessed in the early 1980s. One journalist described the new body as a 'toothless tiger' (Maslen, 1988).

The third dimension of the governing framework was the establishment of institutionalised consultative procedures with the states. Joint planning committees—comprising an equal number of commonwealth and state representatives—were proposed for each state, to be responsible to both state and commonwealth ministers. These bodies are to provide advice on the higher education needs of the states, the distribution of resources among institutions, intended new developments, and the scope of interaction with TAFE colleges (Dawkins, 1988a:72). The committees were seen as a vital component in ensuring the viability of the structure as a whole. It is only 'where the advice of a committee is acceptable to both levels of government', the green paper emphasised, that 'an agreed higher education program follows' (Dawkins, 1987:48).

Dawkins' reforms met with a vociferous reaction from large sections of the academic community. In particular, concern was expressed at the centralisation of control in DEET and the potential of the department to undermine institutional autonomy. By contrast, state governments and state co-ordinating authorities accepted the new format almost without demur. At a meeting of the Australian Education Council in February 1988, two months after the release of the green paper, all state ministers accepted 'in principle' the substance of the new governing structure and agreed to the establishment of interim joint planning committees (Dawkins, 1988b). Though 'some differences in approach' existed between ministers (Dawkins, 1988b), these appear to have been sorted out before the tabling of the white paper. During the first half of 1988, all states also approved the new arrangements for the provision of commonwealth funds for TAFE. The only public criticism from a state minister came two months after the release of the white paper when the Queensland Minister for Education accused Dawkins of promoting 'fascist conformity' in tertiary education and ignoring democratic diversity, 'particularly in Queensland' (Dawson, 1988b). This outburst, however, was probably more a reflection of the declining electoral fortunes of the Queensland government than a substantive attack on policy. There appear to have been a number of reasons underlying the states' ready acceptance of the commonwealth's proposals.

First, Dawkins had been careful to consult adequately with the states before the white paper was released and to put forward a governing framework which made provision for particular state requirements in the evolution of higher education policy. The white paper willingly acknowledged that the development of universities and colleges was a shared exercise; 'The emphasis is on partnership between the states and the commonwealth that best meets the joint interests and priorities of both levels of government' (Dawkins, 1988:73). The new structure, furthermore, gave the states a free hand with regard to the funding of courses and research projects relevant to regional needs. Dawkins also made no attempt to inhibit state efforts to encourage the emergence of private-sector institutions.

Second, the states strongly supported the managerialist rationale underlying Dawkins' governing framework. Concern for enhanced ministerial control and accountability over government activity was as prevalent in the states as it was at the commonwealth level. Indeed, a number of the states had preceded their federal counterparts in reforming their public sectors and state authorities along such lines (Yeatman, 1987; Painter, 1987). Furthermore, the introduction of corporate principals into the TAFE and secondary school sectors was well advanced in some quarters by the time the green paper was tabled (Duignan, 1987; Bessant, 1988). The direction proposed by Dawkins, therefore, was viewed as a logical progression of existing practice and very much in the interests of the provision of efficient state services. Perhaps indicative of state attitudes in this respect was that, shortly after the release of the white paper, the Victorian co-ordinating authority lost no time in preparing an evaluation of the relative performance of its twenty tertiary institutions in terms of educational provision and graduation rates (Slattery, 1988).

The third reason was that Dawkins' reforms—through the process of amalgamations—provided scope for the states to exercise greater control over the development of their campuses and to align their activities more closely to regional economic and social needs. Though the federal government required mergers on a large scale, the format of institutional structures was a state matter. The need to amend existing legislation in order to create new campuses enabled governments to alter the composition of governing councils to include a larger proportion of state government appointments. Moreover, fewer and larger campuses would facilitate state direction. Most states, in fact, set about the task of amalgamations with a zeal that must have surprised even Dawkins. Within a few months of the release of the white paper, the majority of states had drawn up far-reaching proposals. New South Wales intended reducing the number of its institutions to seven 'mega-universities', while Victoria envisaged emerging with eight. There is little doubt that the states welcomed the commonwealth's demands. As the Victorian Minister for Education remarked, 'Victoria sees the Dawkins approach as an opportunity, not an imposition' (Robinson, 1989).

Despite the states' support of the white paper's recommendations, strong elements of conflict began to develop late in 1988 between some states and the federal government when the implementation program began in earnest. Disagreement arose over the diverging interests of the two levels of government in relation to some aims and objectives. In one instance Queensland wanted to upgrade three of its CAEs to university status. A commonwealth task force opposed this move and recommended that a portion of Queensland's triennial grant be suspended unless the three campuses remained as CAEs. Federal opposition was based on grounds of 'national importance' (Dawson, 1989c); the CAEs, it was argued, lacked an adequate research capacity and any attempt to upgrade them would undermine the credibility of the Australian university sector as a whole. The question of amalgamations, in particular, has been problematic. Dawkins has been forceful in his demands for large-scale mergers and has threatened to withdraw federal monies unless appropriate outcomes are achieved. In several cases, however, the states have shown no desire to shoulder the political cost of forcing reluctant partners into an institutional marriage, especially in situations where the educational benefits are questionable. Satisfactory compromises in several of these disputes have been reached through direct ministerial negotiation (Dawson, 1989b). Others, such as the status of Queensland's CAEs, have been referred to the relevant joint planning committee for resolution. Some, however, are likely to fester for a more lengthy period. In the face of Dawkins' considerable displeasure, for example, the South Australian government simply refused to proceed with its proposals for campus amalgamations after strong grass-roots opposition had been expressed (Dawson, 1988a).

Overall, these developments point to the emergence of a more politicised tertiary education environment with regard to broad questions of policy direction. With colleges and universities now perceived as a vital economic and social resource, substantive differences over commonwealth and state objectives are bound to surface from time to time. While the majority of such disagreements will no doubt be settled by the joint planning committees, one longer-term consequence is likely to be a higher degree of ministerial involvement in policy issues and a more strained relationship between the two levels of government. This situation adds a new dimension to past practices in the intergovernmental arena.

Future development

Though governments will adopt a much more active role in the development of the tertiary education sector as a result of the new administrative framework, there nevertheless remains a high degree of continuity between CTEC's approaches and procedures and the structure presided over by DEET. In many respects, Dawkins' reforms build upon the strategies developed by the Commission. Much of the rationale underlying the operation of TAFE colleges, universities and CAEs was derived from CTEC's *Review of TAFE Funding* (1986b) and the *Review of Efficiency and Effectiveness in Higher Education* (1986a). Many of the programs initiated by CTEC in the early and mid-1980s are being maintained by DEET. It is also probable that the manner in which policy is processed under the Unified National System will bear some similarities to CTEC's policy network; that is, the institutions which make up the national system will play a significant role in the determination of broad outcomes. A number of factors suggest this.

First, an effort has been made to safeguard institutional autonomy. The rhetoric of the white paper goes so far as to suggest that universities and colleges now enjoy a higher degree of autonomy than during the CTEC years (Dawkins, 1988a:101). Though educational profiles are the subject of negotiation with DEET, it is up to individual campuses how they go about the actual business of achieving objectives. The department does not become involved in questions of internal management. The detailed implementation of goals therefore is very largely a matter for the institutions themselves. The need for such freedom is seen as essential, both to protect traditional academic functions and to foster entrepreneurial activity. There is recognition that a productive relationship with industry and the broader community will most effectively emerge from initiatives taken at the institutional level. Consequently, campuses will enjoy considerable discretion in the manner in which they carry out general policy directives. The impact of such activity, in turn, must influence the overall thrust of policy development.

Second, the new governing framework implicitly delegates considerable responsibility for policy making to the national system as a whole. The successful operation of the system relies heavily on the emergence of widespread co-operation between its constituent parts. Many of the educational objectives negotiated with DEET cannot be met by institutions in isolation. The implementation of equity programs, for example, requires the easy movement of students between campuses. To facilitate such interaction, and promote accepted procedures on important issues, the green and white papers look to employer associations and academic unions to provide direction. In particular, such bodies are to assist with the development of acceptable policy in relation to credit transfers, consistency in the grading of courses, staff assessment procedures and mechanisms for the evaluation of institutional performance. No doubt this involvement will extend to codes of conduct to regulate dealings with the business sector and other organisations. There are already indications that institutions are willing to collaborate. Several joint teaching and research programs have sprouted. Interest groups have also responded positively. The Australian Vice-Chancellors' Committee announced that it is 'striving for a new, vital image' and intends to play a salient role in the operation of the new governing framework (Dawson, 1989c). A likely outcome of these activities is that the system itself will become a significant factor in shaping the substance and evolution of policy.

Third, the ability of federal and state governments to determine the direction of tertiary education policy may well be limited by the demands of mutual adjustment. As DEET stated in its first Annual Report, educational objectives must be set 'in cooperation with State governments...and tertiary institutions' (DEET, 1988:92). This process inevitably involves bargaining and compromise in order to achieve acceptable outcomes. The result may be so vague as to mean all things to all participants. There is already some suggestion of this in DEET's statement of objectives which, for colleges and universities, are to:

- enhance the contribution of tertiary education towards the achievement of national economic and social development goals
- foster increased participation in tertiary education whilst enhancing quality of outcomes
- foster quality of access to opportunities in tertiary education for the disadvantaged (DEET, 1988:2).

The inherent problems of specifying goals such as 'enhancing quality of outcomes' is compounded by difficulties in the measurement and evaluation of institutional activity. In the absence of clear quantitative indices of success, just what constitutes appropriate performance may also become the subject of bargaining and negotiation between commonwealth and state authorities, institutions and interest groups. The inability to satisfactorily resolve such problems could well contain the managerialist thrust of the new governing structure and widen the degree of discretion possessed by campuses in the national system.

These three factors, taken together, suggest that tertiary institutions will probably end up with a substantial degree of responsibility for the conduct of their own affairs within Dawkins' new framework. While state and federal governments—particularly the latter—will determine overall directions, it is likely that much of the detail and substance of policy development will rest with campuses and related interest groups. Certainly, it would seem, the structure depends upon the co-operation of the organisations within the national system for stability and smoothness in operation as well as for creative initiative. In fact, the national system can be viewed as a community of sorts. It is probable that modes of interaction and negotiation that were utilised during the CTEC era will be refined and adopted to the requirements of the current framework. Commonality of academic values will still act as an adhesive binding campuses together and facilitating compromise between participants.

Yet it is unlikely that a policy environment resembling that of CTEC's community in the early 1980s will again emerge. The national system will be a much less integrated structure. A competitive element now exists between campuses (and between states), fuelled particularly by their recently acquired entrepreneurial functions in terms of fee-paying students and commercial research contracts. Moreover, the sectoral boundaries of the tertiary education arena are not nearly so distinct. The activities of campuses are increasingly merging with the commercial sphere and other policy areas. External groups such as business associations and unions are demanding greater involvement in the curriculum and teaching of colleges and universities. These developments work against the future emergence of clearly defined sectoral identity.

Concluding comments

Dawkins' reforms sprang from a growing conviction on the part of the commonwealth government that universities, CAEs and TAFE colleges had a critical role to play in the achievement of national goals. CTEC's relatively self-contained and internally regulated network appeared unable to respond adequately to the demands of an increasingly unpredictable and complex external policy environment. From Peterson et al.'s perspective the new structure is an appropriate outcome to the need for a more developmental orientation on the part of the tertiary education sector. Co-ordination of the activities of institutions with related areas such as industry and employment necessitates the intervention of political actors. While Peterson et al. suggest that developmental initiatives should usually be left to regional authorities, they make an exception with respect to programs that transcend local boundaries. Tertiary education has long been viewed as having national as well as state objectives and this perception undoubtedly facilitated intergovernmental acceptance of Dawkins' white paper.

Though the changes wrought by Dawkins have resulted in a substantially different approach to the governance of Australian tertiary education, they nevertheless build upon rather than replace the foundations which were laid in the 1960s. There is a strong element of evolutionary continuity. In many respects, the Unified National System consolidates the general thrust of university and CAE activity, a process that began with the AUC and CACAE and which matured under CTEC. While governments will set overall policy directions for the tertiary education sector, the successful implementation of policy—as in the past—really depends on the nature of the infrastructure created within the system and the collective involvement of institutions. The concept of institutional autonomy also remains much the same since the Martin inquiry of 1964. Though the white paper specifies the importance of accountability, efficiency and responsiveness, it must be remembered that the Martin Report similarly viewed the role of campuses in terms of national economic objectives (1964:ch. 1). Finally, the substance of intergovernmental relations in the tertiary education arena has, to a considerable extent, been maintained. Despite the division between the legal authority of the states and the fiscal powers of the commonwealth, interaction between the two levels of government has generally been co-operative. For many years, this was achieved through the medium of statutory education commissions. The pivotal contribution of the commissions has been removed but the institutionalised consultative procedures that evolved during their operation have been retained and refined. While Dawkins' reforms have undoubtedly introduced a new element of friction between the commonwealth and the states, the mutual dependency of their respective roles nevertheless remains and it seems likely that the great bulk of future concerns will continue to be resolved amicably.

Endnotes

1 In later years the AUC became the Universities Commission and the CACAE was redesignated the Commission on Advanced Education.
2 Initially CTEC was called the Tertiary Education Commission.

Bibliography

Anderson, D.S., 1982. 'Planning in a Strait-Jacket: Federal Limits to State Initiatives in Higher Education', in *Federal Intervention in Australian Education: Past, Present and Future*, eds G. Harman & D. Smart, Georgian House, Melbourne.

Anwyl, J., 1987. 'Sliding Towards Anarchy in Higher Education Planning', *FAUSA News: Newsletter of the Federation of University Staff Associations*, 6 May.

Australian Universities Commission, 1960. *Report of the Australian Universities Commission on Australian Universities 1958–68*, AGPS, Canberra.

Batistich, M., 1988. 'Defending the Freedom and Tradition', *The Advertiser*, 9 August.

Bessant, B., 1988. 'The Role of Corporate Management in the Reassertion of Government Control over the Curriculum of Victorian Schools', Paper presented to Australian Association for Research in Education Conference, University of New England.

Chapman, R., 1988. 'Inter-governmental Forums and the Policy Process', in *Comparative State Policies*, ed. B. Galligan, Longman Cheshire, Melbourne.

Chippendale, P.R., 1979. 'Accountability at the Federal Level', in *Accountability in Higher Education*, eds P. Sheldrake & R. Linke, Allen & Unwin, Sydney.

Commonwealth Advisory Committee on Advanced Education, 1966. *First Report of the Commonwealth Advisory Committee on Advanced Education*, AGPS, Canberra.

CTEC, Commonwealth Tertiary Education Commission Act, 1977. *CPP*.

CTEC, Commonwealth Tertiary Education Commission, 1986a. *Review of Efficiency and Effectiveness in Higher Education*, AGPS, Canberra.

—— 1986b. *Review of TAFE Funding*, AGPS, Canberra.

—— 1987. *Report for 1988–90 Triennium: Volume 1, Part 4: Advice of the Advanced Education Advisory Council*, AGPS, Canberra.

Dawkins, J.S., 1987. *Higher Education: A Policy Discussion Paper*, AGPS, Canberra.

—— 1988a. *Higher Education: A Policy Statement*, AGPS, Canberra.

—— 1988b. 'State Ministers Back Direction of Higher Education Reforms', Media Release 30A/88, Canberra.

Dawkins, J.S. & Holding, A.C., 1987. *Skills for Australia*, AGPS Canberra.

Dawson, C., 1988a. 'Bannon "Disappoints" Dawkins', *The Australian*, 28 December.

—— 1988b. 'Reforms Encourage "Fascist Conformity"', *The Australian*, 17 August.

—— 1989a. 'Man of Action Gives AVCC a Tougher, More Vital Role', *The Australian*, 15 February.

—— 1989b. 'Metherell and Dawkins Unveil Updated Plan', *The Australian*, 1 March.

—— 1989c. 'Queensland Army on Canberra Crusade', *The Australian*, 12 April.

Department of Employment, Education and Training, 1988. *Annual Report 1987–88*, AGPS, Canberra.

Duignan, P., 1987. 'The Politicisation of Administrative Reform in Australian Education', Paper presented to the British Educational Management and Administration Society Annual Conference, Southampton, UK.

Employment, Education and Training Act, 1988. *CPP*.

Fensham, P.J., 1981. 'Some Reflections on Four Years as a Member of the Universities Council', in *A Time of Troubles: Proceedings of a National Conference on Australian Tertiary Education and the 1982–84 Triennium*, eds J.E. Anwyl & G. Harman, Melbourne Centre for the Study of Higher Education.

Gallagher, A.P., 1982. *Coordinating Australian University Development*, University of Queensland Press, St Lucia.

Hall, W.C. & Willett, F.J., 1979. 'Accountability at the State Level', in *Accountability in Higher Education*, eds P. Sheldrake & R. Linke, Allen & Unwin, Sydney.

Hannan, K., 1987. 'VEF promises more tertiary places', *The Australian*, 4 November.

Harman, G., 1982. 'The Financing and Control of Tertiary Education: The Search for Appropriate and Acceptable Roles for Federal and State Governments', in *Federal Intervention in Australian Education: Past, Present and Future*, eds G. Harman & D. Smart, Georgian House, Melbourne.

—— 1984. 'Australian Experience with Co-ordinating Agencies', *Higher Education*, 13, 501–15.

Howse, W.J., 1982. 'Commonwealth Government Intervention in TAFE', in *Federal Intervention in Australian Education: Past, Present and Future*, eds G. Harman & D. Smart, Georgian House, Melbourne.

Hudson, H.R., 1985. *Review of the Structure of the Commonwealth Tertiary Education Commission and Arrangements for Co-ordination and Consultation with States and Institutions*, AGPS, Canberra.

Marshall, N., 1988. 'Bureaucratic Politics and the Demise of the Commonwealth Tertiary Education Commission', *Australian Journal of Public Administration*, 47(1).

Martin, L., 1964. *Tertiary Education in Australia: the Report of the Committee on the Future of Tertiary Education in Australia*, Government Printer, Canberra.

Maslen, G., 1988. 'A Difficult Birth, a Tougher Future', *The Age*, 21 July.

Murray, K., 1957. *Report of the Committee on Australian Universities*, Government Printer, Canberra.

Painter, M., 1987. *Steering the Modern State*, Sydney University Press, Sydney.

Peterson, P.E., Rabe, B.G. & Wong, K.K., 1986. *When Federalism Works*, The Brookings Institute, Washington.

Robinson, P., 1989. 'Victoria's Grand Design', *The Australian*, 8 March.

Scott, R., 1985. 'Governance—A Personal Perspective', *Journal of Tertiary Educational Administration*, 7(2), October.

Sharman, C., 1988. 'The University and Government', in *Campus in the Community: The University of Western Australia 1963–1987*, ed. B.K. de Garis, University of Western Australia Press, Perth.

Slattery, L., 1988. 'Deakin, Footscray least efficient, says report', *The Age*, 11 August.

Spaull, A., 1987. *A History of the Australian Education Council 1936–1986*, Allen & Unwin, Sydney.

Tertiary Education Commission, 1979. *Statement to Joint Parliamentary Committee of Public Accounts: Inquiry into Funding of Tertiary Education*, AGPS, Canberra.

Wark, I.W., 1977. 'Colleges of Advanced Education and Commission on Advanced Education', in *The Commonwealth Government and Education 1964–1976: Political Initiatives and Developments*, eds I.K.F. Birch & D. Smart, Drummond, Richmond.

Williams, B.R., 1979. *Education, Training and Employment: Report of the Committee of Inquiry into Education and Training*, Vol. 1, AGPS, Canberra.

Yeatman, A, 1987. 'The Concept of Public Management and the Australian State', *Australian Journal of Public Administration*, 46(4).

12   Housing policy

Andrew Parkin

Housing policy, by which is broadly meant the set of public policies which affect residential accommodation—and in particular its production, location, affordability, quality, mode of tenure and social distribution—is widely acknowledged to be of the utmost political sensitivity. It is, for example, commonplace at both state and commonwealth levels to interpret party electoral prospects and election campaign strategies in terms of their impact on the 'mortgage belt'—those outer-suburban seats, often marginal in electoral terms, which feature disproportionate numbers of home buyers.

Housing policy mobilises a variety of interests. The cost of houses and of mortgage repayments affects huge numbers of voters as well as being a key concern of financial institutions. The building and real estate industries, represented by the federally-organised Master Builders Association and the Real Estate Institute, have an interest in high levels of activity and investment in housing, as do trade unions with members in the building industry. There is also a well-organised lobby for public-rental and community-based co-operative housing, also in a federal structure, represented in Canberra by national shelter and in the states by local shelter committees. Many housing activists from this background are prominent within the Australian Labor Party and some have found their way on to ministerial staff at both commonwealth and state levels.

Unlike many other areas of human-services policy, there is a consensus among these business, union and community groups about many aspects of housing policy. Not only would all prefer lower interest rates, but they would also generally support increased investment in public rental housing, with the private building industry benefitting by the subcontracting of construction work.

The political sensitivity of housing policy has been heightened in recent years by the marked deterioration in many of the indicators of housing provision and affordability (Coopers & Lybrand & W.D. Scott, 1985; Kendig & Paris, 1987:37–47; Wettenhall, 1989). Interest rates have been at very high levels, affecting investment in all housing tenures. Average prices for privately purchased homes have risen markedly, most notably in the Sydney metropolitan area, leaving an increasing number of households unable to enter home ownership. Private rental accommodation is increasingly costly and increasingly scarce, particularly at the lower-priced end of the market. State public housing authorities report huge numbers on their waiting lists, along with serious budgetary problems. Crisis accommodation and emergency shelters also face high levels of client demand.

Corresponding to this range of housing problems are a range of policy instruments which might be brought to bear through the public sector. This chapter argues that intergovernmental relations are a critical factor shaping the public policy responses in the housing arena. The nature of intergovernmental arrangements in Australia is such that some relevant policy instruments are wielded at the commonwealth level but have strong implications for the states. Conversely, others are wielded at the state level but have strong implications for the commonwealth. Importantly, still others have a long history of commonwealth–state intergovernmental negotiation and financial arrangements.

This chapter explores housing policy from this intergovernmental perspective, focusing first on the political interdependencies which result from activities carried out in an ostensibly autonomous manner by either the commonwealth or the states. We then turn to an evaluation of the intergovernmental arrangements associated with the commonwealth–state housing agreements which have, for over 40 years, served as the avenue for conditional grants for housing purposes.

Policy autonomy and political interdependency

In March 1989, the premiers and ministers of housing of each of the states met in Canberra with their commonwealth counterparts in a so-called housing summit. The summit—its rationale and its outcome—revealed much about the intergovernmental interdependencies which characterise housing policy. It quickly became clear that the commonwealth and the states differed in their perceptions of the problems besetting the housing sector.

At the commonwealth level, the Hawke Government was particularly concerned about the impact of rising housing costs on the consumer price index and the consequent flow-on effects on wage demands and social security payments. The commonwealth position was that significant contributors to the problem were the limited supply of metropolitan land for new housing and unnecessarily restrictive regulations governing the density and style of housing construction. These factors could only be directly addressed at the state level.

The states, however, saw the problems in the housing sector as caused primarily by the high cost of finance and by the restrictions on public-sector borrowing imposed by commonwealth macro-economic policies. These policies affected housing affordability in the private sector through the mortgage interest rates charged to home buyers and investors in private rental housing. They also increased the cost of public-sector borrowings for the purposes of acquiring public rental stock and of providing the public service infrastructure necessary for suburban development. The latter problem is of particular relevance to the commonwealth's concerns about limitations on the supply of subdividable urban land.

These differing perspectives, with each level of government tending to locate the primary responsibility for the housing crisis with the other level, illustrate the workings of the federal system in the housing arena. Under the constitution, housing policy, in the strict sense of the provision or regulation of residential accommodation, can be understood as one of the residual powers left to the states. This constitutional demarcation is also a fair reflection of everyday practice: with the exceptions noted below, it is under state authority that Australian property transactions are registered, landlord–tenant relationships are regulated, new housing developments are approved and public housing tenancies are provided.

Yet there is also no doubt that commonwealth policies make a powerful impact on the housing sector and thus on the task facing the states. Table 12.1 summarises the officially reported 'total housing expenditure' for the commonwealth for 1986–87. Several areas of commonwealth spending stand out. The largest single item involves the transfer of substantial funds to the states under the Commonwealth–State Housing Agreement, an intergovernmental program of considerable significance, examined later in this chapter. The next largest item is the Supplementary Rent Assistance scheme, an adjunct to the commonwealth's social security responsibilities, providing extra payments of up to $15 per week to social security beneficiaries who are also private renters. Some 642 000 people were receiving this assistance in 1987 (Gruen, 1988:13). The third largest item is the First Home Owners Scheme, introduced by the Hawke Government in October 1983 to provide up to $7000 to moderate-income first home buyers. By July 1988, it had assisted more than 300 000 applicants and was clearly important in budgetary terms, though there is some dispute about whether it has had any net impact on opportunities for home ownership (Paris, 1987:7–13; Gruen, 1988:12; Orchard, 1989:378–80).

Other programs listed in Table 12.1 cover housing activities incidental to other commonwealth powers, such as benefits for serving or retired defence personnel, public rental accommodation and home-purchase assistance in the Australian Capital Territory, and housing for Aborigines. The latter, as generally applies to Aboriginal affairs, undoubtedly provokes many intergovernmental complexities which require more detailed analysis than this chapter can offer.

Table 12.1 notes the cost to the commonwealth of a temporary subsidy to savings banks for maintaining mortgage interest rates at 13.5 per cent for loans taken out before April 1986, and there is a brief reference under 'tax system assistance' to the financial legacy of a discarded program of tax rebates on mortgage interest payments for certain categories of home buyers. These two items are the only hints in the table, officially headed 'total housing expenditure' by the commonwealth DCS&H, of broader policy instruments by which the commonwealth makes a powerful impact on the housing sector (and thus on the policy and political problems facing the states). Macro-economic policies relating to interest rates and to taxation are particularly significant.

Table 12.1: Housing expenditure—commonwealth government, 1986–87

	$m	%
Conditional grants to states under the		
Commonwealth–State Housing Agreement[a]	700.5	37.9
Other housing programs		
First Home Owners Scheme	200.9	10.9
Defence service homes	123.5	6.7
Supplementary rent assistance	319.1	17.2
Housing for service personnel	111.4	6.0
Aged/disabled	98.7	5.3
Aborigines	118.7	6.4
Housing in the ACT	48.2	2.6
Savings bank subsidies to cover		
protected 13.5% mortgages	86.9	4.7
Other	17.1	0.9
Tax system assistance (mainly		
rebates on home-loan interest)	22.0	1.2
TOTAL	1847.3	100.0

Note: [a] includes funds under the States Grants (Housing) Act which replaced the CSHA for 1971 and 1972, and other minor related programs.

Source: DCSH (l988a:24).

The Hawke Government's deregulation of financial markets and its maintenance of high interest rates have had a powerful impact on housing. For decades, housing finance was accorded a privileged position within the Australian financial system with banks required to make certain proportions of loan funds available for home purchase at regulated interest rates. Deregulation of the financial system by the Hawke Government soon made this privileged position untenable: the banks argued that they were unable to compete with deregulated institutions while restricted in the returns which they could gain from mortgage lending. In April 1986, the 13.5 per cent interest rate ceiling for all new bank mortgages was lifted. Since then, the rate for such new borrowers has been consistently well above the 13.5 per cent still enjoyed by those with older mortgages.

This decision, while unequivocally a responsibility of the commonwealth government, had political ramifications for state governments, particularly Labor governments, who feared that voters might not make fine distinctions about constitutional responsibilities in the course of election campaigns. Indeed, the Hawke Government's earlier resistance to pressure for deregulation of mortgage interest rates can be partly explained as protecting the re-election chances of Labor governments in Western Australia and South Australia. In the course of the South Australian campaign in December 1985, the Prime Minister gave a commitment that the ceiling on mortgage interest rates would be maintained (Orchard, 1989:379). Both the Bannon Government in South Australia and the Burke Government in Western Australia, in the course of their successful re-election campaigns, committed sizeable sums of public money to the short-term subsidisation of building society mortgage lending.

Rising interest rates also affect the states in terms of their own borrowings for capital works. This, allied with effective commonwealth dominance of the Loan Council, which directly limits state government loan programs and sets 'global limits' on borrowing by state instrumentalities, means that both the scope and the real cost of state borrowings are under fairly tight commonwealth constraints. Beginning with the 1986–87 budget year, the commonwealth, pursuing its policy of public-sector financial restraint, has cut back severely on the permitted scope of state borrowings.

Loan Council arrangements have a direct impact on state housing policies because a large proportion of state borrowings through the Loan Council have been used for the construction and acquisition of public rental housing. From 1982, successive commonwealth governments have encouraged the utilisation of Loan Council borrowings for this purpose by charging states a concessionary interest rate of just 4.5 per cent over 53 years repayment for any such borrowings 'nominated' for public housing. The states' responses are worth noting in some detail because they illustrate how states vary both in their policy priorities and in their ability to respond quickly to intergovernmental financial opportunities.

As Table 12.2 shows, South Australia alone, starting in budget year 1983–84, took quick advantage of the concessionary finance by 'nominating' 100 per cent of its Loan Council borrowings. In the next year, 1984–85, it was joined by only Western Australia. With the other

Table 12.2: Loan Council funds nominated for housing

	NSW		VIC.		QLD		WA		SA		TAS.	
	(a)	(b)	(a)	(b)	(a)	(b)	(a)	(b)	(a)	(b)	(a)	(b)
1982–83	100	6.8	100	32.6	100	7.1	100	8.5	100	21	100	15.7
1983–84	100	6.3	100	18.1	100	7.7	100	7.7	100	100	100	26.2
1984–85	100	23.7	100	17.2	100	21.7	100	100.0	100	100	100	25.0
1985–86	30	20.0	30	30.0	30	30.0	100	100.0	100	100	30	30.0
1986–87	60	60.0	60	60.0	60	60.0	100	100.0	100	100	60	60.0
1987–88	100	100.0	100	100.0	100	100.0	100	100.0	100	100	100	100.0
1988–89	100	n.a.	100	n.a.	100	n.a.	100	n.a.	100	n.a.	100	n.a.

For each state, column (a) represents the percentage of its total Loan Council allocation permitted to be 'nominated' for public housing under concessional repayment terms. Column (b) indicates the percentage of the allocation actually so nominated.

n.a. = figure not available

Source: DCS&H (1988b:12–13)

states slowly gearing up to avail themselves of the 'cheap' money, the commonwealth moved (on strong treasury advice) to limit its availability. At the 1985 and 1986 Loan Council meetings, South Australia and Western Australia were permitted to maintain their 100 per cent nomination, but the proportion available to the other states was limited to no more than 30 per cent for 1985–86 and 60 per cent (of a reduced total loan allocation) in 1986–87. In 1987–88 and 1988–89, with the total pool of loan funds even more sharply reduced, all states have been permitted to nominate 100 per cent (with a quarter of these converted by the commonwealth to grants in 1988–89). From 1989–90, as discussed later in this chapter, the commonwealth has proposed terminating the 'nominated' loan scheme altogether.

Commonwealth taxation policies are also an important influence on housing through specific housing-related provisions or exemptions. Historically, there have been a number of tax provisions favouring home ownership. Like most OECD countries, Australia does not tax the 'imputed rent' effectively earned by owner-occupiers. From 1982–83 until 1986–87, rebates on mortgage interest payments applied to first-home buyers. The capital gains tax, introduced with effect from September 1985, exempts the owner-occupied house (as does the assets test on the aged pension). These tax concessions serve as incentives for investment in owner-occupied housing.

Other significant tax measures relate to investment in private rental housing. In 1985, in addition to imposing the capital gains tax on such investment, the Hawke Government abolished 'negative gearing' provisions which had permitted full deductibility of interest payments beyond the rental earned, though it introduced a depreciation allowance in partial compensation. When, subsequently, investment in private rental accommodation declined significantly, the government was under pressure to reverse the decision. It did so in September 1987.

Again, these commonwealth programs and policies have implications for state governments. Taxation-induced variations in the rate of investment in housing affect employment rates in the local building industry and the demand for state-provided urban infrastructure services. They also affect housing costs through the complex interaction of supply and demand. Sometimes this effect seems perverse: the reintroduction of negative gearing, for example, which was surely intended to increase the supply and hence lower the rents of private rental housing, may instead have increased the investor demand for, and the market cost of, established houses (Wettenhall, 1989; Hayward & Burke, 1989). That the commonwealth recognises the political implications of such matters for the states is again demonstrated by the timing of policy changes, with the Hawke Government's reversal on negative gearing closely connected with the re-election campaign of the Unsworth Labor Government in New South Wales.

To this point, the chapter has considered activities under commonwealth jurisdiction which have important implications for the states in terms of housing policy. Correspondingly, activities of state governments in functional areas under their jurisdiction affect and constrain the commonwealth. The commonwealth's position at the housing summit was that the major factors affecting housing prices were the limited availability of metropolitan land for housing sub-division and regulations restricting the density and design of housing. These are clearly matters under state jurisdiction (though states delegate many details to local government).

The states have learned over the past 40 years that metropolitan planning, which aims to ensure sufficient adequately serviced land to meet demand at any particular time, is a complex logistical exercise. The task is complicated because the planning process needs to consider, in addition to the efficient meeting of market demands, the impact of metropolitan development on social equity (such as the access from new fringe suburbs to employment, transportation and community services) and on the natural environment. That policies and procedures have differed between states, and over time within states, reflects both the different circumstances in different metropolitan areas and the inherent organisational and political difficulties involved in regulating private markets in this way (Parkin, 1982, 1989; Alexander, 1986; Wilmoth, 1988).

Likewise, the regulation of the density and design of housing development, much of which is delegated by the states to local government, has several goals, including protecting local amenity and property values, reducing the cost of public infrastructure services and responding to the initiatives of property developers. In recent years, some states have developed 'urban consolidation' policies permitting higher densities, but these remain politically contentious and organisationally tentative (Bunker, 1989).

Despite its keen interest, as manifest in the housing summit, the commonwealth remains relatively powerless over such matters. Attempts in the past (most notably under the Whitlam Government) to intervene in urban affairs from the commonwealth level have demonstrated the intergovernmental difficulties involved (Troy, 1978b; Painter, 1979; Lloyd & Troy, 1981; Parkin, 1982:116–34). An example was the Whitlam Government's attempt to introduce public land banks in the major Australian metropolitan areas, an initiative hampered by the necessity to act through the states (Troy, 1978a). At the housing summit, the commonwealth offered to release some of its own metropolitan land holdings for housing development, a move which will boost supply but which will depend for effective implementation on state planning and development programs.

The commonwealth is also fairly powerless to act in respect of the liberalisation of building regulations. It has co-sponsored, with state and private-sector involvement, the Joint Venture for More Affordable Housing, a project which has achieved cost savings through liberalised planning and building regulations in several small housing developments. However, the value of this program is demonstrative only.

Besides setting the broad developmental parameters for housing construction, the states also directly intervene in the housing market. Two policy objectives—providing public rental accommodation and offering financial assistance to lower-income home purchasers—account for nearly all of the direct state expenditure on housing matters. A long history of commonwealth conditional grants makes the state programs which pursue these objectives particularly interesting from an intergovernmental perspective. The following section evaluates this intergovernmental history.

The Commonwealth–State Housing Agreements

In 1986–87, as Table 12.1 above has shown, $700.5 million was granted by the commonwealth to the states under the Commonwealth–State Housing Agreement (CSHA). Roughly the same nominal amount was provided in the following two years, 1987–86 and 1986–89, equivalent to the minimum amount guaranteed by the commonwealth under the current agreement.

There has been a succession of CSHAs operating since 1945, except for the two financial years 1970–72. An agreement with effect from 1984 has been operating for most of the period of the Hawke Government, and a new CSHA was negotiated during 1989 and early 1990 with financial effect from July 1989.

The CSHAs provide a fascinating insight into the politics of commonwealth grant programs. Some commentators have argued in the past that the policy conditions attached to the CSHA grants significantly constrain state housing policies: 'The State housing authorities operate within the budget limits and policy directives set by the Commonwealth as outlined in successive Commonwealth–State Housing Agreements (CSHAs). Each CSHA provides an explicit statement of what the Commonwealth considers to be its priorities with regard to public housing' (Burke, Hancock & Newton, 1984:76). Newton and Wulff write: 'It is evident that, despite their nominal constitutional rights in regard to housing, the State housing authorities in Australia experience strong centrally imposed restraint on their autonomy via the triennial Commonwealth–State Housing Agreements' (1983:9). A cursory examination of the history of the CSHAs (Pugh, 1976) might well reinforce such an impression.

The first CSHA emerged from the post-war reconstruction initiatives of the Chifley Labor Government, in 1945. The agreement provided finance to increase the stock of public rental housing, the sale of which was strongly discouraged through financial disincentives. In 1956, under the Menzies administration, these conditions were amended to facilitate the sale of rental dwellings by permitting the housing authorities to use CSHA money for vendor financing. Subsequent agreements in 1961 and 1966 reinforced this. Under Whitlam in 1973, major changes were introduced. A means test was imposed for the first time on new public rental allocations. Sales were restricted to just 30 per cent of new completions. CSHA funds were permitted to be used for 'community amenities' in housing estates and for the spot-purchasing of dwellings. Agreements under the Fraser Government in 1976 and 1981 saw new emphases. Public housing rents were henceforth to be raised to 'market-related' levels for those tenants who could afford it, in order to help authorities to be more self-financing and to induce higher-income earners to leave. Sale of public housing was to be at full market value, with no further vendor financing permitted.

The agreement of 1984, negotiated under the Hawke Government, represented, according to one observer, 'a major landmark in housing policy in Australia' (Carter, 1985:10). Among the reforms were the abolition of the market-related rent requirement and its replacement by 'cost rents' (in an attempt to make more equitable the public policy treatment of public tenants and home owners). Housing authorities were to be open to applicants without discrimination on the basis of 'age, sex, marital status, race, religion, disability or life situation'. Home purchase assistance programs had to ensure that any subsidy was repaid by the purchaser during the course of the loan. Several specific programs for community housing and crisis accommodation received earmarked grants.

This potted history seems broadly consistent with the philosophies of incumbent governments in Canberra and thus to represent the imposition of commonwealth priorities on the states through the conditional grants. Such an interpretation is, however, misleading. While states may sometimes invoke CSHA conditions to explain or rationalise aspects of their housing activities (both at the level of overall funding effort and in terms of program administration), CSHAs have not in fact been a major constraint on state housing policies. Those policies can still largely be understood as determined at the state level. Fundamentally, the Agreements need to be understood precisely as 'agreements'. Rarely have they been a vehicle for imposing unacceptable conditions on a reluctant state. Further, the language of the Agreements is characteristically flexible enough for states to find avenues for pursuing their own objectives.

One level of evidence supporting this conclusion is the dramatic lack of uniformity between states in significant housing policies, including those which are ostensibly the subject of CSHA stipulations. The variation between the states in policies and practices is apparent from the following examples:

1   The overall commitment of state funds to housing programs ranged in 1987–88 from $194 per capita in the most committed state (South Australia) to barely a quarter of this amount ($49 per capita) in Victoria (DCS&H, 1988b:18).

2   The relative allocations by states to home purchase assistance programs as distinct from public rental programs ranged in 1986–87 from a 19 per cent allocation to home-purchase assistance in New South Wales to 60 per cent in Queensland (DCS&H, 1988b:54).

3   Eligibility requirements for public tenancies vary from strict means tests in some states to no formal income tests, except in the sense of priority allocations for emergency cases, in others (DCS&H, 1988a:59–61).

4   Levels of rent for public rental units vary significantly, with a typical full rent for a three-bedroom house in June 1987 being $66 in Adelaide but $123 in Sydney (DCS&H, 1988a:142).

5   Rent rebates provided to public tenants on low incomes differ between states, with, for example, a single pensioner in June 1987 paying 17 per cent of the pension in rent had he or she lived in Western Australia but 24 per cent in Queensland (DCS&H, 1988a:67).

6   Eligibility and repayment requirements for subsidised home-purchase loans vary between states (DCS&H, 1988a:48–55).

7   Decisions on the design and location of public housing stock, and on opportunities for tenant participation in management, have quite distinct interstate variations.

These differences between states in housing policies and practices, and the historical developments which have produced them, are fully documented elsewhere (Parkin, 1988).

The CSHAs should be understood as an intergovernmental process which has conceded rather than challenged these interstate differences. Evidence for this conclusion comes from throughout the history of the CSHAs.

The original 1945 agreement was effectively restricted to rental housing largely because, as Troy and Lloyd (1986:5) argue, the commonwealth 'could not win the support of state governments' for more radical programs. Kilner (1989:439) agrees: 'Commonwealth dreams of a comprehensive housing policy failed because it lacked the power to enforce [such a policy] and because the states would not voluntarily oblige the commonwealth'. The Playford Government in South Australia actually refused any funds until 1953 because it could raise its own finance at comparable cost and did not wish to be restricted to rental housing (Pugh, 1976:29; Badcock, 1986:171–73; Kilner, 1989:444–47). The agreements of 1956, 1961 and 1966 deliberately loosened controls even further, consistent with the Menzies view of federalism.

While the commonwealth intention under Whitlam in 1973 may have been to redirect the states, that was hardly the result. Restrictions on the sale of rental stock were ineffective. The states successfully opposed the original intention to enforce a complete ban and agreed only to limit sales to 30 per cent of new dwellings. Thus they could still sell existing stock, and three states (Victoria, Queensland and Western Australia) did so at an accelerating rate.

The means test was also a watered-down version of the original proposal. Carter (1980:109, 111) concludes that 'it is doubtful whether the clause had much practical impact' and in any case 'the motley of existing state means tests seems to have achieved the same outcome'. With the test imposed only at an aggregate level (85 per cent of allocations were to be to households with incomes below 85 per cent of average weekly earnings), it seems unlikely that it produced any significant changes in allocation patterns. Even a state like South Australia, with virtually open eligibility, was apparently unaffected; in fact, the precise percentage figures adopted in the Agreement were those which could accommodate without change the actual allocation practice in South Australia. The other goals of the 1973 Agreement seem to have been similarly bypassed (Carter, 1980:113–14).

The Agreement under Fraser in 1978 is consistent with that government's more conservative approach, but again it would be misleading to interpret it as a Canberra imposition. At the outset, the states simply refused to endorse the commonwealth's proposal to provide all grants at market interest rates (with compensating cash grants), and so this idea was abandoned (Harris, 1978:9–10; Dalton, 1979:85–86). A revealing clause was included in the agreement which affirmed that 'the states will be able to exercise maximum autonomy and flexibility in the administrative arrangements necessary to achieve these principles.'

The move towards market rents was not a unilateral Fraser Government initiative. It followed the recommendations of two reports, from the Commission of Inquiry into Poverty (1975:164–66) and the Priorities Review Staff (1975:101), instigated under the Whitlam Government, and was also independently proposed by a number of states (Carter, 1980:110; Dalton, 1979:114; Harris, 1978:12). After negotiation, the Agreement was worded to suggest gradual evolution to 'market-related' rents; what this might mean was left to the states, and their practices varied as widely as before (Burke, Hancock & Newton, 1984:105). Western Australia, for example, described its market-related rent in 1984—six years after the agreement—in the following terms:

> Rents are now market related though not market matching. Only 63 percent of the weighted average rent for similar accommodation in the private sector was charged as rent for a medium standard 3 bedroom house by the State in September 1983.
>
> Similarly, a two bedroom flat rented for about 45 percent less than its private sector equivalent. (Western Australian Minister of Housing, 1984:16)

Under this strange logic, any level of rent could be described as 'market-related'. Further, Queensland's introduction of income-related rent in 1982 was simply an abandonment of any pretence at market-related principles (Jones, 1983).

Even more than before, the 1984 Agreement was the product of discussion, featuring this time the four Labor states negotiating with a fairly compliant and sympathetic commonwealth government (Bethune, 1985; Carter, 1985). This consensus-building was in part a reaction to the cutbacks in commonwealth grants under Fraser, in part the coincidence of four Labor governments in state office dealing with a new consensus-oriented Labor government in Canberra, in part reflective of the state-based policy experiences of key advisers on housing to the Hawke Government. The ideas which became part of the 1984 Agreement (cost rents, non-discrimination, triennial reviews, a ten-year agreement, equity between tenures, a focus on housing-related poverty) can be found almost entirely in papers and submissions from the Labor states and from the lobby group National Shelter (Bethune, 1983; National Shelter, 1984; Victoria, 1984a; Victoria, 1984b; New South Wales, 1984; South Australia, 1984).

The clause bestowing 'maximum autonomy and flexibility' on state administration was retained, and the implementation of the 1984 CSHA followed the familiar pattern of interstate variation. 'Cost rents' have been as variable between states in interpretation and calculation as had 'market-related rents' (DCS&H, 1988a:62); a later review commissioned by the commonwealth Minister for Housing argued that in any case 'the cost rent system remains unworkable' (Flood, 1988:8). Queensland was, this time, specifically exempted from compliance because cost rents were merely specified as the minimum to be charged. Elsewhere, rent increases have on several occasions been publicly attributed by state ministers to 'commonwealth requirements' (Homeswest, 1986; South Australian Minister of Housing and Construction, 1986), even though the implied counter-factual—that rents would not have increased in the absence of the CSHA provision—is ridiculous.

The non-discrimination clause of the 1984 Agreement contained a major loophole: 'priority in granting assistance shall be determined by the need for assistance'. Such needs and priorities are determined by the states. It was fairly clear from the outset that Queensland intended to do little about opening public housing for young single applicants, and it is equally clear that the CSHA has not been an effective instrument for forcing Queensland to act otherwise (Kendig & Paris, 1987:99). Likewise, the provision in the Agreement that subsidies to home purchasers in the form of reduced interest rates were to be recovered in later years carried the rider 'except in circumstances determined by the state minister [which] have regard to movements in house prices and in the income of home purchasers' (DCS&H, 1988a:90). At least some states have made no move whatever to recover the interest subsidies.

Under the 1984 Agreement, the states have been required to match the untied funds provided by the commonwealth on a dollar-for-dollar basis, with a clear implication that these funds be used for capital purposes. However, as observed in a background paper commissioned in 1988 by the commonwealth minister, 'these requirements are now more honoured in the breach' (Flood, 1988:6). The Agreement has allowed the states' 'matching' to be achieved in a way which does not necessarily commit them to large amounts from their own budgets. The states are permitted to include the revolving funds arising from the repayments of home-purchase assistance loans. In South Australia, the money passing through this revolving fund in 1986–87 more than matched the untied commonwealth grants under the CSHA. The states have also increasingly used the commonwealth grant for recurrent purposes in order to cope with a revenue shortfall as recurrent costs exceed rent receipts.

Other aspects of the 1984 negotiations further weaken any hypothesis about commonwealth domination. Much of the discussion consisted of the states pressuring the commonwealth rather than vice versa. In particular, the states argued that the commonwealth should assume the full cost of rent rebates as an item in its social security budget. The case for this was virtually conceded by the commonwealth minister (AHMC, 1984:11), though it was financially too daunting to be adopted. The agreement did, however, permit the use of CSHA money to offset rent rebates up to a certain level—'a *de facto* recognition by the commonwealth' of the states' case (Carter, 1985:8).

The negotiations also involved the states pressuring each other. While the states have been remarkably united on several recent occasions (as manifest in an unprecedented joint submission for the 1986–87 commonwealth budget (New South Wales, Victoria, 1986)), the distribution of CSHA funds between states is a zero-sum game which strains interstate unity. Until 1981, commonwealth untied funds for housing were allocated on a basis that rewarded states which themselves made a greater financial commitment. Some states, notably South Australia, in this way received more than a *per capita* proportion. During the 1981 negotiations, demands by the larger states for *per capita* funding led to an undertaking to phase in such an arrangement by 1991. South Australia continued to oppose the redistribution (AHMC, 1984:24–34) and the 1984 negotiations produced a compromise in the form of a Grants Commission review of the arguments and figures. The phasing-in has since continued, and South Australia's share of untied commonwealth CSHA grants has fallen as a consequence from 14.2 per cent in 1981–82 to 9.8 per cent in 1988–89 (DCS&H, 1988b:11, 33).

Included under the 1984 CSHA were three specific programs for which separate earmarked funds have been provided on a *per capita* basis. These funds were earmarked presumably in an attempt to restrict state-level discretion. Together, however, these programs—the Mortgage and Relief scheme, the Crisis Accommodation Program and the Local Government and Community Housing Program—accounted for just 7 per cent of all CSHA grants in 1986–87.

The Mortgage and Rent Relief scheme in particular, though an earmarked allocation, has given the states remarkable autonomy. Initiated in the last year of the Fraser Government as a response to rising mortgage interest rates, it has allowed each state to choose its own pattern of spending. Queensland actually refused the money in the first year; it has since used the money mainly as capital for accommodation managed by other agencies. Victoria attempted direct rent relief and, overwhelmed by the demand, suspended the scheme before restructuring it. New South Wales has concentrated on financing community-based low-income rental accommodation. South Australia has been prepared to provide direct rental subsidies. It is not unlikely that the interstate variations represent responses to housing accommodation problems which themselves vary between the states (Kendig & Paris, 1987:102).

Table 12.3 documents this diversity in funding allocations under the Mortgage and Rent Relief scheme. It actually understates it because there has been further variation in eligibility and application criteria *within* each category of spending reported (DCS&H, 1988a:78–82, 158–59) and some variation within states from year to year. States have been required to match commonwealth funding on a dollar-for-dollar basis, though all states—to significantly varying degrees—have contributed more than the required matching sum.

Table 12.3: Mortgage and Rent Relief Scheme, 1986–87, allocation of funds by the states

	NSW	VIC.	QLD	WA	SA	TAS.
Mortgage relief	13.3	8.6	26.1	6.4	10.2	0.1
Rent relief	24.8	61.7	28.1	80.5	88.9	66.5
Capital projects	0.0	17.4	32.9	0.0	0.0	23.1
Community housing	49.3	0.0	0.0	0.0	0.0	0.0
Administration	12.4	12.2	12.9	13.0	0.0	10.3
Other	0.0	0.0	0.0	0.0	1.0	0.0
TOTAL	100.0	100.0	100.0	100.0	100.0	100.3

Source: DCS&H (1988a:83).

The South Australia figures, which allocate nothing to administration, almost certainly need adjustment before making comparison. If a notional 12 per cent is attributed to administration in South Australia, then its 'mortgage relief' figure becomes 8.9 per cent while its rent relief figure becomes 77.3 per cent.

The other two earmarked programs—the Crisis Accommodation Program and the Local Government and Community Housing Program—have involved commonwealth and state officials jointly recommending project allocations to their respective ministers, followed by joint announcements. Despite this close commonwealth interest, the outcomes have still varied between the states (Butler, 1986a, 1986b; King, 1986; Thompson & Purcell, 1986). The commonwealth has been investing an extraordinary level of staff resources to help oversee programs which are, first, a trivial proportion of their total CSHA funding and, second, display little tendency to national uniformity as a result.

The evidence presented in this chapter strongly suggests that CSHA grants do not significantly constrain the states; as Kendig and Paris (1987:60) conclude, 'the CSHA provides little scope for actual commonwealth influence once the accountants transfer dollars to the states'. A further factor promoting relative state autonomy is the decreasing proportion which those grants comprise of state housing funds. Whereas in 1976–77, 75 per cent of state expenditure on housing programs came from commonwealth CSHA grants, the figure was just 33.5 per cent in 1987–88. In South Australia, the decline has been even more dramatic: from 80 per cent to 21 per cent.

These funding trends are illustrated in Figure 12.1, which plots real levels of funding for housing programs under the CSHA since 1974–75. Steep declines under the Fraser Government provoked increased effort by the states to find alternative sources. Real increases in commonwealth grants in the first few years under the Hawke Government still did not match the increasing state effort. In the last few years, the commonwealth contribution has again declined in real terms, and the states' use of alternative funds at their disposal has again increased.

Though the 1984 Agreement specified a ten-year period of operation, the commonwealth Minister of Housing and Aged Care, Peter Staples, proposed to the states in May 1989 that a new commonwealth–state housing agreement be negotiated, to take effect from July 1989. The Premiers' Conference and Loan Council had agreed to consolidate the 'nominated funds' previously allocated under the Loan Council into the commonwealth's CSHA grant. For the states, this carried the advantage of replacing loan monies (albeit at low interest rates) with grant monies, but on the other hand, it brought these funds within the CSHA ambit. (It also, incidentally, brought these funds under the *per capita* formula, even further annoying 'high effort' states like South Australia.)

The commonwealth Minister appeared to have taken this funding change as an opportunity to increase the commonwealth's involvement in determining how the CSHA funds are spent. The Minister had just received the recommendations of a major review of housing policy conducted within his department and the proposed elements in the foreshadowed 1989 Agreement emanated largely from that review.

Figure 12.1: Funding by commonwealth and states for CSHA housing programs, 1974–75 to 1987–88

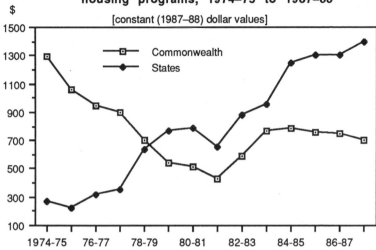

Source: DCS&H (1988a:101).

The commonwealth proposed that its CSHA grant be used strictly for capital purposes in acquiring further public rental stock, with the states required (after a phase-in period) to match this dollar for dollar. At least half of the state matching funds would be 'real' budget allocations (rather than revolving funds or loan monies) required to be spent on public rental stock. The other half of the state matching funds could be allocated to home-purchase assistance and could include revolving funds. The states would be able to draw on the rental capital account to repay principal and interest to the commonwealth from previous loans, but they would not be permitted to fund rent rebates from the account. The commonwealth proposal, in effect, provided for grants as the capital basis for acquisition of public rental stock, and then expected state housing authorities to cover their recurrent costs through rents or extra state funding.

The commonwealth further proposed that the expenditure of funds in the rental capital account would be covered within each state by a bilaterally-negotiated commonwealth–state plan. If the commonwealth and a state did not reach a consensus on such a plan, the commonwealth proposed that the new 1989 agreement would permit it to earmark funds within that state alone for a particular, commonwealth-specified purpose.

The commonwealth Minister and his advisers appeared to have recognised the autonomy which the states have enjoyed in the expenditure of commonwealth grants under the previous CSHAs. The new proposals represented an attempt to limit this autonomy and to impose some commonwealth priorities (such as increasing the public rental stock and promoting tenant participation in management). The suggestion about bilateral commonwealth–state plans, and the threat of the earmarking of commonwealth grants in recalcitrant states only, were novel steps in this direction, perhaps generalising the process already used for the Crisis Accommodation and the Local Government and Community Housing programs.

The 1989 Agreement thus represents another attempt by the commonwealth to increase its influence over the expenditure of CSHA funds and, more broadly, to influence state-level housing policies and priorities. The essential features of the commonwealth proposals survived the intergovernmental negotiations through 1989 and early 1990 with some amendments in terms of detail, with the most vociferous opposition coming from South Australia on the grounds of the effect of the accelerated *per capita* funding rather than on major housing policy grounds.

The analysis presented in this chapter suggests that the common-wealth will find it difficult to significantly increase its capacity to control details about the expenditure of CSHA funds. Implementation of the new Agreement is still likely to leave the states with considerable autonomy. It is difficult to envisage the proposed bilateral commonwealth–state plans as being much more than an endorsement of the broad directions and general spending plans devised by the state authorities. The commonwealth simply does not have the staff resources or expertise for detailed involvement.

The commonwealth's most important influence through the CSHA will remain its overall level of funding allocation. On this matter, commonwealth housing officials have tended to act within Canberra as budgetary advocates for increased CSHA grants to the states. There is probably a deeper bureaucratic rift between the commonwealth housing portfolio and the commonwealth financial portfolios than between commonwealth and state housing policy advisers.

Conclusion

This chapter has argued that housing policy in Australia is paradoxically characterised both by strong intergovernmental interdependencies and by relatively autonomous activities by the two levels of government within their respective spheres. The commonwealth is powerful in the setting of macro-economic parameters, but the states dominate the detailed formulation and implementation of policy with respect to the delivery of services to consumers. Commonwealth conditional grants under the CSHA act as only a minor constraint.

Though housing policy of course displays some idiosyncrasies, the findings here are consistent with recent scholarship on Australian federalism, which portrays a complex interaction between state and commonwealth governments and, in particular, denies any simple portrayal of overall commonwealth policy dominance (e.g., Sharman, 1985). That interdependency co-exists with autonomy in this way illustrates the robust nature of the Australian federal system.

Bibliography

AHMC (Australian Housing Ministers' Conference), 1984, Hobart.

Alexander, I., 1986. 'Land Use and Transport Planning in Australian Cities: Capital Takes All?', in *Urban Planning in Australia: Critical Readings*, eds J.B. McLoughlin & M. Huxley, Longman Cheshire, Melbourne.

Badcock, B., 1986. 'Land and Housing Provision', in *The State as Developer: Public Enterprise in South Australia*, ed. K. Sheridan, Royal Australian Institute of Public Administration and Wakefield Press, Adelaide.

Bethune, G., 1983. 'Public Housing, Welfare Housing or Both?', Paper presented to Urban Research Unit, Australian National University, Canberra.

—— 1985. 'Unfinished Agenda: The 1984 Commonwealth–State Housing Agreement', *Australian Urban Studies*, Special Issue.

Bunker, R., 1989. 'A Decade of Urban Consolidation', Urban Research Unit, Australian National University, Canberra.

Burke, T., Hancock, L., & Newton, P., 1984. *A Roof Over Their Heads: Housing Issues and Families in Australia*, Institute of Family Studies Monograph No. 4, Melbourne.

Butler, K., 1986a. 'Common Equity Rental Co-operatives in Queensland: LGACHP and the Future', *Shelter National Housing Action*, (1).

—— 1986b. 'Community Housing in Brisbane—Better Late Than Never', *Shelter National Housing Action*, 2(3).

Carter, R.A., 1980. 'Housing Policy in the 1970s', in *Public Expenditures and Social Policy in Australia, Volume II: The First Fraser Years, 1976–78*, eds R.B. Scotton & H. Ferber, Longman Cheshire, Melbourne.

—— 1985. 'Emerging Housing Policy Issues in Australia: Deregulation, Tenure Neutrality and All That', *Australian Urban Studies*, Special Issue.

Commission of Inquiry into Poverty, 1975. *Poverty in Australia*, First Main Report, AGPS, Canberra.

Coopers & Lybrand & W.D. Scott, 1985. *Study into Homelessness and Inadequate Housing*, Report to the Department of Housing and Construction, AGPS, Canberra.

Dalton, T., 1979. 'The Victorian Housing Domain', Diploma of Public Policy thesis, University of Melbourne.

DCS&H (Department of Community Services and Health), 1988a. *Housing Assistance Act 1984: Annual Report 1986–87*, AGPS, Canberra.

DCS&H, 1988b. *1984 CSHA: Background Information and Statistics*, Canberra.

Flood, J., 1988. *Financing Public Housing: The Need, The Options and the Risks*, Report to the National Housing Review, CSIRO Division of Building, Construction and Engineering, Canberra.

Gruen, F.H., 1988. Some Economic and Social Aspects of Housing in Australia, Economic Planning Advisory Council Discussion Paper 88/08, Canberra.

Harris, J., 1978. The Commonwealth–State Housing Agreement of 1978, Paper presented to Urban Research Unit, Australian National University, Canberra.

Hayward, D. & Burke, T., 1989. 'Gearing Up For Inflation', *Australian Society*, 8(3).

Homeswest, 1988. 'Cost Rents', pamphlet.

Jones, A., 1983. 'Tying Rent to Income', *Australian Society*, 2(1).

Kendig, H. & Paris, C., 1987. *Towards Fair Shares in Australian Housing*, National Committee of Non-Government Organisations, International Year of Shelter for the Homeless, Canberra.

Kilner, D., 1989. *The Evolution of South Australian Urban Housing Policy 1836–1987*, PhD thesis, University of Adelaide.

King, S. 1986. 'Late Starter: LGACHP in Tasmania', *Shelter National Housing Action*, 3(1).

Lloyd, C.J. & Troy, P.N., 1981. *Innovation and Reaction: The Life and Death of the Federal Department of Urban and Regional Development*, Allen & Unwin, Sydney.

National Shelter, 1984. Submission on the Commonwealth-State Housing Agreement, Canberra.

New South Wales, 1984. 'Renegotiation of the Commonwealth-State Housing Agreement', Sydney.

New South Wales, Victoria, Queensland, Western Australia, South Australia, Tasmania and Northern Territory, 1986. 'Housing the Other Australia', Adelaide.

Newton, P.W. & Wulff, M.G., 1983. 'State Intervention in Urban Housing Markets: A Case Study of Public Housing Development and Change in Melbourne, 1945–1980', *Urban Policy and Research*, 1(3).

Orchard L., 1989. 'Housing Policies', in *From Fraser to Hawke: Australian Public Policy in the 1980s*, eds B.W. Head & A. Patience, Longman Cheshire, Melbourne.

Painter, M., 1979. 'Urban Government, Urban Politics and the Fabrication of Urban Issues: The Impossibility of Urban Policy', *Australian Journal of Public Administration*, 38(4).

Paris, C., 1987. 'Housing Under Hawke: Promise and Performance', *Australian Journal of Political Economy*, 21.

Parkin, A., 1982. *Governing the Cities: The Australian Experience in Perspective*, Macmillan, Melbourne.

—— 1988. 'Housing Policy', in *Comparative State Policies*, B. Galligan ed., Longman Cheshire, Melbourne.

—— 1989. 'Metropolitan Planning and Social Justice Strategies', Working Paper, Urban Research Unit, ANU, Canberra.

Priorities Review Staff, 1975. *Report on Housing*, AGPS, Canberra.

Pugh, C., 1976. *Intergovernmental Relations and the Development of Australian Housing Policies*, Research Monograph 15, Centre for Research on Federal Financial Relations, Australian National University, Canberra.

Sharman, C., 1985. 'The Commonwealth, the States and Federalism', in *Government, Politics and Power in Australia*, 3rd edn, eds D. Woodward, A. Parkin & J. Summers, Longman Cheshire, Melbourne.

South Australia, 1984. 'Renegotiation of the Commonwealth–States Housing Agreement', Adelaide.

South Australian Minister of Housing and Construction, 1986. 'Housing Trust Rents Rise', news release.

Thompson, G. & Purcell, C., 1986. 'More Thoughts on Community Housing in NSW', *Shelter National Housing Action*, 2(3).

Troy, P.N., ed., 1978a. *A Fair Price: the Land Commission Program*, Hale & Iremonger, Sydney.

—— 1978b. *Federal Power in Australia's Cities*, Hale & Iremonger, Sydney.

Troy, P.N. & Lloyd, C.J., 1986. 'Innovation and Federal Political Constraints—the Australian Experience', Paper presented to World Planning and Housing Congress, Adelaide.

Victoria, 1984a. 'The Reintroduction of Cost Rents: A Proposal from Victoria', Melbourne.

—— 1984b. 'A Submission from Victoria on the Renegotiation of the Commonwealth/State Housing Agreement', Melbourne.

Western Australian Minister of Housing, 1984. 'Housing Problems! Needs!', Perth.

Wettenhall, G., 1989. 'No, Prime Minister', *Australian Society*, 8(3).

Wilmoth, D., 1988. 'Sydney's Metropolitan Strategy', Paper presented to Seminar on Metropolitan Planning, Urban Research Unit, Australian National University, Canberra.

13 Aboriginal affairs

Will Sanders

Government policy towards Aborigines underwent a major change of philosophy and institutional form in the late 1960s and early 1970s. As part of this change the previous pattern of predominantly co-operative intergovernmental relations over Aboriginal policy gave way to a potentially more confrontationist one. State dominance and a largely parallel operation of commonwealth and state government involvement gave way to a far more complex pattern of intergovernmental responsibility sharing. While the commonwealth claimed priority in matters of general policy and co-ordination, it did not seek to exclude the other levels of government from Aboriginal affairs. Indeed, the commonwealth actively encouraged them to take greater responsibility for the provision of a wide range of services to Aborigines, as to other Australians. Confrontation between the various levels of Australian government over just who was responsible for what became, if not endemic, at least always a potential. Intergovernmental relations in Aboriginal affairs changed quite dramatically.

This chapter begins with an historical elaboration of this transform-ation. It characterises the period of co-operative parallelism prior to the late 1960s and identifies the seeds of change which emerged around that time. It elaborates on the new era of potential intergovernmental confrontation by discussing in turn the periods of the Whitlam, Fraser and Hawke Governments. Although the periods of each of these common-wealth governments differs somewhat in its pattern of intergovernmental relations, they have all been caught up in the new sharing of responsibility in Aboriginal affairs. They are, as a group, to be contrasted with the earlier commonwealth governments, just as the period of potentially confrontationist responsibility sharing is to be contrasted with the earlier period of co-operative parallelism.

The chapter also briefly addresses the role of local governments in this changing pattern. Though in many ways minor players in comparison with the commonwealth and state governments, local governments are by no means irrelevant to Aborigines and were certainly implicated in the 1970s change of policy approach. Finally, the chapter turns to some more normative analytic issues. First, it addresses the issue of whether these developments reflect general trends in intergovernmental relations that are evident in other policy areas, or whether in fact Aboriginal affairs is a unique policy area in its intergovernmental relations. Second, it addresses the even more evaluative issue of whether greater commonwealth intervention in Aboriginal affairs has been beneficial to Aborigines.

Historical analysis

The co-operative parallelism of the assimilation/welfare authority era

From the late 1930s to the late 1960s, the central term of Australian government policy towards Aborigines was 'assimilation'. The central institutions of Aboriginal policy during this period were special-purpose state/territory-level agencies variously entitled Native or Aboriginal welfare authorities. Each state authority, and the commonwealth's in the Northern Territory, looked after its own Aborigines under special legislation enacted specifically for that purpose. Often this involved management of Aborigines in supervised or semi-supervised institutions on reserves of land specifically set aside for them—as had been done in previous years under the central policy term of 'protection'. This management task was often delegated to non-government bodies, such as church missions. However, it was always undertaken under the special body of state/territory laws applying to Aborigines and under the supervision of the state/territory Aboriginal welfare authority. The assimilation approach also involved provisions under which individual Aborigines could be exempted from these special state/territory laws. These 'assimilated' Aborigines were dispersed among the larger community, officially unrecognisable from other Australian citizens and notionally beyond the realm of government Aboriginal welfare policy.

The intergovernmental aspect of this period from the 1930s to the 1960s was largely one of mutual information sharing and support among the various Aboriginal welfare authorities. As early as 1937, as a result of some discussions at the Premiers' Conference of the previous year, a meeting of the various chief administrators of these Aboriginal welfare authorities had been convened. Paul Hasluck, who was not a direct participant at the time but had cause to be informed of the history some years later, recounts the sequence of events as follows:

> The Premiers' Conference had decided that it would be impractical and
> undesirable for the Commonwealth to take over the activities of the
> States in regard to the protection of Aborigines so the conference of
> administrators sought such goals as uniformity of legislation and
> agreement on general principles while leaving details of administra-
> tion to each state. The discussion, which rambled from topic to topic,
> disclosed the wide diversity of conditions over the continent and the
> wide difference between the measures appropriate to one situation and
> another. (Hasluck, 1988:66)

The commonwealth's participation in this meeting was dependent on its
role in the Northern Territory rather than on any claim to providing a
higher-order national approach. The commonwealth representative was
very much an equal among others, the territory administrator among his
state counterparts, rather than in any sense a national representative.

With the intervention of World War II, a similar intergovernmental
forum of Aboriginal welfare administrators was not convened again until
1948. Neither Tasmania nor Victoria attended. Some of the state
authorities, which did attend, pushed hard for special-purpose Aboriginal
welfare grants from the commonwealth, but without success. As Hasluck
again reports, the 'question of doing more for the Aborigines was still
subordinate to the question of federal–state financial relations', and the
commonwealth resisted these demands on the grounds that 'it had no
obligation to pay for undertakings under the control of the States'
(Hasluck, 1988:77–78).

In 1951, Hasluck became the new commonwealth Minister for
Territories and set about convening a third of these intergovernmental
meetings, this time inviting ministers to attend as well as officials.
Again Victoria and Tasmania did not attend, arguing that they had only
'assimilated' part-Aborigines within their boundaries. They were,
however, soon persuaded to attend future meetings by the argument that
this was an 'Australian question' which required an 'Australian answer'
(Hasluck, 1988:90). Thus was born, in the mid-1950s, the Australian
Native Welfare Council, or the Australian Aboriginal Affairs Council as
it later came to be known. This intergovernmental meeting of ministers
and a parallel meeting of officials involved in Aboriginal affairs was
convened approximately once every two years until the mid-1960s and
has become an annual affair since that time. These meetings are now the
centre-piece of intergovernmental relations in Aboriginal affairs, though
by no means the limits of such relations.

Hasluck remained commonwealth ministerial representative to the
Native Welfare Council meetings from 1951 to 1963. He reflects in his
recent writings that the early meetings were not always considered a high
priority by the states, since the 'old contention' about commonwealth
special-purpose grants was something of a problem:

> Basically State governments thought it was not worth attending a
> meeting about Aborigines unless there was some prospect of obtaining

more money from the Commonwealth for welfare expenditure. The Commonwealth Government maintained the view that it should not open any side doors into the established system and procedures for the distribution of funds; that any claims by the States for extra funds should be made only in the annual meeting of the Premiers' Conference and the Loan Council; and that the Commonwealth did not lightly give money away without having some control over the way it was spent. (Hasluck, 1988:91)

Hasluck also suggests that he personally did not agree entirely with this commonwealth view, but was bound to abide by it. As commonwealth representative at the Aboriginal welfare ministers' meetings, he attempted to avoid debates on special-purpose commonwealth grants and directed discussion instead to other issues: 'we concentrated on seeking co-operation on policy and administration and on settling the occasional problems that might arise between the seven governments in giving effect to policy' (Hasluck, 1988:91). On the situation at the end of his time on the ministerial council in 1963, Hasluck reflects that:

We had arrived at a point where the seven governments in Australia had a common purpose, had come to know each other's local problems and difficulties and were sharing experience, ideas and skills. This co-operation among ministers had been achieved regardless of the political complexion of governments and was reinforced by the fact that public servants had come to know each other and understand more of each other's work. (Hasluck, 1988:92)

Although Hasluck's reflections are somewhat self congratulatory in tone, there is no reason to suggest that intergovernmental relations in Aboriginal affairs during these years were other than cordial and co-operative. They were based on a mutual respect for separate and diverse state and territory Aboriginal circumstances and clearly operated as an amicable information exchange between equals. The one element of contention was the demand by some states for commonwealth special-purpose grant funding. But while the long standing Menzies Coalition Government, of which Hasluck was a part, remained in power, commonwealth resistance to these demands was unlikely to change. The demand for special-purpose commonwealth grant funding was, by the 1960s, an old thorn of intergovernmental relations in Aboriginal welfare, but not one which overrode the general spirit of co-operation and mutual respect which predominated in the Native Welfare Council meetings.

The 1967 referendum and the roots of change

Despite the obvious success and co-operative nature of the Native Welfare Council meetings of the 1950s and early 1960s, there were within public attitudes of the time prospects for the demise of the whole assimilation/welfare authority approach to Aboriginal policy. Increasingly the state and territory level welfare authorities were seen as the entrenched interests of Aboriginal policy and as somewhat outdated in their approach. The commonwealth was seen by many as the appropriate new broom which could bring a national approach to bear on what was increasingly being seen as a national problem and responsibility. The commonwealth parliament was already busily expunging provisions from its earlier legislation which had explicitly excluded Aborigines from such things as social security benefits and the electoral franchise. The new commonwealth legislation granted Aborigines these rights and benefits either explicitly or implicitly by making no reference to them in the legislation whatsoever. As part of this process, a constitutional referendum proposal was put forward to delete two such exclusionary provisions relating to Aborigines from the commonwealth constitution; the one in section 51(xxvi) which gave the commonwealth parliament power to make laws with respect to the 'people of any race, other than the aboriginal race in any State', and the other being section 127 which provided that 'in reckoning the numbers of the people of the Commonwealth...aboriginal natives shall not be counted'. These proposed amendments were put to a referendum without major opposition in 1967. They were passed by a majority in all states and a majority of over 90 per cent nationwide. The constitution was duly amended.

In the wake of the 1967 constitutional change, the new Liberal Prime Minister, Harold Holt, established both a new Advisory Council of Aboriginal Affairs and a small Office of Aboriginal Affairs within his department. Nothing in the referendum had necessitated these initiatives, but clearly the whole process of constitutional change had heightened public awareness of Aboriginal policy and had, in the Prime Minister's judgment, demanded some greater commonwealth response. Interestingly, this new commonwealth advisory council and office were kept well away from the existing commonwealth institutional commitment to Aboriginal welfare within the Northern Territory administration of the territories/interior department. This clearly was to be a council and office with national concerns, rather than one restricted to the commonwealth's role in the Northern Territory. The commonwealth minister with responsibility for the new council and the office joined the ministerial Native Welfare Council alongside his territory counterpart and created a more prominent commonwealth presence there. Also, within a year the new council and office had convinced the commonwealth to revise its long-held opposition to special-purpose grants to the states for Aboriginal welfare. The commonwealth's reluctance to take a leading nationwide role in Aboriginal policy was now seen to be waning. However, the generally co-operative nature of relations between the commonwealth and the states was not at this stage in question. The new specific-purpose grants would be paid to the state Aboriginal welfare authorities and used by them as they saw fit, albeit with some commonwealth conditions attached. This co-operativeness in intergovernmental relations was to be challenged a few years later with the election of the Whitlam Labor Government in December 1972.

The Whitlam Government's confrontationism

After the 1967 referendum, Labor opposition leader Whitlam became a strong critic of successive commonwealth coalition governments for not assuming a greater responsibility in Aboriginal affairs. He saw the referendum result as having given the commonwealth a clear 'mandate' to assume such responsibility. When the Whitlam Government came to power in late 1972 it moved quickly to do so.

It introduced both a new central policy term and new institutional arrangements to Aboriginal affairs. The new policy term was 'self-determination' and the new institutions included a fully-fledged commonwealth ministry and Department of Aboriginal Affairs (DAA). The new Department was created in the first instance by combining the 1967 Office of Aboriginal Affairs with the Welfare Branch of the commonwealth's Northern Territory administration. Whitlam also approached the states asking them to transfer their Aboriginal welfare authority personnel and policy responsibilities to the commonwealth's new Department. Explaining his government's intentions to the council of commonwealth and state ministers for Aboriginal affairs early in 1973, Whitlam noted that the aim was not to establish a new 'omnibus' department of Aboriginal affairs, but rather to create a new commonwealth DAA which:

> will instead seek to devolve upon a wide range of Federal, State and local authorities, as well as upon organisations of Aboriginals them-selves, responsibility for carrying out the policies decided upon by my Government. These authorities would be responsible for Aboriginals in the same matters and in the same way as they now are functionally responsible for the community generally (Whitlam, 1973:697)

This combination of central policy direction via the commonwealth DAA and devolved functional responsibility for Aborigines among a large number of government and non-government bodies was to be achieved in a number of ways. Functional federal government departments, such as social security and the commonwealth employment service, were to be encouraged to develop programs and appropriate service mechanisms for the newly-recognised Aboriginal portion of their clienteles. State government departments with responsibilities such as health, housing and education would be offered special-purpose commonwealth grants to encourage them also to cater more adequately for Aborigines. Local governments, too, would be encouraged to take greater responsibility for providing services to Aborigines living within their boundaries, either as individuals or as discrete communities. More important and more clearly enunciated as a strategy at the local level, however, was to be the encouragement of Aboriginal communities to incorporate as community organisations for the conduct of their own affairs—either as general community councils in remote areas or as more specialised community service agencies and enterprise organisations in both remote and more settled areas. The Whitlam Government also wished to establish a nationwide mechanism for consultation with Aborigines and to this end established a National Aboriginal Consultative Committee elected by Aborigines Australia-wide.

All the states, except Queensland, seemed generally to accept the Whitlam Government's new approach to Aboriginal affairs, despite the fact that all except South Australia had non-Labor governments at the time. All except Queensland agreed in principle to transferring their former Aboriginal welfare authority personnel to the commonwealth's DAA and negotiations were set in train with individual states. As these negotiations came to fruition during the years of the Whitlam Government, the commonwealth DAA gradually grew in size and stature. The states, on the other hand, lost their Aboriginal affairs administrations and their ministers of Aboriginal welfare one by one. There was at this time some discussion at the annual Aboriginal Affairs Council meetings as to whether the Council should continue. All governments agreed that it should and the state governments, except Queensland, came to be represented by a variety of ministers usually with responsibilities such as community welfare or community services, though in the case of Victoria it was the Minister for Housing. The Aboriginal Affairs Council meetings of these years became somewhat less cordial in their tone and considerably less of a meeting among equals. The commonwealth wished to establish its clear national dominance on matters of Aboriginal affairs policy and Queensland was busily entrenching itself as the bastion of resistance to this commonwealth push. The community welfare or housing ministers from the other states found it difficult to talk for their colleagues in other portfolios such as health and education, who were also being encouraged to take some responsibility for Aborigines. Intergovernmental relations necessarily moved more outside the Council meetings as the commonwealth DAA and its minister dealt serially and often bilaterally with different state governments and different functional areas of state government responsibility.

In most instances these relations remained surprisingly cordial, given that the commonwealth was undertaking nothing less than a total rearrangement of the institutions of Aboriginal policy. This, I think, can be largely attributed to the rapidly increasing level of commonwealth Aboriginal affairs funding during these years (see Table 13.1). Major new special-purpose grants for Aboriginal programs were available to the various functional state government departments and the problem for them was getting organised to take on this additional funding. The exception was Queensland.

Table 13.1: Commonwealth Aboriginal assistance expenditure

Year ended 30/6	A—Total Aboriginal affairs portfolio expenditure on Aboriginal assistance/ advancement programs ($m)	Annual growth rate of A	B—Total commonwealth expenditure on Aboriginal assistance/ advancement programs ($m)	Annual growth rate of B	A as a percentage of B
1971	19.6		24.0		82
1972	23.4	19.4	28.4	18.3	82
1973	42.3	80.8	56.4	98.6	75
1974	71.4	68.8	89.8	59.2	80
1975	113.6	59.1	147.7	64.5	77
1976	125.9	10.8	173.1	17.2	73
1977	107.6	-14.5	148.1	-14.4	73
1978	110.5	2.7	160.0	8.0	69
1979	116.1	5.1	135.1	-15.6	86
1980	125.3	7.9	166.5	23.2	75
1981	143.2	14.3	203.4	22.2	70
1982	152.1	6.2	242.1	19.0	63
1983	179.9	18.3	282.3	16.6	64
1984	222.3	23.6	376.2	33.3	59
1985	256.9	15.6	442.9	17.7	58
1986	268.8	4.6	493.9	11.5	54
1987	302.5	12.5	542.5	9.8	56

Source: DAA, 'Aboriginal Statistics, 1986':69

Queensland refused to transfer its Aboriginal welfare personnel and policy responsibilities to the commonwealth throughout the years of the Whitlam Government. In 1975, therefore, the commonwealth DAA moved to set up an office in Queensland in direct competition with the existing Queensland Department of Aboriginal and Islander Affairs (DAIA). The Whitlam Government also invoked its international treaty obligations under the 1965 international convention on the elimination of racial discrimination in its attempts to confront the Queensland government. It asked the Queensland government to amend its Aborigine's and Torres Strait Islander's Affairs Act, arguing that this legislation discriminated against Aborigines on racial grounds and therefore presented a problem for the commonwealth in ratifying the 1965 convention. When the amendments which the Queensland government did make in 1974 still did not satisfy it, the commonwealth moved to enact its own overriding legislation, the Aboriginal and Torres Strait Islanders (Queensland Discriminatory Laws) Act and the Racial Discrimination Act. This legislation, however, had little day-to-day practical effect. The Queensland DAIA's entrenched control, particularly over reserve-dwelling Aborigines within the state, was little changed.

Even the lure of special-purpose commonwealth grants could do little to undermine the Queensland government's resolve. Indeed, for a number of years during the Whitlam Government and afterwards the Queensland government willingly forwent some special-purpose commonwealth grants for Aboriginal affairs in order to guard its independence from the commonwealth's new policy approach.

Commonwealth domination of the states and confrontation with any who were recalcitrant was clearly part of the Whitlam Government's new order in Aboriginal affairs. There were, however, limits to the extent of confrontation in which the Whitlam Government was prepared to engage and on the extent of domination to which even the generally compliant states were prepared to submit. These emerged most clearly in the area of Aboriginal land rights policy and are worthy of a little attention.

None of the states was willing, in the process of handing over policy responsibility to the commonwealth, to transfer to the commonwealth ownership of their former Aboriginal 'reserve' lands. Nor did the Whitlam Government demand that the states did so, since it saw the ownership of what remained of these reserves as more appropriately vested in incorporated Aboriginal community bodies. Also, in its own initiatives to grant further land rights to Aborigines, the Whitlam Government specifically restricted its attention to the Northern Territory—though with the proviso that this could be a model for things to come elsewhere. In explaining this restriction on the land rights initiative some years later, Whitlam identified several reasons. Prominent among these reasons was that 'State Governments could not resist and delay Federal legislation and administration in the territory. The Federal Government would have full jurisdiction and could gain immediate experience on land rights in the Territory' (Whitlam, 1985:469). Clearly, Whitlam was conscious of the potential delays and resistance which state governments could, and probably would, offer in this most contentious area of Aboriginal affairs policy reform. He was, it would appear, cognisant of the potential political costs of prolonged confrontation with the states on Aboriginal land issues and modified his government's approach accordingly. In retrospect, this appears to have been good political judgment. For, as is generally well known, even in the Northern Territory land rights legislation did not become a reality during the term of the Whitlam Government. The Bill which arose from the Whitlam Government's land rights initiative had to rely for its passage on the incoming Fraser Coalition Government. A Northern Territory land rights Act did get passed, albeit in amended form. Clearly, however, given the incoming Fraser Government's strong rhetorical commitment to a new brand of federalism which would return responsibilities to the states, this land rights legislation almost certainly would not have been passed had it involved any element of the commonwealth overriding the states.

The Fraser Government's 'new federalism'

The rhetoric of the incoming Fraser Coalition Government was very much concerned with reversing the growth of commonwealth power which had occurred during the Whitlam years. However, in Aboriginal affairs not much reversal occurred. Funding levels to the commonwealth's Aboriginal affairs portfolio were cut considerably (see Table 13.1). However, all the major institutional and policy changes which the Whitlam Labor Government had set in train essentially remained intact, although not without some reworking over time. The commonwealth DAA remained, and so too, as already discussed, did Aboriginal land rights for the Northern Territory. The DAA continued to bring pressure to bear on the mainstream functional departments of commonwealth administration to cater for the Aboriginal portion of their clienteles and the commonwealth continued to pay special-purpose grants to the states for Aboriginal health, housing, education, etc. The incorporation and funding of local Aboriginal community bodies for the conduct of their own affairs and the delivery of their own services also continued, as too did a national level Aboriginal consultative body—albeit slightly restructured and renamed as the National Aboriginal Conference.

In an attempt to introduce some greater sense of responsibility and accountability into the disbursement of commonwealth Aboriginal affairs funds, the central policy term of Aboriginal affairs was changed by the Fraser Government from 'self-determination' to 'self-management'. However, these were in many ways fairly minor changes when compared with those that the Whitlam Government had made. The Fraser Government's changes in no way undid the major institutional rearrangements and changes in policy approach which had been initiated during the years of the Whitlam Government. They also in no way reversed the change from co-operative to potentially confrontationist relations between the commonwealth and state governments, particularly in Queensland. Indeed, the Fraser years saw as much commonwealth confrontation with the Queensland Bjelke-Petersen Government over Aboriginal affairs as the Whitlam years had done, despite the similar party political persuasions of the Fraser and Bjelke-Petersen regimes.

During the years of the Fraser Government, competition between the commonwealth DAA and the Queensland DAIA for the support of Queensland Aborigines became quite intense. Initially the 'reserve' Aborigines remained loyal to the DAIA, which continued to control most of the resources available to them. However, those outside the reserves began to gain access to new commonwealth DAA resources and to develop loyalties in this direction. It was perhaps only a matter of time before this administrative competition for clientele in Queensland would erupt into some more overt and more political intergovernmental confrontation. Such confrontation did occur in 1978, in relation to the two reserve settlements of Mornington Island and Aurukun. These two communities had previously been administered by church missionaries in conjunction with Aboriginal community councils and under the indirect guidance of the Queensland DAIA. Now the Queensland DAIA wanted to assume direct administrative control. The church missions and the two Aboriginal community councils looked to the commonwealth to intervene to sustain their existing arrangements for community administration. This the commonwealth duly attempted to do by passing the Aboriginal and Torres Strait Islanders (Queensland Reserves and Communities Self-management) Act. However, before the commonwealth Act was proclaimed, the Queensland government had revoked the status of the two communities as Aboriginal reserves and reconstituted them as small local-government bodies. The communities were now beyond the reach of the new commonwealth legislation and the commonwealth declined to proceed further with the confrontation (Tatz, 1979:ch. 4). As in the days of the Whitlam Government, there were clearly limits to the confrontation in which the commonwealth was willing to engage. The political costs of confrontation could be high, so commonwealth action on the Aurukun and Mornington Island affair was not pursued as far as it might have been on legal or constitutional grounds alone.

Concentration on these warlike skirmishes between the commonwealth and Queensland governments in both the Whitlam and the Fraser years does serve to identify the potentially confrontationist nature of the new commonwealth approach to Aboriginal policy which developed during the 1970s. However, it may do so partly at the expense of some greater appreciation of the more routine administrative types of commonwealth/state intergovernmental relations which were developing in other states. Before leaving the term of the Fraser Government it is, therefore, worthwhile to give some greater attention to what was happening Australia-wide in normal day-to-day administration.

While the problem during the Whitlam years for state government departments like education and housing had been one of gearing up to spend the additional commonwealth money being offered to them for Aboriginal programs, the problem of the Fraser years was much more one of meeting rising expectations with less. In this tighter fiscal environment, some of the consequences of intergovernmental and interdepartmental responsibility sharing for the servicing of Aborigines were beginning to become apparent. Disputes became common between various departments at both the state and commonwealth levels over which of them was in fact responsible for what elements of funding and service provision to which types of Aboriginal communities. The Northern Territory, which gained territorial self-government in 1978, began such wrangling with the commonwealth over respective responsibilities almost immediately. This was perhaps not surprising, given the high proportion of Aborigines in the Northern Territory, but the intergovernmental wrangling over responsibilities was by no means restricted to there (see, for numerous examples, Loveday, 1982). From the commonwealth DAA's point of view, the problem was one of getting functional state and territory government departments to take some greater responsibility for the servicing and funding of their Aboriginal clienteles, rather than just spending the DAA's specific-purpose funds and doing no more. From the point of view of the state and territory government departments, the very fact that the commonwealth DAA existed and that it offered specific-purpose grants seemed to suggest that it rather than they should meet all or the major part of the costs of servicing Aborigines. Standoffs were common, while the DAA tried desperately to get others to take some greater degree of responsibility for funding and service provision, but also tried not to leave the Aborigines concerned with no services at all. The potential for ongoing conflict in the new responsibility sharing arrangements of Aboriginal affairs was now becoming apparent, and much, though by no means all, of such conflict was intergovernmental in nature.

The Hawke Government's revisionism

When the Hawke Government was elected to power in March 1983, its policy platform appeared to endorse the strongest yet assertion of commonwealth dominance in Aboriginal affairs. On the central issue of land rights, the federal Labor platform identified five 'principles' of an acceptable land rights approach. The states were to be encouraged to enact land rights legislation meeting these principles, but if this failed the program stated that the commonwealth would be prepared to intervene and exercise the constitutional power it had gained in 1967.

This more assertive national land rights platform had been fashioned by the federal Labor Party while in opposition and had in many ways been designed to set it apart from the Fraser Government, which had passed the Aboriginal Land Rights (Northern Territory) Act in 1976, and the South Australian Liberal government, which had passed the Pitjantjatjara Land Rights Act in 1981. Once in government, however, the implementation of Labor's platform was not as assertive as might have been expected from a reading of that platform. Most of the state governments were also Labor by this time and most had already begun moving towards their own programs for the granting of greater Aboriginal land rights. These Labor state governments, particularly the West Australian, now argued strongly that the commonwealth should hold back on its threat to intervene. They argued the need for flexibility on the platform's land rights 'principles' in the different circumstances that each of the state governments faced and the need for time to allow the state governments to work things through in their own way. After some initial hard-line assertions from the commonwealth Minister for Aboriginal Affairs, the Hawke Government did revise markedly its assertive national land rights stance. The 'principles' were weakened to become a 'preferred model' which the states were encouraged to follow, and the threat of commonwealth intervention was totally withdrawn (Bennett, 1988:33–37). Once again, the potential political costs of commonwealth confrontation with the states over Aboriginal land rights seemed to have been recognised. In circumstances where most of these state governments were of the same party-political persuasion as the commonwealth, the avoidance of such confrontation took on an added dimension.

In the process of developing their own land rights proposals in the early 1980s, most of the Labor state governments had re-established Aboriginal affairs ministries and administrations. There was, it seemed, a new assertiveness among the compliant states of the 1970s who now saw anew that they did have something distinctive to contribute to Aboriginal affairs policy at the state level. They were no longer quite so willing to bow to commonwealth dominance of Aboriginal affairs policy and the meetings of the Aboriginal Affairs Council returned somewhat towards being meetings among equals. The state ministers at those meetings did once again have Aboriginal affairs clearly identified among their primary responsibilities and in the case of the Northern Territory, the representative was often the chief. The Queensland government, of course, had never lost its assertiveness in the Aboriginal affairs policy area, but now found itself not quite so much out on a limb. The Hawke Government's revisionism was as much forced upon it by this reassertion of state and territory government roles in Aboriginal affairs as it had been of the commonwealth's own choosing.

Ironically, such reassertion of a state government role through the re-establishment of state-level Aboriginal affairs ministries and administrations may have contributed significantly to the further realisation of the original Whitlam Government goal of widely based responsibility sharing for Aborigines among all state and commonwealth functional departments. As well as developing state land rights programs and reasserting the state presence at Aboriginal Affairs Council meetings, these renewed state ministries have also often helped focus the attention of other state government departments on their servicing of Aborigines. Comprehensive program lists and expenditure statistics are not available, but there are certainly a large number of functional government departments at the state level which now have their own Aboriginal assistance programs and which in many instances are doing considerably more than just spending commonwealth specific-purpose grants. The exception to this functional responsibility sharing model is still Queensland, which, particularly in relation to Aborigines living on reserve communities, still adopts the old model of a single special-purpose department delivering most, if not all, services to them. Ironically, at a time when other states have been re-establishing administrative offices with Aboriginal affairs in their titles, Queensland has chosen to rename this 'omnibus' department without making specific reference to Aborigines in its title.

The growing degree of responsibility sharing for Aborigines among functional government departments in recent years is also evident at the commonwealth level. The DAA's share of commonwealth expenditure on special Aboriginal assistance programs has fallen steadily from over 80 per cent in the Whitlam years to around 70 per cent in the Fraser years and now down to approximately 55 per cent in the Hawke years (see Table 13.1). This has occurred because an increasing number of functional commonwealth government departments have over the years gradually developed their own programs of Aboriginal assistance; from departments such as health, education and employment in the early years through to housing, community services, arts, heritage and environment and communications in more recent times. The Whitlam vision of widespread responsibility for the servicing of Aborigines does seem to be slowly being realised.

One of the consequences of this growing responsibility sharing has been that it has become almost impossible for the Aboriginal Affairs Council to retain much sense of being the focus of intergovernmental relations in Aboriginal affairs. The trend towards bilateral and functionally specific intergovernmental relations over Aboriginal assistance programs which was evident in the 1970s has become even stronger since then. No longer is it just the commonwealth Aboriginal affairs ministry dealing with state ministries of health, housing or education. It can now in fact often be the housing or education ministries at the two levels of government negotiating over structures for Aboriginal assistance programs which are totally outside the special-purpose Aboriginal affairs portfolios. The commonwealth Aboriginal affairs ministry tries hard to keep an eye on what is going on across the whole spectrum of government responsibility as part of its proclaimed 'co-ordinating' role in the policy area. But it is now an almost impossible task. Aboriginal assistance programs have become the responsibility of so many state and federal government departments that intergovernmental relations in Aboriginal affairs can no longer be solely or even primarily discussed in terms of the workings and concerns of the Aboriginal Affairs Council. The annual Council meetings have in some ways become much more of a forum for discussion and stand-taking in relation to select matters of high political salience at the particular time, rather than in any way covering the now enormous range of established intergovernmental relations in Aboriginal affairs. Recent examples of such matters of high political salience have been the commonwealth government's attempt to restructure its Aboriginal affairs administration through the introduction of an Aboriginal and Torres Strait Islander Commission and the response of both commonwealth and state governments to the Aboriginal deaths in custody royal commission. Both are, of course, important matters and both have understandably consumed large amounts of the Aboriginal Affairs Council's time. But they do not reflect the great range of intergovernmental relations in Aboriginal affairs which now exist.

The role of local government

In Whitlam's vision of devolved responsibility sharing for Aborigines among a large number of government and non-government bodies, local governments also had a role to play. The reality in the welfare authority/assimilation era of Aboriginal affairs had been that local governments were often bastions of local resistance to the movement of 'assimilated' Aboriginal families into towns (see Rowley, 1971:ch. 10). They also generally regarded Aborigines living as discrete communities within their boundaries as beyond their responsibilities. Servicing these non-rate-paying communities was, as the local governments then saw it, the responsibility of others, such as the state-level Aboriginal welfare authorities. These attitudes in local government have been slow to change. Commonwealth government reports of recent years still catalogue the failure of local governments to provide even the most basic of physical services to Aboriginal communities within their boundaries (see, for example, House of Representatives Standing Committee on Aboriginal Affairs, 1982:ch. 7; Human Rights Australia, 1988:ch. 6). Commonwealth injunctions to local government to improve their provision of roads, water, sewerage and electricity to Aboriginal communities generally follow. However, little action results, with local governments often continuing to argue that the responsibility lies elsewhere.

This inaction has also reflected the fact that over the last twenty years there have been very few financial incentives for local governments to act on these commonwealth injunctions. The commonwealth has had no tactical equivalent in its relations with local government to the specific-purpose grant to functional state government departments for the provision of services to Aborigines, no way of extracting some greater degree of local government commitment to Aboriginal residents in return for some financial gain. In the absence of such a financial incentive structure, the devolution of responsibility for Aborigines to this level of government has hardly yet begun, even though it is now over a decade and a half since the Whitlam Government first pushed in this direction. There are, however, some recent signs that this may be beginning to change.

As the result of a national inquiry into local government finance in 1984, a new commonwealth Local Government (Financial Assistance) Act was passed in 1986. This provided local government with its share of the general revenue sharing of personal income tax under a formula which identifies 30 per cent of all such commonwealth funds to be used for 'horizontal equalisation'. In gaining access to this portion of commonwealth grant funds, local governments now have an incentive to identify their areas as disadvantaged. Numbers of Aboriginal residents and the servicing of Aboriginal communities within their boundaries are one obvious claim to disadvantage which local governments may use. Clearly, however, the effective devolution of responsibility for Aborigines to local government is yet to occur in any significant way, so intergovernmental relations in this area have not yet moved beyond the initial posturing of commonwealth injunction and local resistance. The intergovernmental manoeuvring which results from the realisation of significant responsibility sharing is still in the future.

Another interesting development in the area of local government which arose out of the national inquiry into local government finance was the potential for Aboriginal community councils in remote areas to themselves receive commonwealth local government funding under the income tax sharing arrangements. These Aboriginal councils may in time come to constitute a rather special remote area category within the Australian system of local government and hence open up the potential for new forms of local/commonwealth intergovernmental relations in Aboriginal affairs, though ones that will clearly be restricted to the most remote areas of Australia.

Analytic issues

General trend or unique policy sphere?

One of the analytic issues arising from this historical account is the extent to which Aboriginal affairs can be seen to be a unique policy area in its intergovernmental relations or the extent to which it reflects general trends evident in other policy areas. Can the growth of commonwealth involvement in Aboriginal affairs, and the consequent change in the nature of intergovernmental relations from co-operative parallelism to potentially confrontationist responsibility sharing, be seen just as part of the general commonwealth postwar push towards greater involvement in many policy areas? To some extent it can, but there are some peculiarities and differences.

First, Aboriginal affairs was clearly not part of the early postwar efforts at commonwealth intervention in the late 1940s. It only came into the picture in the second, Whitlam round of intervention in the early 1970s. The argument that Aboriginal affairs was a national problem requiring commonwealth intervention only really became dominant during the 1960s. Previously, there had been a strong presumption in favour of policy and administration being conducted at the state and territory level. This presumption relied heavily on the argument that the circumstances of Aborigines were considerably different in the various states and territories and therefore required different approaches, or at least different local adaptations of the one general assimilation/welfare authority approach. It was only when this long-established state-dominated policy approach began to be regarded as inadequate and out of date in the 1960s that the normative presumption in favour of commonwealth action in Aboriginal affairs began to predominate. So Aboriginal affairs, like some other welfare/social policy areas, was in many ways one of the late starters in the push for greater commonwealth involvement.

The other significant difference in comparing the growth of commonwealth involvement in Aboriginal affairs with other policy areas is the existence of the 1967 referendum. Whereas other referendums for the extension of commonwealth powers failed to be passed, the 1967 referendum was passed with a resounding majority. Unlike other policy areas where the commonwealth had to rely for the extension of its involvement on judicial re-interpretations of existing constitutional provisions, in the case of Aboriginal affairs the commonwealth did have a clear change of the constitution to which it could refer. Though the actual content of the 1967 changes have been fairly widely misunderstood and misrepresented ever since, there is little doubt as to the commonwealth's clear concurrent constitutional power in Aboriginal affairs (see Hanks, 1984).

What has been of greater doubt over the years since 1967 has been the commonwealth's political and administrative ability to get its own way in Aboriginal affairs policy when it has had to rely so heavily on state government and non-government organisations for the delivery of so many basic services to Aborigines. The commonwealth's problem has not been a constitutional one, but rather a political and administrative one. In attempting to co-ordinate policy centrally through the DAA, while devolving responsibility for the servicing of Aborigines to so many functional departments and levels of government, successive commonwealth governments have set themselves a task of massive intergovernmental and interdepartmental proportions. Gaining compliance with central policy wishes among this increasing array of involved authorities is by its very nature a major task and, not surprisingly, has often not been achieved.

Commonwealth intervention: beneficial or dysfunctional?

A second set of even more evaluative analytic issues relates to the question of whether the commonwealth's intervention in Aboriginal affairs can be counted as beneficial to Aborigines or not, and on what grounds?

For a long time after 1972 it was difficult, indeed almost unrespectable, to argue that commonwealth intervention in Aboriginal affairs could be seen as anything other than beneficial to Aborigines. So great was the disowning of the state welfare authority era and the critique of its methods that commonwealth involvement and the new policy approach was merely taken to be better by mere assertion. For a long time problems with the new approach could be analysed away in terms of the legacies of the past policy approach and thereby excused. However, as time has gone on and the reality of the new responsibility sharing in Aboriginal affairs has become more established in its own right, such an uncritical attitude to commonwealth beneficence is now no longer so readily sustainable. There are criticisms which have been made of the new responsibility sharing in its own right which need to be addressed.

Perhaps the most substantial and persistent criticism of recent years has been that in advocating shared responsibility for Aboriginal affairs the new approach has often lessened the probability that any public authority will be held responsible on a particular matter. So great is the fragmentation of responsibilities between levels and functional departments of government that it is difficult for Aborigines to know which public authorities to turn to in relation to what matters and what to reasonably expect in response. Different departments have different programs with different eligibility requirements for Aboriginal individuals, families and communities offering them very different types of funding and services. The result is not Aboriginal self-management under a regime of shared intergovernmental and interdepartmental responsibility so much as chronically fragmented management of services to Aborigines in accordance with a labyrinth of bureaucratic rules and priorities. One frequent suggestion for reform in Aboriginal affairs of recent years has been to move towards greater block funding of Aboriginal communities and to allow local Aboriginal (self-managed) setting of priorities. Such a move would almost inevitably involve a retreat of Aboriginal affairs policy into a smaller number of government agencies, if not in fact into some single portfolio defined in terms of its Aboriginal clientele.

This criticism of fragmented responsibility sharing in Aboriginal affairs is, I believe, somewhat overdrawn. It overlooks the extent to which it has been this very fragmentation of responsibility which has increased resources available to Aborigines and increased Aboriginal room for manoeuvre over the last twenty years. Government administration is not a coherent monolith. The fragmentation of government responsibility for Aborigines has also meant a 'pluralisation' of possible funding sources. What Aborigines cannot get from one department or level of government, they may well be able to get from another, albeit under a different guise. Somehow or other, playing one public authority off against the others, an Aboriginal community or family unit might just be able to put together enough of the things they desire to make life viable. It is certainly a fragmented process, restricted by different bureaucratic rules and priorities, but it is also much more open to Aboriginal influence and manoeuvre than the single Aboriginal welfare authority hierarchies of the assimilation era ever were. The excesses of the present responsibility sharing arrangements are also their strength: fragmentation is also pluralisation.

A second criticism of commonwealth intervention in Aboriginal affairs that has been voiced in recent years is that in seeking nationwide uniformity in Aboriginal policy the commonwealth has restricted the local adaptability of policy and program appropriateness. Though this argument may have had some significant credence during the early days of the Hawke Government's push for uniform national land rights, it is generally without great substance. One of the more striking aspects of commonwealth intervention in Aboriginal affairs over the past twenty years has been the way in which it has not been greatly concerned with achieving uniformity. Programs have been applied to different types of Aboriginal communities in different parts of Australia in quite different ways. Indeed, apart from the rather uncharacteristic 1984 episode, commonwealth governments have really only been concerned with uniformity at the level of policy rhetoric and ideology. While the central policy terms and the program names are the same, what occurs on the ground at the local community level can be very different. Local appropriateness and adaptability are probably no more restricted than they were under the earlier state and territory-dominated approach to Aboriginal policy. Achieving uniformity has never really been an issue.

There is then still a strong case to be put that commonwealth involvement in Aboriginal affairs has been of considerable benefit to Aborigines. It helped bring to an end a highly rigid single authority approach to Aboriginal affairs and replaced it with a more flexible, if fragmented, responsibility sharing approach. Perhaps it was not anticipated by many of the supporters of this change just how messy and potentially conflict-ridden the ensuing responsibility sharing arrangements would be. But that probably only underlines their lack of appreciation of the nature of Australian intergovernmental arrangements more generally, rather than any wish to turn back the clock in Aboriginal affairs. Few of the supporters of commonwealth intervention in Aboriginal affairs would have wanted a commonwealth reincarnation of the single-purpose state Aboriginal welfare authorities, and that in many ways may have been the only alternative to a fairly messy system of intergovernmental and interdepartmental responsibility sharing.

Bibliography

Bennett, S., 1988. *Aborigines and Political Power*, Allen & Unwin, Sydney.

Department of Aboriginal Affairs, 1987. *Aboriginal Statistics, 1986, AGPS, Canberra.*

Hanks, P., 1984. 'Aborigines and Government: the Developing Framework', in *Aborigines and the Law*, eds P. Hanks & B. Keon-Cohen, Allen & Unwin, Sydney.

Hasluck, P., 1988. *Shades of Darkness: Aboriginal Affairs 1925–1965*, Melbourne University Press, Carlton, Victoria.

House of Representatives Standing Committee on Aboriginal Affairs, 1982. *Strategies to Help Overcome the Problems of Aboriginal Town Camps*, AGPS, Canberra.

Human Rights Australia, 1988. *Toomelah Report: Report on the Problems and Needs of Aborigines Living on the New South Wales–Queensland Border*, House With No Steps Printing, Belrose, NSW.

Loveday, P., ed., 1982. *Service Delivery to Remote Communities*, Australian National University, North Australia Research Unit Monograph, Darwin.

Rowley, C.D., 1971. *Outcasts in White Australia: Aboriginal Policy and Practice Volume II*, Australian National University Press, Canberra.

Tatz, C., 1979. *Race Politics in Australia: Aborigines, Politics and Law*, University of New England Publishing Unit.

Whitlam, E.G., 1973. 'Aborigines and Society', *Australian Government Digest*, April–June.

—— 1985. *The Whitlam Government*, Penguin Books, Ringwood, Victoria.

14 Rural policy

Rolf Gerritsen

Australian agriculture policy results from the complex interaction between three institutional 'sets'—usually organised at both federal and state levels—within the parameters created by agricultural commodities markets at both the domestic and international levels. Thus the governmental set comprises the commonwealth and the state governments (with the added complication that invariably different political parties hold power in the different governments). The statutory authority set includes the Industries Commission, the CSIRO, national commodity organisations such as the Wool Corporation, and state-level authorities such as irrigation boards. As well there are formal intergovernmental authorities such as the Plague Locust Commission and the Murray-Darling Basin Commission. Similarly, producers' organisations are organised both at the industry/commodity and at the state and national levels. Even without the well-known vagaries of market access and commodity prices, the field of agricultural policy is thus necessarily multiplex. The political and policy interactions between governments, statutory agencies and producer organisations are not confined to their designated federal or state jurisdictions but persistently intersect or override these constitutional boundaries.

Within this elaborate maze, the single arena of intergovernmental relations is a further seamless web. Yet it is a web with a fair degree of formal institutional expression and legitimacy, with largely accepted patterns of interaction, and where the timeframe is usually long term in a policy community that shares many common values. Intergovernmental relations in agriculture are reasonably co-operative. Compared with intergovernmental relations in general, they are very co-operative. Partisan political differences usually do not prevent co-operation.

Division is mostly confined to the discontented mutterings of officials or intemperate press releases from politicians and, relatively rarely, spills out of the institutional frameworks into debilitating political conflict and policy atrophy.

The dominance of co-operativeness in Australian agriculture's intergovernmental relations is neither a happy accident nor solely the product of an Olsonian 'distributional coalition' (Olson, 1965) operating to the detriment of consumers or taxpayers. Distributional coalitions, for example between the unions and manufacturing capital in support of consumer-subsidised tariffs, are rife in the Australian political economy. If they were widespread in Australian agriculture, then it would consequently be less internationally competitive than is undoubtedly the case. The prevailing co-operation occurs for two good reasons: it creates *de facto* economies of scale, in effect 'risk pooling', and there is some (slight) gain to the organising participants.

Agricultural economists explain the public sector's preponderance in agricultural research by arguing that each individual farm enterprise is too small to risk the capital outlays required to conduct research. Consequently farmers share ('pool') the risk through contributing to governmental carriage of the research (in Australia usually directly, through production levies). *Intergovernmental relations are co-operative because they replicate the same risk pooling incentive.* Co-operation reduces the costs of research, policy development, and operational management of services such as agricultural extension. Each government co-operates because 'defection' (in the language of collective action theory), whilst it may reduce short-term costs, will probably increase long-term costs. This is partly because the intergovernmental system acts as a pooling device through common access to collective capacity and experience. One agent's mistakes or experience can save money or administrative time for agriculture policy managers in another jurisdiction. The formal intergovernmental system detailed below facilitates the efficiency of such information transfer.

The incentive for intergovernmental co-operation parallels the market experience of most producers and draws on the same dominant rural philosophy. The bulk of Australia's agricultural produce has to compete in highly distorted international markets (Miller, 1987). Consequently, co-operation at the national level assists farmers to maximise their productive efficiency and market power and so spreads market 'risks'. The assumptions behind its intergovernmental relations thus replicates one aspect of agriculture's central social ideology, the intersection through co-operation between the private and the public interest.

Admittedly, once the institutions of the intergovernmental system are created there is some (relatively small) inbuilt gain to the bureaucratic and scientific participants. The administrators in the various state departments have access to a wider corpus of knowledge, reinforcing their

effectiveness and thereby their careers. The larger community of administrators constituted by the intergovernmental institutions creates larger
peer referent groups and consequent improved access to reputation, the
primary career enhancement tool for administrators. Similar incentives
apply for the scientists in the research sections of the state departments.
But, given that there have to be administrators and researchers (whether
public or private sector), and that there is no evidence that currently they
are adversely affecting the economic efficiency of agriculture as such, this
is far from being a distributional coalition in the Olsonian sense. The
inefficient sectors of Australian agriculture—such as the dairying,
tobacco, dried vine fruits, and egg production industries—are the product
of distributional coalitions between producers and various governments,
to the detriment of consumers. But, as distinct from past experience (see
Seiper, 1982), these inefficient industries are now exceptions to the
general rule in contemporary Australian agriculture.

The advantages of co-operation, plus the centrality of the bureaucratic
input, explain both the low level of politically partisan conflict in the
intergovernmental system and the system's persistence in the current
period when such 'traditional' agricultural policy-making institutions are
increasingly being marginalised by changes to the institutional format
and policy foci of commonwealth primary industry policy. Partisan
conflict, if unchecked and public, may force defection to save electoral
honour; hence the mechanism of the non-public, bureaucratic Standing
Committee on Agriculture. This meets before the ministerial council as a
device to encourage lowest common denominator levels of agreement
before the politicians convene (Gerritsen & Abbott, 1988:10). The Agricultural Council provides an arena for bureaucratic career enhancement
and so fosters the dogged attachment to its institutional forms.

The institutional web 1: the Agriculture Council and the Standing Committee

The ministerial council, the Australian Agricultural Council (AAC), and
its associated Standing Committee on Agriculture (the SCA), a
committee of commonwealth and state officials which meets formally
before the Council, are at the centre of the intergovernmental web in the
rural policy field. They operate on three different levels: as formal
institutional mechanisms for intergovernmental co-ordination and
co-operation; as a 'clearing house' for activities requiring the imprimatur
that the legitimacy of the council provides; and as a minor arena for
'symbolic' and 'issue deferral' politics.

The apex of the formal intergovernmental system is the AAC; this
was formed in 1934 and is the longest-lived of Australia's ministerial
councils. The Council comprises the agriculture ministers from the six
states, the Northern Territory and the commonwealth and is chaired by

the commonwealth minister responsible for agriculture. Papua New Guinea and New Zealand have observer status on the Council (and on the Standing Committee). The role of the AAC is the making of 'policy', the secure dichotomy between that activity and 'administration' being part of the 'sacred' ideology of intergovernmental relations in agriculture. The Council meets formally and biannually. It may meet in special session when an 'intermittent' crisis occurs (Gerritsen & Murray, 1987:7–8), such as in the dairy industry example discussed below. The AAC has the role of formally legitimating intergovernmental agreements and processes.

The Standing Committee of officials has a wider membership than the Council, including in addition delegates from the CSIRO and the commonwealth Department of Finance. The chairmanship of the SCA circulates between the states and the commonwealth. It is considered a prestigious appointment and keenly awaited, particularly by senior state agriculture officials. The Standing Committee's role is the bureaucratic 'administration' of the technical detail of intergovernmental agreements and processes. Most of the matters dealt with at the SCA do not come up at Council or are only formally endorsed there. The SCA carries the delegated authority of the AAC to deal by itself with ongoing 'recurrent' (Gerritsen & Murray, 1987:7–8) technical and management matters. These cover subjects like insect pest control, food and product standards, veterinary drug residues, scientific and information exchanges, technical workshops, official attendance at professional conferences.

The complexity that is historically endemic to the operations of intergovernmental relations was expressed in the plethora (over 300!) of SCA sub-committees and working parties. To ease the administrative burden on the Council secretariat of monitoring this multitude of groups, the July 1988 AAC meeting reduced the SCA's 91 sub-committees, either by amalgamation or abolition, to 24. These were basically structured around the animal–plant divide traditional in state agriculture departments. Over time, and as new issues arise, the number of SCA sub-committees and working parties can be expected to resume their incremental upward creep.

Most of the work of agricultural intergovernmental relations is actually done between the formal meetings. It is done by officials and not necessarily through the AAC secretariat. Working parties operate informally. They may address the issues for which they have been formed without actually meeting, teleconferencing sufficing for such instances. SCA technical committees meet biannually and more formally. Given their relatively permanent nature, their memberships are likely to be consciously more representative of the total SCA membership than is that for a working party. The acceptability of the AAC/SCA framework means that often state officials will engage in some bilateral activity that will be invested with the imprimatur of the AAC or the SCA without actually involving it institutionally. State agriculture officials will seek the endorsement of the SCA as a means of persuading their treasuries of the importance of their attendance at overseas conferences.

In fact, the intergovernmental agriculture policy system exhibits a high degree of efficiency. For example, the participating governments may decide that a particular international conference requires monitoring. A delegate from one of the governments is selected to represent the AAC or the SCA. On returning the delegate's report is circulated to all state and federal agriculture departments. In addition, the delegate's department, which has paid for the trip in the first instance, directly bills all other Council participating governments. The AAC secretariat is not even administratively involved, costs are minimised and efficiency maximised. Such 'clearing house' operational modes enable the Council secretariat to operate on a minimal annual non-salary budget of $35 000 (for 1988–89).

The forums of agricultural intergovernmental relations also serve political ends; not those of political parties so much as those of the system's constituent governments. Occasionally the AAC and the SCA provide convenient arenas for 'symbolic' contestation and interest representation of an issue 'deferral' nature. A state government can raise an issue it knows has no chance of implementation; but in so doing it can defer a political demand from its own constituency. The aggrieved, unsuccessful suitor can then be fobbed off with the story that the matter received no support at the Council. One illustration of this occurred in 1987 when new fee-for-service meat inspection charges were introduced. One economically marginal Queensland abattoir, primarily servicing the domestic market, believed itself to be peculiarly disadvantaged by what was an export-driven impost and petitioned the state government to secure redress from the commonwealth. Accordingly Queensland officials sought to get the new meat inspection charges re-evaluated. They raised the matter at the SCA level (SCA141, February 1988 *Minutes*:7). The other states overrode Queensland and that state did not even persist with the matter at the following AAC meeting. Presumably political honour and convenience had been satisfied.

Conflicting interests between states, or between the states and the commonwealth, are more readily expressed at the SCA level than at the AAC. At the Council disagreements are usually 'noted' rather than debated, the parameters of the different viewpoints having been informally established at the SCA. The legitimacy (respectability?) and utility of the Council's institutional framework should not be sullied, or threatened, by too much 'politics'. At the SCA level divergent interests between states can be expressed as such without the complications of political partisanship and the consequent temptation to render differences more public so as to advance the electoral interests of any particular governing political party.

In 1985, the Interstate Commission reported to the commonwealth on the Tasmanian Wheat Freight Subsidy Scheme. It recommended that existing arrangements continue (*viz.* that the subsidy be paid for by a levy on all domestic wheat consumption). The Commission also recommended that the Australian Wheat Board, which acted as the purchasing agent for Tasmania, should only buy wheat from the least costly source. At the subsequent SCA meeting Victoria and South Australia opposed the latter recommendation. Historically these states had supplied most of the wheat subject to the subsidy scheme. The Labor government of New South Wales joined with the then only conservative state governments in Australia, Queensland and Tasmania, in support of the cost-reduction recommendation (SCA 122, 21 July 1985 *Minutes*:27). The Council noted the states' positions and did not seek to impede the commonwealth in implementing the Interstate Commission's recommendations.

The states take the AAC and the SCA more seriously than does the commonwealth government. This is partly for the career enhancement reasons discussed above. But it has also been a historical tendency that has been powerfully encouraged by the activities of the Hawke Labor Government's Primary Industries Minister, John Kerin. Probably more than any federal agriculture minister since the 1950s, Kerin has sought to change the structures of agricultural policy making (initiatives he foreshadowed before coming to government—Kerin, 1983:59ff.). Kerin has restructured commodity policy by establishing a standardised framework for each industry. This usually comprises three institutions: a policy council, a marketing corporation, and a research council (Gerritsen & Murray, 1987:10–11; Gerritsen & Abbott, 1988:19). To this format has been added a 'corporatist' embellishment; representation on these bodies is usually a mixture of governmental delegates and industry producer representatives. The producers are chosen by new mechanisms explicitly oriented towards merit, rather than the (alleged) political favouritism of the past (Gerritsen & Abbott, 1988:11). These new institutions are rapidly achieving policy centrality. To that extent they contribute to the downgrading of the formal intergovernmental institutions. Perhaps revealing Kerin's attitude to its priority, the position of secretary of the AAC, held at section head level in the commonwealth department, became a half-post in 1986. The current Council secretary simultaneously heads the Ministerial and Cabinet Liaison Unit in the Department of Primary Industry and Energy (DPIE).

Kerin's corporatism has sought to devolve control over commodity policy and marketing to the producers. It has made the private-sector producers much more explicit, equal and accountable participants in policy making, thereby implicitly devaluing the roles both of the National Farmers' Federation and its affiliates and of the state governments. The AAC and SCA mechanisms are in that sense relics of an earlier period in retaining the states as equal *and exclusive* participants in formal agricultural policy making.

Kerin's disinclination to accord policy making centrality to the AAC and the SCA was strengthened after the ministerial reshuffle following the 1987 federal election. This made Kerin one of the 'super ministers' with the amalgamation into the portfolio of a division from the former Department of Trade and most of the former resources and energy portfolio. The incorporation of mineral commodities into the central concerns of the new 'mega' DPIE began a shift to a broader commodity trade policy focus, a shift that has not been emulated in the primarily agricultural state portfolios. This divergence of intergovernmental structural and policy foci was exacerbated in 1989, when the DPIE was restructured to centralise 'policy' into divisions directly responsible to Kerin, leaving the bulk of the 'administrative' matters to his 'junior', the Minister for Resources, Senator Cook. Unless a future coalition government reverses the departmental amalgations of 1987, the structural divergence between the commonwealth and the states will continue.

Consequently, the states accord more importance to the formal institutional structures of rural policy intergovernmentalism than does the commonwealth. In these structures they are central managers, rather than interested observers. The structures provide a means to constrain commonwealth 'centralism' (as the states see it, although from Canberra it is 'co-ordination'). The co-ordination of developing export markets in the mid 1980s is an instance. The 1985 commodity prices crash provided a stimulus for the states and the commonwealth to encourage diversification of both products and markets. The commonwealth vehicles for this were Austrade and the emerging Horticultural Research and Development Corporation (formally established in 1988—Gerritsen & Abbott, 1988:19). The states used the vehicle of the SCA to resist the direction of the commonwealth. In late 1986, the SCA established a 'working group' to categorise and evaluate the new initiatives, claiming that 'the diversity of "new" production and product development and "new" market development suggests that initiatives taken at a commonwealth level will not necessarily be of common interest to all states' (AAC 125, 6 February, 1987 *Minutes*) .

These divergent states' interests, as proclaimed by the SAC's actions, were recognised in the formation of the Horticultural Policy Council. When established, the Council, apart from the usual representatives of growers, processors and employees, uniquely had delegates representing the Agricultural Council, *ex officio*. To underscore the states' independence the newly-elected New South Wales Greiner Liberal Government in 1988 established AGSELL, a 'high profile' departmental unit to facilitate agriculture export diversification from that state ('Agsell to push exports of farming products' *Australian Financial Review*, 4 April 1989). This was claimed to be a significant up-grading of the previous New South Wales Labor government's Export Development Unit. The Labor government of Western Australia also embarked on a separate export establishment drive in 1988.

The institutional web 2: 'agency' and co-operative federalism structures

Outside the centralised policy clearing house of the AAC, most rural primary industry policy is even more akin to a seamless web.

Large policy areas of Australian intergovernmental relations can be best described as 'agency federalism' where one government acts as an agent for another. In the web of intergovernmental relations in rural policy the usual type of agency federalism is where the states carry out the functions of the commonwealth. Thus the states' agricultural extension services provide the applied implementation of the research carried out both by their own departments as well as by the CSIRO. Such co-operative-style federalism is especially a feature of fisheries management. This arises because the commonwealth and the states constitutionally share control of the physical resource: the states from the high-water mark to the old three-mile limit, the commonwealth from there to the limit of the economic exploitation zone. Where the declared management zone of a fishery does not cross any state boundary the state fisheries service usually manages the fishery on behalf of itself and the commonwealth. Such is the case with the Spencer Gulf Prawn Fishery, which is managed by the South Australian government (Bowen & Hancock, 1985).

Other fisheries which cross state boundaries, such as the Southern Trawl and Northern Prawn fisheries, are regulated by management committees comprising commonwealth and state government represent-atives as well as industry representatives (Bowen & Hancock, 1985; Gerritsen, 1987). Some other fisheries which are under the sole constitu-ional purview of the commonwealth are managed by individual states. Thus the Australia—Taiwan agreement governing Taiwanese access to the deepwater Northern Trawl Fishery in the Timor Sea is administered by the Northern Territory Fisheries Service as sole agent for the commonwealth. To complete the seamlessness of the intergovernmental relations of fisheries management the Bass Strait Orange Roughy Fishery is administered by the commonwealth even though the Tasmanian and Victorian Fisheries Services are joint managers with the commonwealth in other Declared Management Zones for fisheries in adjacent areas.

The fiscal web

The most obvious demonstration of co-operative intergovernmental relations is when a program is jointly funded. The Brucellosis and Tuberculosis Eradication Campaign (BTEC) began in the early 1980s to secure the freedom of Australia's beef and dairy herds from these diseases. This was seen as a long-term measure to protect Australian access to the United States beef market. By the late 1980s, these diseases had been eradicated from everywhere but the northernmost parts of Western Australia, the Northern Territory and Queensland. The southern states became restive about their continuing contributions to the costs of the BTEC as their territories were cleared and the expense rose in the more difficult environment of northern Australia. Proposals were periodically made simply to cordon off the northern reaches of Australia's cattle range in an effort to restrict the now-irksome imposts. But the issue was never seriously put to the AAC. That the BTEC scheme will continue until all Australia's herds are free by 1991 is testament to collective obligations ultimately overriding fiscal irritation.

Apart from planned, formal programs like BTEC, many co-operative intergovernmental activities create a 'trigger' levy system of contributions if a pest or disease outbreak occurs. Each state's contribution to the activity is assessed by a rough-and-ready system which takes into account its relative importance in the activity or industry, the state's fiscal and administrative capacity, or some other such relevant measure. These arrangements can lead to minor stresses in interstate relations. For example, during the 'pesticides crisis' in 1987 (Gerritsen & Abbott, 1988:24) all the states except Victoria objected in some degree to the comprehensive (and expensive) testing for organochlorides in 'low risk' areas (AAC 129, 5 February, 1988 *Minutes* :3).

A similar situation had occurred in 1983 when the Northern Territory called into effect the arrangements for a threatened foot and mouth outbreak. This turned out to be a false alarm, fuelling the feeling in the larger states that they are sometimes at the mercy of the staff and infrastructure inadequacies of the smaller states. Again, in July 1988 the Northern Territory triggered the procedures for a screw-worm fly outbreak when two dead flies were found on a ship in Darwin harbour. South Australia cavilled at contributing its $3000 share of the $100 000 expended because the flies were dead and technically, it argued, an outbreak or threat of infestation did not exist. Nonetheless, when its bill arrived South Australia paid.

Occasionally the disproportionate benefit accruing to a particular state of these co-operatively funded agreements creates more serious intergovernmental tensions. Such has been the case for drought relief, of which Queensland has obtained more than 80 per cent over the last five years. Currently the commonwealth is changing the parameters for drought relief under the National Disaster Relief arrangements. These trigger automatic commonwealth payments after a state has expended a specified amount on relief in declared drought areas. The commonwealth action follows persistent reports that Queensland has been over-hasty in declaring areas drought-affected. For this that state is not fully fiscally penalised, both because these expenditures are accounted into its fiscal equalisation needs in subsequent commonwealth Grants Commission relativities reviews and because the commonwealth meets the further outlays after the state's initial triggering expenditure. Action by the commonwealth in April 1989 was prompted by a leaked internal memorandum of the Queensland DPI's Drought Secretariat that revealed widespread and systematic abuse of the scheme.

In practice, even without Queensland-style abuses, strict equity between the various governments' contributions is difficult to achieve. For example, the 1986–87 Western Australian potato cyst nematode eradication campaign apportioned the states' share of the costs in proportion to their share of the gross national value of potato output. Despite it benefiting disproportionately, Western Australia paid only $5687 of the campaign's $125 000 costs in 1986–87. This contribution did not reflect the economic importance of the Southeast Asian market to Western Australia's potato production (see also AAC 131, 10 February 1989 *Minutes*:42).

Of course equity is not the reason for the common levy arrangements for dealing with insects or plant diseases. In fact, the equity implications of these procedures are less clear than this example indicates. *The primary impetus comes from the demonstrable, manifold benefits of co-operation.*

The advantages to co-operating governments of sharing the costs of insect infestation or crop disease eradication are considerable. At its simplest the mechanism utilises risk pooling. Contributing to such levies is a form of co-operative insurance. Enhancing this effect are the positive externalities. By assisting one state government to deal with a disease or pest outbreak the other governments avoid the greater costs of dealing with it entirely by themselves should the affliction spread. The process also has fiscal attractions. Levies are smaller, fiscally smoother, charges than the costs of unanticipated, unassisted sole action. Co-operation, as institutionalised by common levies, is also exhibited in the research activities associated with agricultural pest control. The system facilitates the mobilisation of collective research and management expertise to create *de facto* economies of scale. Finally, the process rewards co-operativeness and legitimates the importance of AAC and its institutional system. In co-operation fiscal, political and administrative benefits coincide.

The management of intergovernmental 'crises'

Two contemporary agricultural 'crises' allow evaluation of the significance of intergovernmental processes in agricultural policy making. These are the dairy industry crisis and the wheat deregulation issue.

The dairy 'crisis'

The dairy industry, along with the egg and tobacco industries, for some time has been one of the least efficient industries in Australia's agricultural sector. Successive efforts at reform in the decades after World War II produced little improvement (Hefford, 1985:171–96; IAC, 1987:38). Essentially the principal states have different interests in the dairy industry. Because it was restricted to its domestic market, Victoria had relative over-production of market milk, which required a collective states levy subsidy for the conversion of this surplus to less-profitable manufactured milk exports. New South Wales, with a smaller-scale, less efficient industry, sought protection from Victorian market milk penetrating its market (the problem is essentially the large price differential between market and manufactured milk). All states also operated marketing mechanisms to protect milk vendors.

The advent of the Hawke Labor Government inaugurated another round of attempts to remove uneconomic producers, along the lines recommended by the Industries Assistance Commission (IAC, 1983). These culminated in the so-called 'Kerin Plan' of 1986. This instituted a common levy to facilitate the restructuring of the industry. This was required because of another externality, the certainty of New Zealand milk entering the market after the Closer Economic Relations agreement came into force in 1990. In 1987 the delicate balance was threatened when a Victorian producer began selling bulk milk to a New South Wales retail chain. The New South Wales government retaliated by threatening to suspend its contributions to the national all-milk levy. In October, a hastily convened meeting of the AAC achieved a compromise. This gave Victoria access to 3 per cent of the New South Wales market (plus incremental annual increases) at New South Wales prices. All trade was to be through the state Dairy Industry Authorities (AAC Special Meeting, 2 October 1987 *Minutes*).

The fragility of the compromise was demonstrated in early 1989 when Coles supermarkets in New South Wales began buying Victorian milk. New South Wales producers retaliated by discounting their supplies to large purchasers (thereby assuring the demise of the vendors). The situation is prone to another flashpoint with large private-sector retailers set to assume the initiative and overturn the intergovernmental milk policy compromise. Probably the most economically rational method of resolving the crisis of the dairy industry is to create negotiable milk quotas and allow efficient, large-scale Victorian producers to buy out the quotas of uncompetitive New South Wales dairymen (Lembit et al., 1988). But the electoral exigencies of New South Wales politics mean that this remains an unpopular option.

The dairy produce market arrangements, arguably continuing in clear breach of section 92, provide a clear illustration of the implied prohibitions and restraints in agricultural policy's intergovernmental relations. Victoria cannot use section 92 to capture the New South Wales market because that will lead to a breakdown of the national levy subsidies for its market milk exports. As a price for the exclusion of Victoria from its domestic market, the New South Wales government has to continue its levy contributions to maintain the price of (overwhelmingly Victorian) manufactured milk. This intergovernmental stand-off lends some superficial credence to the Olsonian distributional coalition hypothesis about such stability in intergovernmental relations. The weakness of the Olson hypothesis is that the intergovernmental relations of the dairy industry are unstable and conflict-prone and moving beyond the control of Australian governments.

Paradoxically, despite there being a high degree of intergovernmental tension in contemporary dairy policy developments, the residual co-operative sinews of the system continue unabated. The February 1989 SCA meeting decided that future meetings of the Chief Dairy Officers Subcommittee of its Animal Production Committee should concentrate on three sets of subjects. These were: dairy technology and regulatory matters; review of dairy research and extension programs in the host state; and review of co-ordination of priorities in national dairy research and extension (SCA 143:7–8 February 1989 *Minutes*:2). No mention was made of the Victoria–New South Wales imbroglio.

The significance of this case study for present purposes is in the determination of the states to maintain the effectiveness of the AAC system. The October 1987 meeting reaffirmed the legitimacy of the Council as a vehicle for resolving interstate conflict. The participation of the unaffected states, both in the meeting and in contributing to the national all-milk levy, exemplify this point. For example, Western Australia, which is protected by the isolation and small scale of its market, is not threatened by the eventual irruption of New Zealand milk. So its contribution to the intergovernmental milk arrangements can be seen as exhibiting a concern for the preservation of the collective intergovernmental system.

The 1989 wheat deregulation 'crisis'

After the 1987 election the federal Labor government committed itself to comprehensive microeconomic reform of the Australian economy. This emphasis fitted easily into Kerin's rationalisation of agricultural commodity marketing organisations. Following the 1988 McColl Royal Commission on grain handling and storage, the commonwealth determined to begin deregulation of the Australian Wheat Board's monopoly of grain purchasing. It determined to begin this by removing most of the Wheat Board's monopoly powers over domestically-marketed grain.

The deregulation threatened the distributional coalitions of unions, state rail authorities and bulk handling authorities that had been built up over 40 years. State governments, alarmed at the fiscal implications, became the champions of these coalitions of interests. Initially the states voiced their concerns at the July 1988 AAC meeting. In addition, they were able, through the SCA's processes, to slightly modify the commonwealth's proposals. In 1989, the impetus for deregulation of the Wheat Board's powers was powerfully aided by the dismay and confusion this caused in the coalition parties' ranks. But the poltical advantage of this to the federal Labor government may be negated if the matter attracts concerted opposition from the states. Some states increasingly appeared ready to move beyond the formal intergovernmental process in attempting to secure their viewpoint.

Currently the states are examining their positions. Most point to heavy investments in grain storage and handling facilities. Servicing the capital costs of these will allegedly be difficult in a deregulated environment. Victoria stressed the potential losses to recurrent revenue from its railways, plus the concomitant increased costs of road funding. Differential commonwealth funding for roads supposedly prevents a 'level playing field' if deregulation occurs. The Victorian government was reportedly prepared to introduce prohibitive road tolls or mount a High Court challenge to prevent the implementation of the deregulation proposals ('Kerin will keep AWB exporting monopoly' *Australian Financial Review* 12 April 1989).

But the prevailing co-operative tendency in intergovernmental agriculture management remained, even with the high levels of conflict associated with wheat deregulation. The July 1988 AAC meeting set up a Working Party of the SCA to report on the effect of deregulation on wheat quality. The February 1989 meeting of Council was able to receive a set of workable arrangements to secure minimum wheat quality (AAC 131, 10 February 1989 *Minutes*:9–11).

The wheat deregulation issue reveals much about the significance of the intergovernmental system in policy determination and management. The states were initially content to use the formal system to press their reservations about the direction of wheat policy. Disagreements were expressed in the language of the technicalities of the issue. And the commonwealth was prepared to accept some compromise to facets of its original position. But because the commonwealth was not willing to alter fundamentally its proposals, and because the AAC mechanism does not provide even united state opposition with a veto power over the commonwealth, the states were driven outside the formal intergovernmental system in pressing their interests. The demands for consensus and the inhibitions on overt conflict in the AAC made the intergovernmental system of marginal relevance to resolution of this dispute.

Conclusion: the aggrandisement of the commonwealth?

The evidence is very mixed for the proposition of commonwealth control over the intergovernmental relations of agriculture policies. In some areas there has been an assumption of commonwealth dominance, even monopoly. In 1982 the commonwealth established an export meat inspection service to operate in parallel with the states' services. Following the 1983 meat substitution 'scandal' and the subsequent report of the Royal Commission into the Australian Meat Industry, which recommended the creation of a single inspection service, the commonwealth gradually assumed a monopoly over meat inspection. The states, with greater or lesser degrees of willingness, vacated the function. But a contrary tendency is evident in the operation of the Rural Adjustment Scheme (RAS). This is a joint commonwealth–states subsidy scheme designed in theory to provide temporarily unfinancial farmers with carry-on finance or to assist non-viable farmers to leave the industry. In 1988 the RAS guidelines were changed to reduce the commonwealth role and to provide the states with more autonomy, control and direct accountability (AAC 130, 14 July 1988 *Minutes*:Annex A; Gerritsen & Abbott, forthcoming).

In 1987 Australian beef exports to the United States and Japan were threatened by the discovery of high levels of organochlorides in Australian meat. Victoria was the most severely affected state and its government immediately bought back all pesticide stocks from the farmers. Other states either requested commonwealth subsidy for their buy-back programs, as did Western Australia, or, like Queensland, refused to act without the provision of a 100 per cent commonwealth subsidy. The commonwealth eventually obtained funding compliance for a National Monitoring Service for pesticides, its trade power giving it the necessary leverage.

The inertial effects from intergovernmental industry management can leave governments pursuing contradictory policies and belies the general picture of Australian agricultural efficiency. In July 1988 a new Tobacco Industry Stabilisation Plan was finalised. To apply for seven years, the agreement between the commonwealth, Queensland, New South Wales and Victoria, plus the growers and manufacturers, provided for a concessional tariff of 47 cents per kilogram and for a 57 per cent local leaf content rule. This arrangement contradicted both Kerin's priority on microeconomic efficiency reforms in agriculture (Gerritsen & Abbott, forthcoming) and the near unanimous governmental restraints on tobacco advertising. This example, besides illustrating the inertial constraints on commonwealth policy, provides a further minor caveat to the argument that intergovernmental relations do not necessarliy foster distributional coalitions.

Again, some states persist with policies that defy the creation of uniform national markets. Thus Western Australia has a range of internal quarantine measures for plant products and live animals that effectively restrict competitive market entry from the other states. The continuation of these measures is yet another indicator that the commonwealth is not overwhelmingly dominant in agricultural policy making. The initiative may reside with the commonwealth, as in the case with wheat deregulation, but this example is successfully qualified by the commonwealth's reactive role in the dairy industry's restructuring.

A federation creates, *de facto* as well as *de jure*, the necessity for intergovernmental relations. Yet it may not create a similar necessity for relatively amicable co-operation. The success of intergovernmental management of Australian agricultural policy is that co-operation has been created despite a very complex web of organisational interests. It is a system that is reasonably efficient administratively and which has not led very often to the creation of inequitable winners and losers with the economic inefficiency of distributional coalitions.

Bibliography

AAC (various meeting nos; various dates) Australian Agricultural Council, Minutes of Resolutions from Meetings.

Bowen, B.K. & Hancock, D.A., 1985. 'Review of Penaeid Prawn Fishery Management Regimes in Australia', in *Second Australian National Prawn Seminar*, eds P.C. Rothlisberg et al., NPS2, Cleveland, Queensland.

Gerritsen, R., 1987. 'Collective Action Problems in the Regulation of Australia's Common Property Renewable Resources', *Australian Journal of Public Administration*, 46(4), 390–401.

Gerritsen, R. & Murray, A., 1987. 'Rural Policy Survey, 1986: The Battle for the Agenda', *Review of Marketing and Agricultural Economics*, 55(1), 7–24.

Gerritsen, R. & Abbott, J., 1988. 'Shifting to Certainty?: Australian Rural Policy in 1987', *Review of Marketing and Agricultural Economics*, 56(1), 9–26.

—— (forthcoming). 'Again the Lucky Country? Australian Rural Policy in 1988', *Review of Marketing and Agricultural Economics*, 57(1)(April).

Hefford, R.K., 1985. *Farm Policy in Australia,* University of Queensland Press, St Lucia, Qld.

IAC, 1983. *The Dairy Industry,* Industries Assistance Commission Report No.333, AGPS, Canberra.

—— 1987. *Assistance to Agricultural and Manufacturing Industries*, Industries Assistance Commission Information Paper (June), AGPS, Canberra.

Kerin, J., 1983. 'Rural and Regional Policy', in *Labor Essays 1983: Policies and Programs for the Labor Government*, eds J. Reeves & K. Thomson, Drummond Books, Melbourne.

Lembit, M., Topp, V., Williamson, G. & Beare, S., 1988. 'Gains from a Negotiable Milk Quota Scheme for New South Wales', *Quarterly Review of the Rural Economy*, 10(3), 255–60.

Miller, G., 1987. Department of Primary Industry, *The Political Economy of International Agricultural Policy Reform*, AGPS, Canberra.

Olson, M., 1965. *The Logic of Collective Action*, Harvard University Press, Cambridge, Mass.

SCA (various meeting nos; various dates) Standing Committee on Agriculture, Minutes of Resolutions from Meetings.

Seiper, E., 1982. *Rationalising Rustic Regulation*, Centre for Independent Studies, St Leonards, NSW.

15 Mining

Ciaran O'Faircheallaigh

A very large literature now exists on various aspects of mineral development in Australia, reflecting the mining industry's importance in economic, social and political terms. However, with few exceptions this literature does not deal explicitly with the issue of intergovernmental relations. For instance, much has been written about Australia's mineral taxation system; most works on the subject raise the issue of federalism, usually as an explanation for inefficiencies and complexities which are perceived to exist in the system and as a barrier to their removal, but they make no attempt to analyse the nature of intergovernmental relations in the area of resource taxation. Thus, while the possibility of applying a resource rent tax (RRT) to Australian mining has generated a great deal of academic (and polemic) writing, no one has yet examined in detail the process through which the commonwealth and the states resolved the RRT issue in 1984–86.[1]

This chapter reviews the literature which does deal with intergovernmental relations in mining, and identifies some key issues which it raises. It then outlines the constitutional division of powers in relation to mineral development, and discusses intergovernmental relations as they affect a number of key policy areas, examining mineral taxation in detail and the provision of mine infrastructure, export controls and foreign ownership more briefly. On the basis of this analysis, some conclusions are drawn regarding the nature of intergovernmental relations in mining and their impact on mineral development.

Intergovernmental relations in mining

Stevenson's 1977 monograph was the first major work to focus explicitly on intergovernmental relations and mineral development, and it had a substantial impact on subsequent work in the area. Stevenson argued that mineral-rich states were becoming more wealthy and powerful relative both to the commonwealth and the mineral-poor states, and that the response of the commonwealth was to initiate policies aimed at redistributing the benefits of mineral development away from the producing states and towards the resource-poor but populous industrialised states. He claimed that the inevitable outcome was extensive intergovernmental conflict, which might eventually lead to a weakening of Australia's federal system (Stevenson, 1977).

A number of authors subsequently developed Stevenson's arguments, claiming that mineral development created mutual interests between the mineral-rich states and foreign investors and mineral consumers, and conflicts of interest between Australia's mineral-rich and industrialised states, threatening to fragment the Australian political system (see, for example, Catley & McFarlane, 1978; Crough & Wheelwright, 1982:ch. 6). Others accepted the assumption that a shift in wealth and bargaining power had occurred, but believed that as long as the mineral-rich states were permitted a commensurate increase in political power and were not prevented from fully exploiting their wealth, political fragmentation could be avoided and Australia as a whole would benefit from mineral development (West, 1983). Galligan (1982) adopted a somewhat different focus, examining Stevenson's argument that a federal system of government would, by fragmenting political power, necessarily result in mineral policies more favourable to the interests of resource developers. Galligan concluded that this need not be the case, arguing that state and federal governments might compete for revenue from resource exploitation, and in the process produce a high level of direct government intervention and appropriate a high share of mining industry profits.

Head reassessed the basic assumptions shared by Stevenson and subsequent proponents of the 'bargaining shift' theory, arguing that the industrialised states and the commonwealth have been successful in preventing any sudden shift in power to the mineral-rich states, and questioning whether the latter were in fact retaining the wealth generated by exploitation of their minerals (Head, 1984). Drysdale and Shibata argued that while resource development has certainly increased the weight of mineral-rich states in Australia's economic life, it has at the same time reinforced centralist tendencies within Australia's federal system, because the commonwealth's control over mineral exports has enhanced its bargaining power relative to the states (Drysdale & Shibata, 1985:19, 22).

A common theme throughout this literature is the emphasis on the competitive and conflictual nature of intergovernmental relations. Another common characteristic is the emphasis on overall shifts in bargaining power perceived to be associated with large-scale mineral development, and with the implications of such shifts for Australia's political system.

The Advisory Council for Inter-government Relations (ACIR) adopted a different approach in what is the most detailed and comprehensive study of intergovernmental relations in mining (ACIR, 1984, 1985). ACIR set out to identify the main intergovernmental issues associated with major resource projects and their infrastructure, to identify any problems associated with the division of powers in this area, and to suggest ways in which such problems could be minimised by improving intergovernmental relations.

ACIR saw intergovernmental relations in the mining area as being 'characterised by conflict and competition'. In its view they involved horizontal tension between state governments resulting from competition for resource investments and over the economic benefits of resource development; and vertical tensions between the three levels of government as each used its particular powers in pursuit of its own policy objectives. It concluded that major problems do result from the division of powers over mining between federal, state and local governments, given the conflicting objectives and perceptions of different governments and their consequent failure to co-ordinate programs.[2] These problems include unwarranted complexity in governmental arrangements for the regulation and management of resource development; inconsistency and functional overlap between commonwealth, state and local governments; excessive delays in the project-approval process; over-regulation of resource development activity; and a piecemeal and disjointed policy approach to the resources sector. In turn, this last problem creates difficulties in dealing with longer-term policy issues, and in undertaking the long-term planning required for resource-linked public infrastructure (ACIR, 1984:9–10, 85–86, 148–50).

Thus two distinct sets of issues emerge from the literature. The first relates to shifts in the distribution of power between state and federal governments. The second relates to the impact of intergovernmental relations on the formulation and implementation of mineral policy and on the management of resource development. Both tend to be treated in a conflictual/competitive framework. Governments are seen to have conflicting interests in mineral development; this leads them to compete for control over it, which in turn has a major (and often deleterious) effect on the way in which policies are formulated and mineral development is managed.

The constitutional and legal framework

A key element of the framework for intergovernmental relations in mining is the division of powers over resource development effected by the Australian constitution. None of the identified legislative powers given to the commonwealth relate to mining, from which it could be concluded that resource development is an area of state jurisdiction (ACIR, 1985:26). However, certain of the commonwealth's general powers provide it with the capacity to exert considerable influence in this area. The extent of its involvement in resource development has reflected both changing perceptions among federal politicians regarding the need for the commonwealth to apply its powers, and changing judicial interpretations regarding the applicability of general powers to the resources field. Some of the most important powers are discussed below.[3]

Trade and commerce

Section 51(i) of the constitution provides that the commonwealth can legislate with regard to trade and commerce between Australia and other countries and among the states. As nearly all large mining projects in Australia export a substantial part of their output, this power gives the commonwealth an effective veto over the establishment and continued operation of major mining projects, which in turn can allow it to influence the terms under which resources are developed. The commonwealth's capacity to use the trade and commerce power in relation to issues not strictly related to trading policy was confirmed by the High Court in 1976 in *Murphyores Incorporated Pty Ltd* v. *the Commonwealth*.

Taxation

Section 51(ii) confers powers over both personal and company taxation and duties of customs and excise on the commonwealth, though these cannot be used to discriminate against, or give preference to, individual states. However, they can be applied differentially to individual mineral commodities. These powers give the commonwealth considerable scope to influence the rate and nature of resource development.

Corporations

Section 51(xx) empowers the commonwealth to legislate with respect to foreign corporations, and trading or financial corporations formed within the limits of the commonwealth. The power to legislate in relation to foreign corporations is of particular relevance to large-scale mining projects, many of which have been established and/or funded by foreign investors.

External affairs

The power to make laws with respect to external affairs (section 51(xxix)) enables the commonwealth to give effect to international treaties to which it is a party, and confers sovereignty on the commonwealth over offshore areas and the continental shelf. The latter power is, of course, of crucial importance in the area of oil exploitation (see chapter 6); the 'treaties power' has been utilised, for example, to enforce quotas on tin production under the International Tin Agreement.

Currency, coinage and legal tender

Section 51(xii) enables the commonwealth to regulate the import and export of foreign exchange. As mentioned above, many of Australia's major resource projects have drawn on foreign capital, and this power is consequently of very direct relevance to resource development. It has been utilised to delay and to modify the ownership of a number of major resource projects.

These powers relate to the capacity to make valid laws. The commonwealth can also use its financial dominance to become involved in areas which the constitution assigns to the states, and its capacity to do so has been seen as having a major impact on the effective division of powers between the states and the commonwealth and on the nature of Australian federalism in the postwar period (see chapter 1).

In its 1984 discussion paper, ACIR states that much of the commonwealth's recent involvement in resource development has been based on its spending powers, and provides a list of resource-related special-purpose grants made by the commonwealth during the early 1980s, for example, to fund feasibility studies, coal exploration and water supplies (ACIR, 1984:B.11). Some of these grants are certainly significant, but they are far from being central to resource development. Almost all mineral exploration and a high proportion of mineral development is funded (directly or indirectly) by private capital. Thus special-purpose grants are not nearly as significant in relation to mining as in areas such as education, housing and health. Probably more important is the commonwealth's role in the Loan Council; state governments may require Loan Council funds to assist in developing infrastructure for resource development, and in the postwar period the commonwealth has developed a stronger position in the Council. This issue is discussed in more detail below. However, in general, the key point to note is the relative *insignificance* of commonwealth funding to resource development activity, a crucial point to keep in mind in comparing intergovernmental relations in mining and in other areas.

As the constitution does not specifically confer on the commonwealth legislative powers in relation to resource development, they reside with the states, which consequently retain major responsibility for resource projects. The states' constitutional powers are reinforced by the fact that minerals in Australia are, with few exceptions, owned by state legislatures.[4] Thus the states can exercise control over many aspects of resource development, including allocation of exploration and mining leases, production levels, royalties, provision of infrastructure, location of processing industries, and safety, training and environmental requirements.

It should also be remembered that, like the commonwealth, the states possess general powers whose exercise can have a major impact on resource development. This point is well illustrated by Stevenson, who cites cases where state governments used legislation in relation to pipelines, registration of companies, and railways to resist attempts by the federal government to increase its control over resource development (Stevenson, 1977:70).

To summarise, both the states and the commonwealth possess strong and unambiguous powers in relation to development of large mining projects in Australia; in Drysdale's terminology, both possess 'jurisdictional vetos' over resource development (Drysdale, 1985:220).

Mineral taxation

As a result of their ownership of minerals, states have the right to impose royalties on mineral production, while the commonwealth has the power to impose income tax on mining companies, excise on mineral products and duties on mineral exports. Until the 1970s, both levels of government accorded relatively low priority to obtaining revenue from mineral development. Their major concern was to ensure that Australia's minerals were discovered, exploited and exported as quickly and on as large a scale as possible, so as to maximise direct and indirect employment, development of industrial and social infrastructure, and export income. Consequently royalties were, with a few exceptions, at low or even nominal levels, while the commonwealth offered partial exemption from income tax for a range of minerals and applied favourable depreciation provisions to capital expenditure by mining firms.

Royalties were generally charged on a unit or *ad valorem* basis which bore no relationship to profitability, and their rate and the method of their application varied greatly both for individual minerals within each state and for the same mineral in different states (for details see Galligan, Kellow and O'Faircheallaigh, 1988:219–26). These characteristics of the royalty system had the potential to distort production and investment decisions (see below), but while royalty levels were low any such impact was likely to be minor.

High commodity prices and the first 'oil crisis' altered perceptions regarding the value of Australia's minerals among both politicians and the public, and, in combination with a growing concern regarding foreign domination of Australia's mining industry, led to a reassessment of mineral taxation policy. A number of state governments significantly increased royalty levels and Queensland, and to a lesser extent New South Wales, also extracted substantial net revenues from construction and operation of mine infrastructure. The commonwealth government reduced the concessional element in income tax provisions and introduced a crude oil levy and a coal export duty.[5]

The effect of these measures was to substantially increase the overall level of mineral taxation, though they did nothing to remove the variability in rates and methods of taxation between individual states and commodities. In general, each new taxation measure was introduced unilaterally by the government concerned. Little account was taken of the impact of the combined measures on the efficiency of the mineral taxation system as a whole, or of the effect of initiatives by one government on another's tax base (for example, of the way in which higher rail freight charges reduced the commonwealth's income tax base). The result was a tax system widely recognised as creating significant barriers to the efficient exploitation of Australia's mineral resources.

When it came to office in 1983, the Hawke Government hoped to reform Australia's mineral taxation system through introduction of a resource rent tax.[6] Initially, Labor intended to apply a RRT to all crude oil production, onshore and offshore, and envisaged that its application to oil would serve as a model for other mineral industries. The justification for its introduction rested primarily on considerations of economic efficiency (Walsh, 1983, 1984). The existing royalty and excise arrangements were believed to deter investment in new, economically-marginal projects and to shorten the life of existing operations by preventing the extraction of economically-marginal minerals. Their impact was thought to be particularly severe in the petroleum sector, because of the high levels of excise (equivalent to 87 per cent of wellhead value on marginal production from large Bass Strait fields). Another difficulty was the variations in royalty regimes among the states, which was believed to create distortions in the allocation of investment both geographically and between individual commodities. If generally applied, a system based on taxation of resource rents, that is the portion of revenue which remained after deduction of all costs (including a 'normal' return on capital), would avoid these problems, first because it *would* be generally applied and second because, by definition, a RRT could not apply to marginal projects or production and so could not deter investment in them.

Prior to the 1983 election, Labor spokesmen had taken a hard line on the issue of state involvement in resource taxation, criticising the proliferation of state taxes and charges, their lack of uniformity, and the tendency of state governments to compete through their royalties and charges for investment in resource projects. Paul Keating, then opposition spokesman on resources and energy, foresaw that a solution to these problems would require the exclusion of the states from mineral taxation, and argued that the commonwealth could do this 'by reaching agreement with the States and if the States are not prepared to reach any agreement then the Commonwealth could reduce reimbursements to the States by the amounts which they collect by way of new taxes to remove any incentives they think they might have to find new areas of mineral taxation'.[7] However, very shortly after coming to office the Hawke Government recognised that the co-operation of state governments would be required if mineral taxation was to be reformed. In the words of the Minister for Resources and Energy, 'With oil we can do almost anything we want. With everything else, if the states do not co-operate there is nothing much we can do'.[8] By October, the Senator acknowledged that the commonwealth was also powerless to take unilateral action in relation to onshore oil (*Commonwealth Record*, 24–30 October 1983:1821).

Senator Walsh claimed that the federal government had no intention of undermining existing state mineral revenues, and that its aim was simply to move to profit-based (and so more economically efficient) taxes. 'I am far more concerned about the nature of the tax—that it should be fair and efficient—than about who levies it'.[9] In May 1983 the Senator invited mines ministers in Queensland and New South Wales to discuss the possibility of introducing profit-based taxes for the coal industry. However, it was immediately apparent that state governments would require some persuasion that the commonwealth's intention was merely to render mineral taxation more efficient, rather than to redistribute revenue from resource projects.[10]

The possibility of rationalising mineral taxes was raised by the commonwealth at the next meeting of the inter-ministerial Australian Minerals and Energy Council (AMEC), which deals with resource issues. The immediate reaction of the states was negative, but Senator Walsh remained convinced that they could eventually be persuaded to accept the commonwealth initiative (*Commonwealth Record*, 24–30 October 1983:1818). In December 1983 the commonwealth Department of Resources and Energy (DRE) released a discussion paper containing proposals for a RRT (DRE, 1983). This focused on the petroleum sector; it envisaged that a RRT would replace existing excises and royalties on petroleum in 1984–85, and that a similar arrangement would be introduced in certain other parts of the mining sector in later years. The paper outlined broad parameters for the proposed tax, but left open both detailed aspects of its operation and the issue of how and to what extent states would be compensated for loss of royalty revenue.

Senator Walsh and departmental officials discussed the proposal with representatives of state governments prior to a meeting of AMEC in February 1984. Queensland was totally opposed to the proposal, arguing that it represented commonwealth interference in the sovereign rights of the states to obtain royalties from resource projects and to distribute those royalties as they saw fit. Labor governments in Western Australia and South Australia also regarded the RRT proposal as a demand that they surrender their powers to collect royalties, which they were unprepared to do, a position shared by Tasmania. The Victorian government was concerned at the implications of a RRT for its royalty revenue from Bass Strait; New South Wales and the Northern Territory, though less vehemently opposed than some of the other states, were still uneasy about the proposal.[11] The states were clearly not persuaded by the commonwealth's assurances that it wished to achieve a more efficient tax system rather than increase its share of the revenues generated by resource exploitation, and their concern was heightened by the DRE's failure to specify how they would be compensated for loss of royalty income.

In March 1984 Senator Walsh admitted that these 'difficulties' rendered it impossible to apply a RRT to resource projects onshore. In addition, aspects of the government's proposal had met sharp opposition from oil producers, and when the DRE released more detailed proposals in April 1984 the scope of the RRT had been substantially curtailed. It would apply only to new offshore oilfields, and there was no longer any mention of extending the tax to other mineral commodities.

Having failed to introduce a RRT, the Hawke Government was forced to adopt a more piecemeal and *ad hoc* method of dealing with problems created by the existing tax regime. These included an attempt to facilitate implementation of rent-type taxes in individual states by introducing a Petroleum Revenue Bill. Under this Bill the commonwealth undertook to waive its crude oil excise wherever a state government introduced an acceptable resource rent royalty. Western Australia quickly negotiated an arrangement under this legislation for the Barrow Island oilfield. The Minister for Resources and Energy, Senator Evans, expressed optimism that the legislation would eventually apply to all onshore oil production,[12] but to date Barrow is the only field covered. During 1984–87 the commonwealth also introduced a series of modifications to the crude oil levy, the coal export duty and to income tax provisions for resource projects, in response to claims that the existing arrangements were inhibiting the development of specific resource projects or categories of projects.[13]

These initiatives failed to deal with any of the fundamental problems associated with the existing tax regime, and indeed probably added to them. They certainly created a marked inconsistency and a lack of stability in the tax treatment of crude oil production. By the end of 1987 seven different tax and excise arrangements applied to oil production in Australia depending on the size, age and geographical location of the field concerned, while six major changes had been made to crude oil taxation provisions within three years.

State governments were suspicious of the commonwealth's motives in pursuing reform of mineral taxation, and concerned with the implications of its proposals for their control over mineral development. They used their 'jurisdictional veto' to force the Hawke Government to abandon its attempt to develop a more consistent and economically-efficient tax regime for onshore mineral production. The RRT proposal was replaced by a number of *ad hoc* initiatives designed to overcome particular problems created by the existing tax arrangements; the outcome was a worsening of the inconsistencies which the RRT proposals had sought to address in the first place.

Provision of infrastructure for resource projects

The rapid growth of mineral output since the 1950s has required massive investments in industrial and social infrastructure, much of it located far from Australia's major population centres. The commonwealth has little direct, formal role in the provision of industrial or social infrastructure for resource projects; constitutionally, the states have virtually exclusive responsibility in this field. Consequently the six states and the Northern Territory have independently developed policies regarding the provision and financing of infrastructure and the setting of charges for its use. The policies of individual governments often differ, and have been modified over time in response to changing circumstances. In particular, substantial variations occur in the extent to which state governments fund infrastructure from their own resources, and in the degree to which they recover the costs of publicly-operated infrastructure services.[14] However, the federal government has not been without influence in this area, particularly because of its control of relevant income tax measures and its influence over state government borrowing (exercised through the Loan Council).

Under provisions of Division 10 of the Income Tax Assessment Act implemented in 1968 and prior years, the commonwealth permitted mining companies to make infrastructure-related deductions for tax purposes which were more generous than those generally available. The concessional element in these deductions was substantial (see O'Faircheallaigh, 1987:17–18 for details), and through them the commonwealth bore part of infrastructure costs which otherwise would have fallen on developers or on state governments. The concessions were removed by the Labor government in 1974 as part of a general reassessment of mining industry taxation. They were partially restored by the Coalition government in 1976 as one of a series of measures designed to largely reverse the impact of Labor's policy changes towards the mining sector, and subsequently amended on a number of occasions by both Coalition and Labor governments.

While the tax treatment of investments in infrastructure is clearly of considerable significance to state governments, changes to commonwealth policy have generally reflected the federal government's broader tax policy agenda rather than consultation with affected states. On the other hand, the states have at times exploited provisions of the Income Tax Assessment Act for their own purposes, most notably by organising arrangements which relieved them of the burden of paying for resource-related infrastructure while allowing the private interests involved to gain considerable tax benefits (as in the case of the Eraring power station, for example). The commonwealth responded by amending the relevant legislation so as to remove the incentive for private companies to participate in such ventures (Perkins, 1985:158).

State governments depend on loan monies to fund much of their infrastructure spending; the level of their borrowing is determined by the Loan Council, within which the commonwealth has a dominant position (Mathews, 1985:58; Perkins, 1985:155). During the 1970s the Queensland and Western Australian governments pressed Canberra to increase their borrowing limits to help meet the additional infrastructure required for large-scale resource developments. In June 1978, in response to this pressure, the Loan Council initiated a new category of loans for state government authorities, approved on a case-by-case basis, to fund major items of infrastructure related to economic development. Many of these items have been associated with major resource projects, including additions to electricity-generating capacity required for mineral processing.

Initially, the resource-rich states believed that these loans would make a substantial net addition to the funds available for infrastructure funding. However, it soon became apparent that the Fraser Government was determined to maintain existing ceilings on overall state government borrowings in pursuit of its fiscal and monetary policies, and in order to achieve this it restricted the total funds made available for infrastructure loans and curtailed other elements of the Loan Council program. In addition, while all proposed projects were approved initially, the commonwealth decided in 1980 that the program was partly responsible for what it regarded as excessive public-sector borrowing; it also believed that the availability of infrastructure loans might have encouraged state governments to provide facilities which developers could have provided themselves and to compete for resource investments through infrastructure provision. As a result the commonwealth refused to approve any new projects for the program after 1980–81, a decision which caused considerable hostility among state governments. They responded by devising ways in which infrastructure could be funded outside Loan Council guidelines, for example through leverage leasing and supplier credits (Perkins, 1985:157; Mathews, 1985:59–60; Head, 1984:323).

In 1982 the Loan Council decided to exempt electricity authorities, which accounted for a substantial proportion of borrowing by state agencies, from borrowing controls on a trial basis. In 1984 it adopted a system of global limits on loans which allowed state governments greater flexibility in their borrowing programs. These changes have been interpreted as increasing state government control over infrastructure provision and as easing intergovernmental conflict (Perkins, 1985:158; ACIR, 1984:124–25). The slowdown in resource development since the early 1980s has reduced the pressure on the states to provide infrastructure for resource projects and this has also tended to ease conflict, at least for the time being.

The commonwealth's general powers in relation to taxation and state government borrowing have given it significant influence in relation to infrastructure provision for resource projects, an area which constitutionally is the responsibility of state governments. In the taxation field the commonwealth has generally taken unilateral decisions, so that it is not really appropriate to speak of policy reflecting 'intergovernmental relations', though the impact of specific commonwealth policies has been modified by the reactions of state governments. In relation to state government borrowing, policy has certainly been influenced by intergovernmental relations at the political level, with the Loan Council as the key institutional forum. In the late 1970s and early 1980s the concerns of state governments had some impact on policy outcomes, though most commentators take the view that the federal government's macro-economic policy concerns played a dominant role. However, some adjustment towards the interests of state governments did occur in 1983–84.

Export controls

Since the mid-1960s, export controls have been used by the commonwealth in attempts to influence the outcome of price negotiations between Australian mineral producers and foreign (especially Japanese) buyers; to prevent development of particular mining projects; and to impose environmental conditions on projects which have proceeded.

Export controls were occasionally used to enforce floor prices for iron ore and zircon during the 1960s, and were applied to all minerals by the Whitlam Government in a systematic attempt to influence export prices, particularly by forcing mineral producers to adopt a concerted approach in their negotiations with foreign buyers. Export controls were initially wound back by the Fraser Government, but reintroduced in 1978 because of fears that iron ore and coal exports to Japan were being undervalued. Their scope was reduced in 1979, and they were largely dismantled by the Hawke Government in 1986.

The states, particularly Queensland and Western Australia, have generally opposed the commonwealth's use of export controls to intervene in price negotiations, regardless of which party is in power at the federal level. Intergovernmental conflict in this area is often thought to reflect fundamental differences between state and commonwealth interests regarding price levels and the rate of mineral exploitation. (Where Australia is a major supplier of a commodity to the world market, the rate of mineral exploitation and the level of export prices are related, since the former will have an impact on the latter.) It is argued that the commonwealth favours a slower rate of mineral development than do the states, because it has a strong interest in maximising export prices (and so national export income) and is consequently anxious to prevent over-production and a subsequent decline in prices. State governments, on the other hand, are thought to be primarily concerned with maximising the volume of production within their own jurisdictions, and thus favour a rapid pace of development (see, for example, Stevenson, 1977:48–49; Drysdale & Shibata, 1985:17; Harris, 1985:86).

However, Smith has questioned the extent to which commonwealth and state interests diverge in this area, pointing out that federal governments have in general been as supportive as the states of rapid resource development (Smith, 1985:217). And Harris has argued that the states have not opposed concerted action to maintain prices *per se*, but rather have rejected commonwealth intervention in this area, viewing it as a major threat to their own control over mineral development (Harris, 1985:85–86). On this latter point, the states are vehemently opposed to the use of export controls to give the commonwealth power over aspects of resource development traditionally regarded as their own prerogative (see below), and this would certainly incline them to resist the use of export controls in principle.

Until the mid-1970s decisions regarding whether individual mineral deposits should be developed were entirely the preserve of the states,[15] but since then the commonwealth has used its export powers to halt a number of mining projects. The Fraser Government was the first to do so, preventing exploitation of mineral sands on Fraser Island in Queensland. The Hawke Government stopped the development of a number of uranium deposits (Ben Lomond in Queensland, Honeymoon and Beverley in South Australia, and Yeelirrie in Western Australia), and has also used its control over uranium in the Northern Territory (under the Northern Territory Self Government Act 1978) to prevent development of the Koongarra and Jabiluka deposits. It should be stressed, however, that these examples represent a very small proportion of the mineral deposits considered for development over the last fifteen years; in the vast majority of cases the commonwealth did not intervene, leaving decisions on whether to develop mines in state hands.

The commonwealth's export controls have also underpinned its role in influencing the environmental conditions under which mineral projects proceed, and in particular represent the ultimate sanction for application of the Environment (Impact of Proposals) Act 1974. This legislation requires developers of major resource projects to submit an Environmental Impact Statement (EIS) to the federal government, and provides for the conduct of public environmental inquiries where the commonwealth believes they are required. Only two inquiries have actually been held, the Fraser Island Environmental Enquiry (1975) and the Ranger Uranium Environmental Inquiry (1976–77); however the EIS process does permit the federal government to attach environmental conditions to a project before allowing it to proceed. In practice, this is most likely to occur when the project involved has a high public profile, as for example with uranium deposits and currently with the Coronation Hill gold/platinum prospect (located inside Kakadu National Park). Again it should be stressed that the number of mineral projects significantly altered as a result of the commonwealth's environmental legislation constitutes a small proportion of the total.

Governments in affected states and in the Northern Territory have complained long and bitterly about the commonwealth's use of its export powers in the ways discussed above. However, in most cases they have been powerless to change federal policy in the face of the commonwealth's unambiguous constitutional powers over trade. Where Canberra has curtailed its use of export controls, this has usually been as a result of the federal government's own policy agenda, rather than of consultation with, or pressure from, the states; thus the relaxation of controls in 1986, for example, came about as part of the Hawke Government's general push to deregulate key sectors of the economy (O'Faircheallaigh, 1990). Perhaps the only significant exception occurred in 1979, when pressure from the Premiers of Queensland and Western Australia led the Fraser Government to modify the application of export controls. In this case, the commonwealth agreed to consult state governments before imposing controls, and removed a requirement for case-by-case approval of export contracts from most minerals, though not, significantly, from two leading export income earners, bauxite/alumina and coal.

On the other hand, except during 1972–75 the commonwealth has applied its controls to only a small proportion of projects which have high profiles in the electorate or to components of Australia's mineral trade which cause substantial public concern (e.g., bauxite exports within vertically-integrated corporations, coal and iron ore exports to Japan). This reflects the fact that federal governments share with the states a fundamental interest in having Australia's mineral resources developed quickly and fully.

Foreign ownership of mineral projects

Until the early 1970s state and federal governments shared a positive enthusiasm for foreign investment in Australia's mining industry. Since 1973 all federal governments have used their powers over corporations and over foreign currency flows to apply restrictions on foreign investment in mining, mainly to ensure a higher level of Australian participation in foreign-owned projects. Foreign investment controls were most stringent under the Whitlam Government. They were relaxed in 1976 and applied leniently during 1976–79, but were enforced more strictly (especially to energy projects) in the wake of the second oil crisis in 1979. In 1987 the controls were relaxed further by the Hawke Government, and effectively abolished in relation to the oil and gas industry in January 1988.

The commonwealth's role in this area has not had major implications for its relations with some states, for example Tasmania, Victoria and South Australia, where few foreign-owned mining projects have been developed during recent years, arfd New South Wales, which shared a belief in the need for restrictions and introduced its own foreign investment controls. However, the federal government has encountered sharp opposition from the Queensland, Western Australian and Northern Territory governments, all of which viewed restrictions on foreign investment as depriving them of valuable economic opportunities.

Particularly during the 1970s and the early 1980s, these governments were highly critical of the commonwealth's policies, though they did not challenge the constitutional basis for its actions. On a rhetorical level, state premiers and senior ministers attacked the assumptions on which foreign investment restrictions rested, for example that domestic capital is 'closed out' by foreign investors and that foreign control of resource projects involves significant costs for Australia. On a practical level they provided public support for potential foreign investors in their negotiations with the commonwealth and the Foreign Investment Review Board (which is responsible for administering foreign investment guidelines).

It has been standard practice for Foreign Investment Review Board officials to consult state governments regarding major projects within their jurisdictions, and their views are reportedly taken into account in making recommendations on investment proposals (Pooley, 1982:116; 1985:149–50). However, there is little to suggest that the attitude of state governments has had much impact on general commonwealth policies in relation to foreign investment guidelines; these appear to reflect more general influences, such as economic conditions in Australia, world demand for Australia's minerals and foreign investor interest in developing them, and the commonwealth's broader policy agenda. Thus, for example, the stricter application of foreign investment controls during 1979–81 reflected strong interest by foreign investors in Australia's energy resources; and, as with export controls, the relaxation of foreign investment guidelines in 1987–88 was part of Labor's broader deregulation strategy (O'Faircheallaigh, 1990).

The federal government has not sought to use its powers to prevent foreigners from developing Australia's resources, but only to alter the terms on which they do so in favour of Australian investors. In order to ensure that projects proceed it has been prepared to negotiate with foreign investors on the timing and precise level of Australian participation in their projects, and at times to interpret its own guidelines 'flexibly'. Very few major projects (if any) have been halted solely on the grounds that they did not meet foreign investment guidelines, though a number have been held up while alternative ownership structures were organised. This reflects the fact that, though the commonwealth had policy concerns not felt by some state governments, it did share with them a strong interest in maximising resource development and the employment and export income associated with it.

In the case of foreign investment, the commonwealth's constitutional right to intervene has not been in question, but nevertheless its imposition of restrictions has been sharply resented by states anxious to see mining projects proceed regardless of their ownership. This has given rise to intergovernmental conflict, but its extent has been contained as a result of a fundamental unity of interests between both levels of government in having mineral resources developed.

Conclusion

Both the states and the commonwealth possess unambiguous constitutional powers whose exercise confers substantial control over mineral development. In particular, ownership of mineral resources and constitutional responsibility for their development are vested in the states. The commonwealth controls exports and this, in most cases, gives it *de facto* control over whether minerals can be exploited or not; in conjunction with its powers in relation to income taxes, corporations and currency, this also allows it a significant say in determining by whom and under what conditions minerals can be developed.

There is no clear evidence that a major shift in power has occurred from one level of government to another as a result of Australia's resources 'boom' or 'booms'. The commonwealth has certainly intervened during recent years in areas traditionally regarded as the prerogative of the states, particularly in response to public concern regarding foreign ownership and the impact of mining on the environment. However, this intervention has generally had an impact on only a small minority of projects, and the states' capacity to bring the Hawke Government's tax reform proposals to a grinding halt shows clearly the continued strength of their position. This resilience reflects, in part, the fact that mineral development does not require or involve significant federal government expenditure, with the result that the commonwealth has not been able to use its fiscal dominance to diminish the practical impact of the states' constitutional position.

Because of the unambiguous nature of each government's powers and the relative unimportance of fiscal issues, many important policy decisions are taken by one level of government in terms of its own policy agenda, leaving the other to adjust to the decision as best it can. For example, the states and the commonwealth both increased mineral taxes unilaterally during the 1970s. In 1983–84 the states refused to consider commonwealth proposals for mineral taxation reform, leaving the federal government to deal with problems generated by the existing system as best it could. The states in their turn have had to adjust to federal policies on borrowing for infrastructure, income tax treatment of mining companies, and application of export controls and foreign investment guidelines.

As noted above, much of the literature on intergovernmental relations in mining stresses their conflictual nature. Conflict certainly occurred in each of the policy areas analysed in this chapter. This is hardly surprising. Mining plays a central role in Australia's economy, particularly in balancing the external account; it is also vital in maintaining economic activity in specific states and regions. Consequently it is to be expected that both state and federal governments will wish to control mineral development and, given the unambiguous nature of their constitutional and legal powers, that this desire will result in intergovernmental conflict.

However, it must be stressed that this conflict has in fact been contained within quite narrow limits. It has tended either to effect only a very small proportion of mining projects, as in the case of the commonwealth's use of export controls to prevent deposits from being exploited, or it relates to the exact terms on which projects will proceed, for example the proportion of private foreign ownership, rather than to fundamental issues, such as whether minerals should be developed by the private or public sectors.[16] The limited nature of intergovernmental conflict is reflected in the fact that it has not significantly hampered the development of Australia's mineral resources. In 1949, Australia's mineral production was relatively insignificant in world terms, and its output of minerals was largely accounted for by a small number of commodities. Forty years later it is one of the western world's three largest mineral producers and exports a wide variety of minerals.

It may of course be the case that mineral output would have expanded even more rapidly in the absence of intergovernmental differences and problems of co-ordination, that the cost of establishing Australia's resource industries would have been somewhat lower and the benefits obtained from them by Australia somewhat greater. This possibility is most apparent in the area of taxation, which affects all mining investments. The division of taxing powers between two levels of government, and the rivalry and suspicion which this creates, has clearly complicated the task of devising a tax system which would both encourage the efficient development of Australia's mineral resources and ensure an adequate return to the nation from their exploitation.

Thus the implications of mining's central economic position for intergovernmental relations are ambiguous. On the one hand, each level of government will wish to exert as much control as possible over mineral development, indicating the likelihood of intergovernmental conflict. On the other hand, all governments have a strong economic interest in ensuring that mineral development proceeds smoothly, and they are under considerable political pressure to ensure that they are not responsible for slowing growth in a key economic sector, both of which indicate the necessity for co-operation and compromise.

Endnotes

1 The issue is discussed briefly in ACIR, 1985:29–30.

2 Conflicting objectives and perceptions reflect, in turn, differences in resource endowment, economic structure, and economic and political history.

3 Other relevant powers include Territories (s. 122), Bounties (s. 51(iii)), Defence (s. 51(vi)), Race (s. 51(xxvi), Banking (s. 51(xiii)), Incidental (s. 51(xxxix) and Acquisition (s. 51(xxxi). For a discussion of these, see ACIR, 1984:Appendix B.

4 For a detailed discussion of mineral ownership, see Crommelin, 1985:90–91, and ACIR, 1984, C.1–C.3.

5 For details of these developments see O'Faircheallaigh, 1984:178–85; Galligan, Kellow and O'Faircheallaigh, 1988:219–26.

6 This section draws on material from a detailed analysis of the Hawke Government's minerals and energy policies: see O'Faircheallaigh, 1990.

7 P. Keating, 'ALP Launches New Resources Platform', *Energy*, June 1982:33.

8 'How Labor Plans to Tax The Miners', *Bulletin*, 3 May 1983:109–10.

9 'Walsh Gives New ALP Policy', *Mining Monthly*, May 1983:4.

10 See, for example, the comments of the Western Australian Minister, Mr Bryce, reported in the *Commonwealth Record*, 30 May–5 June 1983:766.

11 'The Resource Rent Tax: Countdown Starts This Week', *Australian Financial Review*, 23 January 1984.

12 'Evans Wrestles With Price Dilemma', *Australian Business*, 29 January 1986:29.

13 See O'Faircheallaigh, 1990 for details of these tax and excise changes.

14 State infrastructure policies and the factors which shape them are discussed by Galligan, Kellow and O'Faircheallaigh, 1988:226–35.

15 The commonwealth ban on iron ore exports may have prevented development of iron ore reserves, but its action was not directed at specific deposits.

16 This latter issue did arise during the Whitlam Government's term of office, and it did result in severe intergovernmental conflict; see O'Faircheallaigh, 1984:170–74.

Bibliography

ACIR (Advisory Council for Inter-government Relations), 1984. *Intergovernmental Aspects of Major Resource Projects and Their Infrastructure*, ACIR, Discussion Paper No. 15, Government Printer, Hobart.

—— 1985. *Resource Development and Intergovernmental Relations*, ACIR, Report No. 9, Government Printer, Hobart.

Catley, R. & McFarlane, B., 1978. 'Minerals and Multinationals', *Arena*, 50.

Crommelin, M., 1985. 'The Mineral Exploration and Production Regime Within the Federal System', in Drysdale & Shibata, *Federalism and Resource Development: The Australian Case*, Allen & Unwin, Sydney.

Crough, G.J., & Wheelwright, E.J., 1982. *Australia: A Client State*, Penguin, Ringwood.

DRE (Department of Resources and Energy), 1983. *Discussion Paper on Resource Rent Tax in the Petroleum Sector*, AGPS, Canberra.

Drysdale, P., 1985. 'Summary and Comment', in Drysdale & Shibata, *Federalism and Resource Development: The Australian Case.*

Drysdale, P. & Shibata, H., 1985. 'Perspectives', in Drysdale & Shibata, *Federalism and Resource Development: The Australian Case.*

Galligan, B., 1982. 'Federalism and Resource Development in Australia and Canada', *Australian Quarterly*, Spring.

Galligan, B., Kellow, A., & O'Faircheallaigh, C., 1988. 'Minerals and Energy Policies', in *Comparative State Policies*, ed. B. Galligan, Longman Cheshire, Melbourne.

Harris, S., 1985. 'State and Federal Objectives for the Use and Development of Resources', in Drysdale & Shibata, *Federalism and Resource Development: The Australian Case.*

Head, B., 1984. 'Australian Resource Development and the National Fragmentation Thesis', *Australian and New Zealand Journal of Sociology*, 20(3).

Mathews, R., 1985. 'Federal–State Fiscal Relations in Australia', in Drysdale & Shibata, *Federalism and Resource Development: The Australian Case.*

O'Faircheallaigh, C., 1984. *Mining and Development: Foreign-financed Mines in Australia, Ireland, Papua New Guinea and Zambia*, Croom Helm Ltd, London.

—— 1987. *Mine Infrastructure and Economic Development in North Australia*, Australian National University, North Australia Research Unit, Darwin.

—— 1990. 'Minerals and Energy Policy', in *Hawke and Australian Public Policy*, eds C. Jennett & R. Stewart, Macmillan, Melbourne, forthcoming.

Perkins, F., 1985. 'Financing and Charging for Infrastructure', in Drysdale & Shibata, *Federalism and Resource Development: The Australian Case.*

Pooley, F.G.H., 1982. 'Foreign Investment Controls', *Australian Mining and Petroleum Law Journal*, 2(2).

—— 1985. 'State and Federal Attitudes to Foreign Investment and its Regulation', in Drysdale & Shibata, *Federalism and Resource Development: The Australian Case.*

Smith, B., 1985. 'Resource Markets and Resource Trade Issues', in Drysdale & Shibata, *Federalism and Resource Development: The Australian Case.*

Stevenson, G., 1977. *Mineral resources and Australian federalism*, Centre for Research on Federal Financial Relations, Australian National University, Canberra.

Walsh, P., 1983. 'Speech to Coal Association Seminar', *Commonwealth Record*, 11–17 April.

—— 1984. 'Speech to Economics Society', *Commonwealth Record*, 13–19 August.

West, K., 1983. 'Federalism and Resources Development: The Politics of State Inequality', in *Australian Federalism: Future Tense*, eds A. Patience & J. Scott, Oxford University Press, Melbourne.

16 Business

John Wanna

The relationship between government and business transgresses state boundaries. Unlike many other policy recipients or objects of government regulation, business is not necessarily confined to a particular state or even to the nation, and this is especially so as the size of business enterprise increases. Accordingly, for state and commonwealth governments policy issues associated with business possess a high potentiality for requiring some mechanisms of intergovernmental co-operation.

Yet government relations with business are inherently complex. Business is not constrained within a discrete policy area, but its interests trespass on many policy fields. Because of this it is difficult for governments to address business needs and demands through one single government department or agency charged with implementing policies for business. There are few administrative agencies specifically devoted to business. Rather, to some extent most commonwealth, state and local government administrative departments and agencies maintain some direct policy interface with business. Policies affecting business are thus administered by multiple agencies within each level of government and by multiple levels of government.

There are two principal dimensions of relevance here. On macro issues the general relationship between government and a broadly defined business community involves many policy areas, some of which may impact on the activities of intergovernmental forums. At the micro level, much specific government policy toward business is often mediated through regular governmental arrangements, many involving intergovernmental negotiation. These micro policies may affect only certain industries or narrow sectors of business, or they may address particular concerns across spheres of business practice, as with company law reforms (CAI, 1987b; Hogg, 1987; Ostry, 1987; ACTU/TDC, 1987).

Like government, the main interest associations of Australian business are organised on a 'federal' basis; a division influenced by the constitutional division of powers. These associations operate with relative organisational strength at the state level but with representative national bodies operating at the federal level (Matthews, 1983). Membership, personnel and financial resources are located principally at the state level. Clientele dependencies with state governments have traditionally arisen through a mixture of formal institutional linkages, consultative practices and informal contact. The main administrative-policy involvement of business associations with government has generally been at the state and regional level (Loveday, 1982:54–68).

Nevertheless, as policy problems beyond or above one state arise federal-level peak business associations tend to become more active in their own right in policy making. In particular, if business policy issues emerging between different Australian governments become more highly politicised (Galligan, 1988), then federal organisations of representative associations tend also to assume greater policy significance relative to their state counterparts. Their increased role depends upon their capacity to advocate and participate in policy agendas and work toward a concerted view. Initially the federal bodies may serve as conduits of policy opinion from their organisational affiliates. They are then involved in securing acceptance of policy adjustments once decisions or policy documents take shape. This can often mean having to deal with resistance from state-level bodies, leading to intra-organisational conflict. Hence, their policy involvement is not restricted to participating in particular intergovernmental exercises, but more often involves them in pressuring and negotiating with their own state memberships.

This chapter presents an assessment of the scope and arrangements of intergovernmental relations affecting business. It is organised around a number of key questions. There are the related questions of what attempts at policy harmonisation have intergovernmental agencies taken up, and what have they been able to pursue? What issues have they not taken up, or been prevented from taking up? How have the constitutional and political limitations in Australia affected policy making? In examining cases where intergovernmental bodies already exist, have such institutions and administrative arrangements produced a more constructive dialogue or impeded policy making? Has business sought policies from government but been frustrated by the lack of intergovernmental machinery? Do intergovernmental relations make policy outcomes more effective in this policy area? Is policy making made more effective when business is involved in the policy processes?

The chapter also provides a classification of the range of intergovernmental agencies relating to business. The characteristics of business participation in the policy making process and in implemention are assessed. The latter part of the chapter focuses on the policy developments over government preferencing schemes, which were co-ordinated by intergovernmental means after Australia entered into closer economic relations with New Zealand.

Analysing intergovernmental relations

Existing typologies of program implementation involving intergovernmental relations have limited usefulness in explaining the array of policies toward business in the Australian federal context. This is because typologies are generally static and constrain analysis of the richness of policy development. Some typologies also tend to be taken as more than analytical categories, becoming elevated to normative status in policy making.

For instance, in Lowi's terms distributive, regulatory and redistributive policy areas have been applied to business. Each policy area is considered to have its own arena of power and its own politics involving specific structures, processes, elites and group interactions (Lowi, 1964). This typology essentially disaggregates interactive policy modifications and suggests different levels of business involvement across the three types of policy areas. Distributive politics become micro-pluralism based on firms and corporations, regulatory politics figure as sectoral group pluralism, while redistributive politics involve elite peak associations of business. This arbitrarily divides policies into given typologies with accentuated patterns of politicking. Methodologically there is little appreciation of policies that straddle the types, lie outside these types, do not conform to the assumed pattern of politics, or involve business mobilising over existing arrangements of specific policies. Lowi's framework is similarly based on centralised formal political institutions with an assumption that business is inherently national in its political focus. Allowing for its elite-pluralist bias, Lowi's typology is suggestive but ultimately inadequate.

In Peterson, Rabe and Wong's classification of policy effectiveness their typologies artificially separate developmental program from redistributive ones, and expert administration from 'political' administration (1986). In the Australian context this model of policy management involves a vertical descent in financial management from central governments through intermediaries to program deliverers. Such transfers of funding may characterise particular developmental policy fields, such as health or housing, where finances originating from the commonwealth are largely implemented by acquiescent state or local governments. But this argument tends to downplay the significance of 'local power structures as growth machines' (Domhoff, 1986). Peterson's model is less applicable to business policy areas in that business is not solely a 'policy recipient' dependent on centralised federal funding with a set range of programs and defined outcomes. Instead business has a more complex relationship to government involving the ability to set agendas and negotiate over policy directions, multiple access points to all levels of government, the capacity to circumvent or bypass given decision-making levels, and where necessary to play off one government or administrative agency against another (Loveday, 1982).

Similarly the logic of redistributive policies is often different for business than for the range of other client groups. Business generally regards redistributive policies with interest not because it is a prime recipient but because business sees itself as the main source providing resources to be redistributed (Lowi, 1964). Of recent years the issues of social equity or regional equalisation have been of less concern to business than arguments over the capacity to pay (CAI, 1987b; BCA, 1988a, 1989). Hence, under such circumstances the centralisation of redistributive policies advanced by Peterson et al. is seen as neither essential nor desirable for some sectors of business.

Other typologies of business influence in policy making also have limitations. Two examples illustrate this point. Lindblom's characterisation of business as a 'privileged' structural group relying on their control over investment is often taken to imply that this power readily enables business to force policy changes from governments. However, while some aspects of Lindblom's argument can be supported, the application of the argument to actual policy is problematic and cannot be substantiated without qualification (Marsh, 1983; Bowler, 1987). Similarly Offe's view that the economic power of business makes collective organisation less important to business than organised labour does not appreciate the role of business associations in agenda setting or in the consultative processes surrounding government policy making (Offe, 1981). In circumstances where business cannot exert its structural economic power (which may be frequent), the dependence on business associations and other forms of direct contact with government increases (Wanna, 1989).

Governments and business: reciprocal clients

Most assessments of intergovernmental program implementation presume an inherent government–client relationship, with the community, client or consumer dependent on government funding, largesse or regulatory provisions. However, business does not adopt such a straightforward 'client' role. Governments continually make efforts to foster business by enticing new business investment or promoting the expansion of existing businesses. Governments provide various forms of assistance, promotion, cross-subsidies, regulatory protection, policy interventions, marketing and management advice. Because much of their success is premised on economic growth, governments remain solicitous of the interests of business (Coleman, 1988:5). In short, governments are often captured by their 'clients'.

Part of the reason for this is that business occupies a structurally 'privileged position' relative to other groups in society because of its fundamental influence over economic decision making (Lindblom, 1977; Abbey, 1987; Bowler, 1988; Ravenhill, 1989). Policies decided in the boardrooms of major corporations or at managerial levels shape our economy and many of the day-to-day policies of society. Business, unlike many other 'client' groups, initiates much of its own policy agenda. Indeed, government and business are reciprocal 'clients', each relying on the other for conditioning the terms of their own performance. Business is thus both a client of governments and a non-client. Governments for their part operate as the reciprocal 'clients' of business for many economic and social provisions. Some of the studies into 'policy communities' and 'policy networks' implicitly recognise this dual role in government–business relations (Wright, 1988; McFarlane, 1987; Wilson, 1985; Atkinson & Coleman, 1989).

As a client of government, business relies on both the authoritative power of government to maintain regulatory provisions as well as the use of monetary and fiscal power to provide subsidies. Business associations and lobby groups provide an advocacy framework to influence and negotiate with government over such special interests. As a non-client, business operates as an external and in many ways preponderant power. Its international and extra-state sources of power serve to modify government policy directions whether or not business groups actually lobby. Government economic management remains particularly dependent on the decisions and investment policies of big business (Hall, 1986; Katzenstein, 1985; Zysman, 1983). Hence, state 'managers' and government ministers of all parties frequently seek to appease corporate opinion leaders in an attempt to sustain business confidence (McEachern, 1986; Galligan, 1988).

Moreover, in its policy interface with governments business is able to rely on a variety of long-established patterns of direct access. On matters of major concern business maintains both extensive formal-open and informal-confidential access to all levels of government in Australia. In this process intergovernmental agencies are not particularly important access points. Indeed, when special intergovernmental bodies are established for ad hoc reasons (mostly initiated by the commonwealth government), business tends not to be actively involved in the formulation of policy changes but may be consulted extensively in the deliberative process.

Although business leaders are largely uninterested in intergovernmental agencies, they are concerned about the ability of such bodies to shape the policy environment. In this regard the decisions of many intergovernmental agencies impact upon the environment for business.

Accordingly, business cannot afford to be unconcerned about the activities of existing intergovernmental bodies. This is especially so insofar as these bodies directly affect the intermediate or specific interests of business and issues relating to regional policy discretion. Usually business associations and large companies are extensively briefed on policy amendments arising out of intergovernmental negotiations.

As a client group, business has few general interests of significant collective concern. Even such fundamental policies as wage restraint, the impact of tax regimes or the legal form of private companies are unable to produce collective business support. The heterogeneity of interests among the sectors of business effectively means that policies toward business are unable to be formulated from a specific institution of government or a multi-agency forum. There is very little scope for co-ordination within the machinery of government while there exists a diverse range of governmental bodies dealing at least partly with business. Indeed, given the diverse nature of business interests, a scattered response by governments may perhaps be more appropriate or effective than a co-ordinated one. Nonetheless, such factors both restrict the capacity for 'problem-oriented' intergovernmental activity and make it difficult for the latent concerns of business to be expressed within this administrative framework. To date there remain few intergovernmental bodies that deal principally or exclusively with business, and those which do, like the Economic Planning Advisory Council, tend to be advisory committees rather than implementation agencies.

Because the interests of business are both specific and competitive in nature, the various sectors of business have considerable concerns across the entire spectrum of intergovernmental agencies. These concerns may appear as subtle and unstructured. Unlike Canada, where business involvement in intergovernmental forums is extensive, in most cases in Australia business is not reliant on direct involvement in the formal processes of intergovernmental interaction (Coleman, 1988; Skogstad, 1987).

For instance, business is not represented on the intergovernmental Australian Fisheries Council. This annual ministerial body consists only of top-level government representatives. The agenda emanates entirely from government, is confidential, and tends mainly to deal with minor and administrative issues. Each year the meeting of ministers lasts for one day, but is preceded by a two-day heads of departments get-together which discusses 'standing elements' and functions such as an agenda-clearing operation. Although much of the council's time is spent on unresolved or inconclusive discussion, business learns of any specific decisions after the event through a concluding statement released to the media. The more significant policy adjustments adopted within this ministerial council to influence catch sizes, limit netting or regulate the importation of fish clearly interest not only those businesses directly involved in fishing, but also those in canning, processing, steel supplies, labelling, distribution, accountancy firms, restaurants and retailing.

Yet business is not directly represented and has no voice on such ministerial bodies. In the above case of the Fisheries Council, the business sectors involved often may be disorganised and have difficulty presenting a collective case, but this is not always so at the sectoral level. More importantly, these councils with their two levels of negotiation are conducted entirely as government-to-government meetings concerned with administrative and largely incremental policy matters. Business representatives are not invited to participate. The interests of the business sectors affected can only be heard to the extent that government administrators acknowledge such claims, and these are inevitably mediated through the administrative and cultural traditions of the departmental officers and their ministers.

Initiating intergovernmental activity

State and commonwealth governments each have particular reasons for engaging in intergovernmental initiatives. Each can have its own agenda and expected outcomes, and these may not necessarily correspond with the declared intentions of the intergovernmental exercise. Over time the original reason for the establishment of such initiatives may be entirely supplanted by concerns of more recent origin. Some are occasionally abolished, like the Advisory Council for Inter-government Relations (1976–87), because they lack political support or become marginal (Chapman, 1988). Significantly, too, the respective administrative support staff of the various governments can entertain different reasons for participating in these initiatives. Senior administrators concerned to steer a particular minister toward a line of policy may use intergovernmental agendas and agreements to lock their own minister into the policy. Hence, ministerial councils typically operate with two levels of agendas which may not be complementary; a short but selective ministerial agenda, and a separate but more discursive agenda intended as a dialogue for senior officials. Ministerial councils have often been used in Australia not only to negotiate compromises between ministers of different governments, but also between ministers and policy advisers from the same government.

Occasionally, political commentators imply that intergovernmental agencies have arisen as a sensible evolution designed to extend the effectiveness of federal government (Sawer, 1967; Wettenhall, 1985; see also Reid & Spann, 1974). The acknowledgement of sensible policy adjustment certainly has some seductive appeal. Such political common sense is seen to emerge from a maturing process based on an awareness of the problems encountered when the responsibility or authority for policy is displaced. Yet, historical evidence suggests that intergovernmental activities in Australia have generally resulted from the appreciation between governments of specific material incentives (as with federal finance or debt restructuring), or the impending likelihood of liabilities and in some cases penalties.

Ministerial industry councils, for instance, aim 'to encourage commonwealth–state co-operation on industry matters and to pursue greater harmonisation in industry policies' (AITC, 1986). In recent years 'economically rationalist' commonwealth governments have strenuously argued that state industry policies should be systematically harmonised. Yet state industry administrators have only moved in a very limited way to 'harmonise' their industry policies, mainly because of the perceived political benefits for state governments in maintaining some distinctive comparative advantage for industry. Contrary to the commonwealth view, these policy makers have tended to adopt a more phlegmatic view, seeing no reason why in a federation policies of state governments should necessarily be harmonised. On the contrary, specific policies to develop industry are by nature designed to offer comparative advantages to the host state relative to others (QDID, 1988:3–passim).

Where some 'harmonisation' of state industry policies has occurred it has not been due to rational problem anticipation with broad agreement on the nature of the major problems. Rather it has been largely the result of governments agreeing to minimise administrative responsibilities, and at the instigation of the commonwealth government reduce minor disparities in industry policy areas of low politicisation. Harmonisation has involved salvage operations, not an intergovernmental strategic plan. A number of cases illustrate this point: the 1985–86 agreements to co-ordinate national and state preference policies and other regional discriminations, the harmonisation of the offsets program, and the adoption of a national standards and specifications scheme for tendering throughout Australia. These examples, although they may appear as major achievements for those previously charged with the administration of the separate state schemes, provide evidence of such administrative 'salvage' of policies of limited concern to business and low political interest.

The existence of 'real policy problems' in itself does not appear to stimulate intergovernmental participation. Certainly, insofar as business policies are concerned, it is not the major policy problems which have attracted intergovernmental co-operation. Instead, federal and state governments participate as a result of the identification of selective 'irritants' to specific administrative agencies and business sectors. Two additional considerations affect participation. Governments in some instances routinely participate in order to share information and consult. But mostly they decide to participate in intergovernmental bodies as the apparent chances of conflict resolution increase, however slightly. In other words, governments participate in intergovernmental processes to the extent that some tangible political or administrative advantage is perceived. Hence, the establishment of specific intergovernmental bodies implies not only that policy 'irritants' exist outside one government's responsibilities, but also that information sharing is intrinsically valued or some means of resolution are at least available or expected.

As an illustration of this, a form of intergovernmental co-operative agreement on standardising legislation covering companies, takeovers, and the securities and futures industries was entered into in 1976 and implemented by 1978 (SSCCLA, 1987). This co-operative agreement resolved some company law issues by implementing under concurrent legislation a national body, the National Companies and Securities Commission (NCSC), which operated under the Ministerial Council for Companies and Securities consisting of the attorneys-general of each government. For commonwealth and state governments the co-operative agreement operated as a consultative scheme, without adopting a unified national arrangement (SSCCLA, 1987:65–74). Each government continued to retain separate corporate affairs offices. Accordingly, rather than a uniform code of company legislation operating across Australia, the intergovernmental exercise produced many administrative inconsistencies. In the words of the New South Wales Attorney-General it was a 'hybrid institution', which imposed 'severe limitations on developing necessary policies' (SSCCLA, 1987:73). The NCSC represented a co-operative attempt to deal with policy and legal irritants without confronting the more significant issue of a national uniform scheme of company legislation. The Senate Standing Committee's recommendation after reviewing the companies scheme was for the commonwealth to enact comprehensive legislation superseding the co-operative agreement. During 1988–89 the commonwealth passed legislation intending to give itself the power to legislate alone in the area of corporation and securities law (McQueen, 1989). Despite some problems with the states, this legislation was strongly supported by the Business Council of Australia (BCA, 1988a). Initially the commonwealth had intended to establish the Australian Securities Commission (ASC) in July 1989, but due to a High Court challenge by New South Wales (and other states) this was delayed. The High Court decision (by 6:1) in February 1990 declared that the commonwealth did not have the power with respect to the incorporation of trading and financial corporations. As a result the commonwealth did not proclaim the ASC Act, although the ASC commenced its existence essentially as the NCSC, relying on the previous co-operative agreements with the states.

Over business policies, therefore, intergovernmental forums exist in the main as contingency measures to deal with policy 'irritants' rather than as federal lubricants addressing the inherent difficulties in a multi-government political structure. When such mechanisms are adopted, they are generally accepted by different governments either because the respective issues are already of low political interest or occasionally out of a concern to avoid high politicisation. In this sense the principle of selective administrative harm to more than one government appears to have stimulated intergovernmental activity.

The development and range of intergovernment agencies

The Australian constitution did not allocate policy responsibility for business to either level of government exclusively. At the time of federation, micro-business policy was essentially seen as a state responsibility. Initially business development was narrowly conceived around the industrial expansion of agriculture and mining. However, states were required to surrender some important regulatory responsibilities such as tariff and trading restrictions, even though they retained the rights to make policy with respect to the pursuit of business within their territories. States exercised the rights to develop the particular legal framework under which business operated, and as a consequence developed significantly different legal regulations.

Commonwealth governments extended their powers over business incrementally, especially at the macro-policy level. Early commonwealth intervention in establishing protective trade barriers was conceived as a 'national' policy administered by central government. The central government used customs and excise duties, bounties and quotas as a direct regulator of types of business activity. Increasingly taxation schemes were also used as both positive and negative stimuli, and these became elaborate by the 1980s with research and development tax concessions (revenue foregone) of 150 per cent to new manufacturing research investment. Beyond these direct policy interventions, other commonwealth economic measures affected business. Fiscal policy, monetary and exchange rate policies, foreign investment guidelines, wages policy and wider productivity policies (education, training, sponsorship schemes, 'buy Australian' policies), were each significant influences over firms and industries throughout Australia.

Yet there existed no prominent intergovernmental machinery for business matters. Indeed a likely candidate, the Board of Trade, and later the Tariff Board, was not established as an intergovernmental forum. Its legal position, administrative arrangements and political directions were commonwealth-centred largely to minimise or monitor regional and sectoral sensitivities involved in its regulatory and redistributive decisions (Glezer, 1982). Certainly in later years of its operation, as the Tariff Board and then Industries Assistance Commision, state governments became involved in protection cases under review by the commonwealth statutory authority, but they participated as petitioners, not as partners in an inter-agency forum (Warhurst, 1982).

Other more important intergovernmental bodies were institutionally tangential to business but significant in terms of their macro-economic impact. The Premiers' Conference, established in 1901 but with its origins back to the 1850s, became a significant formal but non-statutory federal financial institution (Sharman, 1977). This body was instrumental in the later establishment of both the Loan Council (1928) and Grants Commission (1933) as formal statutory bodies (CGC, 1983; Mathews & Jay, 1972). Together these three dealt with some issues of general importance to business, such as capital works programs, debt redemption, borrowing levels and state taxation. During the 1970s experiments with 'new federalism' some of the fiscal guidelines were removed. But over the years 1981–85 the commonwealth successively imposed restrictive guidelines under its macro-policy of limiting the 'global' borrowing requirements of all governments. In general, though, the role these three had in direct policy making for business was marginal.

A further range of intergovernmental institutions and administrative arrangements was incrementally grafted onto Australian federalism, often with the intention of emphasising central or national requirements (Warhurst, 1983). For the most part such institutions and practices were specific and *ad hoc* in origin. When they involved issues of business policy they tended to take up business concerns indirectly through governmental representatives from more than one government, or in some instances directly used business representation in intergovernmental initiatives.

As the number of these intergovernmental bodies expanded (principally from the 1960s but with many arising in the Whitlam Labor Government's term 1972–75), it is possible to classify them according to institutional characteristics. On a scale of formal organisation business involvement in such bodies ranges from peak institutions to informal discussions, and from standing policy or administrative committees to one-off specialised working parties on technical concerns. The following groups of intergovernmental initiatives relating to business indicate both the diverse nature of business concerns attracting political responses and also the plethora of economic and regulatory issues existing between different governments.

The first group consists of standing formal institutions without direct business participation. They include the Loan Council, Premiers' Conference, Grants Commission and ministerial councils covering business-related fields. Business has no representative participation but is often involved in agenda setting for these bodies, as in influencing the level of public-sector borrowing requirements, debt-GDP ratios, the provision of capital works, and (coming under ministerial councils) aspects of the financial, commercial law, industrial and trading environment of portfolio areas of responsibility.

A second group of standing formal institutions involving direct business participation may be distinguished from the former. These include the Economic Planning Advisory Council, the Australian Manufacturing Council, the National Labour Consultative Council, various industry councils and tribunals, the Indicative Planning Council, the Promotion and Productivity Councils (Auslang), and some federal–state marketing boards (CAI, 1987–88:3). Although these 'meso-level' bodies maintain an ongoing institutional presence, they do not constitute corporatist policy making structures (Matthews, 1988; Loveday, 1982). Indeed, many are merely advisory or consultative forums, rather than committees charged with executing policy. For the most part these bodies practice information sharing and consultation over selective mutual adjustments to policy.

Thirdly, for *ad hoc* purposes specific formal bodies are regularly created with limited time spans. Because these are highly specialised the membership tends to reflect status, expertise or industry representation. These *ad hoc* bodies include specific working parties, intergovernmental parliamentary inquiries and policy advisory committees. Business is selectively represented on occasions, as in the case of the working parties formed to redress disparities in state preferencing schemes and provide proposals for a unified national system. On other policy areas of significance, business has not formally participated, such as in the committees formed to investigate business regulation in 1984–85, or the working party into offshore banking set up in 1984–85 as a result of the Martin Report, which consisted entirely of governmental officials (CSWPOB, 1985).

The fourth group involves attempted resolutions of highly politicised conflicts through special high-level negotiations. Such negotiations are frequently contingency measures and usually have no enduring formal structure. Because of the potential for political conflict these negotiations are rarely assigned to officials. Cabinet ministers tend to conduct these personally but, unlike the routine ministerial councils, they do not necessarily involve all governments, only those affected. Such political conflicts include major disputes such as the New South Wales–Victorian dairy 'war', which led to the intergovernmental Kerin dairy plan; the drought aid and sugar aid negotiations between the commonwealth, New South Wales and Queensland; and the disputes over the legislative provisions governing company and securities activity.

Finally, informal contact between governments and between government and business regularly includes seminars, discussion forums, meetings, lobbying, telephone communication and the circulation of position papers. This activity may surface in the form of formal submissions to ministers or to review bodies. Over time such contact can result in shared understandings among governments and business which may lead to 'co-operative' arrangements over such issues as the self-regulation of industry, the initiation of voluntary guidelines over business practices or commitment to codes of market behaviour as monitored by the Prices Surveillance Authority.

Intergovernmental relations in preferencing policy

Preferencing policy has existed in Australia since colonial times. Against the spirit of section 92 and the various historical interpretations of freedom of interstate trade and commerce (Cranston, 1987:136–37), continued state preferencing sought regional advantage by restricting interstate economic exchange. Historically preferencing was by nature a 'highly politicised' policy. It reflected a form of decentralised decision making, without co-ordination and laced with irregularities. At the national level this 'problem' was often viewed as too hard to resolve, especially as states in the postwar period had administratively codified forms of preference.

The broader 'problem' of state-based selective preferencing schemes had arisen frequently in intergovernmental forums, but was left unresolved because all states retained a political interest in maintaining their own scheme. As business was also decentralised and state-oriented, preferencing was not problematic except for large or expanding enterprises. Business in some states sought the retention of their own protective preferences while supporting the abolition of preferences from other states.

As a policy outcome, state preferencing was designed to protect local business clients by preserving their access to state contracts. The various policies operated in the main as mutually exclusive protectionism; businesses producing in one state gained access to that state but were denied access to others. In Lowi's terms preferencing operated as both a distributive and regulatory policy. Peterson et al.'s typology presents preferencing as a program for local developmental purposes with provincial regulatory overtones. According to both these classifications, policy development should continue at the micro-level, sustained by local pluralist pressure and by program deliverers anxious to meet specific local needs.

In Australia preferencing had become largely routinised and depoliticised. By the 1980s state preferencing came under increasing commonwealth pressure for national consistency. The commonwealth, as part of its decentralist manufacturing objectives, operated an Australian preference policy and sought tender bids for government supplies from all states (BIE, 1988). This policy allowed tenderers in each state to compete on an equal basis regardless of their location or where the goods were required (DOLGAS, 1986b:109–15). However at the state level, after years of discouragement interstate businesses had all but given up tendering in states outside their own. Accordingly, preferencing policy became less contentious as it was invoked less frequently. As part of more general concerns over economic restructuring, preferencing policy was administratively pushed toward a co-operative national system with uniform rates of preference applying only to overseas tenderers. The local political interests aligned with the state schemes were overcome by a combination of national initiatives and a more economic 'rationalist' thinking permeating sections of Australian business (CAI, 1985–86:17; CAI, 1987a:3).

As part of its centralisation and rationalisation of national preferences, the commonwealth government established a series of specialist review committees to inquire into the procedures and effects of preferencing on industry development. The main thrust of the reports increasingly argued that the existence of preferences was largely ineffective and impeded industry restructuring. A rising chorus of economic advice was forwarded to the commonwealth government from these committees, including the Scott Committee on government procurement (1974), the Lusher Committee on commonwealth purchasing (1981), the Utz Committee for defence purchasing (1982), the Australian Science and Technology Council review of preference margins (1984), Industries Assistance Commission reports on heavy engineering (1984–85) and (once the policy changes were underway) the Inglis Committee on purchasing policies for high technology (1987) (BIE, 1988:49–51).

One of the immediate 'political' catalysts of the policy change was the signing of Closer Economic Relations (CER) between Australia and New Zealand in 1980, to take effect from 1 January 1983. As trade policy became more liberalised, 'second generational' issues emerged between Australia and New Zealand in the national-level deliberations over the period 1983–89. One of the main concerns flowing from the CER negotiations within Australia was to secure some intergovernmental agreement on removing the formal or overt system of local preferencing. In particular the New Zealand government protested over the continuation of state preferences which discriminated against their access to real Australian markets. The signing of this international commitment also placed the commonwealth government in a stronger constitutional position relative to the states over restraint of internal trade.

Yet, international trade and economic integration, mutual access to markets and the dismantling of trade barriers between nations has reciprocal implications. Business associations in Australia were often lukewarm toward the specific proposals to cut preferences while supportive of the concept in general (CAI, 1987–88:11; CAI, 1987a:2). Australian business operating from relatively risk-averse environments in the states accepted their improved access to New Zealand markets, but were reluctant to accept New Zealand access to their own.

The CER initiative stimulated a series of intergovernmental contacts through *ad hoc* formal working parties of senior administrators from industry departments. In late 1984 the Australian Industry and Technology Council (ATIC) of commonwealth and state industry ministers signed an agreement in principle to scale down state preferences. To negotiate the details the AITC established a specific intergovernmental committee of department officers with two representatives each from the peak union and employer bodies (ACTU, CAI/MTIA), and with New Zealand officials attending as observers (even though New Zealand was invited as a participant). This committee, the State Preference and Industry Restructuring Advisory Committee (SPIRAC), held six meetings during 1985 and early 1986 (AITC, 1986:10–11). In addition, further meetings were held involving only commonwealth and state senior administrators, as were ministerial meetings which focused on the politics of whether to cut preference levels across the board or phase down gradually and selectively.

In a separate move the Bureau of Industry Economics (BIE) issued a report on heavy engineering in Australia which urged the removal of state preferencing to 'open a way for increased efficiency' (BIE, 1985:235). Following the release of this report together with the two IAC reports on the same industry (IAC, 1984; 1985), a draft national agreement was prepared by December 1985 which proposed the curtailment and removal of state preferencing. The agreement was secured in Melbourne on 2 May 1986, with implementation dating from 1 July 1986 (DOLGAS, 1986a). By December 1987 the Northern Territory had joined the agreement, and New Zealand, after withholding participation from the advisory process throughout 1983–86, signed the agreement effective from 1 July 1989 (DAS, 1988). Two other committees established to investigate the related matters of government purchasing of high technology products (Inglis Committee) and the Department of Local Government and Administrative Services' (DOLGAS) review of purchasing pricing complemented the SPIRAC agreement. Nonetheless, with the adoption of this national agreement not all state preferences were abolished; indeed, as in Queensland, non-metropolitan preferences still applied within state boundaries to encourage decentralisation when tendering from interstate was not involved (QDID, 1987).

The position of the Confederation of Australian Industry (CAI), as part of a more general restructuring, argued that Australian businesses needed to move beyond the confines of one state. Members in some of their affiliated organisations were highly critical of state schemes, regarding the preference policies of individual states as 'lock out' positions making tendering outside the host state 'almost a waste of time' (CAI, 1983). The CAI defined their peak employer role as one of securing agreement from industry and state governments that internal preferences should be abolished and that consistency should prevail, but that a national preference of 20 per cent should remain on overseas suppliers (CAI, 1985–86:17). The Confederation's participation was intended to bolster the commonwealth government's commitment through the Department of Industry, Technology and Commerce (DITAC) to convince the states to co-operate. Previously the CAI had not regarded the intergovernmental processes as effective in dealing with this issue, largely because 'too much politics were at stake' (CAI, 1988). Their centralised support for the abolition of internal preferences meant that the CAI officials often antagonised their state-based organisations which had established cosy arrangements with their own states. To gain feedback on the policy positions taken at the federal level, the CAI officials adopted a 'request and response' procedure, initially soliciting points of view from their respective member organisations, and then seeking comments on the line taken by the CAI in negotiations.

At the state level SPIRAC members consulted with business associations and other groups. But apart from written requests for comments from the CAI, the state business associations were not closely involved in the policy process. The state departments of industry generally contacted their respective state associations and consulted directly with the larger employers affected. This consultation was largely to explain the policy changes and give notice of the likely removal of preferences. These departments did not involve the state business associations in the formation of policy proposals or principles. This was because departments saw the issue as one to be decided by 'the politicians' and because state business associations were often not held in high regard. One Western Australian department officer justified administrative autonomy on the grounds that industry departments really 'carry the banner for business at the state level'. Once the December 1985 draft agreement was prepared the state departments tended to float the proposals with the local business associations for comment. In Queensland the Department of Industry Development and the State Stores Board surveyed between 50 and 100 firms across all sectors of local industry for their responses to the administrative draft. But generally on this issue the involvement of state business representatives was minimal and *post hoc*. As one state business representative suggested, because no formal consultative mechanisms existed over these intergovernmental issues, state business associations tended to be 'frozen out' of the policy making process and relegated to the role of providing subsequent comment.

Finally, the intergovernmental initiative to remove internal preferences appeared to be taken either as an act of faith in economic rationalist doctrine or the merits of federal harmony, without much detailed assessment of the likely impact of such a policy change. SPIRAC presented one paper on the impact of removing state preferencing (AITC, 1986:10). DITAC and most state industry departments did not undertake an impact study, nor did the business associations at federal and state levels. In 1984 the BIE, reflecting commonwealth and rationalistic views, had undertaken a general assessment of regional policies including state preferencing (BIE, 1984). Some minor surveys were conducted to ascertain whether any major objections were likely on the draft plan and on New Zealand's re-entry into the national scheme. But, other than the circulation of information about the intended scheme, little sustained research on the state schemes was conducted.

The BIE was charged under the national agreement with the task of monitoring and assessing the impact of the national scheme. But during the first three years of operation the BIE had not undertaken an impact assessment on the removal of preferences on regional development, for a number of reasons. The BIE allocate internal priorities to research work they are expected to conduct, and clearly state preferencing was not given sufficient priority relative to other projects. Furthermore, by the 1980s comparatively few firms tendered outside their state of residence for state contracts, and abolishing internal preference arrangements was not considered likely to produce marked changes in such well-conditioned business behaviour. Finally, although no state evaluation was conducted, in 1988 the BIE released an evaluation of the commonwealth's national purchasing preference scheme. This report provided evidence that the policy was administratively costly, discriminative, and conflicted with other industry development objectives, yet found that in 'only an extremely small number of cases did the preference margin play a role in determining the eventual winner' of contracts (BIE, 1988:34). This suggests once more that preferencing had become an administrative irritant rather than a substantive problem for business.

Conclusion

Business occupies a structurally 'privileged position' relative to other groups in society, but this potential for power needs to be qualified in light of empirical investigation of actual policy processes. Certainly business achieves a level of access to government at commonwealth and state levels that other groups would not consistently have. Business also has the capacity to play one level of government off against another. Paradoxically, while business has stronger links with state governments, it is often more integrated into commonwealth-level policy making processes. This is largely a consequence of the range of commonwealth consultative arrangements which relate to business policy issues. Ironically, despite its close links to state governments, business often relies on its peak associations when confronted with intergovernmental policy issues.

From the government's side business issues are not a single policy area. The range of policies relating to business is not capable of being implemented by a discrete government agency. Diversity and fragmentation in policy responses are the norm, and given the diversity of interests among business this characteristic is not generally unacceptable to business. What is more, policy alternatives involving greater co-ordination, while they exist theoretically, have rarely achieved political support.

One criticism made by business of the nature of intergovernmental machinery is that it tends to work toward alleviating administrative issues between different governments rather than the problems of business. Thus, most of the initiative for aligning and removing prefer-ences originated with the commonwealth government, with some support from the CAI federal officers. The policy changes were designed to simplify government tendering and purchasing even though the issue was depicted as redressing the fragmentation or misallocation of economic resources within Australia. Intergovernmental arrangements concerning business tend to be oriented toward the administrative processes involved in economic management. As such, intergovernmental relations tend to concern themselves principally with patching exercises, filling policy gaps, standardising relatively 'depoliticised' procedures, marginally extending provisions, taking up specific cases, or aligning some aspects of regulatory frameworks.

Business representation on intergovernmental forums is not extensive. Where it does occur it is likely to be as a result of involvement in existing commonwealth consultative processes. Business is also repres-ented more on the advisory committees than direct policy making bodies, including highly politicised advisory groups such as the Economic Planning Advisory Council. Typically, the composition of this representation is derived from the federal level of business associations or directly from major companies. State-based representatives of business are generally not incorporated in the decision making processes of intergovernmental machinery, but may be consulted.

Many minor policy areas involving more than one government are handled exclusively by federal and state administrators. The administrators and their policy agencies limit the terms of the policy issues, and the communication with affected others. On these issues administrative specialists rather than business occupy a privileged position in relation to influencing policy outcomes. As outsiders, business considers that these examples, as illustrated in the changes to preference policy, provide them with a *fait accompli*. The structural privileged position of business does not translate readily to a privileged position over micro-policy setting.

Bibliography

Abbey, B., 1987. 'Power, Politics and Business', *Politics*, 22(2).

ACTU/TDC, 1987. *Australia Reconstructed: Report by the Mission Members to the ACTU and the TDC*, AGPS, Canberra.

AITC (Australian Industry and Technology Council), 1986. Annual Summary of Proceedings 1985–86, AGPS, Canberra.

Atkinson, M. & Coleman, W., 1989. 'Strong States and Weak States: Sectoral Policy Networks in Advanced Capitalist Economies', *British Journal of Political Science*, 19(1).

BCA (Business Council of Australia), 1988a. 'Critical Role of the States in the National Economy', *Business Council Bulletin*.

—— 1988b. 'Companies and Securities Regulation', *Business Council Bulletin*.

—— 1989. 'The Economy and the 1989–90 Budget', *Business Council Bulletin*.

BIE (Bureau of Industry Economics), 1984. *Regional Impact of Structural Change: an Assessment of Regional Policies in Australia*, Research Report 18, AGPS, Canberra.

—— 1985. *Heavy Engineering in Australia: Problems and Prospects*, Research Report 19, AGPS, Canberra.

—— 1988. *The Commonwealth Purchasing Preference Margin as an Industry Development Mechanism*, Program Evaluation Report 6, AGPS, Canberra.

Bowler, S., 1987. 'Corporatism and the "Privileged Position" of Business', *West European Politics*, 10(2).

—— 1988. 'Government–Business Bargaining and the Impact of EC Institutions: the Lindblom Problem', *Political Studies*, 36 (September).

CAI (Confederation of Australian Industry), 1983. Membership Correspondence, Business and Labour Archives, ANU, ABL-Z196 Box 47 AS-1401.

—— 1985–86. *Annual Report*, CAI, Canberra.

—— 1987a. 'CAI's Industry Policy Objectives', CAI, Canberra.

—— 1987b. *Confederation News*, 10(2).

—— 1987c. 'Statement on Economic Policy', CAI, Canberra.

—— 1987–88. *Annual Report*, CAI, Canberra.

—— 1988. Interview with senior CAI economic advisor.

CGC (Commonwealth Grants Commission), 1983. *Equality in Diversity; Fifty Years of the Commonwealth Grants Commission*, AGPS, Canberra.

Chapman, R., 1988. 'The Australian Advisory Council for Inter-Government Relations as a Moderating Institution', *Australian Journal of Public Administration*, 47(2).

Coleman, W., 1988. *Business and Politics: a Study of Collective Action*, McGill-Queen's University Press, Kingston.

Cranston, R., 1987. *Law, Government and Public Policy*, Oxford University Press, Melbourne.

CSWPOB (The Commonwealth/State Working Party on Offshore Banking), 1985. *Report*, AGPS, Canberra.

DAS (Department of Administrative Services), 1988. 'Amendment to National Preference Agreement', DAS National Policy Coordination, Canberra.

DOLGAS (Department of Local Government and Administrative Services), 1986a. 'Commonwealth Purchasing Circular CPC86/3: National Preference Agreement', Canberra.

—— 1986b. *Local Purchasing Officers Workshop: Background Papers*, Purchasing and Disposals Division.

Domhoff, G.W., 1986. 'The Growth Machine and the Power Elite: a Challenge to Pluralists and Marxists Alike', in *Community Power: Directions for Future Research*, ed. R.J. Waste, Sage, Beverly Hills.

Galligan, B., 1988. 'Politics and Business in Australia: Towards Economising Government and Governing for Business', Conference Paper, IPSA World Congress, Washington, Sept.

Glezer, L., 1982. *Tariff Politics*, Melbourne University Press, Melbourne.

Hall, P., 1986. *Governing the Economy: the Politics of State Intervention in Britain and France*, Oxford University Press, Oxford.

Hogg, T.M., 1987. *'Industry Policy and Economic Growth'*, CEDA Study, *Protection, Industry Policy and Economic Growth*, Growth 35, Melbourne.

IAC (Industries Assistance Commission), 1984. *The Heavy Engineering Industry, Interim Report*, AGPS, Canberra.

—— 1985. *The Heavy Engineering Industry*, AGPS, Canberra.

Katzenstein, P., 1985. *Small States in World Markets: Industrial Policy in Europe*, Cornell University Press, Ithaca.

Lindblom, C., 1977. *Politics and Markets*, Harper, New York.

Loveday, P., 1982. *Promoting Industry: Recent Australian Political Experience*, University of Queensland Press, St Lucia.

Lowi, T., 1964. 'American Business, Public Policy, Case-Studies, and Political Theory', *World Politics*, 16(4).

McEachern, D., 1986. 'Corporatism and Business Responses to the Hawke Government', *Politics*, 21(1).

McFarlane, A., 1987. 'Interest Groups and Theories of Power in America', *British Journal of Political Science*, 17 April.

McQueen, R., 1989. 'The New Companies and Securities Scheme: a Fundamental Departure?' (mimeo), Griffith University.

Marsh, D., 1983. 'Interest Group Activity and Structural Power: Lindblom's Politics and Markets', *West European Politics*, 6(2).

Mathews, R.L. & Jay, W.R., 1972. *Federal Finance: Intergovernmental Financial Relations in Australia Since Federation*, Nelson, Melbourne.

Mathews, R.L., ed., 1974. *Intergovernmental Relations in Australia*, Angus & Robertson, Sydney.

Matthews, T., 1983. 'Business Associations and the State, 1850–1979', in *State and Economy in Australia*, ed. B. Head, Oxford University Press, Melbourne.

—— 1988. '"Vitally Important Allies"? The Role of Interest Groups in Government Decision-making: a Review Essay', *Australian Journal of Public Administration*, 47(2).

Offe, C., 1981. 'The Attribution of Public Status to Interest Groups: Observations on the West German Case', in *Organizing Interests in Western Europe*, ed. S. Berger, Cambridge University Press, Cambridge.

Ostry, S., 1987. 'From Fine Tuning to Framework-setting in Macro-economic Management', in *OECD, Interdependence and Co-operation in Tomorrow's World*, OECD, Paris.

Peterson, P., Rabe, B. & Wong, K., 1986. *When Federalism Works*, Brookings Institution, Washington.

QDID (Queensland Department of Industry Development), 1987. *Queensland State Purchasing Policy*, Brisbane.

—— 1988. *Annual Report, 1987–88*, Brisbane.

Ravenhill, J., 1989. 'Business and Politics', in *Politics in Australia*, eds R. Smith & L. Watson, Allen & Unwin, Sydney.

Reid, G.S. & Spann, R.N., 1974. 'Political Decentralisation, Co-operative Federalism and Responsible Government' / 'Responsibility in Federal Systems', in *Intergovernmental Relations in Australia*, ed. R.L. Mathews, Angus & Robertson, Sydney.

Sawer, G., 1967. *Australian Federalism in the Courts*, Melbourne University Press, Melbourne.

Sharman, C., 1977. *The Premiers' Conference: an Essay in Federal State Interaction*, Department of Political Science, Research School of Social Sciences, Australian National University, Canberra.

Skogstad, G., 1987. *The Politics of Agricultural Policy-making in Canada*, University of Toronto Press, Toronto.

SSCCLA (Report by Senate Standing Committee on Constitutional and Legal Affairs), 1987. *The Role of Parliament in Relation to the National Companies and Securities Scheme*, AGPS, Canberra.

Wanna, J., 1989. 'Centralisation Without Corporatism: the Politics of New Zealand Business in the Recession', *New Zealand Journal of Industrial Relations*, 14(1).

Warhurst, J., 1982. *Jobs or Dogma?* University of Queensland Press, St Lucia.

—— 1983. *Central Agencies, Intergovernmental Managers, and Australian Federal–State Relations*, Research Monograph No. 29, Centre for Research on Federal Financial Relations, Australian National University, Canberra.

Waste, R.J. ed., 1986. *Community Power: Directions for Future Research*, Sage, Beverly Hills.

Wettenhall, R., 1985. 'Intergovernmental Agencies: Lubricating a Federal System', *Current Affairs Bulletin*, 61(11).

Wilson, G., 1985. *Business and Politics: a Comparative Introduction*, Chatham House, Chatham.

Wright, M., 1988. 'Policy Community, Policy Network and Comparative Industrial Policies', *Political Studies*, 36(4).

Zysman, J., 1983. *Governments, Markets and Growth:Financial Systems and the Politics of Industry*, Martin Robertson, Oxford.

17 Telecommunications

Owen Hughes

Some intergovernmental public policy issues are inevitably more contentious than others. At one end of the scale are issues like financial arrangements, which are always important; at the other end are policy issues which are apparently settled and intergovernmental relations only rarely difficult. These areas are likely to be those in which constitutional powers are quite clear or in which administrative arrangements are formalised so that conflict does not arise. However, there is probably no policy area which, seemingly settled, cannot return to the agenda of intergovernmental relations. One such area is that of telecommunications.

Since federation, Australian telecommunications policy has quite clearly been a commonwealth government responsibility. Unlike in Canada and the United States, the interaction of telecommunications and federalism in Australia has been relatively harmonious; the constitutional power over telecommunications was given to the central government at federation and has not been seriously challenged. More recently, however, state governments have become increasingly interested in telecommunications matters. There are two facets to this. The major one is the setting up of state private communication networks for telephony and data communications between different parts of the state governments. Even the name 'private network' is misplaced; these are *government* networks. So far there is no recognition of this fact in policy or legislation; the state networks are treated in exactly the same way as private industry. However, given that state government communications is variously estimated at up to 15 per cent of Telecom telephone revenue, the development of state private networks is not an insignificant development by itself. It has led, in part, to the second facet; that while there is no serious attempt to overthrow the commonwealth constitutional power, the states are now attempting to influence telecommunications policy.

Changes in the regulatory environment which started in July 1989 will give other governments more scope to influence policy. Before this time regulatory policy was made by Telecom under its Act, but the creation of Austel, an independent statutory authority with powers to regulate the industry, changes the ground-rules of telecommunications policy. Some state governments have previously declared their dissatisfaction with regulatory policy interpretations made by Telecom regulations. On some key points, notably interconnect charges, the states have been rather happier with the independent regulator. Having another avenue means that the states, either separately or together, can approach Austel or the federal government with arguments to broaden the interpretation of regulations for their own communications.

There is also increased interest shown in broader policy questions. The increasing commercial orientation of carriers and the interests of the states in development, as well as concern for particular groups—rural and remote areas—may mean more political complaints from those in the community who see their communications interests being adversely affected. In a federal system political complaints may be aggregated at any level of government, and state governments are likely to also approach Austel on behalf of their constituents. Austel will provide an avenue which did not exist before and state governments will be among the first to take advantage of such an opportunity.

These developments in telecommunications are interesting not only because of their implications for the Telecom monopoly or the regulatory environment, but for the federal system as a whole. Taken together these suggest changes in the relationship between governments as well as the commercial relationships between the states and Telecom as the traditional provider of telecommunications services. Therefore, recent regulatory and technological developments have implications for intergovernmental relations and for the federal system in Australia.

The constitutional position

Before federation the states administered their own postal,telegraph and telephone services with some intercolonial co-operation on matters of joint interest. However, in 1901, the constitution quite clearly gave the commonwealth full responsibility for telecommunications. Section 51 (v) establishes commonwealth jurisdiction over 'postal, telegraphic, telephonic and other like services'. This was a departure from both the Canadian or American federalisms, but was not given to the commonwealth government without discussion or without opposition. At several times during the 1890s Convention debates some delegates,

especially from Western Australia and South Australia, opposed the
takeover of services they had provided for many years. Mr Holder, a
Convention delegate from South Australia, argued 'It seems to me
that postal and telegraphic matters are matters of purely local concern,
and that to transfer them to the federal authority would be a great
mistake. The effect would be to bring about centralisation in its worst
form, and cause great detriment to outlying districts' (Convention
Debates, 17 April 1897:767). Western Australian delegate Sir John
Forrest tried several times to retain state control over the various
communications services. Speaking on a South Australian amendment to
make central jurisdiction only 'outside the limits of the commonwealth',
Forrest argued:

> Seeing that these colonies are only in their infancy, and that their post
> and telegraph systems are part of the social life of the community, it
> seemed to us that to intrust to a far away authority the building of
> telegraph lines and the extension of postal services, would be most
> vexatious...As far as the commonwealth is concerned, it is not
> necessary to have a federal government in order to federalise the post
> and telegraph services, because they are federalised at the present time.
> (Convention Debates, 22 September 1897)

This amendment was lost by a margin of 24 votes to 10. The arguments
which eventually prevailed were those of Barton, Deakin and Reid, that
national development would be better served by giving the power to the
commonwealth. Barton, for example, argued, 'If a person sending a long
distance message expects to get an answer, then with respect either to the
message or to the answer, he may be in a very queer position unless the
whole responsibility rests with the Commonwealth of keeping the whole
system as clear as possible' (Convention Debates, 17 April 1897).
Speaking against the South Australian amendment, Sir George Reid
argued:

> This attempt to separate the post and telegraph services will, I think,
> be disastrous. It is impossible to work these two services by two
> different departments. One of the strongest reasons for including the
> post and telegraph service within the Commonwealth, is that, instead
> of having seven Ministerial Post and telegraph Departments and seven
> staffs for the Australia colonies, the whole business can be managed
> under one federal head. If there is an argument in favour of federalising
> any service, it applies more strongly to this than to any other I can
> think of. (Convention Debates, 17 April 1897)

Although the postal and telecommunications parts were never *that*
well suited, it was arguably administratively convenient for there to be
one national department rather than one for each state. This was not a
particularly strong argument by itself. But as was often the case in the
1890s Convention debates, the arguments made by Alfred Deakin—in
this case for central power—were the most persuasive. In his view:

It is not essential to the principles on which the Federal Government is to be established that either the post office or the telegraph service should be transferred to the national Government. But I submit that the post and telegraph office in both its branches comes first in the long list of services in which it is evident there are national interests to be dealt with rather than State interests. (Convention Debates, 17 April 1897)

In fact, there was and is no *axiomatic* reason why telecommunications services were given to the central government. As Deakin correctly argued, it was not *essential* for the federation that powers over posts, telegraphs, telephones and other like services be given to the central government. This can be shown by looking at other federal systems and at the general principles of division of power in federal states.

Although there cannot be fully-agreed principles for division of powers between governments in federal states, some powers are always given to the central government—foreign affairs, immigration, the currency—while others are reserved for states or provinces, such as land-use. There is an assumption that each level of government, rather than attempting to perform all functions of the public sector, does what it can do best. The central government accepts primary responsibility for stabilising the economy, for achieving the most equitable distribution of income, and for providing certain public goods and services which are national, like defence. Other services are provided by governments that are of primary interest only to the residents of their respective jurisdictions (Oates, 1972).

Even against these vague rules, telecommunications policy is an area which is clearly both local and national. The primary interest is not easy to identify, although most telephone traffic is local and intrastate, rather than interstate. Some federal countries see telecommunications as a central function, while others see it as a provincial function with administrative arrangements for matters of joint interest. It would have been possible to run the communication services in Australia as in Canada and the United States where the state administrations were left to themselves and co-operate on matters of joint interest, or in other words, the arrangements stated by Forrest as already existing in Australia before federation.

After 1901 the merits of central control over telecommunications policy was not at issue, although some states were in no hurry to hand over assets to the new Department of Posts and Telegraphs. Commonwealth control was perhaps helpful in providing some cohesion and national purpose. Posts and Telegraphs started and remained the largest commonwealth department, and was the visible manifestation of the very existence of a new government in even sparsely settled parts of the nation. Deakin's 'national interest' argument was persuasive in the Convention and a case can be made that the development of the telecommunications network was assisted by this. However, central government control in what is not a fundamental central power has obscured the legitimate interests of other levels of government.

The constitution and public policy

A superficial interpretation of the constitution is that policy is totally made by the level of government which has the formal constitutional power. However, in any federalism, governments are often able to influence policy in areas where they do not have formal power. If a government has the power it can make laws; but if not it can make representations to the level of government which does have the power. The effectiveness of this should not be ignored. For example, local governments complained for many years that commonwealth authorities were exempt from council rates. The commonwealth government has heeded their representations and now local rates as well as state payroll taxes are to be paid by some statutory authorities. There are other examples such as the dismantling of the two-airline policy. While there are clearly a range of factors at work in this policy change, state ministers for tourism have argued for many years that this commonwealth law damaged their interests and these arguments had some effect.

A more significant case is that of offshore fisheries and other offshore resources discussed in chapter 6. In a series of High Court cases in the 1960s and 1970s the commonwealth won full rights over all territory beyond the low-water mark. The states were most unhappy about this and kept pressuring the commonwealth even though it was quite clear they had no constitutional power in these matters. The Fraser Government passed an Act giving the states administrative responsibility, or in effect acting as agents of the commonwealth.

Governments and telecommunications

In one part of the May 1988 telecommunications policy statement is the comment, 'Australian Governments have long faced the problems of providing an integrated telecommunications infrastructure for economic and social activity across a large national territory' (Evans, 1988). It is not clear whether the word 'governments' refers here to the *temporal* or historical sense or 'governments' in the *spatial* sense, that is the various governments at the commonwealth, state and local level. Both meanings are quite accurate. All levels of government have an interest in telecommunications, regardless of whether the supplier is owned publicly or privately and regardless of the formal constitutional position. These interests are in two main categories—government communications and government policy interests.

Government communications

Governments require communications links in order to function, arguably to a greater degree than other parts of the community. These are:

1 Internal communications within government and its agencies, including both telephony and data links between government employees in the same or other government organisations; these can be either (a) in the same workplace, or (b) in work places at varying degrees of remoteness.
2 Government communications with the public. Quite obviously all governments need to communicate with the general public and the business community. Two-way links with the community must be provided for what can be assumed to be mainly government business.

Government policy interests

Given the importance of communications links to the economy, no government can ignore the condition of the service provided. Telecommunications is a genuine utility; an essential service for business and the community as a whole; specific groups in the community may make a case that it is so important for their interests—for example, those in rural and remote areas—that political demands will be made to government generally. This can occur regardless of level of government and regardless of the formal constitutional position. The importance of telecommunications to the economy, and the increasing realisation of that fact, means that governments at all levels have legitimate interests in matters of policy.

The government communications category may simply involve a particular government as a consumer of telecommunications services. It could, and has, been regarded by the telecommunications provider as exactly the same as any other subscriber. This is a mistake. Governments have interests and powers beyond those of companies or other subscribers and are in a position to change or influence policy in a way other subscribers cannot.

Recent changes in Australian telecommunications affect both government communications and policy interests in the wider sense. Although they more directly affect the former category, representations on policy are already being made and more will follow with the clearer specification of commonwealth government policy and the beginning of regulation by Austel.

Government communication networks

The past few years have seen all state governments either set up their own private communications networks (PCNs) or have serious proposals almost at the stage for tenders to be called. The Queensland government was the first with its development of Q-Net in 1986; Victoria established Vistel in 1987; South Australia announced a new state government network called Statelink in July 1988; the New South Wales cabinet was considering tenders when the government changed in 1988, and in 1989 the Greiner Government appointed consultants to assist in calling for tenders; the Northern Territory is likely to establish NT-Net; Western Australia called for expressions of interest in 1988 and is to call for tenders in 1990 while Tasmania is establishing a government link between Hobart, Launceston and Burnie. Even the commonwealth government has investigated the desirability of establishing its own communications network organised by the Department of Finance.

The initial motivation for these developments is to reduce the cost of government communication, although there are advantages in improving access to services and to improving efficiency and effectiveness in government administration. Estimates of the extent of saving vary widely, but a realistic estimate is that Telecom derives about $500 million a year from internal calls between government departments— about 15 per cent of its total telephone revenue (*Financial Review*, 23 June 1988). A report to the New South Wales government estimated that between 60 and 80 per cent of New South Wales public-sector calls were to people within the same department or to other government departments and a state network would pay for itself within four years (*Financial Review*, 18 January, 1988). The potential savings are substantial, or from another perspective, the potential loss of revenue to Telecom, if not large initially, could be quite substantial over the longer term. Telecom's revenue from this source does not cease because (i) there is still a need to use the public network for some purposes, and (ii) Telecom charges are still incurred for the lease of private lines. Using a private network can lead to savings in several ways.

Call charges

The cost of private networks is in establishment and maintenance, not in the price per call. Until the establishment of government networks it was normal for each office to communicate with other offices or its branches through the Telecom network. However, with a private network most calls need not enter the public network at all. Those calls which do can avoid the high cost parts of the network. Traffic which originates in the public network can be switched anywhere within the private network, while traffic from within the private network can be switched anywhere inside and out again at any interconnect point. This has obvious advantages for government networks, particularly for communication with rural or remote areas. For example, the police station at Broome could access the police computer in Perth and stay in the network. But a local telephone enquiry to the Broome police station could also stay in the network and be answered in Perth, or a public servant in that department could ring a private number in Broome and remain in the private network until the final link to the subscriber's home. This flexibility extends to all members of the allowable 'common-interest group'. The above example could extend to a number of government departments or agencies, to the allowed limit of the common-interest group.

Data communications

State government agencies are major users of data links, but these are often incompatible with other agency lines and their use is often unco-ordinated. While savings are large by using a private telephony/data network, there are also savings to be made by sharing data links between different agencies and by agreeing on standards. Clearly, substantial money could be saved by better organisation and standardisation. While the amounts saved are reasonable now, with the growth in data traffic far greater savings could result. While Telecom will not lose much revenue initially from this source it will miss out on much of the growth. South Australian government data costs are growing at 25 per cent a year while telephony is growing at 10 per cent; another state reports a 30 per cent growth rate in data costs and another state estimates a 45 per cent growth rate in data traffic.

PABX links

Substantial savings can be expected simply by better co-ordination of telecommunications in government departments and agencies. Better choice of PABXs and bulk purchases have the advantages of saving in initial cost, maintenance and in standardisation of features. Modern PABX features enable them to run as exchanges, as in, for example, Vistel's optical fibre link around the Melbourne business district connecting various state government PABXs without going into the ordinary network.

Overall efficiency

Although it is not possible to quantify this factor, there are certainly economies to be made by better integration of telecommunications into the management of the public sector. While this is true of any bureaucratic organisation, it is probably especially true in government departments. If efficiency and effectiveness can be improved then functions could be carried out with less staff, or, more likely, a lower rate of increase in staffing numbers. Productivity could be increased by better utilising communication links; having a private network should lead to some co-ordination of standards and equipment which would lead to more innovative use of technology with corresponding improvement in productivity. Governments, particularly state governments, are involved in delivery of services to the community. The improvement in technology should enable services to be delivered more effectively to more of the public in more parts of the state. This should especially assist those departments and agencies which have traditionally provided services to rural areas, such as education, agriculture and police, but will also enable country areas access to a wider range of services than was available before.

The first state government network, Q-Net, was established by Queensland in 1985 to determine if interdepartmental communications could be carried out more cheaply by using a private satellite network. Vistel in Victoria is mainly terrestrial but with some satellite links to remote places. Vistel is based on an optical fibre cable around the Melbourne city centre to link state government PABXs as well as optical fibre links with eighteen major regional centres.

The two established cases show quite different strategies. Queensland set out to use the satellite and designed its system around it. There were some doubts expressed about its economic viability and the Queensland government subsequently sold Q-Net to Bond Media. Exactly why Queensland wished to sell its government network is not known, but it raises some questions. Telecom spokesman Bill Rowlings said of the deal with Bond:

> We can't fathom the economic and technical rationale used in the decision—it's clear from what the Queensland Government has said in its Q-Net documentation that the cost of providing voice and data services via Q-Net is far higher than Telecom's standard charge for the equivalent capacity. What that means is that Q-Net, for an independent operator, is not likely to be commercially viable without substantial subsidy. This means that either Bond Media or the Queensland Government will be paying more for the voice and data services than if Telecom provided those services in the normal way. (*The Australian*, 21 March 1988)

Perhaps the satellite link was never economic, or there is some other explanation of the conditions of the sale; whatever the case, there are questions which require an answer.

There can be economies made from the state governments' setting up private networks, as well as economies in regarding telecommunications links as rather more important than office equipment. However, there are two major problems. The first is the difficulty of persuading the state bureaucracy of the advantages of some centralisation. Senior public servants may not be willing to give up their autonomy, while computer specialists may prefer their own data communications standards to state-wide standardisation and sharing facilities. But as the cost of communications for government increases, state treasuries will increasingly demand cost cutting, although Vistel for one has tried to operate by persuasion rather than force. Most state governments now have an agency or even a department to co-ordinate telecommunications, so the bureaucratic problem may not be major. The second problem though is rather more difficult and requires separate treatment. As the monopoly provider, Telecom is currently empowered to make regulations on a variety of matters affecting the state networks. This means that the networks are subject to rules many see as inadequate.

Regulatory aspects

For the states, the biggest obstacles to achieving even greater cost saving in telecommunications are the various regulatory interpretations formerly made by Telecom and now made by Austel. On the other hand Telecom has argued that it is the statutory monopoly provider and allowing the state governments or anyone else total freedom in the use of private networks will destroy the monopoly by taking away the ability to cross-subsidise from profitable parts of the network to unprofitable parts. The Telecom view of private networks was spelt out in 1988 by Telecom spokesman Roger Banks:

> As for the regulation of private networks, Telecom has identified three basic issues: first, identifying the sources from which private network operators may derive their transmission capacity; second, defining the circumstances under which private network operators may use and share their private networks with third parties; and third, formulating the conditions and charges under which private network operators may interconnect their private networks with public networks and with other private networks, thereby extending their scope and facilities. Telecom's present position on these matters is, firstly, that private network operators may derive their transmission capacity, for uses which extend beyond their own land, from any source other than the private provision of cable-based capacity. And, secondly, sharing must stop short of fullblood third party carriage, otherwise the concept of common carriage has no separate meaning. At the same time, point-to-point and point-to-multi-point private radio communications links should be permitted. As for leased line private networks, customers are free to lease private lines from any carrier for their own use and the carriage of their own, as opposed to third party, traffic. (*The Communications Newsletter*, April 1988)

Only private lines leased from Telecom or Aussat may be interconnected with the public network; there is strict control over sharing of leased lines and resale of any excess capacity; and Telecom sets the fees and technical standards by which the PCN can be connected to the public network. In Telecom's view the state government networks are exactly the same as the private networks operated by the banks and the travel

industry. Particular parts of regulatory policy which cause problems are
listed below.

Common-interest groups

Private networks must be part of an authorised common-interest group in
order to be connected to the public network. The interpretation of who
may or may not be permitted to join a common-interest group is of great
interest to the states, as it affects the viability of any private network.
The ruling on common-interest groups used by the commonwealth
government and Telecom is that provided by the Minister for
Communications in 1983, in answer to a parliamentary question on
notice. This is as follows:

> For any group of persons (individual or corporate) to constitute a
> 'common interest' group to operate a telecommunications facility
> (including a private network) the group must have a common interest or
> business and meet the following criteria:
>
> (i)   the prime business or interest of the group must be something
>   other than operating a telecommunications facility or service;
> (ii)   the operation of a telecommunications facility or service by the
>   group must be no more that ancillary to, or facilitating, the
>   group's business or interest;
> (iii) the relationship between a company and its subsidiaries is
>   sufficient to constitute a common interest group, subject to (i)
>   and (ii) above;
> (iv)   the relationship between a company and its shareholders, by
>   itself, is insufficient to constitute a common interest group.
>
> It should be noted that the concept of common interest groups who
> share or operate telecommunications facilities or services is a limited
> exception to the Commission's role of national common carrier, and
> the exception is, for that reason, strictly administered. (Australia,
> House of Representatives, *Parliamentary Debates*, 23 August 1983)

Obviously, if common-interest groups were less restricted the monopoly
would be threatened, but the state governments feel that the Telecom
interpretation of their networks is overly restrictive.

A problem for state governments is the definition of 'business or
interest'. They argue that anything belonging to the state government is
part of the business of government and is therefore eligible to join the
common-interest group. Telecom's interpretation is that while inner
government budget agencies are allowed to be part of the
common-interest group, outer budget agencies and statutory authorities
are excluded. The allowable boundaries of common-interest groups can
appear arbitrary. For example, state government electricity suppliers are
excluded, as are the railways. The Telecom rationale is that these
authorities are in the electricity business or the railways business, with
their government ownership being incidental. Even though the railways

in Queensland are under the control of a ministerial department, they are treated in the same way as the railways in other states which have statutory independence. The state police forces operate with statutory independence but are permitted in the common-interest group.

Some governments have expressed dissatisfaction with the interpretation of common-interest groups. The Western Australian government common-interest group currently approved by Telecom contains 75 000 staff with 23 000 excluded, mainly in Westrail and State Electricity Commission of Western Australia. But the Western Australian government has what it calls a 'whole of government' approach to its administration generally; it 'disputes the restrictive interpretation placed by Telecom Australia on membership of the common-interest group and contends that all agencies of the Western Australian Government are entitled to membership' (WA, 1988:22). Graham Smith, from the Queensland government Centre for Information Technology and Communications argues:

> Administrative policy devices such as 'common interest groups' are adopted by Telecom to spread the inevitable costs it has incurred over the years but that particular policy has to be questioned from the user's point of view. In Queensland, government departments such as the Railways and the Centre for Information Technology and Communications (CITEC) are not allowed to transmit data down the same Telecom line. As a result each has to procure a separate line to Townsville although one line could handle the traffic, and in addition, associated equipment such as protocol converters and communications equipment have to be duplicated...The TAB needs weekend and evening communications for racing and is ideally placed to share resources with traditional public service departments working from 9 a.m. to 5 p.m. Monday to Friday. This is not permitted and Telecom costs therefore are needlessly exaggerated with the consequent duplication of hardware.
> If Telecom were to free up their common interest group regulations and allow the Queensland Government to become the one group, savings would be significantly increased. (Smith, 1988:43)

Telecom argues that common carriage is the fundamental policy and that the policy on common-interest groups is a policy exception. Applicants must demonstrate they have a clear common interest and that the other requirements of the common-interest policy have been met. In cases of doubt it is Telecom's 'firm practice to refuse applications for common-interest group status' (Telecom, 1986). Thus far state government statutory authorities in some other 'industry' are excluded even though the boundary of an 'industry' of government must be hard to draw. What industry is the TAB example above? It could be argued to be in the racing business, but this is a business under its own minister in Queensland. The TABs began as part of the law-enforcement industry—to stamp out SP bookmakers and their associated criminal activities—and the police and justice industries are permitted in state common-interest groups. The TABs could also be seen as parts of the state taxation industry. Of course, under current policies, the line must be drawn somewhere, but state governments engage in so many activities or industries that the dividing line can seem arbitrary.

Interconnection policy

The advantage of a private network is that each use is not charged and this means that the average cost of a call is very much less than through the switched network. However, a totally private network is far less useful than one which allows interconnection to the public network at some point. While 60 to 80 per cent of state government communications may be 'in-house' there are obvious demands for access to the public network. Interconnection policy is strictly controlled by Telecom by two major restrictions. First, fees are charged for interconnection and Telecom's reasons for making interconnect charges are:

1 Telephone subscribers using the trunk network for calls make a contribution to the establishment, development and operation of a national asset—the public telephone network, through the payment of a social contribution included in STD and other trunk call tariffs. Operators of private networks extending over a trunk distance should pay this share when they wish to interconnect to the public network to gain the benefits of using that network.
2 Local call areas in Australia, particularly the capital city calling zones, are priced on the basis of unit call fees and represent an undervalued resource, bearing in mind their size and scope and the high level of connectivity and other forms of utility involved. The value of connection from outside to local call areas is reflected in STD charges for Public Switch Telephone Network (PSTN) users and, in the case of private network operators interconnecting with the network, in interconnect charges.

Thus interconnect charges reflect both a contribution to the improvement and maintenance of the public network, and the commercial and utility value of interworking with large local call areas (Telecom, 1988).

The second restriction for interconnection for any other private network is that interconnection is only allowed for lines comprising Aussat and/or Telecom leased lines.

The two restrictions substantially reduce the attractiveness of private networks. It has been argued that these regulations are 'even more stringent' than those for the use of leased lines, and that the second restriction means that 'if an organisation wishes to connect its PCN to the PSTN then it is constrained to using Telecom or Aussat technology regardless of technological developments occurring elsewhere' (BIE,

1988:6). More recently the interconnection policy has been changed. Telecom has simplified its pricing to $2000 for each logical voice circuit connected to the public network, rather than the previous complicated formula which was usually more expensive.

Community service obligations

The reason expressed for maintaining tight regulations is Telecom's statutory requirement community service obligations (CSOs). This concept lies behind the relatively restrictive interpretations placed on common-interest groups and the interconnect policy. If too many private networks were allowed this would undermine the ability of the monopoly provider to supply services to unprofitable parts of the Australian public network. Charges are made for private network interconnection which explicitly attempt to recover part of this cost of providing CSOs. The price charged for private lines and interconnection includes a component for Telecom CSOs that will be avoided by the use of private networks rather than the public network. The key problem for state governments is that, in their view, while the policy is not unreasonable in the abstract, it is unreasonable to treat their networks exactly the same as private industry. As discussed further below, the states do not dispute that Telecom has CSOs but would like some recognition that their own services, especially to remote areas, also involve substantial CSOs.

State policy interests

As well as improving their own communications, state governments are likely to further articulate their general policy interests in telecommunications. Any government can be assumed to wish to develop its economy and will see a fundamental need for an adequate communications network in the community for which it is politically responsible. As a political question it will become 'interested' in some way if communications are seen as inadequate for any of its constituents. This will occur regardless of whether the government involved has any ownership or regulatory responsibilities. For example, the Western Australian government 'is committed to a policy of equitable community access to the benefits of communications technology, particularly for those who are disadvantaged by distance.' This is not simply a matter of the government's own information links but indicates interest in the general provision of an adequate service. A Queensland perspective is similar:

> The states have a large range of federal legislation-based
> responsibilities for the delivery of services to the people of Australia
> (eg, health, education, power, water, police). It is important that they
> have mechanisms by which they can effectively influence the
> development of telecommunications policy as it relates to these

responsibilities. This is particularly pertinent at a time when such technologies have the ability to assist in the effective delivery of such services (Rowell, 1985:46).

In federal systems it is a common mistake to assume that what happens in public policy is that which follows from the constitution and High Court cases. Constitutionally the commonwealth has complete power over telecommunications and the states cannot challenge that. However, they still want a say in policy matters which affect their interests.

All governments have community service obligations. The provision of a police station at Broome is a CSO, as is a school on Thursday Island. While these examples would be allowed to be part of their common-interest group, they would have to pay interconnect charges identical to private industry. The provision of electricity or railways to many parts of Australia is also undoubtedly a CSO, as well as being inherently unprofitable, but telecommunications for such services is currently excluded from state government common-interest groups. The current Telecom view may be that the provision of banking services to the country could be argued to be a CSO, as could many other things in the private economy. The difference is that state governments are governments elected by their community to look after its interests, following a political agenda. The increasing importance of communications for all governments will mean that if one level of government is dissatisfied with the regulatory or delivery decisions made by another, it will take up the issue at one of the many forums of intergovernmental relations.

The forum in which this might occur is not clear but it is likely to be demanded. Ministerial conferences are possible given that many state governments have established departments or specialist agencies to co-ordinate telecommunication policy for their state. Austel now provides an additional avenue which the states will use to their advantage, and for which they lobbied in the first place. In a submission to the Hutchinson inquiry in March 1988, Western Australia Premier Peter Dowding stated:

> The Western Australian Government is an interested party both on behalf of its people, and as a major user of telecommunications. We are particularly concerned to have our views considered on the question of regulation of telecommunications in Australia. The Government of Western Australia considers that our community would be better served if the regulatory control of telecommunications in Australia is vested in a separate body from the carriers and providers of telecommunications services. (WA, Department of Computing and Information Technology, 1988)

Governments are not only users of telecommunications but see themselves in some way as *responsible* for their constituents. The states welcome Austel as a forum for representations on policy and also as a mechanism for influencing the telecommunications policies of the commonwealth government.

Will Austel make a difference?

From July 1989 telecommunications regulation was administered by Austel. In September 1990 the government foreshadowed its intention to merge Telecom and OTC, and to allow full network competition. This will mean an even greater role for Austel which will then have to monitor the boundaries of competition as well as other regulations in the industry. It is too early to see whether these developments will be beneficial to the states or not. However, Austel has signalled it is far from being 'captured' by the large players in the industry. But, on the matters of most concern to the states, there are some possible positive changes outlined in the May 1988 telecommunications statement and carried through into the new Telecommunications Act 1989.

At first glance there seems to be no great change in policy, and the determinations made by Telecom to date will have substantial continuity. The original intention was that 'the shared use and resale of simple carriage of all traffic over private networks will continue to be restricted' (Evans, 1988b:47). This restriction would apply both to facilities leased from Telecom and OTC and to services obtained from Aussat. For example:

> Protecting the carriers' monopoly against intrusion, by policing the boundaries of the monopoly services, is required to ensure that other telecommunications suppliers and users do not infringe the monopoly services and thereby undermine the ability to meet community service and other obligations. AUSTEL will administer the boundary policy which has been determined by the Government.
>
> AUSTEL will administer value added services and private network licensing arrangements to safeguard the boundaries of the reserved facilities and services.
>
> AUSTEL will review present arrangements for allowing joint use of private networks by closed user groups and will report to the Government. (Evans, 1988a:12).

The reason for this policy to remain was to maintain the cross-subsidy arrangements. With the introduction of competition in the provision of services this will presumably all change, and cross-subsidies themselves have a limited future.

Previously competition was precluded to the extent necessary to ensure continued protection of Telecom's ability to finance its specific CSOs and 'the government's primary concern here is to protect the source of present and future cross-subsidy revenues' (Evans, 1988b:45).

Although it is likely to change in the near future, the rationale for the interconnect policy was:

> Given the substantial cross-subsidies operating within the Australian network, and the substantial distortions from costs in Telecom tariffs, the Government considers that the continued payment of appropriate charges for the interconnection of private and leased networks is warranted, in principle, where inter-connections without such a charge would otherwise limit or undermine Telecom's ability to meet the community service and other obligations which the Government has placed upon it (Evans, 1988b:144).

The Telecommunications Act 1989 has now been passed and carries out most of the Evans recommendations. Private networks or other diversions from the monopoly are allowed but these are to be limited exceptions to the monopoly in reserved services. But still there are signs of possible policy change in the future. For example, in Evans the interconnect policy will be subject to future review by Austel. That review will 'examine whether the charges and other conditions are necessary and reasonable, both in structure and level, to protect Telecom's ability to continue to discharge its prescribed CSOs and to prevent competition undermining reserved services'. Also, the government will determine the boundaries of monopoly, and make regulations defining boundaries to be administered by Austel. This may mean that the commonwealth government, following representations, could change, for example, the boundaries of state common-interest groups. In addition, there is to be appeal against regulatory decisions made by Austel, through the complete system of commonwealth administrative law.

Austel will be directed to investigate two important areas where 'ongoing policing will need to be undertaken', that is, value-added services and private networks. While there is a concern expressed in the report that private networks may undermine Telecom's monopoly on reserved traffic and erode its capacity to meet the CSOs from profits made on switched-voice trunk traffic, there is to be a re-examination of closed-user group concepts so that the allowable arrangements for such groups may subsequently be more clearly established by the government, while still recognising the need to maintain cross-subsidy arrangements (Evans, 1988b:133–36). Without any doubt these policy reviews will be seen as opportunities by the states to have the regulations changed in their favour.

As noted earlier, the states do not like paying for the CSOs of another level of government. The May policy statement indicates that 'CSOs bearing on Telecom will be more clearly specified as a matter of government policy' and 'Telecom will be required to obtain the approval of the Minister for Transport and Communications for its plans to meet its CSOs and for the associated levels of costs and cross-subsidy' (Evans, 1988b:153). While no change could be expected immediately, the mere fact that CSOs are more visible parts of government policy will give states greater opportunities to influence the commonwealth through the usual avenues of intergovernmental relations.

Conclusion

In a federal country the powers allocated by the constitution may not be closely related to what happens in the day-to-day operation of intergovernmental relations. They are parts of a written constitution which appear quite settled, but interpretation or events can change their impact and meaning. The power over telecommunications was unequivocally allocated to the commonwealth government in 1901 and, for most of the years since then, the states were content to let the commonwealth make policy without comment. There are now signs that Australian state governments wish their interests to be heard, although there is no serious suggestion of constitutional challenge.

The newly-acquired interest of state governments in telecommunications has three implications. These are, first, a potentially serious challenge to Telecom revenue, both now and in the future; second, a challenge to the commonwealth's regulatory ingenuity; and third, a policy challenge to the commonwealth in an area where there has been little intergovernmental conflict in the past. The states are concerned that their operations are not unduly hampered by policies made by the commonwealth, but also that communications links are adequate for their constituents. Their views on telecommunications are being put forward to Canberra more than before. This has happened in other federal countries. A recent Canadian book on telecommunications regulation noted:

> Competition between the levels of government in the determination of objectives and the provision of public services was not expected. Yet intergovernmental rivalry and competition are a fact of life today for many citizens and businesses. Telecommunications until very recently was relatively immune from such a development. (Schultz, 1982:53)

The same applies in Australia but with a lag of some years. The states' interest in policy is one which is just beginning. It is likely to intensify as state policy interests are affected by the operation of their own networks. But also the states are involved in delivery of services to the public in which communications links can play a major role, as noted by another Canadian study: 'Provinces invoked a rationale for provincial jurisdiction similar to that of the federal government. Communications policy was vital to the provinces, they argued, because they "have responsibilities in the social, cultural, educational and economic spheres"' (Schultz & Alexandroff, 1985:92).

Australian state governments are starting to make similar comments. For example, the Western Australian government argues 'government agencies are increasingly dependent on telecommunications for effective delivery of their wide range of educational, health, social, public utility and other vital services throughout the state' (WA Govt, 1988:5), and is therefore interested in influencing the policy for delivery of telecommunication services.

The state governments are clearly unhappy with current interpretations of common-interest groups. They should press for some specific exemptions, or preferably agree amongst themselves as to what they want. This could be the 'whole of government approach' or some other point on a line in that direction. Also the overall argument about CSOs makes no recognition of the fact that states have their own obligations. But under present arrangements if the states press for changes there would be ramifications for the entire regulatory environment and for other large private users. The states should press for some realisation that their communication needs are vital, precisely because they are *governments*. Communications are important to any level of government; by establishing their own networks and starting to ask for a say in policy, the states are simply showing their realisation of that fact.

Bibliography

Australia, Constitutional Convention Debates, April, September 1897.

Bureau of Industry Economics, 1988. *Regulation of Private Communications Networks in Australia*, Information Bulletin 11, Canberra, AGPS.

Convention Debates, 1987. *Official Record of the National Australasian Convention Debates*, Government Printer, Adelaide.

Evans, G., 1988a. Australia, Minister for Transport and Communications, *Australian Telecommunications Services: A New Framework: Summary.*

—— 1988b, Minister for Transport and Communications, *Australian Telecommunications Services: A New Framework*, Canberra, AGPS.

Oates, W., 1972. *Fiscal Federalism*, New York, Harcourt Brace Jovanovich.

Rowell, D.M., 1985. 'AUSSAT: Its Socio-Economic Development and Q-Net', in *Media Information Australia*, 38, November.

Schultz, R., 1982. 'Partners in a Game without Masters: Reconstructing the Telecommunications Regulatory System', in *Telecommunications Regulation and the Constitution*, R.J. Buchan, C.C. Johnston & T.G. Kane, Montreal, Institute for Research on Public Policy.

Schultz, R. & Alexandroff, A., 1985. *Economic Regulation and the Federal System*, Toronto, University of Toronto Press.

Smith, G., 1988. 'Networking the Distant North', *Directions in Government*, May.

Telecom, 1986. *Telecom Policies on Common Carriage, Common Interest Groups and Authorisation of Leased Lines.*

—— 1988. *Interconnection of Private networks with Telecom Networks*, 2nd edn.

Western Australian Government, 1988. *Regulation of Telecommunications in Australia*, Submission to Telecommunications Task Force, Department of Transport and Communications, March.

WA Department of Computing and Information Technology, 1988. *Western Australian Government Strategic Telecommunications Plan: Request for Proposals*, Perth.

18 Disaster management

Roger Wettenhall

It is arguable that Australian public administration has accorded disasters—which are, in this country, mostly natural disasters—and disaster relief a less secure and continuous place on its policy agendas than any of the other fields of governmental activity surveyed in this volume; and that, for this reason, the policy and management outcomes are somewhat atypical.

From their series of case studies of disaster situations in the United States, May and Williams (1986) have shown that most changes in disaster policy occur at moments of heightened awareness following the visits of 'disaster agents', and that compassion rules at such times. They argue that the cause of more rational disaster policy making requires that governments should confront disaster seriously as an ongoing policy problem, but that this rarely happens. It seems likely that this analysis is applicable to many countries besides the United States, including Australia.

When a flood, hurricane, tornado, earthquake, volcanic eruption or bushfire strikes, it is inevitable that all levels of government functioning in the stricken community will be involved. The special significance of disaster for the understanding of intergovernmental relations (IGR) processes is that it shows these levels interacting at crisis-point, when humanitarian need is very likely to override constitutional nicety. In their study, May and Williams show also that these disaster situations shed important new light on 'shared governance', where federal agencies provide funds and have significant management responsibilities but service delivery is mostly in the hands of state and local officials. Especially in disaster, they observe, 'what occurs at the point of service delivery shapes emerging policy more than big decisions at the "top"'

(May & Williams, 1986:14). To put this in terms suggested by Deil Wright in chapter 4, it might be said that this is a field in which intergovernmental management largely drives the policy making exercise.

Mapping

This section opens with a note on the concept of disaster, which needs to be clearly placed before its IGR connections can be explored. Then follows an account of the constitutional position in Australia, together with a discussion of the extent to which Australian public administration has put in place special intergovernmental agreements or institutions to deal with disaster.

Disaster: concept and incidence

Disasters are social, not physical events: they happen to human communities. A widely accepted definition of disaster is that of United States sociologist Charles Fritz: 'An event, concentrated in time and space, in which a society, or a relatively self-sufficient division of a society, undergoes extreme danger and incurs such losses to its members and physical appurtenances that the social structure is disrupted and the fulfillment of all or some of the essential functions of society is prevented' (Fritz, 1968:202). If the physical agent strikes an uninhabited piece of territory—or the ocean floor—disaster effects are likely to be minimal.

Our understanding of disaster events has been greatly facilitated by a systematic program of research generated in the United States after World War II, invigorated by a network of scholars centred on the Disaster Research Center originally set up by Professors Dynes and Quarantelli at Ohio State University and now located at the University of Delaware. Ironically much of the early work was civil-defence funded: ironic because the government funders assumed that their investment would aid in coping with nuclear attack, whereas the nuclear attack did not come and the research actually assisted in coping with more and more civilian disasters.[1] This has relevance also to the Australian constitutional position, to be noted shortly.

This body of research has focused mostly on natural disasters—the products of destructive agents of nature—rather than on man-made disasters, a term usually used to cover acts of war, rebellion and riot.[2] It has also, consistently with Fritz's definition, focused on *sudden* disasters, which has tended to exclude drought and famine. There has nonetheless been some comparative work done, leading to the important finding that patterns of human behaviour vary considerably across the different disaster forms—thus looting is observed as a central feature of riot events, but is rarely present in natural disasters (Dynes & Quarantelli,

1968). More recently, with the growing incidence of industrial and chemical disasters (e.g., Three Mile Island, Bhopal, Chernobyl), all similarly sudden in their effects, this research has expanded to embrace them within its portfolio.

Australia has been spared the mammoth disasters which strike from time to time in some parts of the world, with death-tolls of tens or even hundreds of thousands. Nonetheless we do have a long history of cyclones, floods and bushfires, occasional earthquakes and tornados, and over the years many human settlements have been severely damaged in the sense of Fritz's definition. In the seven-year period 1967 to 1974, four major cities were hit: Hobart (bushfires 1967), Townsville (cyclone 1971), Brisbane (floods early 1974), Darwin (cyclone December 1974). Though major centres have again been spared since 1974, smaller communities have continued to suffer: the Ash Wednesday fires in the Victorian and South Australian countryside in February 1983 are of recent memory, and as this chapter is being written many people in Queensland are still suffering very directly from the scourges of Cyclone Aivu. Many Australians have been killed and injured in these disasters, and property loss, including the loss of homes and places of work, is sometimes immense. There has been much disruption to public utilities, and the rehabilitation of the victim-communities has often taken years to accomplish.

I once speculated, without much hard evidence, that natural disasters were 'Australia's summer fate' (Wettenhall, 1976). Data compiled by the Insurance Council of Australia now suggest that most natural disasters and lesser emergencies hit Australia between December and March (see Figure 18.1), and that the total insurance loss on about 250 such events recorded in the twenty–year period since early 1967 amounted to around $3400m (adjusted to January 1987 dollar value: ICA, 1987). As a rough guide, the insurance loss may be assumed to represent between one-third and one-half of total disaster-caused losses.

Constitutional position

In this field the states have constitutional priority, for power over (or administrative responsibility for) disasters was not referred to the commonwealth when the commonwealth constitution was adopted, nor has it been referred since. Disaster is thus one of the residual matters which have, since federation in 1901, remained with state governments. Local governments have become heavily involved in disaster management, but of course they have done this by virtue of powers vested in them under state (or Northern Territory) legislation.

This last comment relates to disaster as a discrete event, or as a discrete field of activity. The commonwealth does, however, have constitutional power in some congruent areas, notably defence, postal, telegraphic and telephonic services, meteorology, finance, territories and external affairs. Through the exercise of its power in these areas, it has inevitably acquired an important role in disaster policy and disaster management (see also discussion in Wettenhall, 1975:ch. 3).

Figure 18.1: Number of nature-caused emergencies and disasters producing insurance loss in Australia between 1967 and early 1987, by month of occurrence

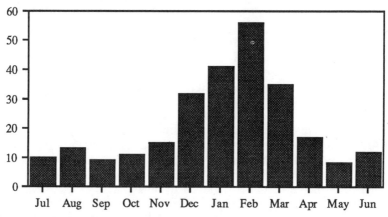

Source: Based on data in ICA 1987

Defence. An important strand of commonwealth involvement is clearly defence-related. The seeds of civil defence activity were sown during World War II and, in the ensuing atmosphere of cold war and fears of nuclear attack, they grew into a Civil Defence Directorate formally established within the Department of the Interior in 1956. This Directorate soon opened a Civil Defence School at Mount Macedon in Victoria, and the states were encouraged to establish their own civil defence units to complement the federal directorate and to send their officers for training at the Macedon college. The commonwealth insisted with constitutional propriety that its co-ordinating role applied to civil defence in relation to enemy attack only.

But, as in the United States, the enemy attack did not come, while natural disasters did. With no such constitutional impediments, the state units demonstrated their usefulness in coping with such disasters, one example being the perennial problem of flooding in the north-eastern river valleys of New South Wales. A stream of people from the states—business leaders as well as a veritable army of private citizens attached in one way or another to local civil defence units—passed through the Macedon college, which increasingly came to realise that it was training for the alleviation of the effects of natural disaster, not enemy attack. Eventually titles changed, even if the formal constitutional position did not: the state civil defence units became State Emergency Services (SESs), the federal directorate became the Natural Disasters Organisation (NDO) within the Defence Department, and the training facility became the Australian Counter Disaster College.

The military forces are often able to make available manpower resources and transport facilities at very short notice to aid stricken communities. In this, they assist the relevant state to discharge its own constitutional responsibilities, and the NDO has an important co-ordinating role here, as well as serving today as a focal point for the whole SES network.

Postal, telegraphic, telephonic. Here the commonwealth provides services which are vital to the states in coping with disaster events. Moreover these (and other) commonwealth facilities may well share in the ravages of disaster, in which case the commonwealth itself becomes an affected party in the recovery operation.

Meteorology. The Bureau of Meteorology, a commonwealth institution, plays an equally vital role in forecasting the build-up of climatic conditions likely to produce disaster events, and in its post-impact reports it provides what are often the most comprehensive records of particular disaster experiences.

Finance. It is in this area that most of the overt policy activity takes place. Apparently beginning with a grant of $2000 for bushfire relief in Tasmania, a gesture to mark the first-ever meeting of the commonwealth cabinet in Hobart in 1939, commonwealth funds have frequently been allocated to the states for disaster relief purposes under section 96 of the constitution, which is the general authority for specific-purpose grants from the commonwealth to the states. A recent study has identified several stages in the development of these grants (Butler & Doessel, 1988; see also Butler, Doessel & Wettenhall, 1981), and a further stage was heralded with the announcement of the Minister for Finance, Senator Peter Walsh, that the commonwealth would no longer provide drought assistance funds as part of its natural disaster relief arrangements (*Canberra Times*, 13 April 1988).

Territories. If disaster strikes in a non-self-governing territory and there is no state (or state-like) machinery to cope, then the commonwealth stands automatically in the place of a state. This was the situation when Cyclone Tracy struck Darwin in 1974, but it would not be so today in the self-governing Northern Territory.

External affairs. There is an international face to disaster, a matter of United Nations-sponsored and bilateral relief arrangements, and as Australia looks outwards in support of other disaster-stricken or disaster-prone lands the commonwealth is again involved, this time under its external affairs power.

Special intergovernmental agreements and institutions

Although disaster experiences extensively involve all levels of government, they have not produced much in the way of intergovernmental
agreements or institutions. The compendium of such agreements
produced by the (ill-fated) Advisory Council for Inter-government
Relations finds no call to recognise disaster as a category of
governmental activity, and under 'emergency services' it identifies a
single commonwealth–state agreement only—relating to marine search
and rescue operations! (ACIR, 1986a:88).[3]

Nor is there a formal interjurisdictional ministerial council operating
in this area (see list at ACIR, 1986b:70). Awareness of the problem of
administrative fragmentation which compounds the costs and disruptions
associated with disaster (on which more below) has produced advocacy of
a co-ordinating intergovernmental body, possibly a Natural Hazards
Council (Heathcote, 1980; Pickup & Minor, 1980; Wettenhall, 1980,
1984), but no official action. The NDO has plenty of operational
connections with state agencies, but it remains unambiguously a section
of a commonwealth department.

When disaster strikes, a state may decide to handle it by itself. But
that is increasingly unlikely, since the availability of commonwealth aid
for all but the smallest disasters is well understood throughout our
governmental system. The commonwealth's own financial formulae will
govern the flow of relief monies, just as the NDO's procedures will
determine the sorts of material assistance that the SESs may expect.
Before the formation of NDO, an affected state tapped into this system
when its premier alerted the 'disaster man' in the then Prime Minister's
Department to the occurrence of a serious disaster (Wettenhall, 1975:48).
But this commonwealth role has now gone to NDO, and despite the
informality there are several well understood IGR mechanisms:

1 There has been an exchange of letters between the prime minister and
the premiers under which the director-general of NDO is nominated as
point of contact for the commonwealth, and each state and territory is
required to nominate an official who has authority to approach him
with a request for 'Commonwealth physical assistance' when a disaster
occurs.

2 The director-general of NDO now meets annually with the directors of
the state and territory emergency services.

3 There was an *ad hoc* meeting between the relevant commonwealth and
state/territory ministers about 1984.

4 The NDO's annual budget includes an item ($4.186m in 1988–89)
enabling it to contribute to the cost of disaster-relevant building and
equipment items required by local governments, and to subsidise the
salaries of regional officers employed by the SESs.[4]

Dynamics

The dynamics of disaster policy and implementation can best be understood by first presenting a disaster time-scale formulated as part of the systematic post-World War II research program noted above, and then noting how institutions and problems have interacted through the several time bands in a number of actual disaster events. It should then be possible to identify the main IGR issues presented by the accumulated experience of disaster in Australia.

A disaster time-scale

By 1956 serious scholars of disaster were reporting that most existing accounts suffered from disorientation in time and space. Thereafter the spatial and time dimensions were both mapped. The latter is the more significant here. A formulation by Powell and Rayner of the University of Maryland has been widely accepted: it proposes that 'disaster time' can usefully be divided into seven periods characterised by the major type of activity occurring during each of them:

1 Warning—when some apprehension arises, based on conditions out of which disaster may arise.

2 Threat—when people are exposed to communications from others, or to signs from the approaching disaster force itself, indicating specific, imminent danger.

3 Impact—when the disaster force strikes, bringing with it death, injury and destruction.

4 Inventory—when those exposed to the disaster begin the task of assessing the damage.

5 Rescue—when activity turns to immediate help for survivors, first-aid for the wounded, freeing trapped victims, putting out residual fires and the like.

6 Remedy—when more deliberate and formal steps are taken for the relief of the stricken and their community.

7 Recovery—usually an extended period during which the community and its members either return to their former stability or adapt to the changed conditions which the disaster has brought about.

This categorisation does not deny that there may be overlapping between the various stages, nor does it infer that they will be of equal duration or equal importance in every disaster. It has, however, served a useful purpose as an analytical tool in several later studies (Powell, 1954; Wettenhall, 1975:11–13).

Organisations in disaster

One other analytical tool deriving from this same body of research is also relevant to the present discussion. It seeks to classify organisations according to their disaster salience. A simple version of this classification posits that there are 'front-line' agencies, and others with back-up responsibilities in disaster. The numbers will surprise. A Californian disaster plan listed 22 state agencies with 'major responsibilities' in disaster, with others too numerous to mention in the back-up category; this listing made no reference to federal or non-governmental organisations (California, 1967). A more sophisticated exercise classifies organisations in terms of the way they respond to disaster, and identifies four main groups (Dynes, 1970; and see Wettenhall, 1975:25–34):

1 Established—may become involved, but perform functions they are used to and seek to follow existing procedures.

2 Extending—like established organisations except that they take on new disaster-generated tasks.

3 Expanding (or standby)—with latent disaster tasks like the Red Cross, for whom sudden and temporary expansion is scarcely a novel experience.

4 Emergent (or 'synthetic')—arising spontaneously in the disaster situation, performing often heroic tasks in very non-bureaucratic ways, and destined to disappear as the community returns to normality.

A major disaster may be thought of as provoking a vortex of organis
ational activity—and, to repeat, it will be no respecter of constitutional niceties. Working through the time phases, it will be apparent that an established commonwealth organisation, the Bureau of Meteorology, will often be the first to be activated, since its normal weather forecasting processes will warn of climatic conditions developing which might produce flooding or bushfires, or estimate the likely course and landfall of a cyclone building up at sea. This forecasting function will in turn—in the threat phase—activate other established organisations at all levels of government, although their response behaviours may follow no settled or predictable pattern. (Some consideration will be given later in this chapter to the function of disaster planning, and the extent to which that may increase the predictability of these response patterns.)

Provided there has been this awareness of threat—in the case of an earthquake there may be none[5]—the front-line organisations will have at least a little time to prepare. In Australia, the operators here will be predominantly established state agencies, notably police and emergency services, fire authorities (often divided between urban and rural) and areas of health administration such as hospitals and ambulance services.

Whether or not there has been warning and threat, these will also be the organisations which must bear the brunt of activity when the disaster force strikes, i.e., in the impact and rescue phases. Their efforts will be supplemented by those of voluntary emergency-relevant bodies like the Red Cross and St John Ambulance, and of local governments in stricken areas—which are often themselves firmly plugged into the SES networks. Someone, usually state, local or voluntary, will have to cope with the 'convergence phenomenon', the crowding into the disaster area of donated goods and money, people and messages—this function is rarely adequately planned for (Fritz & Mathewson, 1957).

Commonwealth agencies are likely to reappear during the rescue period, as available military units are pressed into service, and the commonwealth's utility operators (notably posts and telecommunications) begin to restore damaged services along with state and local utility operators (electricity, water, transport). To complete this brief catalogue of impact and rescue operations, one other commonwealth agency, the ABC, must be noted: together with other established media organisations, it will have reported the early warnings and the impact details—providing, of course, that its own reporting and transmission facilities have survived the disaster force. The inventory process will have already begun, and the damage count will involve many of the organisations already noted and others besides, notably other established state organisations like agriculture and education departments and housing authorities, with the Premier's Department in a co-ordinating role.

By now, as remedy begins, the nominated state authority is likely to be conveying a sense of the early damage inventory to the commonwealth (details are still likely to be vague) via the NDO channel already noted. The Department of Finance will be speedily involved (quick promises of financial aid will be expected), as will any of a range of other departments and authorities whose facilities and expertise might be called in to assist the stricken state. Commonwealth activity will now be at its height, probably highlighted in severe disasters by visits to the stricken areas by the prime minister and other ministers and officials. Of course, once the details are agreed, commonwealth funds will flow right through remedy and well into the recovery period, and in particularly severe disasters the commonwealth parliament is likely to be asked to pass special disaster-relief legislation.

What this description has so far missed is the role of the emergent groups or synthetic organisations. They are a feature of social response to disaster in Anglo–Saxon communities and have been much studied, since they represent an extreme case of interest-group formation and they may, for varying periods through rescue and remedy, acquire executive functions and supplant regular organisations. Non-governmental fund-raising may be one, but only one, of their functions. Their impact is likely to be felt at all levels of government (see, for example, Forrest, 1978).

It is likely that these emergent groups will join with private organisations like the churches and the Red Cross to bring social workers trained and untrained into disaster service. Social workers have performed conspicuously and heroically in all recent large Australian disasters, but their role has not been without controversy. The relevant professional body, the Australian Association of Social Workers, has given serious attention to the disaster problem; and the commonwealth's Department of Social Security has inevitably been drawn into disaster activity, especially where there are large evacuee populations. This involvement can extend well into the recovery period, as can that of medical professionals (especially psychiatrists) and overseeing health departments.

Individual private organisations, other than the voluntaries, will be recruited to disaster activity as they donate funds or relief in kind, or as, being victims themselves, they join the ranks of applicants for government assistance. More generally—across the board as it were—the insurance organisations, which are in Australia both public (state) and private, will be early on the scene, paying out vast amounts on damage claims. They also, through their peak body, the Insurance Council of Australia, played a prominent part in the 1970s negotiations relating to a proposed commonwealth Disaster Insurance Fund, though that fund did not eventuate.

Arising during remedy and continuing through recovery will be the inquiry process. Governments will want to know variously why the disaster occurred, how it might have been prevented or its damaging outcomes minimised, how social and organisational responses might have been improved, whether populations in disaster-prone areas should be relocated, and whether changes should be made in disaster-relevant facilities and systems (such as flood levees, building standards or communications systems). It will be state governments which will initiate the inquiries, but commonwealth and local officials and private citizens may be co-opted to share the work. At this stage also attention is likely to be given to disaster planning, i.e., planning for future disasters in the light of practical experience gained. If such plans already exist, consideration will be given to their adaptation and improvement. And, finally, recovery will see much activity by established government organisations to restore utilities, rebuild the stock of public housing, make loans and grants for the rebuilding of private homes and factories and the rehabilitation of farms, and so on.

Eventually a state of normalcy will return. A few activities will continue, such as the training of disaster personnel at the Macedon college and commonwealth support of overseas disaster relief programs through the Australian International Development Assistance Bureau and its semi-privatised offshoot, the Australian Overseas Disaster Relief Organisation. But, as a particular disaster event for which all this activity has been mobilised fades into history, all the emergent groups will disappear and the expanding and extending organisations will shed their added functions. Until the next disaster comes...

The last few paragraphs have provided a kind of abstracted picture of organisational activity in Australian disasters, based on a number of empirical studies that are now available. These disasters do have many features in common. Of course no two disasters are identical, and differences will emerge especially in consequence of differing scales of disaster. Where a disaster affects an area of countryside, or one or several rural or provincial towns, for example, those responsible for its management can safely expect to be able to call on assistance from the intact headquarters of their several organisations in the relevant capital. But—as in Hobart and Brisbane—the disaster may strike the capital itself, and then, at least for a short period, the central administrative functioning of the whole state will be disrupted. Australia is fortunate that, as yet, it has had no case in which such disruption of a state capital has extended for more than a short period. Should a state capital be more extensively disrupted, it is possible that this might provide a justification for a temporary commonwealth takeover of the reins of state authority. Darwin was, for example, considerably more disrupted than either Hobart or Brisbane. There is now, however, a good deal of evidence to suggest that its capacity to administer itself, even in the agony of Cyclone Tracy, and without the advantages (then) of self-government, was much greater than Canberra was prepared to allow for.

IGR issues

It is suggested that the accumulated experiences recorded above make it abundantly clear that the area of disaster policy and management cannot be other than intergovernmental. The course of IGR in disaster is driven by the nature of disaster itself, by the total involvement of affected communities in it. It is also, unlike many other IGR fields, driven by compassion, which makes it less likely than most to produce large intergovernmental controversies and frictions. The 'therapeutic community' effect of natural disaster is widely accepted in the relevant scholarly literature (e.g., Baker & Chapman, 1962; Barton, 1969): such disaster causes existing social divisions to be put aside while all struggle, out of shared humanity, for the survival and rehabilitation of their communities. It is not therefore likely that governments participating in the relief and recovery operations will often find reason to be in conflict. They may sometimes be critical of each other's performance, but the criticisms are likely to be muted—handled constructively on inquiry committees and the like—for so long as the heightened humanitarian spirit prevails. Like the emergent groups, that spirit is likely to disappear with the return of normalcy.

All this said, it remains true that during the period of a disaster officials at all levels of government face challenges and have to resolve sometimes difficult issues in dealing with those at other levels of government. The next few paragraphs provide some illustrations of such challenges and issues drawn from Australian disaster experiences already referred to in this paper.

In the bushfire disaster in Southern Tasmania on 7 February 1967, the forecasts of the commonwealth meteorologists were assiduously monitored by state forestry officials. The latter group eventually took the initiative in contacting the police commissioner, and together they set in motion the process that led to the declaration of a state of emergency (by the executive council, not the cabinet). The declaration put the police commissioner in supreme command, but he had the good sense to approve the activities (or at least those he was immediately aware of) of some emergent groups that were forming. At the height of the impact (in the three-hour period in which 62 people were either killed in the fires or suffered the burns from which they later died, in which 1400 major buildings were destroyed leaving over 7000 people homeless and a great many others injured or jobless, and in which over 80 000 farm animals were killed and 3000 miles of farm fences, 5 per cent of the state's pastures, the transmitting facilities of three radio stations and vast tracts of the telephone and electricity grids destroyed), the most spectacular group formation was at the Hobart Town Hall, where the town clerk joined with the Red Cross state secretary to establish the Emergency Civil Relief and Rehabilitation Committee. To many, over the next ten days or so, this appeared to be the effective government of Tasmania. Very early in the piece the Army commandant in Tasmania, possessing a camp to accommodate homeless people and with the Citizen Military Force actually mobilised for its summer exercises, looked for the centre of responsibility and action and believed he found it here—so he joined the co-ordinating committee and this vital commonwealth resource was thereafter channelled to the stricken community through an emergent group.

Another case of spectacular emergent group formation in the fire aftermath also took up commonwealth energies. When social workers produced much evidence of the grave difficulties many fire victims were experiencing (especially those not adept at form-filling and identifying or getting to relevant government offices) in gaining access to available relief funds, activists from churches, voluntary societies, the state's Health Department and the commonwealth's Social Services Department got together to form the Fire Victims' Welfare Organisation. This group operated to good effect for seventeen months, for much of this time under the direction of the official of the commonwealth department who had worked tirelessly to secure acceptance of the activity.

When the state government had marshalled its arguments and presented a detailed case to the commonwealth for financial assistance, officers of the Commonwealth Treasury (the Department of Finance had not yet been split off) raised serious questions about some items. They found it difficult, for example, to understand why the state's Hydro-Electric Commission should not be expected to apply its large reserves towards the restoration of the damaged grid—surely this was just the sort of emergency the reserves were for? But, in the climate of goodwill generated by the Prime Minister's post-impact visit to Tasmania, they found that there was then no available avenue for pressing seriously such a question. Indeed, because of the magnitude of the damage toll in the Tasmanian disaster, the commonwealth expanded the categories of relief it was prepared to underwrite and a review of this and other relevant experiences led to the promulgation of a new and firmer commonwealth policy in the 1971–72 budget. In so far as the Tasmanian disaster itself was concerned, it transpired that the state was unable to spend all the $14.5 million of commonwealth relief aid on disaster-relevant projects, so some of it was returned to the Treasury anyway! While the matter of taking advantage of the destruction caused by the disaster to rationalise areas of primary and secondary industry seriously exercised the state authorities, there is little evidence to suggest that the commonwealth involved itself in such considerations until it found itself with its own disaster in Darwin (detail mostly from Wettenhall, 1975; see also Butler & Doessel, 1988:2–3).

The warning-threat stage in the Brisbane flood disaster around Australia Day 1974 produced one spectacular IGR event. As the Bureau of Meteorology issued its flood warnings, it became clear to it that the state government under Premier Bjelke-Petersen was putting pressure on the media to downplay the seriousness of the warnings. It did this because of a desire to avoid panic, but meteorologists were angered because the city was therefore less well prepared than it might have been for a disaster force which soon flooded to a greater or lesser degree some 13 000 homes and other buildings. This episode still rankles among meteorologists whose memories go back that far. It is, for present purposes, especially ironical that one of the media organisations which could well have succumbed to the pressure of the state government was another commonwealth agency, the ABC![6]

This disaster also produced a fairly spectacular collision between the state government and the Brisbane city council under its then lord mayor, Clem Jones, over the organisation of the public disaster relief fund. In Hobart, the state had simply acquiesced when the fund was launched under a direct vice-regal/lord-mayoral partnership, meeting the fund's administrative expenses and providing an audit service. Lord-mayoral initiative is, in this matter, part of a long Australian tradition (Wettenhall, 1975:58–59). But in the Brisbane case long-standing rivalries between state government and city council led the state to launch its own public subscription fund separately from that of the lord mayor. A sometimes bitter competition ensued.

Queensland has figured much more recently in disaster relief policy making, as the commonwealth has moved to remove drought-assistance funds from its normal natural disaster relief arrangements. The reported reason was the conviction held by the present commonwealth government that the state government 'looked on drought relief as a slush fund provided by Commonwealth taxpayers for the National Party to distribute as patronage and reward'. It was further reported that the Queensland government had acted against one state official who raised this issue in a leaked memorandum, and that other state officials feared that they wold be 'sacked' if they gave evidence to a relevant Public Accounts Committee inquiry (*Canberra Times*, 13 & 17 April 1989).

As I have already indicated, Darwin was, in the then non-self-governing condition of the Northern Territory, much more the commonwealth's own disaster than Hobart or Brisbane. This is even more so as local government in Darwin was in an embryonic state when Cyclone Tracy struck on Christmas Eve 1974, so that it played little part in the sequence of disaster events that followed. For this reason this most catastrophic of all concentrated-area disasters yet experienced in Australia scarcely lends itself to IGR analysis. Nonetheless a few observations may be in order, organised around an assumption that, even without self-government, Darwin's own structure of interest groups and resident civil officials constituted a sort of incipient governmental system separate from Canberra.

This disaster (it was one, not two: Major-General Stretton, then NDO director-general, told the National Press Club in Canberra soon afterwards that the after-effects of the mass evacuation of 35 000 people constituted a second disaster) produced an overlay of two waves of Canberra officialdom superimposed over the local system, and each attracted to itself much criticism and bitterness. The first ran for about six days, from the arrival to the departure of the NDO contingent under Stretton (Stretton, 1976). The locals had already taken monumental steps to restore order before Stretton arrived, but this seemed never to have been understood; and there was inevitably great controversy about the evacuation Stretton ordered. The second followed the establishment of the Darwin Reconstruction Commission, with its imported phalanx of National Capital Development Commission officials. In brief, they sought to impose Canberra-style planning regimes on Darwin's reconstruction, which was an incitement to a great deal of organised opposition. Darwin's reconstruction seemed to 'come together' only when a populist mayor experienced in the ways of local and state government (Brisbane's Clem Jones) took over the reins of the Darwin Reconstruction Commission (King, 1979).

Arguably, the commonwealth's record in this disaster stands highest at the point where, subsequently, the Department of Social Security sponsored and then published the results of serious research into the plight of the refugee population, adding fuel to the arguments of those who believe that the evacuation should never have taken place (Chamberlain et al., 1981; and, for example, Milne, 1977a, 1977b). It is clear that there was advocacy of self-government for the Northern Territory before the cyclone struck. It is, however, likely that the very great disenchantment with 'rule from Canberra' which this disaster produced had much to do with the subsequent strengthening of the territorial resolve for self-government, leading to the dramatic constitutional change which took place four years later.

Fiscal and managerial

It has not been possible to separate the fiscal and managerial strands from the description of the dynamics of disaster presented in the last section. It would seem, however, that this is a field where the main weight of political and administrative power remains with the states, notwithstanding the very great importance to them, in coping with disaster relief, of commonwealth grants and loans, and that their own financial outlays may by comparison be relatively small. In the Tasmanian disaster, for example, the commonwealth initially contributed to the relief funds $14.5 million (eventually scaled down to about $10 million), compared with a specific state grant of only $0.75 million. The governor's fire-relief appeal netted over $5 million, and insurance payouts, other less public relief appeals, and amounts spent by commonwealth, state and local government agencies and private bodies on their own rehabilitation outside the main system of relief grants combined with these two contributions to add up to a gross inflow into the disaster area of about $33 million. Only the established machinery of state government could, in the long run, hope to mould this assistance into a comprehensible pattern.

Managerially, however, the relief effort remained fragmentary, even within the apparatus of state government. This condition is customary in disaster relief efforts in many countries. When Stretton said that there were two Darwin disasters, he was falling into Heathcote's 'administrative trap' (Heathcote, 1980). Disaster experience (i.e., all that happens before, during and after the visitation of the disaster force that is connected with that visitation) is a phenomenological unity, and disaster policy making and disaster management are hindered to the extent that this is not appreciated. The fact that it rarely is appreciated makes the field much more problematical than it might otherwise be.

It soon becomes widely accepted that co-ordination of the efforts of diverse agencies must be striven for, and disaster plans now frequently identify senior officials (or perhaps ministers) to assume *el supremo* roles in states of emergency. There is not, however, a great deal of evidence to suggest that the problems of fragmentation have thereby been significantly reduced. In federations, of course, the disaster spreads itself over all levels of government, though, as the above analysis suggests, the IGR issues are muted and do not especially aggravate the relief and recovery effort. The problem is so much more general that, while it involves many IGR issues, essentially it exists irrespective of them. The federal connection does, however, lead advocates of high-level mechanisms to co-ordinate both the handling of specific disasters and the development of a more comprehensive disaster preparedness culture to urge the inclusion of both commonwealth and state leaders in those mechanisms. This was certainly true of the proposal for an Australian Natural Hazards Council noted above.

Whether the 'new managerialism'—or economic rationalism—that is becoming the dominant force in commonwealth government today is likely to alter prevailing Australian disaster-response behaviours is a question awaiting investigation as and when some very recent disaster experiences—such as last summer's crop, the Newcastle earthquake and the flooding of Charleville and Nyngan—are subjected to close case study.

While commonwealth grants are subject to the play of within-Canberra forces, it seems unlikely that a process of centralisation could succeed. The Darwin experience was certainly unusual, but it did reveal that Canberra managers and planners were 'out of their depth' in handling the multitude of grass roots issues raised in such concentrated fashion by disaster. It has more than once been observed that, though the states may be somewhat behind Canberra in developing policy making capability, they have developed through long experience a superior capacity in service delivery and in relating to communities of people. The observation is no doubt a contentious one; but there is nothing I have observed in a long study of disasters to suggest that it is wrong.

A policy challenge

For us, too, the most compelling policy question today is probably that raised by May and Williams in their United States study. In periods of 'normal politics', they argue, disaster policies have high salience only in moments of increased awareness following the visitations of disaster agents. At these times the upsurge of public generosity leads to costly relief 'solutions' but does little to control the growth of disaster losses in the long run. Such remedies have typically involved generous relief payments to help victims re-establish in ravaged areas, along with structural mitigation efforts such as building dams and levees.

There is a measure of what we know as managerialism or economic rationalism in what follows. Today United States policy makers want to cut back on disaster losses and relief outlays, and understand that to do this prevailing response patterns need to be changed. So a shift is advocated to non-structural mitigation efforts, such as tougher land-use planning, limitation of development in hazardous areas, and support for disaster insurance schemes. But to succeed in this, these authors urge, governments must do their disaster policy making in 'quiet periods' well away from the catastrophic visitations (May & Williams, 1986; Wettenhall, 1987).

If we are to move seriously in this direction in Australia, the required policy shifts will need to be preceded by reforms which introduce a disaster organisation much wider in its concerns and capacities than the present NDO, locked in as it is to the Defence Department and constrained by that Department's major functions and the managerial and policy styles that go with them. This new structure will need to have continuous existence and be supported by governments' recognition that disasters keep coming, and that being prepared for them in all their many-sided effects requires much more than the present stop-go approach. Finally, it will need to acknowledge both that state governments do now have, and should continue to have, the central responsibility in coping with disasters, and that they require commonwealth support to discharge this responsibility. This includes not only funding support as in many other IGR fields, but other forms of support besides. To this end, the new organisation will need to be interjurisdictional in its constitution and direction. For disaster and disaster relief are themselves totally intergovernmental in their effects.

Endnotes

1 I have described the earlier phases of this history in more detail in *Bushfire Disaster* (Wettenhall, 1975:ch. I).

2 Bushfires are sometimes caused by arson, and in that sense also 'man-made'. But they share the other characteristics of natural disaster, and thus are usually so considered.

3 Nor is the field noted in Wiltshire's *Administrative Federalism: Selected documents in Australian intergovernmental relations* (1977).

4 This budget item is quite separate from the Department of Finance-administered relief grants and loans.

5 Although in California, of course, earthquake prediction has become a major industry.

6 The potential civil defence implications of such action by a state government were alluded to in Heatherwick, 1980:App. 3.

Bibliography

ACIR (Advisory Council for Inter-government Relations), 1986a. *Compendium of Intergovernmental Agreements,* published by the Council, Battery Point (Tas.).

—— 1986b. *Operational Procedures of Inter-Jurisdictional Ministerial Councils,* Information Paper No. 13, Government Printer, Hobart.

Baker, G.W. & Chapman, D.W., 1962. *Man and Society in Disaster,* Basic Books, New York.

Barton, A.H., 1969. *Communities in Disaster,* Doubleday, New York.

Butler, J.R.C. & Doessel, D.P., 1988. *The Economic Role of the Commonwealth Government in Natural Disasters,* Working Papers in Management, No. 9, Queensland Institute of Technology, Brisbane.

Butler, J.R.C., Doessel, D.P. & Wettenhall, R.L., 1981. 'Disaster Relief', in Australian Water Resources Council, *Proceedings of the Floodplain Management Conference,* Canberra, 7–10 May 1980, AGPS, Canberra.

California (legislature), 1967. Interim Committee on Military and Veterans Affairs, *California's Civil Defense and Natural Disaster Program,* Sacremento.

Chamberlain, E.R., et al., 1981. *The Experience of Cyclone Tracy,* AGPS, Canberra (for Department of Social Security).

Dynes, R.R., 1970. *Organized Behavior in Disaster,* Heath, Lexington (Mass).

Dynes, R.R. & Quarantelli, E.L., 1968. 'What Looting in Civil Disturbance Really Means', *Transaction,* 6.

Forrest, T.R., 1978. 'Group Emergence in Disasters', in *Disasters: Theory and Research,* ed. E.L. Quarantelli, Sage Studies in International Sociology 13, London.

Fritz, Charles E., 1968. 'Disasters', *International Encyclopedia of the Social Sciences,* 4.

Fritz, C.E. & Mathewson, J.H., 1957. *Convergence Behavior in Disasters: A Problem in Social Control,* Disaster Research Group Study No. 9, Washington.

Heathcote, L., 1980. 'An Administrative Trap? Natural Hazards in Australia: A Personal View', *Australian Geographical Studies,* 18(2).

Heatherwick, G., 1980. 'Weather Warning Systems: Bureau–Media Interaction as Components of the Total Warning-Response System', in *Proceedings of Broadcasters Queensland Workshop,* Department of Science and the Environment, Bureau of Meteorology, Brisbane.

ICA (Insurance Council of Australia), 1987. *Insurance Losses on Australian Emergencies and Disasters Between June 1967 and January 1987,* table prepared by the Council.

King, S.A., 1979. 'More Than Meets the Eye: Plans for Land Use Change in Darwin After Cyclone Tracy', in H.H. Ashman & S.A. King, *Two Northern Territory Urban Studies,* North Australia Research Unit, Australian National University, Darwin (North Australia Research Bulletin No. 5).

May, P.J. & Williams, W., 1986. *Disaster Policy Implementation: Managing Programs under Shared Governance*, Plenum Press, New York.

Milne, G., 1977a. 'Cyclone Tracy: I. Some Consequences of the Evacuation for Adult Victims', *Australian Psychologist*, 12(1).

—— 1977b. 'Cyclone Tracy: II. The Effects on Darwin's Children', *Australian Psychologist*, 12(1).

Pickup, G. & Minor, J.E., 1980. *Assessment of Research and Practice in Australian Natural Hazards Management*, North Australia Research Unit, Australian National University, Darwin (North Australia Research Bulletin No. 2).

Powell, J.W., 1954. 'An Introduction to the Natural History of Disaster, University of Maryland Psychiatric Institute' (mimeo).

Stretton, A., 1976. *The Furious Days: The Relief of Darwin*, Collins, Sydney.

Wettenhall, R., 1975. *Bushfire Disaster: An Australian Community in Crisis*, Angus & Robertson, Sydney.

—— 1976. 'Natural Disaster: Australia's Summer Fate', *Current Affairs Bulletin*, 52(11).

—— 1980. 'The Response of Government to Disasters: A Study in Fragmentation', in *Response to Disaster*, ed. J. Oliver, Centre for Disaster Studies, James Cook University of North Queensland.

—— 1984. 'Disaster and Public Administration: Reflections of a Researcher', *Disasters*, 8(2).

—— 1987. Review of May & Williams 1986, in *Public Administration* (London), 65(3), 363.

Wiltshire, K.W., 1977. *Administrative Federalism: Selected Documents in Australian Intergovernmental Relations*, University of Queensland Press, St Lucia.

Index